THE DESTRUCTION OF JERUSALEM, OR TITUS AND VESPASIAN

MIDDLE ENGLISH TEXTS SERIES

The Middle English Texts Series produces scholarly texts designed for research and classroom use. Its goal is to make available to teachers, scholars, and students texts that occupy an important place in the literary and cultural canon but have not been readily available in print or online editions. The series does not include authors, such as Chaucer, Langland, or Malory, whose English works are normally in print. The focus is, instead, upon Middle English literature adjacent to those authors that are needed for research or teaching. The editions maintain the linguistic integrity of the original work but within the parameters of modern reading conventions.

THE DESTRUCTION OF JERUSALEM, OR TITUS AND VESPASIAN

Edited by
Kara L. McShane and Mark J. B. Wright

A publication of the Rossell Hope Robbins Library
in collaboration with the University of Rochester
and the Teaching Association for Medieval Studies

by

MEDIEVAL INSTITUTE PUBLICATIONS
Kalamazoo, Michigan
2021

The text of this book was set in Arno Pro 11pt, a contemporary typeface inspired by books from the 15th and 16th centuries. It was designed by Robert Slimbach at Adobe.

Library of Congress Cataloging-in-Publication Data

Names: McShane, Kara L., 1985- editor. | Wright, Mark J. B., 1985- editor.
Title: The destruction of Jerusalem, or Titus and Vespasian /
edited by Kara L. McShane and Mark J.B. Wright.
Other titles: Titus and Vespasian (Middle English poem) | Titus and Vespasian
Description: Kalamazoo, Michigan : Medieval Institute Publications, 2021. |
  Series: Middle English texts series | Includes bibliographical
  references. | Summary: "The Destruction of Jerusalem, also called Titus
  and Vespasian, is a fifteenth-century fictionalized version of the
  historical Roman siege of Jerusalem. Marked by antisemitism, Christian
  nationalism, and violence, this Middle English poem was nonetheless
  intriguing to medieval and early modern readers. As the poem weaves
  together sources both medieval and classical, it transforms
  first-century Romans into Christian agents of divine vengeance. Here
  presented in the most comprehensive edition to date, the poem will be of
  particular interest to scholars and students of Middle English romance,
  the Crusades, medieval antisemitism, and literary reimaginings of
  historical events. Further, this new edition expands our understanding
  of fall of Jerusalem narratives in later medieval England, bringing
  attention to a long-ignored English retelling of these first-century
  events that captivated Christian audiences"-- Provided by publisher.
Identifiers: LCCN 2021045026 (print) | LCCN 2021045027 (ebook) | ISBN
  9781580444873 (paperback) | ISBN 9781580444880 (hardback) | ISBN
  9781580444897 (pdf)
Subjects: LCSH: Titus, Emperor of Rome, 40-81--Romances. | Vespasian,
  Emperor of Rome, 9-79--Romances. | LCGFT: Romances.
Classification: LCC PR2065 .T4 2021 (print) | LCC PR2065 (ebook) | DDC
  821/.033--dc23/eng/20211022
LC record available at https://lccn.loc.gov/2021045026
LC ebook record available at https://lccn.loc.gov/2021045027

ISBN: 9781580444873 (paperback)
ISBN: 9781580444880 (hardback)
ISBN: 9781580444897 (ebook)

Printed and bound by CPI Group (UK) Ltd, Croydon, CR0 4YY

TABLE OF CONTENTS

ACKNOWLEDGMENTS

Any project of this scale relies on the generosity of editorial staff, librarians, students, and other colleagues. Ursinus College has generously supported image requests and research travel to consult manuscripts. Bailey Ludwig '19 provided research support. Students in the Fall 2018 English department capstone, Violence and Otherness in Medieval England, provided feedback on the in-progress text and notes, and the volume is far better for their engagement with it. Lori J. Daggar and Rosa Abrahams graciously read early drafts of the introduction with a keen critical eye. Beyond this material support, the departments of English and History at Ursinus College have eagerly inquired about the volume and endured extremely unusual conversation over lunch as a result, and thanks are due to them all for their generosity.

Thomas R. Martin and David Levenson provided key guidance about Josephus, his Latin translators, and Ps. Hegesippus. Frank T. Coulson's generosity and expert paleographical eye were invaluable. Fritz Graf and Sarah Iles Johnston guided us through the Sibylline Oracles. Will Batstone, as always, helped us see the poesis in historiography, no matter its genre, while Tim Joseph, Blaise Nagy, Steve Maiullo, Scott Kennedy, David T. Gura, Thomas Bihl, Deanna Singh, and Robert Albis provided support and advice along the way. Sturgis student Grace Rapo, with her own work on the Jewish war and Josephus, proved a critical interlocutor about matters Josephus at an early stage.

We thank staff at the Beinecke Library at Yale University; at the Bodleian Library, Oxford University; the Pierpont Morgan Library; and at the British Library. Staff at the Ursinus College library (most especially Interlibrary Loan), the Sturgis school library (with a surprisingly robust Interlibrary Loan!), and the Rossell Hope Robbins Library at the University of Rochester provided bibliographic support. At the Middle English Texts Series, thanks are due to the entire editorial team, most especially Pamela Yee, assistant editor; Ashley Conklin and Steffi Delcourt; and we thank both our anonymous reviewer and Alan Lupack for thoughtful and meticulous feedback. Russell A. Peck and Thomas Hahn saw the promise of the volume and encouraged the work throughout. Thanks are also due to the National Endowment for the Humanities for their long-time support of the Middle English Texts Series.

This project was inspired in part by the work and teaching of John Wilson, long-time professor of English at the College of the Holy Cross. What we discovered in his dissertation work led us to the poem some years after his death, but his life's work, especially in the classroom, planted the seeds. Sarah Stanbury and James Kee provided crucial foundations that enabled us to take this project on. We are grateful to Karen McShane and Megan Wright for tireless support both intellectual and emotional. Alexander McShane, Freddie McShane, and Bob Wright have also been crucial supporters throughout this work.

ABBREVIATIONS LIST

A	British Library Additional 36523
Addit	British Library Additional 36983
C	British Library Harley 4733
CA	Gower, *The Confessio Amantis*, ed. Peck
Chester	*The Chester Mystery Cycle*, ed. Lumiansky and Mills
Cov	Coventry, City Records Office MS 325/1
CT	Chaucer, *The Canterbury Tales*, ed. Benson
D	Bodleian Digby 230
Douce	Bodleian Douce 126
EH	Eusebius, *Ecclesiastical History*
GN	*Gospel of Nicodemus*, ed. Hulme
Herbert	*Titus and Vespasian*, ed. J. A. Herbert
HJW	Mason, *A History of the Jewish War A.D. 66–74*
JW	Josephus, *The Jewish War*, ed. Thackeray
LA	Jacobus de Voragine, *Legenda Aurea*, trans. Ryan
MED	*Middle English Dictionary*
MS	Bodleian Laud Misc 622 [base text]
Munro	Munro, "Edition and Study"
N-Town	*The N-Town Plays*, ed. Sugano
O	Beinecke Osborn A.11

PL	*Patrologia Latina*, ed. Migne
SJ	*The Siege of Jerusalem*, ed. Livingston
Towneley	*The Towneley Plays*, ed. Stevens and Cawley
Whiting	Whiting, *Proverbs, Sentences, and Proverbial Phrases*
York	*The York Corpus Christi Plays*, ed. Davidson

❧ INTRODUCTION

The *Destruction of Jerusalem*, known also as *Titus and Vespasian*, represents one anonymous writer's attempts to situate the city of Jerusalem as a central pivot point in history: a sacred city of God's chosen people, the site of the execution of God's son, and later the divine vengeance for this act upon God's chosen people that represents God's rejection of salvation for the Jews in favor of the Gentiles and Christians, represented by the future Roman emperors Titus and Vespasian. Like many Roman historical epics, *Destruction* seeks to inscribe a divine, salvific meta-narrative onto human events. The poem is inspired by the historical events of 70 CE and the Jewish War undertaken by the Romans against a rebellious province, Judea. Replete with miraculous healings, cannibalism, graphic violence, and detailed accounts of siege tactics, it presents an historical romance akin to works such as *Richard Coer de Lion*, *Siege of Jerusalem*, or the Middle English Charlemagne romances. At over five thousand lines, *Destruction* seeks to present an authoritative, comprehensive account of the fall of Jerusalem, drawing on a complex range of vernacular and Latin sources to do so.

Yet the poem's form and content both contribute to its ongoing marginalization. This position is not helped by the opinions of the few scholars who study it: Phyllis Moe refers to the poem as "an artistic failure," while Early English Texts Series editor J. A. Herbert observes that the poem "is intended to be octosyllabic . . . but our author cannot have had a very fine sense of rhythm."[1] In addition to the poem's clunky language, it amplifies the antisemitism found in works like the Middle English *Siege of Jerusalem*, making the poem both difficult and troubling for contemporary readers. Indeed, *Destruction* is usually referenced only in comparison to *Siege of Jerusalem*, almost always to suggest that *Siege* is comparatively the superior and more complex work. Yet, as Maija Birenbaum notes, "In its uniquely affective, participatory rendition of the fall-of-Jerusalem narrative, the poem [*Destruction*] engages with fourteenth-century discourses about the importance of the sacraments, specifically penance; cultural and spiritual anxieties about Jews and heretics; and fears of divine vengeance for the sins of Christendom."[2] The poem provides a crucial, if troubling, perspective in ongoing conversations on Crusades literature, Middle English popular romance, and medieval antisemitism. With this edition, then, we hope to bring renewed scholarly attention to this overlooked work.

We deviate here from the title previously given to the poem by editors; that is, we have inverted Herbert's "Titus and Vespasian, or the Destruction of Jerusalem" to call the poem simply *The Destruction of Jerusalem*. This is, of course, itself an argument, and we suggest that this is a more appropriate way to designate the poem. To begin with, this title is entirely editorial; headings given to the poem in manuscripts emphasize either the place of Jerusalem or the violence against Jews, rather than the work's Roman

---

[1]   Moe, "A Study of Two Manuscripts," p. 26; Herbert, *Titus and Vespasian*, p. xliii.

[2]   "Affective Vengeance," p. 331.

1

characters.[3] Inverting the traditionally-given title, then, brings modern practice more into keeping with medieval notions of what the poem is indeed about. It places the focus on the violence that is at the poem's heart. Further, our title links this poem more closely to Early Modern performances and versions of the legend, suggesting the poem's continuity both with its sources and with later adaptations of the narrative.[4]

THE PLOT

Like many Middle English works, *Destruction* is episodic, and the transitions between episodes are often quite abrupt. There are two distinct versions of the poem, a short and a long version; the long version includes an extended prologue and two substantial digressions from the central plot.[5] The first, an account of the birth and early life of Pontius Pilate, appears from line 1483 to line 1622. The second, from line 4461 to line 4858, describes the life of Judas Iscariot, including his birth, abandonment, adoption, and murder of his adopted brother. Judas makes his way to Jerusalem and befriends Pilate. He unknowingly kills his father in a fight and marries his mother, who sends him to Jesus to repent of these sins when they discover that they are related. The episode then describes Judas's eventual death by hanging himself after his betrayal of Jesus.

In the long version of the poem edited here, the first 910 lines serve as a lengthy prologue, retelling several key episodes in the life of Jesus familiar from the Gospels. The first describes Nicodemus's encounter with Jesus, in which Jesus tells him about the future destruction of Jerusalem. The next episode describes Jewish officials who ask Jesus to whom their taxes should be paid; Jesus asks whose image appears on their coins. When the Jews tell them that Caesar appears on them, he advises them to pay their taxes to Caesar but render God what is owed to Him. Then, the officials challenge Jesus by bringing him a woman caught committing adultery. Jesus responds by writing in the earth and then admonishes that the one of them who is without sin should deliver her punishment, and the officials all creep away. Jesus then tells the woman to go and to keep herself from sin in the future. In the next episode, the Jews question Jesus's authority, because they have the law from their ancestors; Jesus responds that he could destroy and raise their temple in three days, which angers the assembly. Jesus continues to defend himself against the charge of Sabbath-breaking for healing on the Sabbath. From there, the poem details events of the Passion, emphasizing an episode in which Jesus entered the courtyard of the temple and, angry at seeing trade and the exchange of coins there, turned over the tables and drove the sellers out. Because of this deed, the poem claims, those whom Jesus admonished led the group that captured Jesus and eventually put him to death.

After these Biblical episodes, the poem transitions to events occurring in Jerusalem after Jesus's death. The central episode here is the martyrdom of St. James the Less, drawing heavily on the *Legenda Aurea*. James, Bishop of Jerusalem, lives a holy life of preaching; indeed, he is so earnest and spends so much time in prayer that the skin on his knees becomes hard from so much time on bare stone. One Passover, the Jews admonish James to stop his preaching, but James preaches all the more, with even greater enthusiasm.

---

[3] Only three of the manuscripts we consider here include any sort of title: L and A both call the poem "The Bataile of Jerusalem," while O's header, added by a later hand, reads "The vengeance of god taken upon the Jewys for Chrystus deathe."

[4] For a more comprehensive account of these Early Modern versions, see Groves, *The Destruction of Jerusalem in Early Modern English Literature*.

[5] See Moe, "A Study of Two Manuscripts," for the most comprehensive discussion of differences between the versions. We follow Herbert and Wilson in privileging the long version of the poem.

Enraged, the Jews strike him with a fulling staff, and James bleeds to death in his church. From there, the poem describes nine others signs, astrological and prophetic, that occur in Jerusalem to foretell the city's destruction. These signs continue through line 1156 of the poem.

Following this lengthy opening, the poem gives an account of Pontius Pilate's treachery and abuse of power in Jerusalem. When Pilate learns that the emperor Tiberius intends to exile him from the city, he sends a messenger, Nathan, to Rome with a letter defending Pilate and recounting Jesus's death. Nathan is blown off course en route and eventually lands in Bordeaux. In Bordeaux, we learn that the king, Vespasian, is ill, suffering from leprosy and a swarm of wasps that have lived in his nose since his birth. Nathan meets Vespasian's son, Titus, who explains that Tiberius is dead and Nero is now emperor in Rome. Titus agrees to help Nathan reach Rome if Nathan can offer any aid to Vespasian. In response, Nathan laments that there was one who could help in Jerusalem, but that man has been killed. Nathan then retells the story of Jesus to Titus and Velosian, Vespasian's steward. The digression on the life of Pontius Pilate falls here. After this, the plot returns to following Nathan, who completes his errand in Rome and returns to Jerusalem.

After Nathan departs Bordeaux, Velosian goes to the king and seeks permission to go to Jerusalem on Vespasian's behalf. Velosian intends to seek some object that once belonged to Jesus, hoping that such an object could heal Vespasian's condition, as well as to make sure he can recognize Pontius Pilate in case Vespasian and his forces ever find themselves attacking Pilate. In incredible pain and discomfort, Vespasian agrees, and Velosian travels to Jerusalem. Upon arrival, Velosian meets Jacob, a secret Christian living in the city, and explains Vespasian's situation. Jacob introduces Velosian to Veronica, a woman healed by Jesus who has secretly kept a cloth bearing the image of Jesus's face. Veronica agrees to accompany Velosian to Bordeaux, since Pilate has been persecuting both her and Jacob because Pilate suspects they are Christians. Before Velosian and Veronica depart, however, Velosian asks Jacob if any of Jesus's torturers are still alive. Jacob explains that he sees them in the street every day and calls them together, and these torturers detail the violence they did to Jesus before his death. Velosian tells them he will tell the story everywhere he can, and once the torturers depart, he vows to bring Vespasian to Jerusalem to avenge their deeds if Vespasian regains his health.

Velosian and Veronica travel to Bordeaux, and upon arrival, Veronica meets Clement, a disciple of Peter's who has fled Rome in exile. When Veronica is summoned before Vespasian, she brings Clement with her, explaining that he can speak words and perform deeds that she cannot. Clement gives a sermon to Vespasian and his court, preaching Christian doctrine. Evidently moved by this preaching, Vespasian vows that if he is healed, he will go to Jerusalem and avenge the death of Jesus. Veronica then presents the cloth to Clement, who bids Vespasian to kiss it. Vespasian is instantly healed, and he rewards Veronica and Clement with land and money. Clement warns Vespasian that he should be baptized before he leaves for Jerusalem, but Vespasian instead makes his son Titus and his men swear to accompany him. Vespasian and Titus receive leave from Nero to go to Jerusalem, leaving Clement in control of Bordeaux. They depart, with Vespasian promising to be baptized upon his successful return. They leave Bordeaux with Clement's blessing.

Titus and Vespasian go first to Acre, take the city easily, and continue to Jaffa. The citizens of Jaffa do not willingly surrender, and many of them kill each other rather than submitting to Vespasian and Titus's army. One man, Japhel, survives and joins their forces, and Vespasian gives him a place of honor both because he is related to the emperor of Rome and because he knows the geography of the area well. Citizens flee from the surrounding area, seeking shelter inside Jerusalem. A frightened Pilate summons the king of Galilee, Archilaus, to help him, and Archilaus advises Pilate to hole up inside Jerusalem's secure walls. Vespasian's forces put the city under siege, and Archilaus encourages Pilate to go to the city walls and challenge Vespasian, which he does. Vespasian takes offense at the challenge, telling Pilate that he will regret it and admonishing Archilaus for siding with Pilate. The fighting begins as Vespasian's forces construct and deploy various siege weaponry. The war lasts for seven years. In the fifth year of the siege, Nero dies in Rome and Vespasian is chosen his successor. A messenger rushes to Jerusalem to bring the news to Vespasian, and Vespasian departs to be crowned. He returns as quickly as he can to the war.

The poem then shifts briefly to events inside Jerusalem. Within the city, Pilate accuses Jacob of helping Vespasian's forces, and Jacob is imprisoned. When Jacob's daughter Marie realizes her father is missing, she prays to Jesus that Jacob will be delivered, and Jesus releases him from his prison. Jacob leaves the city and eventually reaches Vespasian's forces, where Velosian immediately recognizes him and speaks for him. Jacob is able to provide the force with valuable strategic advice, which they quickly take. Many in the city, including Josephus, an advisor to Pilate, sneak out to attack. Josephus is injured in the battle that follows, but he survives because he is secretly Christian.

Inside the city, resources have begun to fail, notably food, leading to mass starvation and suffering. A Christian woman named Marie and her companion Clarice heed an angel's advice and cook and eat Marie's deceased daughter. Pilate is horrified and forbids the people to eat their children, advising them instead to eat their gold and silver. They do so, but mass cannibalism continues in the city.

Jacob leaves Vespasian's camp and goes to the city wall to investigate what is happening inside Jerusalem. He meets Josephus on the wall, and Josephus confesses his faith and describes the wretched conditions inside the city to Jacob. Josephus claims that the Jews would have surrendered already if Vespasian had been baptized, but that they will not surrender to a non-Christian. When Jacob goes back to Vespasian with his report, Josephus returns to Pilate and the assembled Jews to advise that they yield the city. Many of the Jews instead kill themselves and each other as a means to end their suffering. Those who survive bid Pilate to give up the town, claiming that they are suffering due to their sin in the persecution and death of Jesus.

Josephus and several companions escape the city and take shelter in a cave, but without resources, they are quickly reduced to killing and eating each other. When only Josephus and one companion remain, Josephus kills his companion in self-defense and leaves the cave, making his way to Vespasian's forces. At first, Vespasian orders him bound, but Josephus is quickly released when the Romans discover that Josephus is Christian. Josephus then heals Titus of a serious illness, earning honor for himself among the Romans.

After this, the Romans take the city. Pilate pleads with Titus to preserve his position, but Vespasian's forces show him no mercy, binding him to await punishment. Titus and his men begin to destroy the city, and in the process they find a place where the wall seems unusually thick. When they break the wall, they discover that Joseph of Arimathea, who buried Jesus and spoke against the Jews, has been walled in for the entire seven-year siege. The Romans release Joseph and show him great honor, along with other Christians found in the city. Vespasian then conducts a massive sale of the Jewish survivors, selling them thirty for a penny and encouraging the Christians to chop them open and extract the treasure that Pilate told them to eat earlier in the poem. Pilate himself is sealed alive in a barrel and sent to Viene to be imprisoned. Upon arrival, Pilate is removed from his barrel and put in prison, where he receives only water and rough bread for food except on holy days. After some time in prison, Pilate begs a guard for a paring knife and kills himself with it. His guards seal Pilate in the barrel again and toss it into the water. However, Pilate's punishment does not end here: demons torment Pilate by tossing the barrel around, and those who pass the barrel are frightened by the shrieks and other noise. Eventually, the local clergy and people come to the shore of the water and pray, and Pilate's barrel is secured in a hole in the rock. After this, the poem's second major digression, on Judas Iscariot, unfolds.

After describing Pilate's death, the poem then returns to Vespasian, who rewards his men for their faithfulness. Vespasian, Titus, and their army return from Jerusalem and are baptized. Vespasian confirms Clement as Pope. The last episode recounts a "miracle" that occurs when several surviving Jews return to the site of Jerusalem to rebuild the city. After two divine warnings in which red crosses appear first on the ground and then on the clothing of the Jews, the Jews return to the site for a third time and are killed when fire suddenly springs out of the ground.

The Historical Siege: Josephus and the Jewish War (66–72 CE)

In this section we will examine some of the key contexts for our romance. We will start with the history of the event itself, then turn our attention to the historiography of the event in Josephus's *Jewish War*; finally, we will examine the later reception of Josephus's *Jewish War*.

For Jews, the War in Judea was a cataclysmic event that culminated with the destruction of Herod's expansion of the Second Temple.[6] On the other hand, for the Flavian dynasty (69–96 CE), the war provided a basis for their claims to the imperial throne after the disastrous civil discord in Rome of the so-called "year of the four Emperors," 69 CE. Within a few decades, by the end of the first century CE, the early Christians would grow more eager to distinguish themselves from the Jewish faith and people, as figures like Saul (later Paul) of Tarsus expounded the Gospel to Gentiles. These Christians saw the destruction of the Temple as a sign of the greater validity of their faith: now Christianity had "superseded" Judaism, with a new covenant for all people.[7] This idea could quickly turn anti-Judaic, as Christian writers began to blame the people of Judea for rejecting Jesus of Nazareth as the Messiah and for responsibility for his execution at the hands of Pontius Pilate (for which the Gospel of John provides a particularly pointed example).[8]

Looking at these three responses to the war — Jewish grief at the destruction of the Temple, Roman imperial triumph, and Christian supersessionism — it may seem hard to uncover any relatively unbiased narratives of the war. What makes this even more difficult is the fact that there is only one main ancient source for the conflict, the *Jewish War* of Flavius Josephus. Josephus, a Jewish priest and one-time rebel leader who surrendered early in the war to Vespasian, wrote a history of the war in seven books within about a decade of its conclusion. It is the rare history that is, in a sense, written by a loser in the war — for example, Josephus's grief at the fall of the city and the Temple is palpable.[9] Since Josephus did join up with Vespasian, and acted as an envoy for Titus during the siege of Jerusalem, his Jewish perspective is mixed with a Roman, Flavian one. In addition, actual Flavian monuments that provide a more propagandistic perspective remain in Rome; the Arch of Titus is one particularly famous example.

---

6   We choose this wording to reflect the fact that while the Second Temple after the Babylonian exile was the foundation of the actual Temple destroyed in 70, Herod the Great almost completely replaced the Second Temple with his grandiose building projects in the 20s BCE. See Goldhill, *Temple*, pp. 4–8.

7   Gospel passages, e.g. Mark 13:1–2, were cited as evidence of God's plan.

8   Another example (important for our romance) is the Gospel of Nicodemus. See also Gatewood, "Narrative Characterization," pp. 225–92 and Judd, "Pontius Pilate," pp. 73–96.

9   See Josephus's request for indulgence at *JW* 1.9–12; and the destruction of the temple at *JW* 6.249–280. All subsequent *JW* citations will follow this book.section number format.

In the space of this introduction, we can only briefly recount the conflict's vicissitudes.[10] Nevertheless, this will provide a historical "baseline" by which we may better evaluate the changes of later authors and romances. We will begin by discussing the central cultural importance of the Temple for ancient Judaism. Then we will examine the cultural tensions that sparked the Jewish revolt, and the outcome of the war itself, by turning to our main source, Josephus.

Rome and Jerusalem

In antiquity, the Temple was the center of Jewish faith, where sacrifice was carried out to God every day in the morning and afternoon. The first Temple had been constructed by Solomon sometime in the tenth century BCE and survived for roughly 400 years, before its destruction in the Babylonian sack of Jerusalem in 586 BCE, which began the Babylonian exile. After the return of the Jews to Jerusalem several decades later, when Cyrus and the Persians had conquered Babylon in turn, a new Second Temple was constructed by the end of the sixth century BCE. This structure was greatly expanded by Herod the Great in the 20s BCE as part of a building program to strengthen his hold and position in Jerusalem. Herod was viewed with suspicion by native Jews partly because he owed his power to dispensations of the Romans, as he and his father successively impressed Caesar, Antony, and then Octavian. Herod also replaced the previous, Jewish, Hasmonean dynasty that had ruled for a century, though under Roman sufferance for its last few decades. Another problem for Herod was that he was an Idumaean, a nearby people who been forcibly converted to Judaism during an expansionary period in the Hasmonean dynasty; while he had been raised Jewish, his religious commitment was viewed with skepticism by his Jewish subjects. Thus, expanding the Temple was a way for Herod to both demonstrate his political power and commitment to the Jewish faith. What remains of the Temple today is part of the massive foundational platform Herod built for his expanded Temple, now known in modern Jerusalem as the "Wailing Wall."

An elite priestly caste, the Saducees, arranged sacrifice and maintained the temple complex. The complex itself was divided into several areas. Various outdoor courts were set aside for different groups — one for gentiles, one for Jewish women, one for Jewish men, one for priests. Another court, the Temple Court, was set aside for sacrificial offerings. Inside the Temple were three chambers: the *ulam* (antechamber); the *hekhal* (sanctuary), where the menorah, the showbread, and incense altar were located; and the Holy of Holies, where the ark of the covenant was originally placed. These last two chambers were separated from the rest of the Temple structure and access to them was highly restricted — only the high priest could enter the Holy of Holies and even then only on Yom Kippur (the day of atonement). Jews living outside Jerusalem in various parts of the Mediterranean, who could not easily attend Temple services, sent money to Jerusalem each year towards Temple upkeep, a tithe of a half shekel. Transport of the proceeds of this Temple tax to Jerusalem could be hazardous — liable to banditry or the avarice of local potentates along the way. For example, Josephus tells us that Mithridates VI Eupator once seized 800 talents of Jewish money (an enormous sum) from the island of Cos[11] in 88 BCE. Another incident occurred in 62 BCE, when the Roman governor of Syria, Flaccus, confiscated a large stash of Jewish gold bound for Jerusalem, as a defense

---

[10] Steve Mason's recent and magisterial *History of the Jewish War* (hereafter, *HJW*) should be the go-to reference for students of the Jewish War. Mason's cogent analysis and reconstruction informs much of our summary below. The recent translation of Josephus by Martin Hammond and Martin Goodman in the Oxford World Classics series is an excellent accessible rendering of Josephus, with valuable notes and indices.

[11] Josephus, *Jewish Antiquities*, trans. Thackeray, Marcus, Wikgren, and Feldman, 14.112–13; all subsequent citations will follow this book.section number format.

speech by Cicero tells us.[12] Later, the Jews got a decree from Julius Caesar that the money for this tithe was protected, but after the destruction of Herod's Temple, Vespasian redirected these proceeds to the Temple of Jupiter Optimus Maximus in Rome as the *fiscus Judaicus*, or Jewish tax.

While it is doubtful that Titus and Vespasian intended from the outset to destroy the Temple, there is debate about whether its destruction was accidental, or if Titus and his generals decided to destroy it after the frustrations of a long siege.[13] Certainly Judaism was a tolerated faith in the Roman empire, even if individual Romans looked askance at Jewish culture and customs. Either way, the Temple has remained a potent cultural symbol (and its location a site of simmering interfaith conflict) to this day. The Jewish war functionally ended with the destruction of the Temple in 70 CE. It began there as well in 66 CE, when a young priest ordered that the daily sacrifices for the health of the Roman emperor were to cease. This was a response to Roman exaction of Temple funds and, when combined with other rising tensions in the region, sparked the war that would consume the region for the next several years.

The background and causes of the war are complex, and ultimately go back to the origins of the Hasmonean dynasty in the Maccabean revolt of the mid-second century BCE (famously retold in 1 and 2 Maccabees in the Old Testament, and in the context of the story of Hannukah). Put simply: certain revolutionary parties in Judea exploited increased cultural tensions between Jews and Romans to spark a revolt against the Romans, and that revolt was brutally suppressed by Vespasian and Titus. Josephus adds that civil discord between the revolutionary parties and those who wanted to maintain the status quo also debilitated the Jewish state, making it easy for the Romans to win the war.[14]

For centuries, Judea had been a small region caught up in other empires — Persian, Seleucian, and then Roman. Given the limitations of communication and travel in antiquity, and the political changes and upheavals occurring at the imperial centers, Judea and Jerusalem did have periods of comparative independence. The most notable one was the Hasmonean dynasty of 140–37 BCE. The roots of the dynasty were found in the revolt of Judah Maccabeus in the 160s BCE.[15] As retold in 1 and 2 Maccabees and in the first book of Josephus's *War*, the Jews reacted against the attempts of the Seleucian king Antiochus IV to exert control on the region. Eventually, after years of conflict, Seleucid energies were needed elsewhere to defend their kingdom against rival powers (including Rome), and Judah's brother Simon took power in Jerusalem as high priest and prince of Israel, founding the Hasmonean dynasty.

Simon and his successors began to expand aggressively, which created untold resentments between the Jews and neighboring Greeks, Samaritans, and Idumeans, and as a result the Roman general Pompey the Great was enthusiastically welcomed by non-Jews of the region when he clipped the wings of Hasmonean control. Eventually, constant infighting doomed the Hasmonean dynasty and the Idumean adventurer Herod replaced them, founding his own dynasty after successively winning the support of Caesar, Antony, and finally Octavian (the later emperor Augustus).

Rome's entry onto the scene changed the political dynamics. First, it conquered and absorbed the Seleucid empire and by extension Judea. Second, in the figure of Pompey the Great, Rome adjudicated in a civil war between rival fraternal claimants to the Hasmonean throne. Herod's rise to power was aided by

---

[12] *Pro Flacco* 67–69, trans. Macdonald.

[13] On this see Barnes, "Sack of the Temple."

[14] On the cultural contrast between Rome and Jerusalem in this period, see Goodman, *Rome and Jerusalem*.

[15] Interestingly, Judah Maccabeus was familiar to Christian audiences as one of the Nine Worthies, a group of figures seen as chivalric exemplars: three Christian, three pagan, and three Jewish. For a brief overview of the Nine Worthies, see van Anrooij, "Nine Worthies," *Encyclopedia of the Medieval Chronicle*, 2:1150–52.

his adept maneuvering between factions in the Roman civil wars. This meant, however, that Herod owed his power to, and Judea remained a part of, the Roman Empire. Herod's own expansionist tendencies did much to exacerbate Gentile and Jewish tensions that had barely recovered from Hasmonean ambitions.

For the Romans, Herod fulfilled the role of client king — a local potentate who could keep his people under control and do Rome's bidding as necessary, obviating the need for a Roman governor or military legate in the region. While Herod was a ruler of some talent, shown primarily in an enthusiastic liquidation of any potential rivals to the throne and in appointing unknowns to the high priesthood, his descendants were judged by the Romans to be unfit for rule and so in 6 CE, upon Herod's death, Judea was formally absorbed into the Roman Empire and a procurator was appointed to rule over the Judeans.[16] A procurator was not a governor per se, but more of a bureaucratic administrator, who might have a few cohorts at his command to keep the peace but would be outranked by a legate or official Roman governor, in this case the governor of Syria, the main Roman province in the region. The most famous procurator of the Judeans was, of course, Pontius Pilate. Pilate was not a bad procurator by Roman standards, and was certainly not as antagonistic to the Jews as his successors could be, nor the craven and calculating moral monster of the *Destruction of Jerusalem.*

The procurators and other officials sent by Rome were, as often in such cases, of varying quality. The Jews expected that they could have some outlet for complaints with the local Roman governor, or ultimately even appeal to the Emperor himself (Josephus, in fact, had just returned from such a mission when he found himself a general in Galilee). A larger issue, however, was Jerusalem's loss of any kind of regional supremacy. Without a Herodian monarch, the center of power for the Roman officials had switched to nearby Caesarea, while Jerusalem remained a religious center of some importance, due to the presence of the Temple. With Jerusalem's importance and power in the region diminished, there were legitimate Jewish fears that other peoples in the region, particularly the Samarians, would let vent the long simmering resentments over Hasmonean and Herodean rule. Given the fact that Roman auxiliary forces (locals drafted into military units to supplement and assist the actual Roman army) were made up of these locals and not Jews (due to an exemption for Jewish men from military service), there was plentiful opportunity for abuses both trivial and large. With a procurator like Pontius Pilate in the 30s CE, who strove to keep up good relations with the Jews, these resentments and fears of lost status could be minimized. With someone like the later procurator of the 50s CE, Gessius Florus, who cared little for Jewish opinion and was assigned by Nero primarily to acquire money for the imperial treasury, these resentments and fears flared up. Even though the legate at the time, Cestius Gallus, had tried to maintain good relationships with Jewish elites and technically outranked Florus, the latter's remit from Nero constrained Gallus's options to keep the peace.

The Romans respected Jewish monotheism as a traditional religion of some antiquity, and in return the Jews offered sacrifices to God daily on behalf of the emperor's health. Nevertheless, most Romans found Jews to be a strange, highly insular people, and the references in Latin literature to Jews tend to be contemptuous in one way or another.[17] The emperor Nero shared this contemptuous attitude towards the Jews, and his youth (diminishing the prospect of a new ruler, short of war or assassination) seemed to rule out the viability of diplomatic missions to redress Jewish grievances. In short, by the mid-60s, many Jews in Jerusalem

---

[16] Later, the emperor Claudius attempted to install Agrippa I as King of Judea, as a reward for Agrippa's early support of Claudius's succession of Caligula. However, Agrippa I died after only a few years, and Rome reinstalled its own people to take control of the region, deeming Agrippa II, his father's heir, to be unready for rule. Agrippa II's sister Berenice notoriously maintained a sexual liaison with Titus, the son of Vespasian, and emperor from 79–81 CE.

[17] Tacitus, *Histories* 5.3–9 is a representative example of Roman attitudes.

found themselves with diminished regional status, at the implacable mercy of the Romans, and victims of harassment and abuse by the local auxiliary forces. For some, like the revolution-minded Zealots, therefore, war and revolt may have seemed the only option. The regional elites of Jerusalem and Judea, the class that Rome relied on to keep order in the provinces, were unable to tamp down this revolutionary activity, particularly when the Zealots began assassinating their opponents.[18]

The Outbreak of War

For these reasons, by 66 CE, the region was a tinderbox. One day, some Greeks began sacrificing birds in front of a local synagogue. Enraged by this sacrilege against Jewish custom, a priest at the Temple in Jerusalem stopped prayers and sacrifices for the emperor's health. For this sign of loyalty to cease was a strong signal of potential revolt. Florus, who cared only for his mission of raising funds for Nero, immediately made things worse by leading a detachment of soldiers into the Temple and removing seventeen talents from it, a significant amount of money. This outrage plunged the city into reactionary unrest and mockery of the procurator (some people passed a basket around collecting money for Florus, jeering that he must be poor and that is why he stole from the Temple). In response, Florus sent in soldiers to arrest city leaders, who he had whipped and crucified. At this, Jewish rebels rose up and overwhelmed the garrison inside the city, while Agrippa II and his sister Berenice, Herodians who had tried to calm the Jews, fled to Galilee. Next, militants spread out over the region, destroying Roman symbols and terrorizing Romans and pro-Roman inhabitants. Some militants even took over the fortress of Masada. Florus fled, leaving to Cestius Gallus, the legate in Syria, the burden of restoring order.

Unlike Florus, Gallus maintained cordial relations with the Jerusalem elite, as any good Roman governor should have done. He expected that, with some quick retaliatory mop-up operations of rebelling militants in the area, he could arrange a cessation of hostilities and restore order. Upon arrival at Jerusalem, with Agrippa II and Berenice in tow, Gallus's hopes were dashed, and those of Agrippa and Berenice dashed yet again — Judean militants even attacked the baggage train of Cestius's force as they approached Jerusalem. Disappointed by his exclusion from the city and lacking supplies and forces for an extended siege, Gallus turned back towards the seat of his power at Antioch in Syria. The rebels, emboldened by their previous attack on the baggage train and on Gallus's exclusion from Jerusalem, attacked the Roman forces in an ambush in the Beit-Horon pass. The Jews' defeat of Gallus's Roman force all but ensured a forceful response from Rome. Judea was now committed to war.

A frustrated and shamed Gallus returned to Antioch to plan for a more forceful response in the spring, sending some forces and cavalry to keep order amongst the cities of the Decapolis, a group of ten Hellenistic foundations, and in Galilee. In the meantime, the emperor Nero had lost faith in Gallus and recognized the need for new leadership to settle the issue. Nero faced a perennial problem of Roman emperors; he needed to find a general capable of battling the revolutionary Jews, but one who would not outshine the emperor and become, willingly or not, a threat to imperial power. He settled on the seasoned, capable non-entity Titus Flavius Vespasianus. Vespasian took his son Titus with him, and (like Gallus), brought Agrippa and Berenice as well, in order to make the most out of connections to the local elite. At the very least, the Romans would have expected to raze a few towns and then, based on Gallus's experience there, to besiege Jerusalem. This would fulfill the basic policy need: when the Roman Empire was disrespected, reprisal was,

---

[18]   For an analysis of this elite group and its breakdown, see Goodman, *Ruling Class*.

if not always swift, always brutal — a way to both punish the initial transgression and to warn any other province or people thinking of rebelling against Roman rule.

The Jewish elite knew this well and realized that, as much as they themselves deplored the actions of the militants, a penalty would have to be paid and much suffering would ensue, as often happens in war: famine, disease, rape, pillage, sieges, and sacks. Forced into a defensive situation and dreading the arrival of a retaliatory force in the next campaign season, they appointed leading citizens to go out into the region and prepare other cities and towns for the oncoming Roman onslaught. One of these "generals" (for lack of a better term) was the future historian Josephus, who took responsibility for Galilee. Though his exact activities and motivations differ between the earlier account in *War* and the later one in the *Life*, Josephus seems to have done his job competently, despite rivalrous intrigues against him by the notorious John of Ghiscala, who would go on to cause much misery in Jerusalem before the war was done. In fact, Josephus presents himself as Vespasian's most tenacious opponent in the third book of the *Jewish War*.

As Vespasian arrived, he knew he would have to be prepared for a siege at Jerusalem, with all the investment of manpower and resources that such an operation would entail. This was all the more reason to ensure the surrounding countryside was secure first, not least to avoid a repeat of the ambush of Gallus's forces that had led to Vespasian's appointment. Thus, Vespasian began by securing the region of Galilee, which would eventually bring him into contact with Josephus. Upon his arrival in Galilee, most of the cities and towns sent delegates immediately and allowed the placement of garrisons. Part of this was tactical, of course — it was all they could do to avoid the punishing force of the Roman army. Other towns tried to hold out, but those too, like Iotapata, fell to the Romans in the end. Nevertheless, though he was in nearly full control of Galilee by this point without the need for actual military activity, Vespasian still made sure there was minatory and retaliatory violence — Gallus's losses in the ambush at Beit-Horon had to be avenged, after all.

For whatever reason the city of Iotapata was marked for especial punishment.[19] Josephus's remit had been to prepare the cities of the region for just this eventuality. Though he had already successfully fled Iotapata, Josephus returned to the city as the Roman army approached and, perhaps hoping he could negotiate a settlement, chose to face the siege with the people of that city. Whatever else one may think of Josephus, this was a brave choice. He held out until the city fell before being captured in somewhat mysterious circumstances that would haunt his later career. Briefly brought before Vespasian, Josephus claimed that he was versed in prophecy and predicted Vespasian's eventual accession to the Roman throne.[20] Vespasian, understandably seeing this as the rankest flattery, had Josephus put back with the other prisoners. When Josephus's alleged prediction was ultimately proven actually prescient,[21] he was released and made part of the Flavian retinue. Josephus's membership in the Jerusalem elite would allow him the opportunity to fulfill a similar diplomatic role as Agrippa II and Berenice had attempted for Gallus.

With Galilee secure, Vespasian moved further south, receiving the surrender of other towns in the region, Jerusalem excepted — though rich Jerusalemites escaped as they were able to Vespasian and his forces. With just about the entire region secure, Vespasian could bide his time, surround Jerusalem, and prepare as thoroughly as he could for a siege. However, the forces of civil discord active in both the city of Jerusalem itself, and in the larger Roman world, were ready to completely change the character of the war.

---

19   Mason, *HJW*, pp. 365–70. Mason argues that a garrison commander at Sepphoris antagonized the locals and then deceptively chalked it up to recalcitrant rebels in the city.

20   This event happens in *Destruction* as well, at lines 3911–15.

21   The cynic would of course note that since Josephus is writing his account of the war after the victory of Vespasian and Titus, it is all too easy (and convenient) to insert this *post facto* "prophecy."

The Next Phase: Civil Discord in Rome and Jerusalem

While Vespasian was reestablishing Roman authority in the province of Judea, the center of Roman power was in upheaval, culminating in the chaos of the so-called "year of the four Emperors," 69 CE. In 68 CE, Julius Vindex, the governor of Gaul, had revolted against Nero, supported by Galba, the nearby governor of Hispania Terraconensis, one of the Roman provinces in Spain. Though Vindex's revolt ultimately failed, enough of the military and civil authorities in Rome had tired of Nero's reign, with its pretentions to artistry and the bloodletting that followed the exposure of the conspiracy of Piso in 65 CE. Tried and condemned *in absentia*, Nero committed suicide and Galba took the throne. Galba was overthrown in turn by the forces of Otho, who had been frustrated by Galba's choice of heir. In the meantime, Vitellius declared for the throne in Germania. Defeated in an engagement with Vitellius's forces at Bedriacum, Otho committed suicide rather than prolong a hopeless conflict. The senate confirmed Vitellius as emperor, though his reign began with ill omens.

At this point, the legions in Egypt declared for Vespasian, along with the legions in Syria and Vespasian's own in Judea. The governor of Syria, Gaius Lucius Mucianus, also supported Vespasian. Emboldened by their support, Vespasian left the command of the Jewish war to his elder son Titus,[22] and left for Egypt to take command of the legions there. Control of Egypt gave Vespasian a distinct advantage, both because of the province's wealth and because it was the most important grain supplier for Rome. His position was further strengthened when the legions on the Danube also declared for him. Marcus Antonius Primus led these legions in an invasion of Italy, defeating Vitellius's forces at the second battle of Bedriacum. An increasingly desperate Vitellius was soon caught and killed, and Vespasian's forces took the city, though Vespasian himself remained in Egypt. On December 21, 69 CE the Senate declared Vespasian the new Emperor, the fourth and final man to ascend to the throne that fateful year.

Back in Judea, Titus continued to prepare for the eventual siege of Jerusalem. Inside the city itself, various factions struggled for power, and the arrival of John of Ghiscala, fleeing Vespasian's military operations in Galilee that resulted in Josephus's capture, made matters inside the city worse. Various rival factions were packed into the city, which was nominally controlled by the Judean Free Government led by the priest Ananus ben Ananus. It was under their authority that Josephus had gone out to secure Galilee. When John of Ghiscala arrived in Jerusalem, he led the Zealots in taking control of large parts of the city, began fighting with the Judean Free Government, and executed any who advocated surrender to the Romans. The Zealots next lured a force of 20,000 Idumaeans into the city with a false message that the Judaean Free Government had already reached terms of surrender with Rome. The Zealots and Idumaeans attacked the forces of the Judean Free Government, killing Ananus ben Ananus, countless civilians,[23] and seizing the Temple. John later tricked and killed the original leader of the Zealots and began a despotic rule of the city. In response, the remnants of the Free Government invited the rebel warlord Simon bar Giora into the city. Simon had led the forces that defeated Gallus earlier in the conflict, but the Free Government still distrusted Simon and expelled him from Jerusalem. Simon fled to Masada, but eventually left that fortress too, in order to engage in banditry around Idumaea, before coming to Jerusalem once more. Simon and John's respective forces now began a bitter civil war, only joining together when it became clear that the Roman army now led by Titus were investing for a long siege.

---

[22] His second son, the later Emperor Domitian (ruled 81–96 CE), had been left behind in Rome.

[23] Josephus counts out 12,000, which is likely an exaggeration.

All of this was terrible enough for the poor civilians still trapped in the city (most of the wealthy elite would have fled much earlier in the conflict). The Zealots proceeded to make things far worse by burning the food supplies in the city to further induce everyone to fight against the Romans rather than surrender. As the siege began in earnest, there were probably about one million people, by Josephus's estimate, still within the city walls.

The Fall of Jerusalem and the End of the War

By the summer of 70 CE, the siege had been going on for seven months. The suffering inside was ineffably terrible. Titus finally breached the city, aided by the collapse of several walls. The forces of Simon held the upper city, while John and his Zealots occupied the Temple. In July, Titus finally breached the third wall, which had been put up before the siege had begun and was the weakest of all. Though it is debated whether the destruction of the Temple was intended by the Romans or not, it burned to the ground on July 29–30, 70 CE, with monumental consequences for the Jewish and Christian faiths. The city was put to the torch, and Simon and John were captured. Both were marched in the triumph back in Rome, along with treasures looted from the Temple and city, like the Menorah. But while John was sentenced to life imprisonment, Simon was executed at the climax of the triumph.[24]

Even though the Flavians, imperial father Vespasian, and his general son Titus celebrated a triumph after the fall of Jerusalem, the rebellion was not fully stamped out — pockets of resistance remained at Herodium and Machaerus. Finally, there were the forces still at the well-placed fortress of Masada, strategically placed atop a plateau. These rebels held out against the Roman forces until 72 CE. Determined to stamp out every vestige of the revolt, the Romans, now led by Lucius Flavius Silva, built a circumvallation (or enclosing wall) around the plateau to prevent any supplies from getting in or people from getting out. Next, they transported vast amounts of earth in order to construct a siege ramp up to the redoubt itself. When they finally broke through, the Romans found that nearly all of the inhabitants had killed themselves. The remains of the Roman siege works can still be seen at Masada today. This was the bitter end to the first Jewish War.

In the aftermath, Vespasian instituted the *fiscus Judaicus*, a tax upon Jews which essentially redirected the half-shekel tithe to the Temple of Jupiter Optimus Maximus in Rome. He also ordered the Temple of Onias in Egypt to be destroyed, lest that become another center of insurrection. There would be two other major Jewish revolts in the Roman empire. In 117 CE, the Kitos war enflamed Jewish communities across the Eastern Mediterranean for two years before its eventual repression. Finally, in 132 CE, a revolt erupted in Judea led by Simon bar Kokhba, which was also suppressed. Afterwards, the emperor Hadrian built a Roman colony, Aelia Capitolina, on the site of the ruins of Jerusalem. Aelia Capitolina remained the name of the site until the seventh century CE and survives as the Arabic name for Jerusalem (*Iliyā*).

JOSEPHUS AND THE *JEWISH WAR*

The Jewish War (66–72 CE) is the rare ancient conflict where a participant wrote an account of the event afterwards. Josephus thus joins a group of ancient historians that includes Thucydides (a clear and obvious

---

[24]   The Menorah can still be seen on an interior panel of the arch of Titus. See Mason, *HJW*, pp. 4–41, on the triumph and associated monuments.

model in many ways for Josephus) and Julius Caesar. Josephus's text was written in Greek[25] and eventually translated into Latin (perhaps by Cassiodorus) and adapted into Latin by later writers, in particular the author called Pseudo-Hegesippus. In this section we will consider the life of Josephus, his corpus of works, and their transmission into later Latin translations and adaptations.

Life of Josephus

What we can know of Josephus's life comes from those parts of the *War* where he is a participant in the action (first as a leader in the siege of Jotapata, later as a prisoner-turned-advisor in the camp of the Flavians). Late in his life, presumably safely ensconced in Rome on the outer fringes of the new dynasty, Josephus composed a text appended to the *Antiquities* which scholars call the *Life* of Josephus. Rather than an autobiography in our sense, it is really an *apologia* against the calumnies of another participant in the war, whose own writings are no longer extant, as well as rather revised account of Josephus's actions during the revolt from 66–72 CE. Oftentimes, when Josephus describes an event in the *Life* which he had earlier written about in the *Wars*, the account in the *Life* is markedly different from his earlier work. This is not a case of better research or a more detached approach to the conflict years removed, but rather the result of different goals and audiences for the two texts. Nevertheless, these divergences have vexed scholars over the years, especially when trying to put together a convincing account of the early stages of Vespasian's campaigns, much less the life of the author of our main surviving historical account of the conflict.

What we can confidently say about Josephus is that he was born around 37 CE, and was descended from a priestly family on his father Matthias's side and from the Hasmonean dynasty on his aristocratic mother's side. Such parentage and noble lineage ensured a wealthy and comfortable upbringing for Josephus and his elder brother, named Matthias after their father. In the *Life* he describes a typical elite upbringing, and rather too schematically limns his education in the major "schools" of Jewish thought in the first century CE — the Saduccees, the Pharisees and the Essenes.

It is worthwhile to pause for a moment to outline these three schools, both for their importance to ancient Jewish culture (Saduccees) and later Jewish, rabbinical culture (arising out of the Pharisees), and because membership in the sects tended to reflect class distinctions.[26] The Saduccees were primarily composed of the priestly elite and handled the maintenance and sacrifice at the Temple. They kept firmly to the Mosaic law or "written Torah" and eschewed the eschatological beliefs of the other sects. They also tended to be more in favor of Hellenization, and those trying to make peace with Rome would largely be of this group. The Pharisees for their part resisted Hellenization, tended to be of non-elites (Josephus reports they enjoyed broad lower class support),[27] and emphasized the oral Torah — laws and interpretations — over the written one.[28] Members of this sect would tend to want to resist Roman power. With the fall of the Second Temple, Rabbinical Judaism would evolve out of the Pharisaic sect. The last and smallest group, the Essenes, were a more eschatological, communitarian group. They lived apart from others, focusing more on

---

[25] There are references to a supposed earlier Aramaic edition in the preface to the *Jewish War* (*JW* 1.3), but there is no other evidence such an edition ever existed.
[26] A further complication is that Josephus is our only real source of information about these sects.
[27] Josephus, *Jewish Antiquities* 18.12–15.
[28] The "oral Torah" is teachings originally passed down over the generations. It was eventually written down after the destruction of the Second Temple. It is comprised of the Mishnah (the oral Torah itself) and the Gemara, a series of commentaries on the Mishnah. Together these two works comprise the Talmud, the preeminent text of Rabbinical Judaism.

purity than even other Jewish sects. It would not be too far off the mark to call these communities "monas-tic" in character, or at least monastic *avant la lettre*, with their commitments to asceticism and (for priests) celibacy. The famous "Dead Sea Scrolls" were produced by Essenes.

Josephus's first major role in adulthood was membership in an embassy to the emperor Nero, to argue for the release of twelve Jewish priests. While he was in Rome, events in Jerusalem had spiraled out of con-trol. Almost as soon as he returned to Judea, Josephus found himself as governor of Galilee, responsible for its defensive preparations for the expected retaliatory action by the Romans. Although we cannot be sure, given how Josephus changes his account between *War* and *Life*, he may have also been sent by the elites in Jerusalem to feel out sentiment in Galilee, to see if a large-scale conflict with Rome could yet be avoided and a few guilty parties turned over for punishment — for Rome could not let the successful ambush of a legion go unrevenged.

While in Galilee, Josephus successfully fortified major settlements and cities in the region in prepara-tion for the expected Roman retaliation. In both *War* and *Life*, Josephus describes his wrangling with John of Gischala for control of Galilee.[29] Their contest is left unresolved, even if Josephus gets the last laugh in his work with his vicious and caustic characterization of John, who becomes one of the leading villains in Josephus's *Jewish War*. While Josephus would leave Galilee in Roman custody, John would later make his way to Jerusalem to become a pox upon the city and its population, especially in his murderous rivalry with Simon Bar Giora, who emerges as the other lead antagonist in Josephus's account.

The downfall of Jotapata was but a detour in the inexorable march of Vespasian's legions across Galilee. As the city fell, Josephus found himself in a cave with forty other survivors. These holdouts rejected Roman calls for surrender and Josephus suggested a method of collective suicide by counting out amongst the forty lots, where the person who took the first lot would be killed by the one who chose the second. Josephus keeps this account suitably vague (he would have to, since he survived), but somehow Josephus ended up as one of the last two alive and convinced his fellow survivor to just forget about the whole thing. Leaving the cave and the bodies behind, Josephus became a Roman prisoner.[30] He cannily prophesized (suddenly in possession of a heretofore unmentioned gift of divination) Vespasian's eventual accession to the throne, which later led to his release and elevation amongst the non-military coterie in the Flavian camp. He would prove most useful as an ambassador to the Jews of Rome, though his efforts (as in the romance) were in vain.

After the war, Josephus went back to Rome with his new patrons. He seems to have been present at the Flavians' triumphal parade; in fact, he provides us with the fullest account of a Roman triumph we possess.[31] He received lands around Jerusalem from the Flavians and resided in one of their domiciles in Rome (like-ly one owned earlier by Vespasian). He composed all of his extant works during this Roman retirement. Especially for his later works, he benefitted from contact with several leading personages in Rome and boasted of Titus's personal approval of the *War*.[32] Nevertheless, it would seem that he was on the fringes of Flavian patronage.[33] He probably died around 100 CE.

---

[29] While John does not appear in the *Destruction of Jerusalem*, he does appear in its cognate text, the *Siege of Jerusalem*. See *SJ*, line 1137.

[30] See *JW* 3.340–355.

[31] On the Roman triumph see Beard, *Roman Triumph*.

[32] Josephus, *Life*, ed. Mason, 65.

[33] Cotton and Eck, "Josephus' Roman Audience."

As Steve Mason asserts, Josephus is not a sure guide to reconstructing the events of the *Jewish War*. Nevertheless, he is our only substantial guide, sometimes assisted by archaeology.[34] However, Josephus is *not* a historian in our modern sense of academic history. History, in antiquity, was a branch of rhetoric. While writers self-professedly strove to present the truth, much leeway was given to the individual writer of history in filling in the picture, according to the principle of *to eikos* or "what is probable." Josephus, first and foremost, is a literary artist, one whose art involved commemorating the past. Like our romance, Josephus sees the fate of the Temple and Jerusalem as an act of divine vengeance. However, unlike our romance, Josephus attributes this to the civil discord plaguing the city, especially the battles between Simon and John, rather than the execution of Jesus.[35] But like our romance, Josephus sees the Roman army led by Vespasian and Titus as the instrument of God's will.[36]

The Corpus and its Transmission

We possess four works of Josephus, all in Greek. The cultural polemics of *Against Apion*, where Josephus defends the value of Jewish culture against a Hellenic detractor, will not concern us here. Most important for our purposes is the *Jewish War*, a text in seven books that was likely started soon after the war's effective conclusion (i.e., after the destruction of the Temple in 70 CE, but before the fall of Masada in 72 CE) and finished by the end of the 70s CE. This text starts from the origins of the Hasmonean dynasty in the second century BCE and concludes with the fall of Masada in 72 CE. The twenty books of *Jewish Antiquities* trace Jewish history from Adam and Eve to the outbreak of the Jewish War (therefore, here too there is overlap and variation with the narrative in *War*). The *Life* of Josephus was apparently conceived as an appendix to this later work. Both the *Antiquities* and *Life* date to the 90s CE.

As with most surviving works of Greco-Roman antiquity, we owe the preservation of Josephus's text to the hard work of Christians in Late Antiquity and the Middle Ages.[37] There is also a Hebrew transmission, the *Sefer Yosippon*.[38] The Greek text would have been preserved in the Eastern part of the Roman Empire (what modern historians call the Byzantine Empire, which outlasted the empire in the west for nearly a thousand years). The seven main witnesses to the Greek text of *War* are from the eleventh century CE — which means there is still another millennium of transmission between our earliest extant texts and Josephus himself, for which we have no testimonia or evidence.[39] Latin translations and adaptations were made in Late Antiquity. A passage from Cassiodorus's *Institutions of Divine and Secular Learning* tells us that the scholar and statesman had had the *Antiquities* of Josephus translated by monks at his monastery

---

[34]   The limitations on archaeology in Jerusalem, especially around the Temple Mount, mean that much of the additional evidence has been limited to Galilee. See Mason, *HJW*, pp. 466–87 and for a recent survey. See Goldhill, *Temple*, pp. 152–62 for a survey of the last major archaeological work on the Temple mount in the 1960s.

[35]   Josephus remarks on God's vengeance in several places in the *JW*, e.g. 2.539, 3.354, 4.104, 4.288–89, 5.19. Josephus adopts many of his ideas about civil discord from the work of Thucydides. See Mader, *Josephus and the Politics of Historiography*.

[36]   E.g. *JW* 2.390–94, 3.6, 3.293, 5.367–68, 6.38–41.

[37]   See Goodman, *Josephus's Jewish War: A Biography*, for a concise survey of the history of that text.

[38]   See Nisse, *Jacob's Shipwreck*, pp. 1–48 on the *Sefer Yosippon*.

[39]   On the Greek manuscript transmission of the corpus, see Leoni, "Josephan Corpus."

Vivarium, while ascribing a translation of the *War* alternately to Jerome, Ambrose, or Rufinus.[40] There is nothing in their surviving works or testimonia that suggest Ambrose or Jerome ever attempted a translation of the *Jewish War* themselves,[41] and the earliest records of attribution to Rufinus date to the fifteenth century. As Cassiodorus is writing in the sixth century CE and refers to earlier translations of the *War*, it would seem the Latin translation would date to the fourth or fifth century CE (300s–400s), though absent any other information beyond the mere existence of the text and the lone testimonium from Cassiodorus, this must remain a guess.

In late antiquity the most notable adaptation was by Pseudo-Hegesippus, a text that seems to date from the fourth century (300s) CE, usually called *De Excidio Urbis Hierosolymitanae* (*On the Destruction of the City of Jerusalem*), in five books, reduced from the original seven of Josephus.[42] A somewhat compressed account of the war, it mixes elements of Josephus's *Jewish War* and *Jewish Antiquities* with Christian material. The author generally follows the thread of Josephus's account, while explicitly figuring the destruction of the city and the Temple as divine retribution for the death of Christ, rather than Josephus's emphasis on God's anger at Jewish discord. Because of this shared sense of God's divine anger, it is not too difficult for an author like Pseudo-Hegesippus and later Christians to use Josephus's narrative for their own Christian ends.

One factor that allowed the text of Pseudo-Hegesippus to endure is the fact that it was often ascribed to Josephus in antiquity. By the ninth century it had been (mistakenly) identified with the second-century CE Greek Christian apologist Hegesippus (hence the modern addition of Pseudo). Claiming that a text was written by an established famous author was one way to help it find an audience.[43] However, its association/confusion with Josephus's original was also the source of its authority on the subject for centuries.[44] Thus, when it comes to deducing the source of different details of the war in texts like *The Siege of Jerusalem* or our *Destruction*, it can be very difficult to determine whether it is derived from the Latin translation of Josephus's original or Pseudo-Hegesippus. It is likely that the author of *Destruction* encountered Josephus through the Latin translation mentioned by Cassiodorus, Ps.-Hegessipus, or more probably a mixture of

---

[40] Cassiodorus, *Institutions*, p. 149. Some argue that Cassiodorus may have in mind here the work of Pseudo-Hegesippus, but since Cassiodorus explicitly refers to a work on the war in seven books (Pseudo-Hegesippus is only five books), it seems clear he is referring to a Latin translation of Josephus himself, not the adaptation of Pseudo-Hegesippus. Levenson and Martin, "Ancient Latin Translation," p. 323 summarizes this debate.

[41] In *Epistulae* 71.5 Jerome claims he cannot translate the *Antiquities* because the work is too long.

[42] On Pseudo-Hegesippus, see Kletter, "Christian Reception," p. 371.

[43] Hence, for example, the canonical status of the pseudepigraphical letters of Paul. The Hippocratic corpus is also largely pseudepigraphical. Homer, Plato, and many ancient playwrights had many works attributed to them that, even in antiquity, were questioned. On Christian pseudepigraphical writings see Ehrman, *Forged*.

[44] The authorizing function of the figure of Josephus himself may partially explain his presence in our romance. Eusebius cites the authority of Josephus for his details on the destruction of Jerusalem in the *Ecclesiastical Histories*, translated into Latin by the aforementioned Rufinus. This may also be one function of the *Testimonium Flavium*, a brief passage about Jesus of Nazareth inserted into the text of Josephus's *Jewish Antiquities* 18.3.3. See Whealey, "Testimonium Flavianum," and Nisse, *Jacob's Shipwreck*, pp. 19–21.

both. Though work on both traditions is limited, there is hope that more work will be done to expound these neglected aspects of Josephus's reception.[45]

DESTRUCTION IN THE MIDDLE AGES: THE VENGEANCE OF OUR LORD TRADITION

Though *Destruction* has its ultimate origins in the writings of Josephus, Eusebius, and Pseudo-Hegesippus, accounts such as the one in *Destruction* were increasingly common from the twelfth century onward, with a proliferation of similar tales across genres and languages in the fourteenth and fifteenth centuries.[46] The Old and Middle French prose *Vengeance de Nostre-Seigneur* exists in over forty-five manuscripts, and the fifteenth and sixteenth centuries saw over twenty-three editions.[47] Notably, this version as well as the poetic *Venjance de Nostre Seigneur* lack the episode about Judas, the account of Pontius Pilate's birth, and the closing episode in which the Jews return to the site of Jerusalem.[48]

    Destruction weaves together a vast array of sources, the majority of them Latin. The most frequently used include the *Vindicta Salvatoris*, dated to around 700 CE; Jacobus de Voragine's incredibly popular *Legenda Aurea* or *Golden Legend*, a thirteenth-century compendium of saints' lives; and the *Gospel of Nicodemus*, a noncanonical account of the events in Jerusalem after the death of Jesus.[49] The four Gospels themselves, as well as the Book of Acts, provide much of the remainder of the poem's source material.

    Four versions of this narrative exist in Middle English: the short and long versions of *Destruction*, the alliterative *Siege of Jerusalem*, and Roger d'Argenteuil's *Bible en françois*.[50] The best known of these, the alliterative *Siege*, shares some key source texts with *Destruction*, though it is roughly a third of its length. As Adrienne Williams Boyarin notes, besides their similar subject matter, the poems share very little in common.[51] Nonetheless, as *Siege* is a more familiar text for many readers, it may be helpful to address some of the crucial differences between these versions here.

---

[45] On the Latin translations, see Levenson and Martin, "Ancient Latin Translation," with a *cri de coeur* for more work in this area. See too Schreckenberg, *Rezeptionsgeschichtliche*, and more recently Kletter, "Christian Reception." The only scholarly edition of Ps. Hegessipus is that of Ussani. A translation into English of limited utility by Wade Blocker is available at http://www.tertullian.org/fathers/hegesippus_00_eintro.htm; but let the reader beware of the severe limitations and inaccuracies of this translation — a good translation remains a *desideratum*.

[46] We consider the poem a romance, though the issue of genre has also troubled editors of *Siege of Jerusalem*. See Livingston's Introduction (*SJ*, pp. 14–15) as well as Nicholson's discussion ("Haunted Itineraries," pp. 452–54). Though not part of the alliterative tradition, *Destruction* has a strong interest in reimagining historical events; likewise, its episodic structure and interest in recounting battles align it with the popular Middle English romance tradition. See Heng, *Empire of Magic*, pp. 3–10, and Yeager, *Jerusalem in Medieval Narrative*, pp. 11–15.

[47] See Ford, *Vengeance*, pp. 1–2.

[48] Compare Gryting, *Venjance*, pp. 6–22 and Ford, *Vengeance*, pp. 27–35. These details are similarly absent from *The Siege of Jerusalem*.

[49] We track which portions of the text draw on which of these materials in the present edition's Explanatory Notes. For an incredibly thorough account of the poem's sources, see Munro, especially pp. 12–15.

[50] For an edition of Roger d'Argenteuil, see Moe, *ME Prose Translation of Roger d'Argenteuil's Bible en francois*. Higden's *Polychronicon* may well have been a source for the poem, as it retells a portion of Josephus's and Pseudo-Hegesippus's works and was very likely a source for *Siege of Jerusalem* (Millar, *Siege and Contexts*, pp. 64–68.) Its inclusion in *Polychronicon* is particularly interesting given that, as critics have observed, developing nationalism is one of *Polychronicon*'s goals: see Bale, *The Jew in the Medieval Book*, pp. 44–47, for a brief discussion of the work's agenda grounded in its manuscript contexts.

[51] A. Boyarin, *Siege of Jerusalem*, p. 21n2.

Perhaps the most notable difference between *Siege* and *Destruction* is how *Destruction* reinforces binaries that *Siege* selectively blurs, especially around each poem's treatment of its Jewish characters. Boyarin notes that *Siege* condemns Jews at many points in the text while expressing sympathy for their suffering at other moments.[52] In contrast, *Destruction* Christianizes any character meant to be seen as virtuous — notably Jacob, Josephus, and Veronica — while categorizing all the poem's villains as Jewish, including Pontius Pilate and Herod. Titus and Vespasian themselves are the only characters who complicate this binary: they espouse Christianity and are seen as God's agents in enacting revenge, but they remain unbaptized until the end of the poem.[53] Likewise, *Siege* contains far less opening apparatus designed to praise Jesus and vilify the Jews. *Siege* tends to renarrate Christian doctrine more briefly, whereas the telling and retelling of key narratives is central to *Destruction*: the poem contains multiple references to the disciples speaking in tongues from the Book of Acts, as well as considerably expanding Clement's preaching to Vespasian.

On the whole, then, *Destruction* is invested in reinforcing Christian religious structures, which partially explains the poem's preoccupation with Vespasian's deferred baptism. As one who has not been baptized, Vespasian remains a "Saracen" until after Jerusalem has been defeated, and the Jews of the city repeatedly refer to him as such.[54] Belief in Jesus may effect miraculous healing in *Destruction*, but only the sacraments confer Christian status. As Munro notes, the poem's closing material — in which Vespasian honors the Christians who endured in Jerusalem, confirms Clement's status as Pope, and constructs Christian churches — seems to be unique to *Destruction*.[55] These moments align the poem especially strongly with the Middle English romance tradition; indeed, these acts, especially the establishment of churches, appear in a range of romances, transforming Vespasian from Roman emperor to romance hero.[56] Like Gowther or Havelok, Vespasian returns home to live a religiously and politically virtuous life; Christian dominance is established, his faithful men are rewarded with lands and wealth, and he lives out his life in Rome before leaving his status as emperor to his son Titus. Vespasian's deeds make *Destruction* a champion of religious orthodoxy at a moment when English poetry seems particularly concerned with such orthodoxy.[57] From its preoccupation with baptism to its detailed attention to the vernicle as a relic to its ending confirmation of Clement's papacy, *Destruction* promotes institutional orthodoxy throughout.

---

[52] A. Boyarin, *Siege of Jerusalem*, p. 18. For related arguments, see Narin van Court, "'Siege of Jerusalem' and Augustinian Historians," pp. 228–29, and Mueller, "Corporal Terror," pp. 287–89.

[53] This deferred baptism may suggest a parallel to figures like Palomides in Malory's *Morte d'Arthur*, who has Christian beliefs but refuses baptism until he has fulfilled a quest that will prove his worthiness to be baptized.

[54] See, for example, lines 3671–72.

[55] Munro, pp. 105–06.

[56] See, for example, Herzman, Drake, and Salisbury, *King Horn*, lines 1393–94 and Laskaya and Salisbury, *Sir Gowther*, lines 703–08.

[57] The fifteenth century saw new methods of persecution for a heretical group known as the Lollards, who challenged the doctrine of transubstantiation and disapproved of pilgrimage and Biblical drama. It is perhaps not an accident, then, that some Middle English texts that reinforce the church's sacramental authority, such as the short *St. Erkenwald* and the Croxton *Play of the Sacrament*, also appeared during this period. On the Lollards, see the work of Anne Hudson, especially *Lollards and Their Books* and *Premature Reformation*; on the Croxton play in particular as a response to Lollardy, see Cutts, "An Anti-Lollard Piece," where the argument originated.

CANNIBALISM HISTORICAL AND LITERARY

Destruction's story of Maria's cannibalism of her child, familiar to readers of *Siege*, originates in Josephus, where it is the culmination of the horrors of Titus's siege that Josephus describes in book 6.[58] As with other historians in antiquity, Josephus resorts to a number of stock episodes and scenes to flesh out his description of the siege, including cannibalism, but no other surviving ancient historian goes into the kind of horrifying detail that Josephus does in this episode. While Josephus was present outside the city during the siege, he would not have been privy to precise information about what was happening in the city, though he might have had opportunities after the war's conclusion to interview survivors. The cannibalism episode is gruesome enough that Josephus even highlights it as a report that reached the Roman camp and disgusted Titus himself, a detail that *Siege* and *Destruction* do not include.[59]

Cannibalism has a greater cultural force in medieval than in ancient literature.[60] The ancient Greeks and Romans typically discussed cannibalism in two distinct contexts.[61] The first was as an extreme marker of cultural difference. Several ancient ethnographies of areas in and around ancient Scythia (roughly modern Eastern Europe and northern Iran) mention a tribe called the Androphagoi[62] or Anthropophagi,[63] about whom not much more is known than their descriptive tribal name, Greek for "man-eaters." Herodotus also tells of some peoples (the Issedones and the Indians) who consume the flesh of their dead relatives,[64] though this is presented as a specific funerary cultural practice, as opposed to a general gastronomic practice for the Androphagoi, as their name would indicate.

The more common context for cannibalism in ancient sources is during the deprivations of siege warfare, as in Josephus's infamous account, and by extension his many imitators, from Pseudo-Hegesippus and the *Sefer Yosippon*, through the *Vengeance* tradition, down to *Destruction*. Thucydides, writing in the late fifth and early fourth centuries BCE, is our earliest surviving example of cannibalism during a siege. In his description of the siege of Potidea (which finally fell in 429 BCE) during the Peloponnesian war, Thucydides tells how the people in the city, after their grain supplies had given out, were desperate enough to eat their fellow citizens.[65] Such is the typical cannibalism in siege scene — driven by the deprivations of a

---

[58] Josephus *War* 6.201–19. Compare Pseudo-Hegesippus, *Historiae*, 5.40.

[59] Josephus, *War*, 6.214: Ταχέως δὲ καὶ Ῥωμαίοις διηγγέλθη τὸ πάθος. τῶν δ' οἱ μὲν ἠπίστουν, οἱ δὲ ᾤκτειρον, τοὺς δὲ πολλοὺς εἰς μῖσος τοῦ ἔθνους σφοδρότερον συνέβη προελθεῖν [This suffering quickly was announced to the Romans. Some of them didn't believe it, others were moved to pity, but it's agreed that the majority of them came into more vehement hatred of the Jews.] (Translation by Mark J. B. Wright.) Compare Pseudo-Hegesippus, *Historiae*, 5.41, with a more straightforward "pervenit etiam ad Romanos huius facti immanitas," where only *immanitas* conveys any sense of the response in the Roman camp, which Josephus makes explicit.

[60] See Heng, *Empire of Magic*. Heng argues throughout that symbolic cannibalism is a pervasive feature in medieval romance.

[61] One exception to this trend is Tacitus, *Agricola* 28, where a group of Usipii mutineers commandeer some ships and go marauding around Britain. As things increasingly do not go their way, the men are driven to at first eat the weakest among them, and then to eat others by drawing lots (*eo ad extremum inopiae venere, ut infirmissimos suorum, mox sorte ductos vescerentur*). Finally, those left are captured and enslaved. For this strange episode see Ash, "Great Escape."

[62] Herodotus, *The Persian Wars* 4.106, trans. Godley.

[63] Ammianus Marcellinus, *History* 31.2.15, trans. Rolfe.

[64] Herodotus, *The Persian Wars* 4.26, 3.38, trans. Godley.

[65] Thucydides, *History of the Peloponnesian War* 2.70.1, trans. C. F. Smith.

protracted military operation, men inevitably are driven to extremes: war, as Thucydides tells us, is a harsh teacher.[66] There are accounts of cannibalism that feature in three other sieges: Scipio Aemilianus's siege of Numantia in 133 BCE;[67] Sulla's siege of Athens in 87–86 BCE, during the Mithridatic wars;[68] and Gnaeus Pompey's siege of Calagurris in 72 BCE.[69] Plutarch's *Lucullus* provides a slight twist on the siege theme. In this case, Mithridates VI Eupator, King of Pontus, is besieging the city of Cyzicus. The Roman general Lucius Licinius Lucullus successfully cuts off Mithridates's supply lines to the point where the conditions in his own camp become worse than those of the besieged, even as his own advisors attempt to deceive him. Soon enough Mithridates discovers the truth, which includes cannibalism on the part of his soldiers.[70] In all these cases, the emphasis is on the horror of an extended siege and the gruesomeness of this grim act, and the stories from the siege of Numantia, fragmentary as they are, remain the most chilling outside of Josephus. Like us, the ancients regarded cannibalism with, at minimum, strong distaste.[71]

While most of these references are brief, with minimum condemnation or exculpation, two ancient accounts stand out. First, of course, is Josephus's account of Maria and her child, which we discuss below. About a century earlier, Julius Caesar, in his account of his wars in Gaul, describes a speech of an especially fierce Gaul named Critognatus, during the climactic siege of Alesia that finally broke the revolt of Vercengetorix:

> Quid ergo mei consili est? Facere, quod nostri maiores nequaquam pari bello Cimbrorum Teutonumque fecerunt; qui in oppida compulsi ac simili inopia subacti eorum corporibus qui aetate ad bellum inutiles videbantur vitam toleraverunt neque se hostibus tradiderunt.[72]

> [What, therefore, is my plan? To do that which our ancestors did in the war with the Cimbri and Teutones, one that is utterly unequal to this war: men who locked themselves away in their towns and compelled by a similar want of resources nourished themselves with the bodies of those who seemed, because of their age, useless towards the war effort — nor did they hand themselves over to the enemy.]

Caesar's prefatory remarks emphasize the "singular and nefarious cruelty" (*propter eius singularem et nefariam crudelitatem*, 7.77.2) of the speech — it is in fact the entire reason Caesar records it (all the more notable because it is one of the rare speeches in direct discourse in all of Caesar's extant writings). Like the other examples, this is contextualized in a siege; like the Numantines earlier or the Usipi later, the weaker are to be consumed first to support the strong. For Caesar's immediate purposes, this allows him to continue his

---

[66] Thucydides, *History of the Peloponnesian War* 3.82.2, trans. C. F. Smith.

[67] Sallust, *Histories* 3.61, ed. and trans. Ramsey (includes the odd detail that the Numantines took the time to salt the leftover meat from the cadavers for later use), Valerius Maximus, *Memorable Doings and Sayings*, 7.6, ext. 2, ed. and trans. Shackleton; Appian, *Iberica* 96, ed. and trans. McGing, and Florus, *Epitome* 1.34.12, trans. Forster.

[68] Appian, *Mithridates* 38, ed. and trans. McGing.

[69] Valerius Maximus, *Memorable Doings and Sayings*, 7.6 ext. 3, ed. and trans. Shackleton.

[70] ταχὺ δ'ἐξερρύη τὸ φιλότιμον αὐτοῦ καὶ φιλόνικον ἐν αἰσθήσει γενομένου τῶν ἀποριῶν, αἷς οἱ στρατιῶται συνείχοντο, καὶ τῶν ἀνθρωποφαγιῶν [but his ambition and contentiousness quickly flowed away when the deprivations of his soldiers came to his attention, even of the cannibalism.] (Plutarch, *Lucullus* 11, ed. Ziegler and Gärtner, translation by Mark J. B. Wright.)

[71] Compare Appian's disgust at *Iberica* 96 ed. and trans. McGing at the conditions of the Numatines under siege, and Valerius Maximus's condemnation of both the examples of Numantia and Calagurris (*Memorable Doings and Sayings*, 7.6, ext. 2 and 3, ed. and trans. Shackleton).

[72] Caesar, *The Gallic War* 7.77.13–14, trans. Edwards.

characterization of the Gauls as "barbarians" and use it to justify his conquests in the region.[73] It is also an especially memorable summation of a key antithesis in *The Gallic War*, book 7 between *libertas* (freedom) and *servitus* (servitude) — so repulsive is the latter to the Gauls that they would turn to cannibalism before surrender, as Critognatus proposes.

While Caesar's is the most memorable extant passage concerning cannibalism in Latin, it is Josephus's infamous account in the *Jewish War* that really captured the medieval imagination.[74] While these authors were writing for either primarily a Greek audience, or a Roman one,[75] Josephus, as a Hellenized Jewish resident in Rome, seems to have intended his work to be read by all three of these possible audiences: Roman, Greek, and Jewish.[76] As Honora Chapman demonstrates in her reading of Maria's episode, Josephus draws upon both the Hellenic cultural tradition (e.g. Thucydides) and Hebrew scripture in rendering this episode.[77] For all its horror, then, this episode provides a stimulating locus to see how Josephus negotiates these competing cultural traditions. As such, it also makes a good text to see how these cultural traditions are reshaped in the Latin translations, the *Vengeance* tradition, and *Destruction*.

Given Josephus's use of Thucydides as a model,[78] it is likely that Josephus was familiar with the ancient historian's account of the siege of Potidea, and certainly with the horrors of more recent sieges like Sulla's siege of Athens, or Scipio Aemilianus's siege of Numantia. For Greco-Roman historians, bare events (e.g. a siege, a pitched battle) were elaborated by writers of history to provide an entertaining and didactic read for their audience. Cannibalism was a stock resource for this kind of elaboration, but generally not on the scale of Josephus's narrative in *Jewish War*, book 6.

To elaborate this episode, Josephus draws upon Jewish tradition, where not only cannibalism but specifically that of a mother eating her own children frequently figures as part of God's punishment of the Israelites for their failure to keep with Jewish law. Two representative examples come from Leviticus 26:28–29:

> I will also go against you with opposite fury, and I will chastise you with seven plagues for your sins, so that you shall eat the flesh of your sons and of your daughters.

And Jeremias 19:9, where the context is specifically a city under siege:

> And I will feed them with the flesh of their sons, and with the flesh of their daughters: and they shall eat every one the flesh of his friend in the siege, and in the distress wherewith their enemies, and they that seek their lives shall straiten them.

These examples are in the context of warnings from God for Jews to keep within the law.[79] There is one specific case mentioned at 4 Kings 6:28, again in the context of a siege. Here, Samaria is being besieged by King Ben-hadad of Syria, and a woman complains to the King of Israel:

73 On Caesar and barbarians, see Mannetter, "Narratology in Caesar," pp. 1–54; Barlow, "Noble Gauls"; Johnston, "Nostri and 'The Other(s)'"; and Schadee, "Caesar the Ethnographer."

74 On this episode, see Chapman, "Josephus and the Cannibalism of Mary."

75 Most of the Roman elite had long been bilingual in Greek and Latin. In fact, the earliest Roman histories were written in Greek. See Feeney, *Beyond Greek*, on the origins of Latin literature.

76 Josephus, *War* 1.3: Ἑλλάδι γλώσσῃ μεταβαλὼν ἃ ... τῇ πατρίῳ συντάξας. [By translating into the Greek language the things I had arranged before in my native language.] (Translation by Mark J. B. Wright.)

77 Chapman, "Josephus and the Cannibalism of Mary," pp. 420–21.

78 Most notably in the importance of stasis (civil discord) as a reason for Jerusalem's fall to the Romans.

79 See too Deuteronomy 28:52–61, Lamentations 2:20, and Ezekiel 5:9–10.

And the king said to her: "What aileth thee?" And she answered: "This woman said to me: 'Give thy son, that we may eat him today, and we will eat my son tomorrow.' So we boiled my son, and ate him. And I said to her on the next day: 'Give thy son that we may eat him.' And she hath hid her son." When the king heard this, he rent his garments.

Beyond the horrific nature of the cannibalism itself, what is most striking about this passage is that the woman's complaint is not about the deprivations of the siege and the terrible lengths it drove her to, but of her neighbor's dishonesty and deception at not keeping up her end of the child-devouring bargain.

While it is curious that an educated Jewish writer like Josephus would claim that Maria's horrible deed was "of such a kind that has never been recorded by Greeks or barbarians, awful to tell and unbelievable to hear," given the earlier story from 4 Kings 6:28, Chapman notes that in keeping with Josephus's historiographical goals, making claims in his preface for the uniquely great nature of the Jewish war, it is important to omit an earlier Jewish example, the better to emphasize the unique awfulness of Maria's desperate meal.[80] Thus, Jewish readers can recognize Josephus's careful alignment with Hebrew scripture, apt for his contention that God's wrath is responsible for the fall of Jerusalem because of the civil discord within. Meanwhile, for his Greco-Roman readers, this scene is a particularly vivid and grotesque example of a "stock scene" in siege narratives.

As Merrall Price has noted, this account of maternal cannibalism exists across the spectrum of fall-of-Jerusalem narratives; by the thirteenth century, the story was well-known enough as an exemplum of maternal depravity for Dante, Boccaccio, and perhaps even Chaucer to refer to it obliquely and assume their audiences' familiarity with it.[81] However, *Destruction* integrates several crucial changes. In earlier versions, such as that of Eusebius, the child cannibalized is a boy, which, combined with the mother's name, Maria, suggests Eucharistic overtones.[82] By the time the narrative reaches the Vengeance of Our Lord tradition, however, new variants appear; in the French *Vengeance de Nostre-Seigneur*, Marie is not Jewish but an African Christian convert encouraged by her friend Clarice to cook and eat part of Clarice's son, a deed Marie only agrees to upon urging by an angel, much like *Destruction*'s narrative.[83] In this, *Destruction* differs from *Siege*, as well as Josephus, his Latin translation, Rufinus's translation of Eusebius into Latin, and Pseudo-Hegesippus, all of whom omit Clarice and the exhorting angel. We would venture that the *Vengeance* tradition, and *Destruction*, perhaps see the reference to 4 Kings in the original account, and brings their story more in line with that story with the addition of Clarice. Combined with the prevalent mother-devouring-child imagery from other biblical sources (as in Jeremias and Kings), this version allows *Destruction* to figure the downfall of Jerusalem as part of God's divine plan, foretold in scripture.

Historical accounts of cannibalism during the First Crusade are pervasive, and Geraldine Heng has linked the narratives in chronicles of the period to medieval romance as a genre.[84] In her reading of the account in *Siege*, Bonnie Millar notes that in eating her child, "[b]y breaking social taboos [Marie's] actions

---

[80] Chapman, "Josephus and the Cannibalism of Mary," p. 420.

[81] Price, "Imperial Violence," p. 278.

[82] Price, "Imperial Violence," pp. 276–78.

[83] Price, "Imperial Violence," p. 280.

[84] Heng, *Empire of Magic*, pp. 23–43. Katherine Terrell has recently gathered relevant excerpts in translation for her edition of *Richard Coeur de Lion*; see Terrell, *Richard Coeur de Lion*, pp. 227–34. For more extensive discussions, see also Rubenstein, "Cannibals and Crusaders," and Tattersall, "Anthropophagi." Millar, *Siege and Contexts*, p. 103, suggests that the poet of *Destruction* might have been influenced by Crusades accounts.

convey the breakdown of social systems. This is something to which she has been driven by society."[85]   In making this action divinely approved, *Destruction* sanctions the siege and the extreme conditions within the city of Jerusalem, fitting them neatly into God's prophesied plan for the city's downfall. Millar suggests that the narrative in *Destruction* is simplified in several ways that fit the poem's emphasis on horror, suggesting that in this episode, "[t]he emphasis is placed on the fact that Mary must do this against her will to fulfil the judgement decreed upon Jerusalem by God," a necessary outcome of Marie's Christian, rather than Jewish, background in *Destruction*.[86]

Medieval English Antisemitism and Its Contexts

In part because of the broad network of sources it draws on, *Destruction* has links to a variety of literary traditions circulating in medieval England. The scholarship on English anti-Judaic sentiment is substantial, and we cannot hope to examine it all here; nonetheless, an overview detailing the theological and historical situation of Jewish communities in relation to late medieval England contextualizes *Destruction*'s treatment of its Jewish characters.[87]

As many critics have observed, medieval Christians were aware that their own faith developed from and existed in opposition to Judaism: that is, Judaism was the necessary precursor to Christianity, yet its continued existence presented a challenge to notions of Christianity as universal. This tension led to particular vitriol leveled at Judaism and Jews in the literature and theology of the period as well as to violence against Jewish communities. As Geraldine Heng has recently suggested, "Jews functioned as the benchmark by which racial others were defined, measured, scaled, and assessed."[88] This marginalized status was exacerbated by their proximity; while Muslims might occupy Jerusalem, Jews were to be found in communities across Europe. Their geographic position made Jews a convenient way for Christians to present alterity, thus endangering actual Jews. As Bale succinctly puts it, "medieval antisemitic representations allow us to see that which medieval Christians were not, or did not want to be."[89]

The position of Jews in medieval England was particularly fraught. Jews were essential to the developing English credit market, which made them uniquely endangered by Christian views of wealth and a target of resentment for anyone who needed financing; at the same time, they were imagined by Christians

---

[85]   Millar, *Siege and Contexts*, p. 91.

[86]   Millar, *Siege and Contexts*, p. 102.

[87]   While this bibliography cannot be comprehensive, recent and seminal studies include Bale, *The Jew in the Medieval Book* and *Feeling Persecuted*; Lavezzo, *Accommodated Jew*; Kruger, *Spectral Jew*; Krummel, *Crafting Jewishness*; Heng, *Invention of Race*; Rubin, *Gentile Tales*; Cohen, *Living Letters*; D. Boyarin, *A Radical Jew*; Delany, *Chaucer and the Jews*; Tomasch, "Virtual Jew;" Mellinkoff, *Outcasts*; Biddick, *Typological Imaginary*; and Nisse, *Jacob's Shipwreck*. For an excellent, cogent, and brief description of the position of Jews in medieval England as it relates to texts in the Vengeance of Our Lord tradition, see A. Boyarin, *Siege of Jerusalem*, pp. 15–18.

[88]   Heng, *Invention of Race*, p. 55. Heng argues for the construction of Jewish identity as a racial identity in medieval England on the grounds of the particular, marginalized status of Jewish communities: see pp. 15–54, especially pp. 23–24 and pp. 27–31. As she asserts in *Invention of Race*, p. 31, "In England, then, the Jewish badge, expulsion order, legislative enforcements, surveillance and segregation, ritualized iterations of homicidal fables, and the legal execution of Jews are constitutive acts in the consolidation of a community of Christian English . . . against a minority population *that has, on these historical occasions and through these institutions and practices, entered into race*" (italics original).

[89]   Bale, *The Jew in the Medieval Book*, pp. 3, 5.

as ideologically subordinate, further justifying their murder and legal mistreatment. Though it is unclear whether Jews were originally linked to the English crown, they quickly came to be associated with royal authority, and in 1275, Edward I referred to English Jews as the king's serfs, which made any rights and protections offered to Jewish communities subject to royal whim.[90] Scholars have noted that anti-Jewish sentiment resulted in legal action against Jews earlier in England than on much of the continent. England was the first European power to enforce the Fourth Lateran Council of 1215's Canon 68, which required that Jews wear identifying markers on their clothing, with a law introduced by King Henry III on 30 March 1218.[91] Late twelfth-century England also saw multiple waves of violence against Jewish communities by Christians, notably in Lincoln (1189–90), York (1190), Bury St. Edmunds (1181),[92] Norwich (1144), and London (1276).[93] Of particular interest to readers of this poem, Jewish responses to violence wielded against them were sometimes linked to the 70 CE events at the fall of Jerusalem. As Anthony Bale explains, "William of Newburgh, the most eloquent Christian chronicler of the [1190 York] incident, reports that the leader of the York Jews, Rabbi Yom Tov of Joigny, modelled his speech and actions on those of the suicidal Zealots led by Eleazar at Masada (73 CE), as narrated by Josephus (c. 37–100 CE) in *De bello Judaico*."[94] The events surrounding the fall of Jerusalem held imaginative power for both Christians and Jews in the Middle Ages, serving as an affirmation of triumphant Christian violence and a model of Jewish resistance.[95]

England was also the first European power to officially expel Jews, who were removed from the country by royal edict of Edward I in 1290.[96] As Bale notes, however, this seeming turning point had little to no impact on English antisemitism, which continued to thrive in England's cultural products.[97] Spectral, virtual, though legally absent, Jews featured strongly in English cultural production, available for repeated marginalization in post-Expulsion literature by Christians.[98] Though *Destruction of Jerusalem* long postdates official expulsion, it is one of many antisemitic literary texts that circulated in England in the later Middle Ages. Thus, *Destruction* and works like it — including most famously Chaucer's Prioress's Tale but also the *Book of John Mandeville*, Croxton *Play of the Sacrament*, and others — continued to circulate and imaginatively shape notions of English identity.

These tensions rise to the surface especially in texts that focus on the city of Jerusalem. Jews are sometimes erased entirely from literary depictions of the city central to all three Abrahamic faiths imagined as displaced from the holy city;[99] at other times, they are strongly linked to Muslims, who had political control

[90] We draw on this summary from Heng's recent work in *Invention of Race*: see especially pp. 58–60 and pp. 65–67. For a more detailed and comprehensive treatment, see pp. 55–109.

[91] Bale, *The Jew in the Medieval Book*, p. 15; Heng, *Invention of Race*, p. 15.

[92] Bale, *The Jew in the Medieval Book*, p. 29, pp. 9–10.

[93] Heng, *Invention of Race*, p. 28. We are indebted to both Bale's and Heng's account of this history throughout this section.

[94] Bale, *The Jew in the Medieval Book*, p. 29.

[95] For a comprehensive discussion of this event's position as both, see Nisse, *Jacob's Shipwreck*, pp. 23–32.

[96] Bale, *The Jew in the Medieval Book*, p. 15. It is noteworthy that though Jewish communities began to return to the country under Oliver Cromwell, the edict of expulsion has never been formally revoked by the British crown. On Cromwell's involvement in the readmission of Jews to England, see Endelman, *The Jews of Britain, 1656–2000*, pp. 20–25.

[97] Bale, *The Jew in the Medieval Book*, p. 16.

[98] We invoke here Kruger's *Spectral Jew* and Tomasch's "Virtual Jew."

[99] Akbari, *Idols in the East*, p. 115–16.

over the region for the vast majority of the later Middle Ages.[100] *Destruction* resists both these urges, placing its Jews in Jerusalem — though a Jerusalem under Roman authority — and presenting them as a distinct community.[101] Narratives about Jerusalem served a devotional purpose, giving Christians the chance to engage in narrative travel as a kind of meditative exercise.[102] As Susanne Yeager has argued, Jews were both central to literary constructions of Jerusalem and considered a danger to the city. Roger Nicholson likewise notes that Jerusalem is central to notions of European Christendom in the same way as Troy narratives were crucial to developing ideas of national identity.[103] The poem's crusading echoes are thus very much in keeping with its antisemitism, and these echoes extended beyond literary production. As Susanna A. Throop notes, the First and Second Crusades included attacks against Jews; she also describes a forged papal encyclical, allegedly by Pope Sergius IV (1009–1012), that claimed that Titus and Vespasian's destruction of Jerusalem foreshadowed Crusading victory.[104] Thus, it is possible to read *Destruction* alongside texts of the period that celebrate Crusading ideologies and imagine a successful reconquest of Jerusalem despite the poem's first-century setting. These fantasies about Jerusalem hold particular sway in English contexts. As Yeager has suggested, "portrayals of Jerusalem articulated expressions of incipient national identity in late medieval England . . . English writings about travel to the holy city were part of a much larger project of constructing England in the image of Jerusalem."[105] *Destruction* follows in the same trajectory as English works such as *Richard Coer de Lion*, *The Book of John Mandeville*, or its counterpart text, *Siege of Jerusalem*.[106] Thus, English identity and English antisemitism are entangled: *Destruction*, in seeking to rid Jerusalem of Jews, fashions a literary expulsion for the Holy Land that mirrors the legal expulsion of Jews from England several hundred years before.

While the existing scholarly literature on *Destruction* tracks its reinterpretations of Latin sources, the poem's connections to medieval drama have been historically overlooked. These parallels make sense given *Destruction* and the cycle plays' shared interest in reproducing and translating Biblical narratives for vernacular audiences, as well as the shared source material; further, many of the Biblical stories reproduced in *Destruction* also appear in English cycle plays. The episode of the woman taken in adultery, for example, appears in the York, N-Town, and Chester Plays. Diane Munro has identified several other passages that may well draw on the dramatic tradition, including the detail that Pilate's wife's dream came from Satan (present in Chester and N-Town Plays) and Mary's presence at the ascension of Jesus (present in Wakefield and York Cycles).[107] Even the detailed violence with which the crucifixion is narrated and renarrated might be familiar from its dramatizations within the cycle plays; as Michael Livingston notes, the cycles included entire

---

[100] Heng, "Romance of England," pp. 142–50; see also Delany, "Chaucer's Prioress, the Jews, and the Muslims," pp. 44–45, on this connection.

[101] While Muslims are often described as "Saracens" in literature of this period, here it is the Romans who are called Saracens (see lines 3671–72). Muslims are conspicously missing from the poem, leaving Jerusalem's Jews as the primary antagonists for Vespasian and Titus and their forces.

[102] Yeager, *Jerusalem in Medieval Narrative*, pp. 12–13.

[103] Nicholson, "Haunted Itineraries," p. 461.

[104] Throop, *Crusading as an Act of Vengeance*, pp. 45–46.

[105] Yeager, *Jerusalem in Medieval Narrative*, p. 15.

[106] Yeager's larger project compellingly argues that each of these works links territorial ownership, crusading discourses, and a growing sense of English national identity. See *Jerusalem in Medieval Narrative*.

[107] Munro, pp. 80, 103–04.

plays focused on the torture of Jesus.[108] Patricia A. DeMarco suggests that these depictions of the Passion are indeed designed to be traumatizing and that they are thus crucial to Christian identity formation.[109] Yet key to the use of Crucifixion narratives as a mechanism for Christian identity formation is its antisemitism: as Bale observes, "In popular religion, the Passion was reduced to a series of sensational and often crude moments of violence and degradation . . . In texts and images of the Passion we find the most violent and widespread antisemitic images, serving not only to represent Jews as the killers of Christ but also to vitiate and objectify the Jewish image more generally."[110] While there is not an English dramatic version of the siege and destruction of Jerusalem, the narrative was dramatized on the continent, especially in French, as Steven Wright has discussed.[111] From its vernacularizing of Latin source material to its preservation in multiple versions across many manuscripts, *Destruction* was clearly imagined for a wide and interested medieval English Christian public.

For *Destruction*, the destruction of the temple is unequivocally the preordained consequence of Jewish condemnation of Jesus. In its retelling of Jesus's lament over Jerusalem (lines 695–720), the poem narrates this account of the end times as a more focused, specific account of the city's destruction by Roman siege.[112] Indeed, the poem is notable for its repeated assertions that readers should not pity the Jews because their suffering and justification is preordained vengeance.[113] These assertions are crucial to the poem's antisemitism, serving as excuse and justification for its most violent passages.

MANUSCRIPTS AND EDITIONS

There are twelve manuscripts of *Destruction of Jerusalem*.[114] While this fact alone is not necessarily proof of wide readership, the number of extant manuscripts is nonetheless noteworthy, particularly as *Destruction* seems to survive in more copies than *Siege* and many works are preserved in a single copy. The majority of manuscripts are of the somewhat unwieldy long version described above, although several of these are incomplete.

Long Version Manuscripts:

- **A**: London, British Library, MS Additional 36523, fols. 1r–71r

  - Complete; second quarter of fifteenth century

  - 10 ½ by 7 inches

---

[108] *SJ*, p. 20, refers to Towneley Cycle plays 21 and 22; York Cycle plays 29 and 33; and Chester Cycle play 16 as examples.

[109] DeMarco, "Cultural Trauma," pp. 280–82.

[110] Bale, *The Jew in the Medieval Book*, p. 149. This binary is, unfortunately, still deployed; see for example Krummel's "Staging Encounters" on Mel Gibson's *Passion of the Christ* and its connections to the York cycle plays.

[111] Wright, *The Vengeance of Our Lord*, pp. 1, 10.

[112] This passage draws on Matthew 24 and Luke 21.

[113] See for example lines 199–204, 275–84, 3509–18, and 3709–28.

[114] For more comprehensive descriptions of these manuscripts, see Moe, "A Study of Two Manuscripts," pp. 8–25; Herbert, *Titus and Vespasian*, pp. xxvi –xli; Wilson, "Titus and Vespasian," pp. i–iv; Munro, p. 2e–f; and Guddat-Figge, *Catalogue*, pp. 110–11. For comparison, *Siege* exists in six complete and three additional fragmentary manuscripts; see A. Boyarin, *Siege of Jerusalem*, p. 89, and Hanna and Lawton, *Siege*, pp. xiii–xxvii.

- **L**: Oxford, Bodleian, MS Laud Misc. 622, fols. 1r–21v, 71v–72v

  - Complete: first 680 lines appear at end of MS; dated to around 1400

  - 11 ¾ by 10 ¼ inches

- **C**: London, British Library, MS Harley 4733, fols. 40v–127r

  - Complete except a small gap, lines 4702–4730; around 1460

  - 8 by 5 inches

- **D**: Oxford, Bodleian, MS Digby 230, fols. 195r–223v

  - Complete; middle of fifteenth century

  - 15 ¾ by 10 ½ inches

- **O**: New Haven, Beinecke Library, MS Osborn A.11,[115] fols. 1r–38v

  - Partial: contains lines 1–4875, with a gap from lines 3719–3775; early fifteenth century

  - 9 ¾ by 6 ⅜ inches

- **Addit**: London, British Library, MS Additional 36983, fols. 216r–255r

  - Complete: however, lines 2201–2382 transposed with lines 3820–4002; circa 1440s

  - 11 ¼ by 8 ½ inches

- **Douce**: Oxford, Bodleian, MS Douce 126, fols. 69r–84r

  - Partial: begins at line 3913 and continues to end; first half of fifteenth century

  - 9 by 6 ½ inches

- **Douce 78**: Oxford, Bodleian, MS Douce 78, fols. 19r–76v

  - Partial: contains only the first 2295 lines; late fifteenth century

  - 8 ¼ by 5 ¼ inches

- **Cov**: Coventry, City Records Office MS 325/1,[116] fols. 98r–129v

  - Partial: contains lines 80–5039; mid-fifteenth century

  - 12 ⅔ by 7 ½ inches

---

[115] We follow Herbert's designations for manuscripts L, A, O, C, D, B, P, and M for the sake of consistency with existing scholarship. Abbreviations used for other manuscripts are our own.

[116] This manuscript has been overlooked by much previous scholarship: it is not listed, for example, in Herbert's edition, nor in *A New Index of Middle English Verse* (entry 1881). Clifton, "*Alisaunder* and Oxford," p. 40, identifies it as a copy of *Destruction of Jerusalem*, and we have identified it as a long version manuscript using a digital facsimile.

Short Version Manuscripts:

- **P**: Cambridge, Magdalene College, Cambridge University, MS Pepys 2014 (formerly Pepys 37), fols. 23r–35v
  - Late fourteenth/early fifteenth century
  - 10 ⁷⁄₁₀ by 7 ⅕ inches
- **M**: New York, Pierpont Morgan, MS M.898, fols. 1r–100r
  - Fifteenth century
  - 5 ⅝ by 3 ⅞ inches
- **B**: London, British Library, MS Additional 10036, fols. 2r–61v
  - Early fifteenth century (circa 1425)
  - 6 by 3 ¾ inches

Previous Editions:

- Fischer, Rudolf, ed. *"Vindicta Salvatoris." Archiv für das Studium der neueren Sprachen und Literaturen* 111 (1903), 285–98 and 112 (1904), 25–45. [using P as the base manuscript]
- Herbert, J.A., ed. *Titus & Vespasian: or The Destruction of Jerusalem in Rhymed Couplets: Edited from the London and Oxford MSS.* London: Roxburghe Club, 1905. [using A as the base manuscript]
- Munro, Diane A. "An Edition and Study of Portions of MS Laud Misc. 622 of the Bodleian Library." Ph.D. Dissertation: Aberdeen University, 1977. [a partial edition of L that includes *Destruction*]
- Wilson, John Holmes, ed. "Titus and Vespasian: A Trial Edition of the Osborne Manuscript." Ph.D. Dissertaton: Yale, 1967. [using O as the base manuscript]

We have selected Bodleian Library MS Laud 622, abbreviated as L, as our base text. The earliest extant version of the poem, dated to around 1400,[117] the manuscript is in reasonably good condition, with some damage to the outer margins and several small holes.[118] Pricking and ruling is sometimes faintly visible, but not consistently so. *Destruction* appears on folio 1r, but this is not the beginning of the poem. Folios 65–72 contain the first 680 lines of the poem, with two lines of the poem appearing as a single line of text; a *punctus* indicates where the line break should be. Though these folios appear at the back of the manuscript, they contain the start of the poem; thus, the first line in the book is line 681, and the poem continues through folio 21v. As it appears from folio 1 to folio 21, the poem is copied in double columns, with blue capitals surrounded by rubrication. However, the early lines that appear on folios 65–72 are considerably more compressed: the poem is again written in two columns, but with couplets sharing a single line, and the

---

[117] On this point, see Herbert, *Titus and Vespasian*, pp. xxxv–xxxvii, as well as the Bodleian description at https:// medieval.bodleian.ox.ac.uk/catalog/manuscript_7410. Herbert suggests in his edition that L should be considered authoritative based on its dating, but opts to use A as his base text because it is a cleaner manuscript. However, in our view, the unusual binding should not disqualify L as base text, particularly given its interesting manuscript context.

[118] See for example folios 4, 5, 20, 30.

margins are dramatically reduced.[119] We have compared L against all long version manuscripts of the poem, with major variants detailed in our textual notes.

Previous editions tend to be based on a single manuscript or else collate manuscripts from both the long and short versions of the poem. Phyllis Moe has argued that the short version of the poem should be privileged, largely because its narrative holds together more neatly without the digressions of the longer version.[120] It is certainly the case that that short version's narrative is somewhat more coherent; however, given that the majority of manuscripts are of the long version, we have here chosen to edit the more frequently preserved version of the text. L is notable for the works alongside which *Destruction* appears: Laud 622 also contains *Kyng Alisaunder*, a life of Saint Alexis, Adam Davy's visions of Edward III, a single-folio account of the Holy Land, and various biblically-inspired material, including "Fifteen Tokens before the Day of Judgment."[121] As Nicole Clifton has suggested, then, the manuscript may serve as a sort of compendium of writings about the Middle East, broadly imagined.[122] Laud's manuscript context emphasizes the extent to which the poem links current discourses of crusade, antisemitism, and pious violence. It also contextualizes the seemingly long prologue on Jesus's Passion, making these lines part of its presentation of the geographic area's history.

In our editorial practice, we have followed Middle English Texts Series guidelines as follows:

- thorn (Þ) has been modernized to *th*;
- yogh (ȝ) has been modernized to *g, gh,* or *y* as appropriate;
- Middle English *the* has been emended to either *the* or *thee* as sense demands;
- we have normalized *u/v* and *i/j* to their modern spellings to facilitate reading.

Punctuation is editorial. Several paraph markings appear in the margin of the text, which are noted in the Textual Notes. Breaks in the text indicate decorated capitals in the base manuscript, which are also recorded in the Textual Notes.

[119] Indeed, some of the words are obscured by the manuscript's binding; see the Textual Notes.
[120] Moe, "A Study of Two Manuscripts."
[121] See Clifton, "*Alisaunder* and Oxford," pp. 40–41, for a discussion of the varied manuscript contexts of *Destruction*.
[122] Clifton, "*Alisaunder* and Oxford," p. 30. Charles Russell Stone, "Many Man," p. 20, has likewise suggested that texts in Laud Misc. 622 demonstrate the "simultaneous influence of romance and history," and this is in keeping with the poem's other manuscript contexts. *Destruction* appears with *The Book of John Mandeville* in Coventry, City Record Office MS 325/1, with religious verse such as the *Seven Penitential Psalms* in A, and with works by Lydgate in Digby 230. Certainly, it differs considerably in form from *Siege*, but like its alliterative counterpart, the poem is invested in historically-inspired events, like much medieval popular romance.

THE DESTRUCTION OF JERUSALEM

fol. 71va	Listneth alle that beth alyve,	
	Bothe Cristen men and wyve;	*men and women*
	I wil you telle a wonder cas	*miraculous event*
	Hou Jesus Crist bihated was	*detested*
5	Of the Jewes felle and kene	*bitter and cruel*
	That was on hem siththe isene.	*afterward*
	Gospelles I drawe to witnesse	*Gospels*
	Of this mater more and lesse,	
	And the Passioun and Nichodeme,	*Gospel of Nicodemus (see note)*
10	Who that taketh right good yeme,	*heed*
	And the gestes of emperours	*deeds (tales)*
	Of thise wonder aventours,	*events*
	Hou Jesus was don to ded	
	Thorough the Jewes fals red.	*advice*
15	First thai deden hym gret despyt	*disdain*
	Er he died, I tell you it,	
	I trowe that thai bilowen noughth,	*liked him*
	For after that thai dere it boght.	*dearly paid for it*
	As ye mowen forthward lere —	*learn*
20	Listneth now and ye schull here.	
	Ye witen wel, and soth it is,	*know; true*
	That many on giltles honged is;	*That many a guiltless person is hanged*
	Also bifel of Jhesu Crist,	*it happened to*
	Tho us scheweth th'ewangelist;	
25	For oure trespas and noughth for his	
	Suffred he al her schame, iwis.	*their; indeed*
	First thai weren wroth with hym	*angry*
	Als thai weren ful of venym,	
	For he preched everewhore	
30	Among the Jewes, lesse and more,	
	And the more thai gunne hym greve	*anger*
	For he had of hem no leve.	*permission (see note)*
	And oft he tolde hem in his sawe	*speech*
	Where thai trespassed ageins the lawe,	
35	And that in fele manere,	*in worthy manner*
	He rought never theigh thai it here	*cared; hear*
	And proved it hem by holy wright	*scripture*

31

	That thai ne couthe againsaie it;	*could contradict*
	Also he telde hem everywhore	
40	That thai ypocrites were,	
	For thai maden swich cheire	*outward appearance*
	As thai liveden in good manere,	*As if they lived*
	Hou thai the povere robbe and reve	*plunder*
	For al her lawe thai nolden leve	*would not stop*
45	The grettest maisters werst it kepeth,	*kept it worst*
	Her wrong with hem noght ne slepeth.	*Their*
	Yut also he tolde her owen thoughth	
	That thai ne mightten withseie it nought;	*deny*
	That was no maistré to Crist,	*not difficult*
50	Natheles thai wondred hou he it wist.	*knew*
	Graceles thai were and dym of sight,	
	To knowe the strengthe of God almight;	
	Altheigh thai hym in manhode sowe	*Although; saw*
	His godhede might thai noght knowe.	
55	Thai schewed after her mysdede	
	Forth onon thai felle in drede	
	For the wonders that thai sawghe,	
	Of his godhede than had thai awghe;	*holiness; awe*
	For no man migth swich maistré kithe	*show such power*
60	As he dude for hem oft sithe,	*many times*
	As Nichodemus hath witnessed rigth	
	That com to Jhesu Crist by nigth	
	And sede, "Jhesu, we witen wel	
	That thu art maister of Israel,	
65	That knowlechestow noughth to be	*you acknowledge*
	For all the merveiles we sen of thee;	*wonders*
	Among us ne coude we never fynde	
	On so wirche by mannes kynde,	*One accomplish such things*
	Neither lewed man ne clerk,	*unlearned*
70	Bot God were with hym in his werk.	*Unless*
	Therfore, we wolde sum tokne see —	
	Schewe yif thou God almightty be."	
	Tho seide Jhesus to Nichodeme,	
	"Ye taken of me ful litel yeme.	*heed*
75	Theigh I you all aventours telle,	*events*
	Of this werlde ther ye inne duelle,	
	That ben gon and schollen falle,	*have happened; will happen*
	Ye leven never a word of alle.	*believe*
	Forthi of Heven yif I tolde,	*Therefore*
80	Of al that ye witen wolde,	*would know*
fol. 71vb	Hou schold ye therof trowe me ought,	*trust*

Whan ye trowen me therof nought?
Natheles the aventours all
That I saie you schullen bifalle."   *will happen*
85   Nichodemus hym trowed wel   *believed*
And prively held with hym uche del.   *secretly supported; completely*
In the Gospel as men rede,
The Jewes hym tempted oft in dede;
Thai asked hym many a wonder sawe   *difficult question*
90   For to ateint hym bi her lawe,   *condemn*
That thai mightten bi juggement
In sum manere have hym schent.   *harmed*
Agains hym thai wroughtten in vayn   *worked*
That al unbynt and byndeth agayn.   *unbinds and binds*
95   This werldes wytt is bot folie   *foolishness*
Ageins Goddes gret maistré.   *knowledge*
Ones thai asked hym, "Maister dere,
To whom schul we yolde iche yere
Al the trowage of oure londe?"   *truage*
100   Hou he ansuerd now understonde:
"Of whom youre moné hath ymage,   *money (coins)*
With name written, yold hym trowage."
This was of hym asked with scorne
For the wordes he seid biforne,
105   That he was a Jewes kyng.
Tho ansuered thai to this thing,
"Oure moné, we maken the war,
Is made after oure kyng Cesar."
Than seide he, "Yeldeth Cesar his rigth,
110   And that is Goddes to God almight."   *what*
There thai were confounded onon
For thai were concluded everichon.   *answered*
By a womman thai tempted hym yut
That schulde be stoned, fair he quit   *acquitted*
115   For avoutré, a foule synne,   *adultery*
Thai tolde hym thai fonde hire therinne.
Jhesus stouped doun onon;
Thise wordes he wrot the erth upon,
The wrecched erthe that other wried   *covered*
120   Bot God forgiveth that mercy cried.
Tho he had writen what he wolde,
Hy gon the hens to biholde;   *They; from there*
Whan thai had seighen it als he bad,
Sore thai weren all adrad.   *afraid*
125   "Take this womman that hath don mys.   *sin*

Who that withoute synne ys,

Caste on hir the first ston."

Thai stale out tho sone onon,   *crept*

All bot the womman stode alone,

130   And he sat and loked hire on.

"Where ben thise men, womman," he seide,

"That this blame on thee leide?"

"Sir, I not sikerli."   *I do not know, truly*

"Dame," he seide, "no more wot I.   *neither do I*

135   Bot go now forth with joye and wynne,   *delight*

And kep thee forthward fro syn."   *henceforth*

Alwey thus on hym thai soughth,

Bot evere thai founde it halp hem nought;

For Goddes might and mannes wit

140   Mowen nought wel togidre sit.

Than thai gunne hym to defame   *began*

And leide on hym and dude hym schame   *slander*

Tho thai mighth spede with no resoun

With falshede thai thought to bryng hym doun

145   Thei seiden, "Thu seist amys, we leven,

Agayn the lawghe that is us yeven."   *Against; given*

Thai seiden, "Sith we have the lawes   *Since*

That Moises taught us by his dawes,   *in his days*

That he of Messias took,   *the Messiah*

150   As we fyndeth by oure book.

So held oure fader Abraham

And hiderward that after hym cam.

That we cunne wite we brake hit nought,   *can understand*

In werk, in word, ne in thought."

155   He wist wel that thai mistolde,   *knew; misspoke*

That maden the lawes newe and olde.

Than spak Jhesu the Jewes to:

"Moises and Abraham I seigh also.

Moises the lawghe I bitought,

160   That fro me to you it brought.

I seie Abraham and he me;

He was ful glad me to se.

Ye ben wel harder than the ston,

That of you nyl knowgh me non.   *will not know*

165   Tueie doumbe bestes, oxe and asse,   *Two*

Thai knewe me and wist what I wasse,

And bestes wilde under wood lynde —   *linden tree*

Me knowthe al bot mankynde."   *All but mankind know me*

The Jewes seiden that he mistolde:

170	He nas nought fyfty wynter olde.	
	"Moises ne Abraham thu nast noght seen;	
	This may nought in no wise ben.	
	Thu semest but a yonge man,	
	Hou mighttestou have seyen hem than?"	*might you have seen them*
175	"Forsothe," he seide, "I you telle can.	
	I was er the werlde bigan	*before*
	And schal be withouten ende,	
	Theigh al thing asondyr wende.	*go to pieces*
	I am Jhesus, Goddes son:	
180	I saigh Abraham and Salomon.	*saw*
	I com the lawghe to fulfille,	
	Nought o poynt therof to spille,	*one; invalidate*
	Ne the prophetes alle,	
	That han yben, other ben to falle;	*have been, or will be*
185	And also treuly I you telle,	
	Youre michel temple I may felle	*great*
fol. 72ra	And areisen agein the thrid day."	
	"That might noght be," thai swore ay.	
	In all thise wordes he hem blent,	*befuddled*
190	For by his owen body he it ment,	
	That he scholde die and assaie	*strive*
	To arisen the thrid day.	
	For this word thai were neigh mad,	
	For ever thai fond hym trew and sad.	*honest and solemn*
195	Natheles thai ansuered tho right,	
	"Er oure temple were al dight,	*made*
	Yeres weren six and fourty fulle;	
	Hou ever than we trowe schulle?"	
	Right cursed folk men might hem calle,	
200	For the miracles he schewed hem alle,	
	Bot al that he wolde and thought	
	Most sum tyme to ende be broght;	*Must; be fulfilled*
	That folk was loked to do that dede,	
	Therfore thai mightten sore drede.	
205	He blamed hem for her bileve,	*faith*
	And seid it scholde hem sore greve.	
	He might sone such thing han wroght,	
	That made al the world of noght;	*from nothing*
	And for he held noght her Sabath day	
210	To don miracles alway,	
	The seek to hele of yvel and synne,	*sick*
	For her lawe nolde he noght blynne.	*stop*
	Fendes werkes were thai none,	*Devil's*

Bot God Almightties dedes alone.

215 Thai areden hym whi he wroght than. *guessed*

He ansuerd as God and man:

"Is there any of you alle,

Yif youre beest were yfalle

Ded doun in pyt oither in lake, *As if dead; or*

220 Yif it schulde ben up ytake,

Ar it were lorne ye wolden up drawe, *lost*

On the Sabath day, for al youre lawe?"

Thai holden hem abasshed everichon, *perplexed*

That thai ne couthe ansuere hym non.

225 Onon thai axed hym with gret tene *insult*

What his miracles wolden mene,

That was whan he heled the seek

Or seide or dude wondres eek.

After tho thai comen hym to

230 And axeden whi he dude so.

He ansuerd after her thought,

That thai ne couthe withseie hym noght.

The grettest of the princes bolde

Ageins Jhesu wel hard thai holde,

235 And uche made to other present

For to ben at on assent.

But smale folk al aboute *But common people*

Folowed hym with gret route; *in great numbers*

Wonder thik thai fellen hym to

240 For the miracles thai seighen hym do

That thei despyt do hym ne might *would not harm him*

That made thai token hym by nighth.

Whan Jesus seigh the tyme therto,

That it most nedes be do,

245 He bad thai schulden hem amende

Or stronge vengeaunce he wold hem sende;

He hight to fordon hem alle *promised to destroy*

And her cité schulde falle,

Jerusalem that was stronge and heighe.

250 Tho gan to waxen her envie; *increase*

While it stood thai had no doute,

So riche it was and strong aboute,

Natheles of this gret sawe *promise*

All thai weren in michel awe.

255 For his prophecies thai hated hym sore,

And for he was trewe wel the more,

And for his wyt that was so gret,

	And for his ansuer and his thret,	*crowd*
	And for he bare so noble fame,	*carried*
260	That men honoured hym al by name	
	And clepeden hym Jesus verray prophete,	*called*
	Bothe in toun and in strete.	
	Oft thai waited hym to sle,	
	Bot for drede thai lete hym be.	
265	By day thai might hym noght hent	*seize*
	For the folk that with hym went;	
	Many a thousand for his sake	
	Wolde have ben ded or he were take;	*before*
	Yif thai hadden biforehonde wist	
270	Thai scholde so foule have faren with Crist,	
	The princes thai wolden have sleyn	
	And al the cuntré brent ful feyn.	*burnt*
	God wolde nought that it were so;	
	Otherwise it most go.	
275	Whan tyme and terme was ycome	
	That he suffred to be ynome,	*taken*
	Ful wel he had taken his merk	*taken note of*
	What manere men scholde don this werk,	*kind of*
	And sithen it scholde alway be do,	
280	Sum manere folk most nedes therto;	
	Yyt was it better thai hadden the gylt	
	Than any other had ben spylt.	
	For in the book so we it fynde,	
	Thai were the outcast of al mankynde.	
285	He praied for hem on Rode tree,	*Rood (i.e., the cross)*
	"Forgeven hem that it scholde be."	
	In ensample of Cristen menne,	
	That here in eny envye brenne,	*burn*
	That we forgiven as he forgave,	
290	Michel mede schull we have.	*Great reward*
	For he is so gret of curteisie,	*mercy*
	He wil no synful man dye,	
	Bot grace and space he wil hym sende,	
	And he wil hymself amende.	
295	So mightten the Jewes have had grace	
	Of her vileynous trespas;	
fol. 72rb	Jesus suffred a longe stounde,	*for a long while*
	Fourty yer, it is yfounde,	
	For tokne ne for other sight	*sign*
300	Repented thai nevere day ne nighth.	
	Bot in the Passioun as we rede	

There thai wore gadered in everich stede   *every place*
Oft bifore thai spaken his ded,
Hou to don thai couthe no red.   *had no course of action*
305   Thai seiden, "Whan schull we us wreke   *avenge*
Of this prophete that hath thus speke?
For yif we leten hym thus gon,
He schal fordon us everychon;   *destroy*
Romeins and other schull comen us on,   *Romans*
310   And alle oure lawes thai willen fordon."   *undo*
Thai seiden sother than thei wende,   *more truly; knew*
For thai were never in will to amende;
Oft thai casten and wolden sonde   *discussed*
Hou thai might drivon hym out of londe,   *drive*
315   Thorough her lawes by juggement,
Oither thorough privé queintise to have hym schent.   *secret trickery; killed*
Ones thai hadden hym hem bitwene,   *among*
Tho thoughtten thai have wreken her tene,   *anger*
At a stede on an heighe hyll   *place*
320   Thai wolde have sleyn hym withoute skill;   *for no (just) cause*
Thai wolde have done hym thereto stirt,   *have attacked him*
Bot quyt he went away from hirt.   *freely; harm*
And ones thai wolde have stoned hym,
And to drawe hym every lym;
325   Thai seiden he blasfemed hym than,
He made hym God and was a man.
And oft afterward thai lepen   *jumped*
For to take hym with her wepen,   *weapons*
Bot for men that yeden hym by,   *went*
330   There durst non leie honde hym neigh.   *They dared not lay a hand near him*
And ones atte Flum Jurdon,   *Jordan River*
There he baptized Seint Jon,   *John (the Baptist)*
There thai waited to have hym sleyn,
Bot quyt he went with might and meyn.   *miraculous power*
335   Whan thai seieghen thai mightten noght spede,
Thai thoughtten don a lither dede;   *wicked*
Thai maden there a conspiracie
Among the poeple with felony
That Messias ones seide —
340   That is Jesus on oure tunge leide —   *called*
Out of synagoge he schulde be do,
And for cursed man holden also.
This was to hym no vilenye,
Al were it don with gret envie
345   Alway thus failed her cast,

Tyl Jesus wolde it atte last
That the certein day was sett,
Thei hadden no might hym to get;
Whan he wist it most nedes be,
350   Than wolde he hem nothing fle.

Caiphas prophecied there,
Als in the Passioun we mowen here,
That a man schulde deie hem bifore,
That the poeple ne were noght ylore;   *lost*
355   The Holi Gost had brought hym this,
Bot he nas nevere the better, iwis.
Theigh it were seid with good resoun,
It turned hym al to confusioun,
For thorough hym and his felonye,
360   Encreced fast the Jewes envie;   *Increased*
Fro that this word was seide on heighe
In al manere he schulde dyghe.
Her eighen were blynde and nought hym knewe,   *Their eyes*
That mowen thai evermore rewe.   *might; regret*
365   Therfore he went onon hem fro —
Among hem more nolde he go.   *he would not*
He went a litel there biside,
Out of her sight hym to hide;
Nought for drede took he his waie,
370   Bot for to stable us in the faie,   *make us firm; faith*
To abiden his tyme wel and faire.
There he was us a good samplaire   *example*
To prelates and to other men   *clergy*
That in anguisch here ben,   *torment*
375   To kepen us out of her weie
That oure enemyes us nought saie   *test*
Whan men hem seen the more thai synne;
Yif thai ben fer the more thai blynne.   *fierce; fail*

Thus turned Jesus from hem the bake,
380   That thai nought mychel of hym spak;   *much*
In to desert he held the sty,   *path*
To a citee that ther was ney.
The story seith it hat Effroem,   *Effrem*
A litel weie fro Jerusalem;
385   With his deciples he duelled there —
Nought for dred thai might hym dere,   *hinder*
Bot for the poynt I seide biforne.
And yut were summe forsworne,

Tho seiden thai there thai yede

390 That he was yfled for drede.

Bot trewely they liyeden uchon,   *all lied*

Thai nysten nought whi he was gon;   *did not know*

Thai weren nought worthi his conseil to witte

That thoughtten alday don hym despitte.   *injury*

395 Yut eft the schrewus weren forsuorne   *often; villains (shrews)*

In leccherie thai helden hym borne.   *lechery*

There weren tuelve that herden thus;

Thai tolden hem thai seiden amys

That witnessed all with sawe

400 That he was borne in tho right lawe.   *the right law (i.e., in wedlock)*

Thai seiden thai seighen Joseph wed

Marie, that clene lyf lede,

Thai helden hym Joseps son right,

A wrighttes son he was iplight.   *carpenter's; sworn to be*

405 His fader made al thing of nought;

There is non other that so wrought.

fol. 72va The tuelve namis tell I can

That with Jhesu helden than:

Lazar, Asterus, Antonius,

410 Ysaac, Finous, and Cripus,

Jacob, Samuel, and Joras,

Agripta, Amos, and Judas.

Tweie riche men there weren also   *Two*

That helden with Jhesu tho,

415 Evere in word and dedes bothe,

Wherfore the Jewes weren wrothe.   *angry*

For her wraththe thai nolden leve   *cease*

Ne for her love Jhesu greve.

Nichodemus was that on,

420 Prince of the Jewes everychon,

At his dom and at his ded   *command*

He praised hym in every stede.   *place*

Forthi thai prisoned hym sone,   *immediately*

And wolden hym to deth have done.

425 And so thai wolde his other felawe,

For his werk and for his sawe;

That was Joseph of Arimathie,

A riche man and of kynde heighe.   *high rank*

Thise men thai thought to have sleyn,

430 As I schal here after seyn.

Thise were the pointes of her envie,   *grounds*

Wherfore thai deden hym to dye

	Withouten any other thing:	
	Assaies, upbraides, and cursyng.	*Ordeals, reproaches*
435	Love brast Jesus Cristes hert,	*broke*
	And non other pyne smert;	*sharp*
	Love hym drof and love hym brought,	*drove*
	For to fynde that he sought.	
	Whan love thirled Heven kyng,	*pierced*
440	Love passeth al thing.	
	Love is hede and love is ende;	*head*
	Loveth love as ye ben hende.	*gentle*
	Whan that Jesus was broght of lyve,	*killed (i.e., brought out of life)*
	There fel wondres als blithe.	*at once*
445	Centurio biheld and seid thus:	
	"This is sothfast Goddus son Jesus."	*truly*
	And so dude Longens the knight,	*Longinus*
	After that he had his sight;	
	The gret temple atwo toclef,	*cracked in two*
450	And beried men ded and def	*buried; dead and deaf*
	Arisen and walkeden al about	
	From toun to toun in muchel route,	
	That weren wel knowe out and in	
	Of men that weren of her kyn.	
455	Thai tolden whi thai risen thore,	*there*
	For Jesus that dyed hem bifore.	
	The sunne also les her light,	*lost*
	And ston and tre loren her might,	*lost*
	And everich thing in his kynde	*according to its nature*
460	Of Jhesus deth had mynde,	
	Outtake man that scholde be chief,	*Except*
	And most scholde be Jhesu lef;	*Jesus should be dear*
	Thai schewed hym most unkyndenesse	
	Ageins al his gret godenesse;	*In contrast to*
465	Al this was witnesse ageins man	
	That he had ytrespassed than.	
	Sithen al quok bot mannes hert,	*Since; trembled*
	Ne was he worthi than to smert.	*suffer*
	Adam bigan first the game;	
470	The Jewes ended it with schame;	
	Bot Oure Lorde, that curteis is,	*gracious*
	Dude it al for mannes blis;	*joy*
	Also for the Jewes forthi,	*therefore*
	Yif thai hadden sought his mercy.	
475	This dede men bigunnen to telle	
	Whi thai risen in flesch and felle	*skin*

And Jhesus wolde rise the thrid day.

The Jewes weren in gret afray, *dismay*

Bot thai dredden noght aright

480   As thai scholden; hem failed might.

Tho he was risen the thrid morne, *third*

As his Passioun seith biforne,

Aggeus, Phinees, and Escandas,

Thise thre tolden hem hou it was;

485   Tueie clerkes witnessen this also, *Two*

That Sent Mychel schewed it to, *Saint Michael*

Carianus and Elyntheus

Doumbe thai weren til swete Jhesus

Fro that he rose and stighe to Heven *rose and went up*

490   And than tolden thai ful even

Al that was don everych del *entirely*

Of the lore of Seynt Mighel *Michael*

In erthe and helle, in paradys,

What Jhesus Crist had don, iwys.

495   Also it witnesseth in othere stede,

There men of the story rede.

Tho spak Nichodemus onon

To the Jewes everychon,

"Ye wycked men, wat have ye wroght? *what have you done*

500   In muchel sorough ye han us brought. *sorrow*

Al that Josep and I you sede, *said to you*

It might stonde you in no stede."

Than gan Josep speke hem to,

"Agein Jhesu ye han mysdo, *done wrong*

505   For giltles ye han hym slawe; *guiltless; slain*

Therfore ye mowen ben unfawe." *must be joyless*

Onon the Jewes on Josep borne *charged*

That he was to Jhesu sworne.

"Ye," quoth Josep, "to hym I take,

510   All youre lawes I forsake.

I wot wel ye ben wroth with me,

For I beried his body fre;

I ne recche, so Crist me save, *do not care*

Theigh I youre wraththe have.

515   I warne you wel ye schullen abye, *pay for it*

That ye duden hym such vilenye."

fol. 72vb   Than weren the Jewes wel neigh wood,

And though he seide for her good;

He is nought my frende, ye han herd told,

520   That seith as myne hert wold.

Josep withouten more sake   *strife*
Sone onon thai gonnen take;
Thai putten hym in a strong prisoun,
With dubble lok al for tresoun.
525   Annas and Cayphas, thise two
Beren the keies the dore to undo.
The hous was hole withouten hole,   *entirely*
For thai thoughtten so have hym stole   *spirited him away*
That never frende ne scholde have wist
530   Hou ne where he had ben myst.
Bot Jhesus, that is curteis at nede,   *benevolent*
That night com hym out to lede.
The Jewes soughtten hym on the morn;
His deth thai holden among hem sworn.
535   Anna and Caiphas undeden the dore;
They sought and cleped thai hadden hym lor.   *lost*
Thai wepden and weren sory men,   *shed tears*
Out of londe thai thoughtten flen,   *fled*
Body for body thai token hym,
540   To kepen hym uppon lyf and lym;
And also thai hadden mychel care,
Where thai wolden gon or fare,
Among al this so comen the knighttes
That woken Jhesu bi day and nighttes,   *watched over*
545   Therwhiles that he in the toumbe lay
Til it was on the thrid day
That he out of the toumbe aros
Thai weren neigh wood so hem agros   *trembled*
And tolden the Jewes he was arisen
550   And for an aungel they weren agrisen   *terrified*
That put doun the gret ston   *moved*
And set hymself there upon
For dred thai seiden that thai had,
Thai fellen doun as thai wore mad
555   Also wymmen there comen thre
That soughtten Jhesu for to see;
The aungel taught hem where he is,
In to Galilé gon, iwis.
Than ansuerden the Jewes blake,   *wicked (see note)*
560   "Whi nad ye tho wymmen ytake?   *didn't; seize*
Ne were ye armed swythe wel,   *very*
Alle foure in yrne and steel."   *iron*
The knighttes seiden, "Ne witeth us noght;   *Do not blame us*
We hadden no myght hem to have brought."

565	Than axed Pilate hem onon,	
	"Whi lete ye than Jhesu gon?"	
	Than ansuerden the knighttes bold,	
	"Whi nadden ye Josep withholde?	*didn't*
	We han bothe failed of oure pay;	*satisfaction*
570	Jesus and Josep ben gon away.	
	Delivere us hider Joseph now,	
	And we schull take Jhesu to you!	
	He is risen as God ful of might:	
	Evere we mowen dred hys right.	*authority*
575	There com no man hym to stele,	
	Theigh he be risen with good hele;	
	And yut we mowen drede the more,	
	We schullen abie his deth ful sore."	*pay for*
	Than wexen the Jewes all mad	*grew; distraught*
580	To maken her gre thai weren glad;	*To make peace with them*
	Thai gaven hem michel tresore	
	That thai scholden speke no more.	
	Al halp nought that thai ne tolde	
	Where thai comen with wordes bolde;	
585	It might in no wise ben yhid:	*be hidden*
	It most nedes alway be kyd.	*known*
	Than seiden the knighttes, "Secheth ye,	*Seek*
	For Josep is now in his cité."	
	Than senten the Jewes Josep to	
590	Letres of pes to come and go;	*Letters of peace (see note)*
	Josep cam and spak hem with	
	The Jewes all, in pes and grith.	*mercy*
	Thai wente ageins hym with honour,	*greeted*
	Thai kist and graunted hym her socour,	*kissed; protection*
595	And thai axed hym the resoun,	
	Hou he com out of prisoun.	
	"Sires," he seide, "I telle you right,	
	Jesus me fet the first nigth.	*sought (fetched)*
	Whan he com me thought that stounde	*at that time*
600	That the hous res fro the grounde,	*rose*
	Up in to the eir ageins hym right,	*air*
	For he is verray God Almight.	
	Ful the hous me thought he sprad	*dispersed*
	With gret light that he had;	
605	For drede of hym I fel adoun	
	As a man that was in swoun,	*swoon (i.e., a faint)*
	Bot sone he me toke by the honde	
	And bad me I scholde by hym stond.	

	My face he wipte and siththe me kyst;	*wiped*
610	What he was yit I nyst.	*did not know*
	"Ne drede thee ich am Jesus," he seide;	
	"That thu beriedest in that stede;	*place*
	Thu madest my grave in yone orchard:	
	By that tokne be noght aferd."	
615	Onon he led me to the grave,	
	Ful good mynde therof I have.	
	"Josep, here thu beriedest me,	
	And that I schal wel yelde thee."	*reward*
	Whan I had this grave seen,	
620	I nyst nevere hou he com then.	
	In myne owen hous he me set,	
	That non of you might hym let;	*hinder*
	In pes ho bad me duelle thore,	*dwell there*
	And bad me come out no more,	
625	Til fourti daies were comen and gon,	
	And bad I ne schulde drede you non;	
fol. 1ra	And at the fourty dayes ende	
	Whider I wolde he bad me wende.	*He bid me to go where I wished*
	Upon the Mount of Olyvete,	*Mount of Olives*
630	There my Lorde that is so swete	*blessed*
	Steigh to hevene fair and wel,	*Ascended*
	Almightty God in flesshe and fel;	*flesh and skin (i.e., the whole body)*
	And efte shal comen at Domesday	*Doomsday*
	To yelde bothe gode and wick her pay.	*give; wicked; reward*
635	There was a swete compaignye:	
	Fyrst his dere moder Marie,	
	His apostles and othere moo	
	That weren ywoned with hym to goo,	*accustomed*
640	To beren witnesse biforne his foos.	
	I hope yee han herd of this,	
	And bot yee han, yee shullen, iwys!"	
	Whan Joseph had al thus saide,	
	Jhesus upon his heved laide,	*head*
645	Er he up upsteigh, ich understonde,	*ascended*
	Faire and wel his rigth honde.	
	"He kissed me and blissed also	
	And faire he took his leve to go,	
	And bad me drede for no Jew —	
650	By this I wist he was Jhesu.	
	And thusgate I come you fro.	*in this manner*
	Sires, what cone yee seie therto?	*what can you say*

By this me thenketh it may acorde
That he is God Almighty Lorde,
655   And tyl the fourty dayes weren ywent
I nolde have comen, theigh yee hadden sente."
Onon he thought hom to goo,
And took his leve and dude also.
Thoo Josep had tolde hem this
660   Than thoughtten hem thai hadden don amys   *wrong*
Thai seiden, "What chaunce is this bifalle
Of this prophete amonge us alle?"
Josep went into his cuntree
And preched and taughtte the Trinité;
665   Michel poeple he tourned and lerd   *converted and taught*
With the wordes thai of him herd.
And whan the Jewes herden this,
Thai weren sore agreved, iwys.
Eftsones thai laughtten hym queyntlich   *Soon after; caught slyly*
670   And sperred hym up wel pryvelich;   *locked; secretly*
In her toun wal thai shetten hym   *shut him up*
In a vaughtth that was ful dym,   *cell*
And there he duelled seven yere.
Oure Lorde hym kepte ful leef and dere;   *cherished*
675   That nede was he had uche day   *What he needed*
Of Jhesu whiles he there lay.
Bot wel I woot atte last,
With mychel honoure he was out cast;
And his foomen aboughtten it dere,   *enemies paid for it*
680   As yee shullen hereafter here.

fol. 1rb   Listneth you, ich wil you rede;
I shal you telle a wonder dede,
Hou curtes Jesus Crist was   *gracious*
To hem that duden hym that trespas,
685   And so he is yut uche day
To us alle, I telle may.
We wraththen hym with many a synne;
Good it were sumtyme to blynne.   *cease*
Al that he may for us he doothe,
690   Al day yee mowen seen the sothe.
In many manere he us fondeth;   *tests*
To wraththen hym therfore withstondeth,   *angered*
For in his honde he bereth the knyf   *bears the knife*
Of oure deth and of oure lyf.
695   Also we reden of this resoun
Thre yere biforne his Passioun   *Three*

	With his deciples hou he kem	*came*
	Toward the cité of Jerusalem,	
	And hou he weep yee shullen see	
700	And spaak thus toward the citee:	
	"Yif thou wist als mychel as I,	
	Thou mostest wepe, I seie thee whi.	
	The day bigynneth fast to highe —	*to come quickly*
	Bot al that is hyd from thine eighe —	*eye*
705	Swiche a day shal come thee on	
	Thou shalt have enemyes many on,	
	That al aboute shullen thee bicast	
	And destroyen thee atte last.	
	Muchel sorough mowen yee have;	
710	You dar no mercy of hem crave.	
	There shal no ston on othere leve,	
	Bot doun thai shullen thee to-dreve."	*drive*
	Foure prophetes seiden righth thus,	
	Longe biforne oure lorde Jhesus,	
715	Bothe Moyses and Ysaye,	*Isaiah*
	And Hosie and Jeremye.	*Hosea and Jeremiah*
	He stood on the Mount of Olyvete	
	Whan he toward the cité gan grete,	
	Bot his deciples wenden ay	
720	That he had speken of Domesday.	
	Peter ansuered for hem alle:	
	"Lorde," he seide, "whan shal this falle?"	
	And Jesus wyst what he wolde mene,	
	And seide to hem, "Yee shullen sene	
725	Mony a tokne upon heighe,	
	Of sonne and mone in the skye;	*sun and moon*
	Londe shal weren agenis londe,	*war*
	The fader agenis the child shal stonde,	
	The childe agenis kynde also;	
730	Manqualme shal be, with hunger and woo,	*Death (from plague)*
	Qualme of beestes and of othere kynde	*Illness*
	Thorough every londe men shullen fynde;	
	The fruyt shal on erthe faile,	
	Men lyven in tene and in travaile.	*suffering; affliction*
fol. 1va	Yee shullen ben drawen, more and lesse,	*brought*
736	Biforne tyrauntes in destresse,	
	And fele for my love shullen plen,	*many; complain*
	And summe al quyk thai shullen flen.	*alive; flay*
	Grete tribulaciouns men shullen see	
740	Many on suffre for love of me;	

	And I myself shal gon to dede,	*death*
	Ybeten and bounden, bak and hede,	
	And risen agein the thrid day	
	To gladen myne, al that I may;	
745	And many other toknes shullen fall	
	I may noughth now seie you alle.	
	Yut cometh noughth the day so sone	
	That the grete dome shal be done.	
	Heveth up youre heveden from slepe,	*Lift; heads*
750	And out of synne clene you kepe!	
	The dome shal come with grete yre,	
	As theef that steleth or wilde fyre,	
	And alle thai shullen to joye wende	
	That kepen hem trewely to the ende.	
755	By toknes that han ben sen byfore,	
	Dredeth that is to comen the more.	
	Hevene and erthe shulle passe bothe,	
	Al bot myne wordes that ben sothe."	
	Whan this was seide, to toun thai drough,	*go*
760	And there he wraththed summe ynough;	
	In the temple he gan biholde	
	Hou the Jewes boughtten and solde;	
	He wexe ful wrooth als yare	*completely*
	Also thai solden there her chaffare,	*goods for trade*
765	Oxen, kyne, and other score,	*cows*
	Withinne the temple and othere tresore,	
	Golde and silven there thai solde	*silver*
	To alle men that bygge wolde,	*buy*
	And for usure to maken chaunce	*usury*
770	To men that comen out of Fraunce.	
	Natheles thai solden non othere thing	
	Bot that shulde to offryng	
	To pilgrymes sekande that cité	*seeking*
	That comen from dyverse cuntré.	
775	Hym thoughth that thei gunnen apeire	*diminish*
	Of holy chirche to maken a feire	*market*
	"Lete chepyng," he seide, "be there it is.	*trading*
	This hous for bedes alone, iwys."	*prayers*
	A roop he laughth that he fonde,	*rope; seized*
780	With many knottes ful his honde,	
	And droof out alle that there stoode;	
	Thai weren so drad thai weren ner wode.	*crazed*
	Hem thoughtten his lokyng was as fyre,	*appearance*
	And thus he seide to hem with yre:	

785	"Yee maken myne hous a theves den,	
	That first was sett for Cristen men.	
	An hous of orisenus dighth it is,	*prayers; made*
	I wil non other it be, iwys."	
	Bestes for hym bigunnen to fleighe,	
fol. 1vb	And felden boordes with monee,	*knocked down tables*
791	And othere thing that stood to selle,	
	Ne durst abide ne lenge to duelle.	
	There ful faire he hem teched,	
	And sithen ful ofte hem preched,	
795	Til thai token it with envie	
	And bispeken his deth with felonye,	*agreed upon*
	Wharfore siththe whan thai hym took	
	Also we reden in the book,	*As*
	Fyfty knighttes with Judas comen	
800	With her meignee that hym nomen,	*troops; took*
	By the resoun that he uchone	*each one*
	Out of the temple droof alone.	
	Natheles whan thai hym took,	
	For his word so sore thai quook,	*shook*
805	That thai fellen all adoune	
	As ded men oither men in swoughne.	*in a swoon*
	He reised hem up as the hende,	
	For that ded most be broughth to ende,	
	For to saven al mankynde,	
810	Als we in prophecies fynde.	

Gode men understondeth now,
And I shal telle you alle how
The Jewes that duden Jhesu to ded,
Thorough feble conseil and fals red.   *bad counsel; treacherous advice*
815 Thai weren in so gret encombraunce;   *ensnarement*
Therfore thai hadden all meschaunce
That had Jhesus byforne hem highth,
And ay thai token it ful lighth;   *lightly*
Bot sithen it fel in her owen nek,   *on their own necks*
820 Thai nolden non other who dar rek.   *should care*
Yut fourty yer he yaf hem space,   *a reprieve*
To see yif thai wolden seken his grace;
To vengen hym wolde he noughth sende   *avenge*
Yif that thai wolden hem amende.
825 Thre thinges there weren in Israel,
Whiche thai weren hereth hem wel,
Als in storye we redeth and fynde
That fellen on the Jewes kynde.

	The first was cleped pylrynage,	*called pilgrimage*
830	That other thraldom and servage,	
	Dispersioun the thrid was tolde,	*Dispersion (Diaspora; see note)*
	That is to-dreveyng of yonge and olde.	*scattering*
	Thus began her pilrynage	
	Thoo Jacob went with his lynage	*descendants*
835	Into Egipte for mychel nede	
	Thai lyved there longe in mychel drede	
	Thoo Jacob ne mighth no lenger lyven	
	His kynde was out of londe ydryven,	
	Thorough the Rede See as yee han herd,	*Red Sea*
840	There Pharaou and his folk forferd.	*perished*
	Moyses was her leder than	
	Into the londe of Chanaan	*Canaan*
	That was the londe that he hem highth	*promised*
	And there he kepte hem wel aplighth.	*in faith*
fol. 2ra	With aungels mete he fed hem,	*angel's food (i.e., manna)*
846	Her clothes lasted withouten wem	*flaw*
	Fourty wynter in deserte —	
	That was a miracle fair and aperte!	*plain*
	And yut for al his curteisie,	
850	Thai wroughtten ageins hym gret folye.	
	Thai maden goddes of metal	*(i.e., idols)*
	And honoured hem with worthschipp al;	
	Than yolden thai Jhesu his godenesse	*rewarded*
	With ful mychel unkyndenesse.	
855	Nou shal I touche of her servage,	*bondage*
	That evere shal last the worldes age;	
	Ne shullen thai nevere duelle in toun	
	Withouten trowage or raunsoun.	*tax; ransom*
	In Babiloyne first this thraldom	*Babylon; subjection*
860	On her former fadres com,	*forefathers*
	There thai duelleden fifty yere	
	Er than mosten gon quyt and skere.	*go free; safe*
	The fiftithe yer was her solace,	*fiftieth*
	Forthi it is now the yer of grace;	
865	Thai weren than leten out of prisoun,	
	So is that oure yer of gret perdoun.	*pardon*
	Dispersioun was the thrid thing,	*Diaspora*
	Of Jewen kynde the to-drevyng,	*scattering*
	That is now fallen in this cas.	
870	Thorough Vaspasian and Titus it was.	
	As Jhesus er seide thorough prophecie,	
	"I schal delyver hem for her envie	

	Under lordeschipp and swiche honde."	*control*
	There thai shullen duelle, ich understonde,	
875	Withouten skapyng of prisoun,	
	For golde, ne fee, ne raunsoun,	
	For no mercy quyt shulde thai wende	*go freely*
	Hethen to the werldes ende.	*From hence*
	Mesure ne mercy was non in hem,	*Moderation*
880	And swiche shullen thai have and her barnetem	*offspring*
	For thai Maries son forsook	
	That was rigth heire, so seith the book,	*true heir*
	For Marie com of that lynage	*lineage*
	That he shulde bere the heritage.	*inheritance*
885	Of this chaunce was spoken and founde	
	Er than it fel a longe stounde.	
	The noble clerk maistre Josephus	
	Amonge the Jewes seide thus:	
	"The day wil come this toun schall falle	
890	And the Jewes ben confounded alle;	
	This cité shal ben overthrowe,	
	The heighe paleys shal lye ful lowe.	
	Messias shal sende you amonge	
	Sorough and shame and werre stronge.	*fierce war*
895	Fro Rome shullen come princes two,	
	The fader and the son also,	
	And shullen destroye al that thai fynde,	
	This toun with al the Jewes kynde.	
	This shal falle by her werkes,	
fol. 2rb	Taken thai nevere so wel her merkes,	*no matter how much they beware*
901	For thai slowghen Jhesu Crist, iwis,	
	That God Almightty son is,	
	And this is her rightful juggement,	
	Bot thai comen to amendement.	
905	The fader gate there swiche honoure	
	That he shal ben emperoure.	
	Another tyme witnesseth yee	
	Whan that yee the sothe ysee."	*truth*
	Thus wroot he in the Jewes book,	
910	There thai mightten it alway look.	
	After Jhesus deth fellen wondres thicke,	*many wonders*
	Faire and foule, gode and wyk,	*evil*
	Sithen thai slough the yonge Seint Jame,	
	For he preched Cristes name.	
915	Seven yer after Jhesus dede	
	Dyed James in that stede,	

	For whiche deth God was wrooth also.	
	For to amende hem he was sent hem to,	
	With conseil, bedes, and with prechyng,	*prayers*
920	In tokne of the first warnyng	
	To amende hem that thai deden hym dye.	*caused his death*
	This me thinketh was a curteisie,	
	For it was the heighest trespas	*greatest*
	That evere in erthe yarked was.	*ordained*
925	Forthi it is no skyl reuthe to have	*it is not fitting to have pity*
	Of hem ne kepten hemself to save;	
	Forthi we owin make joye and game	*ought*
	That hem bifel sorough and shame.	
	Jesu it grauntte for his mercy	
930	That uche synful be quyt therby!	*freed*
	God sent this James to Jerusalem,	
	As I seide er, to prechen hem,	*before*
	To repenten of her synne	
	That thei weren encoumbred inne,	*ensnared*
935	And so he dude alwaye;	
	He ne spared noughth, the sothe to saye.	
	He wexe of so gret renoun	*grew*
	Thai maden hym bisshop of the toun;	
	He was a man of grete penaunce	
940	And dude his body grete grevaunce.	*injury*
	He wered nevere wollen ne lynnen clooth,	*wore; wool; linen*
	Ne brede ne fyssh ete, ne flesshe that gooth,	*live animals (i.e., meat)*
	For chaungeyng, wasshyng na bathing,	
	Bot a goune of heer to his clothing;	*hairshirt*
945	And kneled so to God alway	
	For the poeple nighth and day,	
	With his knees bare upon the ston,	
	That the hide wexe hard hem upon,	*skin*
	So that thai semeden biforne	*seemed*
950	As chamailes knees that ben of horne.	*camel's; horn*
	This com hym of gret charité,	
	Yif thai mightten the better have be;	
	Wicked thai weren ay and wicked than	
	That kidden than in that gode man.	*That was made known*
fol. 2va	It was upon a Paske Day,	*Passover (see note)*
956	The Jewes gadered with grete deray	*noise*
	And seiden thus to Seint Jame,	
	Al on yrnest and with grame:	*earnest; hatred*
	"Out of this cuntree fer and hende,	*fair*
960	Michel folk wil hider wende	

For to heren thi prechyng.
We bidde thou speke non othere thing
Agenis oure law with Jhesus,
Yif thou wilt have thank of us.
965   For yif the folk after thi sawghe   *words*
Thorough thi prechyng from us drawghe,
Michel pyne than shaltou have,   *Great pain*
The grete lorde shal thee noughth save."
Thai beden hym despise Jhesu   *ordered*
970   Whan he preched of his vertu;
And yif he preised hym wel byfore,
He preised hym than mychel more.
And also he preched upon a day
In the temple ageins her pay,   *against their liking*
975   On went to hym there he stood   *One*
And drough hym doune as he were wood;   *pulled; mad*
Anothere laughtte a fullyng staf,   *seized; (see note)*
And in the hevede therwith hym gaf.   *head; struck*
He smoot hym ther with so gret mayn,   *strength*
980   That in the chirche shad his brayn.   *dashed out*
Thus thai yelden hym his mede   *gave him his reward*
For his travaile and his good dede!
There risen up fele that loveden Jame,   *many*
To taken thise men and don hem shame;
985   Thoo that seighen thai flowen anon   *fled*
So that tyme quyt thai gon.   *free*
Bot thai abiden the grete vengeaunce
For Cristes deth and for his chaunce.   *fate*
Alway they were ylich wyk,   *constantly wicked*
990   Tyl the wreche com to the pryck,   *Until the point of vengeance*
For Goddes righth ne wil no wrong
That dampned hem sithen to pyne stronge.   *condemned*
Thai that wolden James socoure   *aid*
Byriyeden his body with honoure.   *Buried*
995   The Jewes clepid hym on and other   *called*
Noughth bot Jhesus Cristes brother;
Of body, of face, and of feet,
He was liche hym evere yutt.
For the first tokne he was sent   *sign*
1000   To tourne the poeple was his entent.   *convert*

Listneth now, I wil you telle,
Of wondres I may you spelle,   *explain*
That othere tokne that com there than
That shewen amonge the Jewes gan.

1005	There weren gadred on a foest,	*feast*
	Alle the Jewes, lest and mest,	*least and greatest*
	That richest weren of that cité,	
	And also fele of the cuntré,	
	For at morne whan thai arise,	
fol. 2vb	Thai duden her Goddes sacrifise,	
1011	So that nothing shulde hem greve.	
	So bifel hem as thai bileve	
	For the pride that thai were inne	
	And encombred weren of senne,	*sin*
1015	At that fest aross swiche stryf	*strife*
	That uche slough other with his knyf;	
	Thritti thousande there weren sleyn,	
	And that made many a Jew unfeyn.	*unhappy*
	The thridd tokne next was this,	
1020	Agenis kynde it fel, iwys,	*nature*
	To the temple an helefer was broughth,	*heifer*
	That to sacrifice was soughth	
	And sodeynlich amonges hem alle,	*suddenly*
	Er men wyst, it gan doun falle.	*knew*
1025	There com out of the beestes wombe,	
	In the stede of a calf, a lombe.	*place; lamb*
	That abaissht alle that there stood,	*perplexed*
	So that thai weren alle wel neigh wood.	*insane*
	The furthe tokne fel on a nyghth	
1030	In the temple was swiche lighth	*such light*
	That alle the Jewes that it say	*saw*
	Wendeth it had ben lighth of day,	*Thought*
	On Paske Day withinne the nigth	
	It was the nynthe houre ful rigth.	*3:00pm, the office of Nones (ninth hour after dawn)*
1035	As ich rede of this cas	
	This the fyfte tokne was:	
	Anothere nighth fel at cokkes crowe	*(i.e., dawn)*
	That alle the gatus gunne up blowe,	*gates; blow*
	That weren of yren ysperred fast	*locked*
1040	With suche a dyne that thai upbrast.	*din; burst open*
	Thorough the toun was swiche a dyne	
	So that thai wenden that weren thereinne	
	That her toun wal was fallen adoune	
	That enclosed al tho toune.	
1045	Tha sexte token was thai herden a cry	*sixth*
	In the temple al on hygh	
	Thai seide "go we hethen, go we hethen."	*hence*
	Alle thai it herd and noughth ne seighen.	*and saw nothing*

	It was upon the Witsoneeday	*Whitsunday (Pentecost)*
1050	Withinne the even, tellen I may;	*evening*
	The preestes comen the temple unto	
	Als thai weren ywoned to do,	*accustomed*
	For to don her servise,	
	Bot ful sone thai gonnen agrise;	*tremble*
1055	For the cry that was bifore	
	Thai flowen out alle that there wore.	*fled; were*
	The seventhe tokne after that cry	
	Thai seighen a sterre lighth in the sky,	
	Shapen als a swerd it henge,	*Shaped like; hung*
1060	The poynt doun righth as a strenge.	*like a string*
	So it henge til it was daye	
	That al the cité wel it saye;	*saw*
	And so it honge there als yere	
	And alway it semed yliche nere.	

fol. 3ra	The eightteth tokne sithen there kem	*then there came*
1066	Over the cité of Jerusalem;	
	Thai seighen in tho ayre hem above	*air*
	Men on hors yarmed hove	*Armed men on horseback suspended in the air*
	That sumtyme faughtte and sumtyme rest.	
1070	What thai bitokned often thai kest;	*pondered*
	Thai reden it tokneth werre stronge,	*serious war*
	Manqualme oither hunger stronge.	*Plague; famine*
	Thai seiden sother than thai wende,	*truer; knew*
	Yut thoughtten thai noughth hem to amende.	
1075	Hadden thai thoo turned to penaunce,	
	Thai hadden ben from the vengeaunce.	*would have avoided*
	The nynthe tokne after this,	
	Ye shullen heren whiche it is,	
	Chares and waynes also thai say	*Chariots; wagons; saw*
1080	Comande in cloudes hem thoughtten ay;	*Coming*
	Righth now thai alle it sowe,	*saw*
	And or thai wist, away was blowe.	
	The tenthe tokne was the last	
	That made the Jewes sore agast:	
1085	The fierthe yer ar the sege bigan,	*fourth; before*
	Of Jude there was borne a man	*Judea*
	On James, Ananias sone,	*One*
	For alle the Jewes he nolde shone.	*would not fear*
	Ones on a Wytsonenday,	
1090	Whan Jewes weren gadred in her lay,	*according to their religion*
	For to maken joye mest	*great*
	As bifel to the heighe fest,	

He stood up amonges hem alle

And on this werlde he gan loud calle: *world*

1095 "From est and overe al this worlde,

South and north ich have herd,

Fro the foure wyndes a voys kem   *voice came*

Upon the cité of Jerusalem,

And on oure temple for grete synne,

1100 And on the poeple that were thereinne.

Me thenkith that it bitokne may

Us wil befalle a grete affray.   *attack*

Come whan it come shal,

Ful sore I drede me of that fal!   *destruction*

1105 Thus met me by a visioun   *dreamed*

That shal bifalle on this toun."

The Jewes token hym for this

And beten hym and bounden hard, iwys.   *forcefully*

Biforne Pilate thai broughten this man

1110 And as he seide er, so seide he than.

And thoo thai beten hym fele at ones,   *many at once*

That mon mightten seen his naked bones,   *people (men)*

Natheles he cryed for al this cas,

"Jerusalem, allas, allas!"

1115 Of this mighth hym no man stynte   *stopped*

For betynge, thretynge, ne for dynte,   *beating, threatening, nor for striking*

Bot seide always thus onon.

And than thai suffred hym alle to gon,

For they ne might hym noght at holde,

fol. 3rb Bot alway seide as he arst tolde.   *first*

1121 Of thise toknes hadden thai non awghe   *awe*

Bot meynted forth her fals lawghe.   *upheld*

Of her synne thai nolden biknowe   *confess*

What so evere that thai sowe,   *saw*

1125 In toun in felde oither in place,

For thai hadden no better grace:

Natheles her lawghe gan blynne   *cease*

And the niwe lawghe to bigynne.   *new*

Thoo Jhesus on rode his hede doun leide   *At that time; on the cross*

1130 And "consummatum est" seide;   *It is finished (Latin)*

This tokned "The elde lawghe is went,

And the niwe I have you sent,

And my purpose is broughth to ende,

For man that is my dere frende."

1135 Her owen bokes witnesseth this;

Thai weren the more to blamen, iwis,

For alle thinges that weren don,
Pilate dude hem writen onon,
And that was sithen agenis her kynde
1140   As men in the storie fynde.
Whan Seint Eleyne the croice fonde   *Helen; cross*
Sithen in that ilche londe   *same land*
Longe ageins hir thai it forsook
Til she overcom hem by her book.
1145   Whan God alle thise toknes sent,
Yut nolden thai noughth hem repent,
Ne ones of mercy hym bisoughth
For that thai hym to deth broughth.
Thai that willen no mercy crave
1150   Aren non worthi for to have.
Thai duden folye to hurtlen with hym   *fight against*
That kepeth soule, liif, and lym;   *protects soul, life, and limb*
The erthen vessel ne lasteth noughth   *earthen*
To hurtlen with that of metal is wroughth.
1155   No more may mannes kende figth   *mankind*
Ageins the power of God almighth.

Lete we now the Jewes duelle;
Here gynneth her wreche for to telle.   *vengeance*
Jhesus a messagere hath sent
1160   That swithe upon his erande wente   *swiftly*
To the kyng, Sir Vaspasian,
That was a swithe noble man,   *very*
And in meselrie so depe hym cast   *leprosy*
That body and face foule to-brast   *burst stinkingly*
1165   And in his nose a cankre smoot   *tumor afflicted him*
That bothe his lyppes al to boot;   *stung*
And for no cost that he couthe bye
He seighe non other bote bot dye.   *remedy but death*
Natheles in his nose wore
1170   Waspes sithen that he was bore;   *Wasps; born*
Out of the holes thai hem fedden,
Hevedes and wenges out thai spredden,   *Heads and wings*
fol. 3va   And of thise waspes thai cleped hym thus —
His righth name Vaspasianus,
1175   For thoo was no name given
Tyl men seighen the childe shulde lyven.
Of thise waspes his name he took
As we fyndeth ywriten in book.
Swiche meselrie God hym sent
1180   That al his body it overwent;   *covered*

Fole yeres so on hym it left,   *Many years*
Tyl Jhesus wolde it were hym reft.   *taken from*
For yee witen ful wel alle
Of alle thinges that shulden bifalle,
1185   Fro the bigynnyng to the dome,   *judgment*
He hath sette whan thai shullen come   *appointed*
In werkes, in wedres, in al kynde,   *weather*
Thorough holy wrytt as men fynde.
The resoun I you telle can
1190   Whi God sent this on this man:
God dooth nothing withouten skyl,   *reason*
Who so understonde it wil.
Righth als the Jewes with fals red   *counsel*
Duden hym that is God to ded
1195   Of hevene, erthe, and of helle
And weldeth alle that thereinne duelle,   *rules*
As God is lorde of alle thinges
So is the emperour kyng of kynges,
And alle londes thorough resoun
1200   Ben at his subjeccioun.
Forthi by skyl it was kest   *Therefore*
To wreken Jhesu bicom hym best   *it suited him*
The grettest lorde in erthe righth
Bycom to wreken God almighth,   *It was proper*
1205   And so he dude faire and wel
I shal you shewe uche a del.
Yut had he noughth the empire in honde
Bot after sone thorough Goddes sonde.   *sending*
The yvel was on hym so rank   *foul*
1210   That on his folk so foule he stank;
Fro amonge his men he fleigh,   *fled*
And helde his chaumbre biside neigh.   *near beside*
Unnethe hise men for the stynk   *Scarcely*
Mighten hym brynge mete or drynk;
1215   With a viis thai tourned in his mete   *winch*
Whan he shulde any ete.
And thus in his bed he lay
That he ne mighth out nyghth ne day,
To the tyme come atte last   *Until*
1220   That Jesus Crist hym wolde out cast.
Alle yvels comen of Goddes sonde,   *illnesses*
And so dude his, ich understonde.

Also the sept sages us tellen   *seven sages (see note)*
That clerkes in the storie spellen

1225	Whan Jhesus dyed amonges us	
	Was emperour Sir Thiberius;	*Tiberius*
	Of doughttynesse he had the fame,	*bravery*
fol. 3vb	And therfore men writen his name.	
	For in his tyme Jhesus dyed,	
1230	As men it han wel aspyed.	
	In the tyme of his eighttende yere	*eighteenth*
	Jesus Crist took his deth here.	
	Of Rome he bare the dignité;	
	Thre and thritty yere regned he.	*reigned*
1235	In his tyme the Jewes sent	
	A lettre endited by on assent;	*written*
	Thereinne thai biwrayed Sir Pilate,	*accused*
	His grete pride to abate,	*destroy*
	For hem thoughth in werk and sawghe	*deeds; words*
1240	That he trespassed ageins the lawghe.	
	Of his mysberyng thai writen thus	*misconduct*
	To the emperour Sir Thiberius:	
	That he gaf conseil ageins the pes	
	To slen the childer giltles,	*To slay the guiltless children*
1245	And in the temple with grete rages	*madness*
	Of fals goddes set up ymages,	*idols*
	And of her temple the tresore	
	That was of offryng the store	*offerings*
	Withouten her aller assent	*all of their*
1250	In his owen nedes it spent.	
	He made a conduyt merveillous	*conduit*
	With pipe comande into his hous,	*coming*
	And othere fele wicked outrages	*many wicked excesses*
	He dude ageins her usages.	*customs*
1255	And thorough this sonde and this pleynt	*message; complaint*
	In thise defautes he was ateynt	*defects; convicted*
	And was jugged to the exile	
	For his trespas that was so vile.	
	Of this Pilate herd telle,	
1260	And that he migth noughth there duelle;	
	He ordeyned a riche present,	*arranged*
	And with his lettre he hath it sent	
	That was endited fel and hard,	*shrewdly and forcefully*
	As yee mowen here afterward.	
1265	After hym regned Sir Gayus,	
	And after hym Sir Claudyus,	
	And sithen Nero, the cursed soule,	*then*
	That slough bothe Peter and Poule,	

	And after hym com Sir Vaspasyan	
1270	That was an honourable man.	
	God graunted hym thorough his sonde	
	To wreken his deth with his honde;	
	Of Galice and Gascoyne the kyngdome	*Galatia; Gascony*
	Was his ar he come to Rome,	*before*
1275	And yut the storye telleth me thus,	
	He had a son that highth Titus.	
	In the cité of Burdeux on a day,	*Bordeaux*
	Titus out at a wyndow lay,	
	And as he loked in the strem,	*water*
1280	A shipp there com from Jerusalem.	
	He sen where that the shipp went	
	In the cee as Crist it sent;	*sea*
fol. 4ra	Anon he sent a messagere	
	To come to hym that thereinne were.	
1285	The maister com bifore his kne;	*(ship's) master*
	"Felawe," quoth Titus, "wel thee be!	
	Felawe," he seide, "what hattestou?	*are you called*
	And fro whethen comestou now?"	*from what place*
	"Sir," he seide, "I hatte Nathaan;	
1290	Of Jude I am a borne man.	*Judea*
	Leve sir," he seide, "telleth me	*Dear*
	Yif I now at Rome be."	
	"Nay," quoth Titus, "withouten ensoyne;	*without delay*
	This is Burdeaux in Gascoyne!	
1295	From hethen to Rome, forsothe to seye,	*hence*
	Men it holde a wel fer weye!	
	Have ydo and telle me sone,	
	What hastou at Rome to done?"	
	"Sir, thider me sent Sir Pilate;	
1300	A wynde me hath dryven another gate.	*path*
	To Tiberius is his sonde,	*message*
	To beren hym trowage of oure londe."	
	"Felawe," he seide, "Tiberius is ded;	
	There have ben two sithen in his stede.	
1305	Natheles, my leve frende Nathaan,	
	I shal do brynge thee to that man.	
	Upon myne costagus I schal fonde	*At my expense*
	That hath the empire in his honde.	
	For us, I hope, and oure lettre,	
1310	Thou shalt spede wel the bettre,	*fare*
	In a covenaunt thou showe me	*an agreement*
	Hou my fader migth hole be,	*whole (i.e., healed)*

	Of a sekenesse that hym greveth;	
	For we hopen here and bileveth	
1315	That men that in the contré wonen	*go*
	Of al maner yvel thai connen,	*all kinds of evil*
	Oither with gras, oither with ston,	*herb; stone*
	And othere medicynes many on."	*medicines*
	"Sir," he seide, "I am no leche,	*physician*
1320	Bot of on I can you teche,	
	That highth Jhesus of Nazareth;	
	The Jewes duden hym to the deth."	
	He tolde hym the despyt, aplighth	*harm, in faith*
	That Jhesus tholed with unrighth:	*executed*
1325	He was a prophete over alle,	
	He seide always as sooth is falle,	*as truly as it happens*
	He clensed men of yvel and synne,	*purified*
	With his word that bileved herinne;	
	He arered Lazar the knighth,	*raised Lazarus*
1330	That foure dayes lay yplighth.	*in danger*
	Al he tolde hym of Jhesus dede,	
	As men in the Godspell rede,	
	And of his deth and his uprist;	*upraising*
	And of his apostles that he wist;	*knew*
1335	And hou the Holy Gost he hem sent	
	After that fourty dayes weren went;	
	"Ten and sexty langages I herd	
fol. 4rb	That thai of her maister lerd,	*learned*
	And bad hem gon into every londe,	
1340	To prechen his name thorough his sonde.	*message*
	Of alle yvels he gaf hem mighth,	
	To helen the seke that bileved arighth,	
	And tho that wil noughth to hem wende,	
	Shulden ben lorne withouten ende.	*lost*
1345	I woot wel fele of hem lyven,	*many*
	In what londe so thai ben dryven,	*driven to*
	And I am siker and bileve	*certain*
	Non yvel shal thi fader greve	
	That yif he wil bileven arighth	
1350	I dar bihote hym hele, aplighth."	*promise; health, in faith*
	His fader stiward Velocyan,	*steward*
	That was a wel crafty man,	
	Stood and herd her wordes alle,	
	And fayn he wolde it mighth bifalle.	*gladly*
1355	Thai took and gaven hym his mede	*reward*
	And to the emperour dude hym lede,	

Sir Nero that was a cursed man
That slough hymselven sone than.
Tho he had hymself ysleyn,
1360   The court of Rome was ful feyn.   *glad*
Onon thai chosen Vaspasian
To ben her emperoure than,
For the noblest man of the worlde,
And heighest of blood, as yee han herd.   *highest ranking*
1365   After that Nathaan was comen and gon,
It was two yer er it were don
Thus fel it hym for this wonder cas
Righth as God wolde, so it was.
Bot alle that knewen hym more and lesse
1370   Maden grete mon for his sekenesse,   *moan*
In aventure yif he shulde amende   *In case; improve*
His empire for to defende,
Bot thai hoped and wel thai kest,   *knew*
His son shulde don it atte best.
1375   Nathaan com to the emperoure;
He shewed his nedes with honoure,
He broughth hym trowage of fele yere   *many*
And Pilates letter, as yee mowen here:

"Sire, I grete thee also my frende.   *as*
1380   Understonde that I thee sende,
I have perceyved and proved wel
Of Cristes deth uche a del,   *every bit*
What wondres han siththe bifalle   *since*
In Jerusalem among us alle.
1385   The elde Jewes kynde bihighth   *Jewish people; promised*
That Crist shulde to the erthe alighth   *descend*
Into a mayden of her kynde,
As we in oure bokes fynde
That of a mayden he shulde be borne
1390   That the poeple ne were noughth lorne,
And seide he shulde be kyng of hem
And of alle her barnetem.   *offspring*
fol. 4va   And so he com als thai sede;
Ageins hym alle thai gonne plede   *argue*
1395   The prophecies whan he seide hem to,
As her elders hadden do.
And for he withtook hem in her lawghe   *opposed*
Thai wraththed hem sore with his sawghe;   *angered*
Al that he seide thai token in vayn,
1400   Thus thai helden longe hym agayn,   *for a long time*

So that thai token hym atte last
And beten hym and bounden hym fast,
And comen and delyvered hym to me
And demed hym to hangen on tree.   *judged*
1405   And agein hem ne durst I be,   *against them; dared*
Bot yif I shulde of londe fleghe.   *flee*
I sat as justise in domes sted;   *judge*
I nad no gylt of his ded.   *had no*
Riche and povere gaf up the tale,
1410   And maden hym foul, bothe grete and smal.
I dradde and loved the communaulté,   *feared; people of the country*
And durst noughth ageins hem be;
And though I fonde in hym no gylt
Wharfore that he shulde ben spylt,
1415   In my pretorye, in my mete halle,   *praetorium (see note); dining hall*
The princes of the Jewes alle
There thai gaven hym the dome.
That tyme I wolde it had ben come
For he dude non othere wik,   *evil*
1420   Bot shewed wordes fele and thik,   *many and great*
Doumbe to speken, blynde to seen,
Deef to heren, fendes to fleen   *demons; drive away*
Fro wood men many on,   *mad*
And croked men also to gon.   *crippled; walk*
1425   And fele miracles dude that man,
Wel mo than I telle can.
Wharfore, sir, by no resoun
Haveth me in no suspecioun,
That it was in none othere waye,
1430   What so evere the Jewes saye.
For peraventure it may so be   *perhaps*
That thai wolden put this werke on me.
And forthi sir, leveth hem noughth:
It was her dede and her thoughth   *belief*
1435   It was her ded and nought myn!
That wil I prove by al her kyn.
Thai buriyed hym and did hym kepe   *guard*
With her knyttes that felen on slepe;
On the thrid day he aroos,
1440   Almightty God among his foos.   *enemies*
The knightes comen hem onon
And seiden he was arisen and gon;
Thai gaven the knyttes mede thoo   *reward*
To saien that he was stolen hem froo,

1445	And thai ne mightten hem nougth withholde	*restrain*
	Where thai comen that thai ne tolden	
	Al the sothe and al the cas	*truth*
fol. 4vb	Of the prophete als it was.	
	I have done writen gret and smal,	
1450	What this matere touches al,	*All that pertains to this matter*
	So that of hym the storye	
	Evere may last in memorie.	
	Holdeth me excused, sir, herby,	*therefore*
	For any tale, for any cry."	
1455	He was nevere the bettre excused than	
	Ageins God ne ageins man,	
	For his feith was al in wynde	*(i.e., in transitory things)*
	And noughth in herte ne in mynde.	
	He ne mighth excuse hym in none wise	
1460	Of that ilche fals juwyse,	*same false sentence*
	For many faire myracles he say	*saw*
	And hymself witnesseth ay;	
	And Joseph hym warned of Aramathie	
	And Nichodemus with curtesie,	
1465	And so dude Centurio,	
	Fele othere men and wymmen also,	*Many*
	That al that Jhesus dude uche del,	
	It was treuly don and wel.	
	Natheles he took al to lighth	*all too lightly*
1470	That he shulde ben God almighth.	
	He was warned also by his wyf,	
	That he ne raste Jhesu his liif;	*take*
	So bad hir the fende in a visioun,	
	For to have letted Jhesus Passioun;	*hindered*
1475	Fende and man bothe God blent,	*blinded*
	So that the prophecie forth went.	
	Wostou whi he dude so?	*Do you know*
	For that his deth shoulde forth goo:	
	Elles the fende wolde have had alle	
1480	That hadden ben in synne falle,	
	Bot Jhesus er the deth wolde chese	*rather; choose*
	Than he shulde mannes soule lese.	*lose*
	And any man be that noughth hath herd	
	Hou Pilate com into this word	*world*
1485	It was a kyng that highth Tyrus	
	Of Spayne, ich understonde thus;	
	A millers doughtter of his londe	
	He knouleched, ich understonde.	*had intercourse with*

	She highth Pila, her fader Atus;	
1490	Her son was sithen merveillous.	*peculiar*
	Pilatus thai cleped hym thoo,	
	After hem bothe two.	
	The kyng on his wiif dere	
	Gate a son the self yere;	*Begat; same*
1495	This Pila sithen broughth hem her sone	
	With his fader the kyng to wone.	*live*
	Thise children weren togedre longe	
	Til thai weren bigge and stronge.	
	In alle dedes thorough kynde,	*nature*
1500	Pilate was alway byhynde,	*inferior*
	And that agreved Pilate sore,	
	And prively he slough hym therfore.	*secretly; slew*

fol. 5ra   The kyng it herd, sorough he made;
           To slen Pilate his men hym bade.
1505   The kyng wolde noughth don her rede,   *advice*
           Bot sente Pilate on another stede,   *to another place*
           For he shulde by lawghe and by dome   *law and judgment*
           Uche yer a childe sende to Rome.
           Than thoughth the kyng, "by this sonde
1510   May I best delyver myne honde."   *pledge*
           In trowage he hym sent for this chaunce,
           And for trowage the kyng of Fraunce
           To Rome also sent his sone,
           And he and Pilate togedres wone.
1515   The kynges son was mychel praised,
           Ye, more than Pilate, and upreised   *raised up*
           For gentyle thewes and curteisie,   *manners*
           And Pilate had of this envie.
           In pryvé stede togedres thai drough,   *secret place; came*
1520   And there the kynges son he slough.
           The Romaynes token her conseil thoo   *Romans*
           What thai mightten with hym do;
           Biforne he slough his owen brother,
           And now he hath sleyn another.
1525   On there spaak of th'assemblé:
           "Wicked and fel man he wil be;   *evil*
           He wil be mody man of thewes,   *a man of cruel manners*
           For to adaunte felle shrewes;   *conquer many rogues*
           For he hath don to deeth tweyne
1530   He were worthi to dye in peyne.
           Ne can I given no better rede   *advice*
           Bot senden hym on another stede,

	Into Pounthes, the wicked ylde,	*Pontius; isle*
	To abaten his blood that is so wilde,	
1535	And for to kepe that wicked cuntré.	
	The folk is fel and so is he;	
	Oither he shal hem overcome,	
	Or he shal be sone ynome.	*taken*
	And there hym may so ben yolde	
1540	The pyne that he to sholde."	
	Thai senten hym with commissioun	*authority*
	To holde that ylde in his baundoun,	*power*
	And what with paynes and with giftes,	
	Al that ylde to wille he shiftes;	
1545	And so he dude her pride abate	
	That men clepen hym Pounthes Pilate.	
	He was kyd so queynte with pride	*known to be; crafty*
	Thorough that ylde on every side,	
	That men dredden fer and nere	
1550	For to comen in his daungere.	*dominion*
	Thoo Heroudes herd of Pilate this fame,	
	And of his queyntise and of his name,	*craftiness*
	He sent hym giftes and messagers	
	And praied hym to ben with hym chers;	*friendly*
1555	And Pilate onon to hym kem	*came*
	And he hym made keper of Jerusalem,	*protector*
	And als justise of al that cuntré	
fol. 5rb	That men clepeth now Judé.	*Judea*
	He peyned hym longe with hym to duelle,	*occupied himself*
1560	For that thai weren bothe felle.	*evil*
	Bot Pilate wexe so riche than	
	Of the tresore that he wan,	
	And for thai ne parted her wynyng bothe,	*divided*
	Therfore Heroudes was with hym wrothe;	
1565	And so thai lyveden in yre and onde,	*anger and spite*
	Til Crist com thorough his holy sonde	
	And was taken and to Heroudes went	
	As Pilate hym thider sent,	
	And thus thai weren bothe dere	*fierce*
1570	As yee mowen in the Passioun here.	
	Every man that lyveth in hate	
	May be likned to sir Pilate,	*compared*
	That wesshe his handes and noughth his herte,	*washed*
	That dude hym sithen sore to smerte.	
1575	Yut smerteth noughth Pilate alone,	*injured him*
	Bot the Jewes everychone,	

For thai baden his blood shulde falle
On hem and on her children alle.
I shal you shewen it is sooth,
1580   For everyche Fryday so it dooth,
A floure of blood cometh hem on   *menstrual blood (see note)*
And holdeth hem til the day be gon,
And namelich on the Gode Friday   *especially*
Wel harder than thai han it ay
1585   Or than thai han it thorough the yere
For that day ne dar thai noughth out stere.   *proceed*
Bot whan thai taken oure Cristes lawghe,   *take our Christ's law (e.g., convert)*
That yvel bygynneth to withdrawghe.
That yvel shal no more hem greve,
1590   So longe as thai wel bileve,
By this tokne ben thai clene:
Thus is a faire myracle I wene.
For alle that wilten hym mercy crave,
He is so ful that thai shullen have.
1595   And also mighth sithen Sir Pilate,
Bot he bood to longe and bad to late,   *remained; asked*
And therfore he aboughth it dere,   *paid dearly for it*
Als yee shullen herafter here.
God com to seken that was forlorne   *lost*
1600   And to gadre thoo that to-dreved worne.   *were driven away*

Lucifer first and sithen Adam
Maden that he to erthe cam,
For he wolde thorough his grace
Fulfillen agein that empty place
1605   From thethen that the aungels felle   *thence*
Into the deppest pytt of helle.
Forthi Adam and al his kynde
He wolde have thider, as we fynde,
For to beren hym compaignye;
1610   And this gile God gan sone aspye,   *trick; discover*
And for that he fonde non of us than
For this, siker, he bicom man   *certainly*
fol. 5va   And dyed on the Rode tre,   *Rood (i.e., the Cross)*
For to maken us alle fre.
1615   And sithen he roos and helle brast,   *and hell burst*
And his owen out he cast
And ledde hem to the joye thoo.
In helle I hope ne comen no mo
Bot gostes that ay kepen that stede,   *souls*
1620   And thai that duden hym to dede.

Here mowe we seen God ys howre frende: *our*
Agein to the story will we now wende.   *Back; go*

Tho Nathaan had his erande ydo,
"Sire," he seide, "giveth me leve to goo.
1625   The day is gon, sooth to seyn,   *past, truth to say*
That I shulde have ben at home ageyn.
I have so ben letted by the waye   *hindered*
That I noot what me is best to saye."   *do not know*
Thoo seide Nero, "Drede thee no del,
1630   I shal excuse thee fair and wel."
In his lettre he dude to write
To witnesse Nathaan and aquyte   *acquit*
Of al that fel sithen he out went,   *happened*
And of the tresore that Pilate sent
1635   He gaf hym giftes grete also,
And therwith leve for to go.
Now wendeth hom Nathaan;
Now hereth of sir Vaspasyan.

Sithen bithoughth hym Velosyan
1640   What Tytus had herd of Nathaan;
Of his lorde he had grete care   *distress*
And sore byment his yvel fare.   *lamented; painful condition*
Biforne his lorde he gan doune falle
And tolde hym Nathaans wordes alle;
1645   Titus upon a day and he
Reherced this as yee mowen see,   *Reported*
For reuthe of hym sore he grete   *pity; cried*
And seide he wolde his bales bete   *remedy his misfortunes*
Though he shulde of his body take
1650   Yif he wyst his pynes to slake: *relieve*
"For liif ne deth ne wolde I lette   *life nor death*
To wenden ful fer thi bete to fette,   *To go full far to fetch your cure*
For Titus and I this othere day
Herden wordes to oure pay.   *satisfaction*
1655   Sir, hereth me, I wil you telle
What in Cesars tyme bifelle.
There was a prophete in Judé
That preched in al that cuntré;
Of alle sekenesses the poeple he heled
1660   And thus the Jewes with hym deled: *dealt with him*
He ne dude bot grete curteisye,
And toward hym thai hadden envie.
His oo deciple his traitour was,

	A wicked theef that highth Judas,	*was called*
1665	His maister to the Jewes he solde,	
	For thritty pens that thai hym tolde;	*thirty pence (i.e., thirty pieces of silver); paid*
	That ilche theef hymself henge	*same*
fol. 5vb	Upon a tre with a strenge,	*rope*
	His grace was no better to spede,	
1670	For he dude that wicked dede.	
	And than the Jewes with falonus red	*wicked advice*
	Duden that gode man to the ded	
	Biforne the shrewe Sir Pilate,	*villain*
	A false traitour al for hate,	
1675	With wronge al at one voice	
	Nailed hym fast upon a croice;	*cross*
	He dyed and roos the thrid day.	
	That deth we mowen riwen ay!	*regret forever*
	Yif he had lyved and forth went,	
1680	Yut mightten we for hym have sent;	
	Thorough hym thou migth hole have be,	
	Loketh here now, sir, grete pyté.	
	Sir, was noughth Pilate to blame,	
	That dude hym giltles al this shame?	
1685	This prophete that thai duden to deth	
	Highth Jesus of Nazareth,	
	And al this nighth me met a drem	*I had*
	That I was at Jerusalem;	
	Me thoughth I stood, wel witterly,	*clearly*
1690	Bisydes the temple of Kyng Davy,	*David*
	And there bothe I herd and say	
	Fele thinges to my pay.	*Many; pleasure*
	And sir, yif yee willen don after me,	
	I schal wenden to that cité,	
1695	And brynge you tidyng, yif that I can	*news*
	Any thing heren of that man,	
	And yif oughth of hym migth ben founde,	*anything*
	That migth make you hool and sounde.	
	And ek also speken I wolde	
1700	With Sir Pilate, that traitour bolde,	
	For he is shirreve and longe hath ybe	*governor*
	Of Jerusalem that riche cité	
	And yif he aske whennes I come,	*from where*
	I shal telle hym I com fro Rome,	
1705	Fro Vaspasyan that hath power	
	Of Rome and is Neroes viker.	*deputy*
	And yif he aske after Nero oughth,	*at all*

	Yif he be seek or doune ybroughth,	*sick*
	I schal seie nay, bot he graunted thee late	
1710	To ansuere for hym and for his state.	
	Thorough the prophetes help yut may it be so	
	That we mowen seen thee comen therto.	
	To knowe Pilate, sir, have I thoughth,	
	That I ne faile of hym noughth,	
1715	So that we mowen on of thise dawghes	*one; days*
	Yelden hym alle his false lawghes.	*Punish him for*
	I wil seie he holdeth of you despytt,	*disdain*
	Sithen he dooth you no profiit;	*benefit (income)*
	Als men in registré fynde	*public register*
1720	Of longe tyme it is byhynde,	*late*
	And that wil be a grete raunsoun	*sum of money*
	That wil come of swiche a toun.	
fol. 6ra	I wil wende to heren hym seyne	
	Whi he heldeth of you disdeyne.	*holds you in contempt*
1725	Gladnesse in herte ne gete I non,	
	Til that I be comen and gon.	
	Me liketh wel this waie fulfille.	
	Seie me sir, what is thi wille?"	
	Than seide Vaspasian hym to,	
1730	"I praie thee goo and do righth so,	
	And hyghe thee swithe with al thi mayne;	*go quickly; troop*
	I be noughth glad til thou come agayne.	
	And loke that thou no tresore spele,	*fail to use*
	To have sum craft that mighth me hele;	*heal*
1735	For to have myne hele given I wolde	*health*
	More perré and more golde	*jewels*
	And more tresore than I can telle,	
	So sore I smerte and foule smelle.	*hurt*
	And therfore, for love of me,	
1740	Highe thee swithe to that cité."	*Go; quickly*
	The stiward dighth hym as the hende;	*like a gentleman*
	To Jerusalem he gan hym wende.	
	So fel hym aventure fair and wel	*befell*
	After his sweven every del;	*dream*
1745	His in was taken fast by	*lodging was taken*
	Nexte the temple of Kyng Davy.	*Near*
	The lorde of the in Jacob highth;	*inn*
	He was a Jew, bot I thee plighth,	*I promise you*
	He was a pryvé Cristen man.	*secret*
1750	Ful faire he grette Velosyan.	
	Jacob asked hym whennes he com	

And what he soughth there and whom.
"Jacob," seide sire Velosyan,
"I am with Sir Vaspasian.
1755   Galice and Gascoyne he hath in honde;
        Fro hym I come in to this londe,
        For he hath an yvel stronge   *a great evil (e.g., an illness)*
        That hath holden hym ful longe.
        He ne roughth nevere what he gave   *He does not care what the cost*
1760   So that he mighth his hele have.
        It was tolde bothe hym and me
        That on was ded in this contré,
        A noble prophete that highth Jhesu
        Thorough Sir Pilate and thorough you
1765   That heled alle seke and sore
        In this cuntré everywhore.
        And now yif he were unsleyn   *alive*
        My lorde of hym wolde be ful feyn.   *glad*
        Now, sir, I praie thee, seie me this,
1770   Yif any thing be left of his,
        And what it is and in whiche stede,
        And thou shalt have riche mede."   *reward*
        Than seide Jacob the gode man,
        "Yee beeth welcome, sir Velosyan.
1775   Ful wel I shal conseile thee,   *advise*
        Bot loke thou that it conseil be;
        Yus hardilich er wolde I deye   *assuredly I would die before*
fol. 6rb Than I to any man shulde thee wreye."   *expose*
        Jacob seide, "Now am I glad!
1780   It is ful longe that I it bad,   *prayed*
        That I shulde the tyme here
        That Jhesus deth venged were;
        And yut I hope shal come the day
        That I therof heren may.
1785   Yut hope I thorough thi lorde and thee
        That I shal that tyme ysee.
        Now hereth a wonder merveillous
        I telle that is amonges us:
        A fole, sir, walketh in this toun   *fool*
1790   Al day with children up and doun.
        He seith wel often upon his game   *in his revelry*
        That this toun shal goo to shame,
        And the more wo dreden hym alle,
        For als he seith ful often is falle.   *For it often happens as he says*
1795   Sir, I wil tellen thee also I can   *as I understand (it)*

Hou Jhesus dyed, the gude man,

Als I seigh it with myne eighen, *my eyes*

Hou thai duden Jhesu to dyen.

Thai bounden hym and beten als a theef *like a thief*

1800 Al a nigth in paynes greef, *great pains*

And on the morowen with oo voice

Thai nailed hym fast upon the croice;

He dyed and roos the thrid day

Out of the grave there he lay.

1805 Marie my doughtter, I telle thee,

Was on of the Maries three

That to Jhesus toumbe went

With boistes ful of oynement *jars; salve*

To have alithed his body with *soothed (anointed)*

1810 There he was sore in lyme and lith. *limb and joint*

And yif thi lorde leve hym upon, *will believe*

I dar warante hym hele onon, *guarantee*

And he wolde to his feith hym swere

Litel while shal his yvel hym dere. *torment*

1815 Trowe yee, sir, he wil don so?" *Do you think*

"Nay," quoth that othere, "I trowe noughth so,

Er he wolde ben ded and grave, *buried*

Bot yif he wist his hele to have

So that he migth have his hele sone,

1820 He ne rougth what men duden hym to done." *He does not care; order*

Than spaak Jacob the gode man

To the stiward Velosyan:

"Sir," he seide, "I knowe a wyf, *woman*

A curteis lefdy of clene lyf, *lady; virtuous living*

1825 I hope she be my grete frende;

I shal tomorne for hir sende,

And under hir and under me *under her care and mine*

We shullen so conseillen thee

That thine nedes shullen ben sped

1830 And than thar thee no more ben dred." *then you need*

Whan the stiward this herd,

With mychel joye al nigth he ferd, *fared*

fol. 6va And he seide to Jacob onon,

"Tomorowe thou most with me gon,

1835 And lede me to Sir Pilate.

I hope we shullen his pride abate.

My lorde me hath to hym ysent

To fecchen of hym Neroes rent." *fetch; income*

"Sir," seide Jacob, "per ma fay, *by my faith*

1840	I graunte wel tomorowe day."	
	On morne hym roos the gode knighth,	
	Pryvelich and wel adighth,	*dressed*
	And he and Jacob bothe two	
	To the synagoge gonnen go,	
1845	That there was by that dawghe	*at that time*
	The chirche of the Jewes lawghe.	
	Sir Pilate thai founden there	
	That stood his servise for to here,	
	And al abouten hym enviroun	*surrounding*
1850	There stoden the grettest of the toun.	
	Jacob drough hym out of the waye	*drew himself*
	To heren hem bothe what thai saye.	
	Sir Velosyan forth sprong	*bounded*
	Upon his stede styf and strong,	*mighty*
1855	Bot doun wolde he noughth alighth	
	Tyle he com to Pilate righth.	
	"Sir," he seide, "Wel thee be!	
	My lorde thee greteth wel by me,	
	The kyng of Galicé, Vaspasyan,	
1860	He holdeth thee as for his man	
	Under hym thou kepest this cité,	
	I understonde thi lorde is he;	
	Al the trowage is byhynde	*late*
	Of his tyme as we fynde,	
1865	And that wil be a grete raunsoun	*great sum*
	That shulde come of swiche a toun.	
	And therfore gladly witen I wolde	
	Whi thou hast his righth withholde.	
	I rede yif yee willen ben his frende,	*suggest*
1870	By me the trowage that yee hym sende,	
	For bot he it have, he wil it fette;	*fetch*
	Thou no non ne shal hym lette.	*You nor anyone else; prevent*
	Have ydo and ansuere me onon,	
	For homward I most gon."	
1875	"What," quoth Pilate, "Is Nero ded?	
	Hou longe hath he had the lordehed?"	*lordship*
	"Sir, he is bicomen his lieutenaunt,	
	And that I dar wel waraunt;	
	And yif thou wilt noughth leven me,	*believe*
1880	Yut sumday thou shalt hym see	
	And asken yif thou wilt ben aknowe	*well acknowledge*
	Of the trowage thou shuldest hym owe."	
	"Mafay," quoth Pilate, "thou seist amys!	*My faith; said*

Were it so, I had wist er this."
1885   Thys seide Velosyan tharwhile
            Sir Pilate for to bigyle,   *trick*
            That he ne shulde anothere throwe   *at another time*
fol. 6vb   Failen his visage for to knowe.   *face*
            I hote thee he dude this viage   *I assure you; journey*
1890   To knowen Sir Pilates visage;
            He forgate hym never a deel,   *not a bit*
            So he took his merk wel.
            Pilate stared as he were wood
            Upon Velosyan there he stood.
1895   "What," he seide, "have I no man?
            This knighth is comen me to slan!   *slay*
            Helpeth that I venged were
            On this theef that hoveth here."   *waits*
            Than spaak a knighth that highth Barabas,
1900   That out of prisoun delyvered was
            That ilk tyme that Jhesus dyed,   *same*
            Forth he stirte and loude cryed.   *He sprung forth*
            "Sir," he seide, "this knighth is one;
            It were shame to us uchone
1905   To done hym any vilenye,
            For I hote thee he nys no spye.   *spy*
            He semeth to ben a doughtty knighth,   *excellent*
            For he seith his erande arighth.
            Bot be thou of hardy chere,   *resolute*
1910   For thou art most maister here.
            Vaspasyan drede thu no thyng,
            For we shullen make thee oure kyng,   *you (Pilate)*
            And yif he come thee oughth to lette,   *to hinder you any*
            I hope rigth wel he shal be mette,   *confronted*
1915   And er he have of us maistrie   *control*
            He it shal wel dere abye!   *suffer (pay for)*
            And lete we now this gode man go,
            And grete hym wel and seie hym so."
            Velosyan grette thoo alle that there stood,
1920   And out he sprong as he were wood;   *as if he were mad*
            Unto his in he com ful righth
            And of his stede doune he lighth.   *horse*
            Thoo Jacob seigh hym lighth adoune,
            He com to hym as was resoune   *reasonable*
1925   And seide, "Sir, welcome hiderward!"   *to this place*
            "Ye, Jacob," he seide, "I am passed hard,   *escaped with difficulty*
            Bot now I woot that I hym knowe;

	Wel I holde bisett this throwe.	*I consider this time well spent*
	Whan tyme cometh I hope I can	
1930	Knowe hym from anothere man."	
	"Sir," seide Jacob, "I have seen	
	Hou yee han agreved ben,	
	And Jhesus ne lete me nevere dye	
	This despiit er he abye.	*despite*
1935	Ac sir be now glad, I praye thee,	*But*
	And welcome be thou now to me;	
	Conforte thee now and drede thee noughth,	
	That I thee higth I have thee broughth.	
	Sire, take dame Veroyne here,	*Veronica*
1940	She oweth wel to ben thee dere,	*ought*
	For she wil shewe thee every dele	
	Hou thi lorde shal have his hele.	
fol. 7ra	Pilate hateth hir and me,	
	For we have longe frendes ybe;	
1945	Whan she is agreved, she cometh me to,	
	And I wende to hir also,	*go*
	For we ben Cristen pryvely	
	And on us long he hath aspye,	*And he has long spied on us*
	And so weneth he witterly	*hopes; cleverly*
1950	For to done us vileny."	
	Thoo eten thai and maden glade;	
	The stiward mychel joye made	
	For he hath this womman founde.	
	Thai souped togedre that stounde,	*dined*
1955	And after he shewed hir his cas	
	Of his lorde hou it was	
	And seide, "Jacob, I praie thee	
	That this lefdy goo with me	
	Unto my lorde seek and sore,	
1960	I wil hir geve grete tresore."	
	"Yys sir," seide Jacob thoo,	
	"I praie hir that she with thee goo.	
	I hope yee wil hir savely lede,	*safely*
	And also wel ye don hir mede."	*reward her*
1965	Than seide Velosyan hym to,	
	"Al that she wil shal ben ydo.	
	Dame," he seide, "I praie thee	
	That thou graunte to goo with me,	*consent*
	And seie me also sum dele	*in some part*
1970	How my lorde may have his hele."	
	"Sir," she seide, "drede thoo noughth,	

	For therto shal it wel be broughth,	
	Also fer forth also we conne,	
	Yif he wil leven on Goddes sone,	
1975	As Jhesus Crist heled me,	
	In the londe of Galilé.	
	With a flixa I was ysmyten,	*flux (dysentery); struck*
	As Jacob and othere wel it witen;	
	Jhesu Crist I loved and dradde,	
1980	And therfore myne hele I hadde.	
	The yvel lasted longe, me thoughti;	
	To speke with Jhesu hider I soughth	
	And whan that I to toune come,	
	Than hadden the Jewes hym ynome.	*taken*
1985	Thoo I this herd, it was me looth;	*I did not wish it*
	Onon I took a piece of clooth,	
	Toward a peyntour I thoughth to gon,	*painter*
	To peynten his ymage there upon	
	That I mighth uche day it seen	
1990	And it evere in my mynde to ben;	
	For I wyst I had hym forgoo	*lost*
	And than was me, sir, wonder woo.	
	And as I toward the peyntour come,	
	I mette my Lorde toward the dome,	*judgment*
1995	Upon his shulder berande the croice;	*carrying*
	I cryed to hym with loude voice	
	And seide, 'Jhesu, me riweth thi pyne,	*I rue your pain*
fol. 7rb	And that I shal thee so sene tyne.	*And that I shall see you for such a short time*
	I have nede to speken with thee,	
2000	Swete Lorde, loke ones on me,	
	For I have loved thee her bifore,	
	Forthi I trost on thee the more.'	
	A litel bisides yede Marye,	*went*
	And herde me so loude crye;	
2005	Anon fro me this clooth she kipte	*grabbed*
	And therwith Jhesus face wypte,	*wiped Jesus's face*
	So hard swetande than was he	*sweating*
	For the birden of the tree.	*burden*
	I siwed after als he yede	*followed; went*
2010	And handled a litel upon his wede.	*touched; clothing*
	I kneled and wepte and kissed his feet;	
	He blissed me and there me lete.	*left*
	Marie bekened me so gode,	*beckoned*
	Als she yede under the rode.	*went*
2015	My clooth she me took and I it kiste —	

Onon I feled me hoole and triste,   *secure*
And in my clooth thorough his grace
Left the semblaunt of his face.   *image*
In my cofre I have it sperd,   *chest; stored*
2020   And sithen the bettre I have ferd,   *fared*
And every day I knele therto
Als I was woned to Jhesu do,   *accustomed*
And evere the more that I it see
Muchel the bettre fele I me.
2025   And ay sithen have I duelled here,   *ever since*
That hom agein ne wolde I stere.   *go (i.e., steer)*
Natheles I wel thee now telle,
Here may I noughth longe duelle,
For Pilate is my stronge foo;   *vicious*
2030   Me is the lever with thee to goo.   *I would prefer*
To fetce the semblaunt wil I gon   *fetch; semblance*
I shal me dightten and comen onon."   *prepare*

Velosyan was swithe gladd
That he had sped of that he badd: *fulfilled what he promised*
2035   "Jacob," he seide, "here now me,
Oo tidyng I wil telle thee.
Yif I lyve, Pilate shal abye,   *pay*
For that he wolde have don me dye.
Yif my lorde be hayl and fere,   *healthy and sound*
2040   Hiderward I shal hym stere,   *guide*
And on Pilate he shal be wroken   *avenged*
For the wordes that he hath spoken.
Wel may he ben shrewe ageins us,   *a rascal*
That giltles slough swete Jhesus.
2045   Holde thee covert til thou it see   *furtively*
I hote thee wel that it shal be."
"Ye," quoth Jacob, "Crist leve I may   *allow that*
Abiden to seen that ilche day,
And also sonde hym hele sone
2050   That the viage mighth be done."   *journey*
"Lorde," seide Sir Velosyan,
"Jacob, wostou yut any man   *do you know*
fol. 7va   That is on lyve in this toun   *alive*
That was at Jhesuses Passioun?"
2055   "Sir," seide Jacob, "forsothe, iwys,
Many of hem yut on lyve ys.
I may seen hem uche daye,
Gon byfore me in the waye,
And yee willen, I wil for hem sende,   *If*

2060	And thai wille telle you word and ende.	*word and action*
	Her dede willen thai noughth hyde	
	Bot maken therof yelpe and pryde.	*boast*
	To speken therof thai ben so glad	
	That thai ne ben nevere therof sad."	
2065	"Now Jacob," seide Sir Velosyan,	
	My swete frende, for hem sende than.	
	I praie thee, sir, that I had herd	
	With Jhesu Crist hou thai ferd."	
	"Sir," seide Jacob, "I graunte thee;	
2070	Sone onon thou shalt hem see."	
	He sente pryvely for hem alle,	
	And thai comen into his halle.	
	He welcomed hem and dude hem glade,	
	And gret semblaunt he hem made	*made them welcome*
2075	And seide, "Lordynges, welcome yee bee,	
	Unto my gest here and to me!	*guest*
	This is my frende and fayn wolde here	*gladly*
	Hou Jhesus the prophete dyed here,	
	For that to hym were joye and game,	
2080	He migth here tellen of his shame."	
	And onon thai setten hem doun and lough	
	And weren alle glad ynough.	
	"Sir," seiden the two, "we hym bounde	
	To a piler of marbel rounde;	*pillar*
2085	There we hym beten and sore hyrte	
	With longe scourges felle and smerte	*cruel whips*
	Til that he fomed al on blode	*foamed all bloody*
	And sithen we duden hym on the rode."	
	Forthe than stirten othere twoo	*started*
2090	And seiden, "Listneth what we han doo;	
	We hym blenten and buffeted al nighth	*blindfolded*
	And yut us riweth he had it so ligth!	
	Biforne Pilate we herden hym telle	
	That he mighth oure temple felle	
2095	And raisen it on the thridde day,	
	And amonges us we seiden nay.	
	Forwhi we shewed Pilate this pleynt	
	Amonge the Jewes he was ateynt."	*convicted*
	And thus thai tolden on and on,	
2100	Til thai knowleched everychon	*acknowledged*
	Al that pyne thai duden hym	
	At one tyme, in everyche lym.	
	Evere satt the stiward to byholde	

	Til al was seide that thai wolde.	
2105	"Lordynges," he seide, "grete and smale,	
	I thanke you of this faire tale	
	That yee have tolde of this man.	
fol. 7vb	I shal rehercen it yif that I can	*rehearse*
	In another stede hou that it was	
2110	There men desiren to heren this cas."	
	And than weren thai swithe glade	
	For that the gode man swiche joye made;	
	For thai wenden wel to haven ydo,	*to have done well*
	Michel myrthe thai maden thoo.	
2115	Bot I hope that mychel game	
	Turned hem alle sithen to mychel shame!	
	Thai token her leve and wenten away;	
	He thanked hem for her faire playe.	
	"Now," seide Sir Velosyan,	
2120	"Jacob, yut yif that I can,	
	And thou lyve and here duelle,	
	Of thise tales thou shalt here telle;	
	Grete wondres shullen falle and be	
	Amonges the poeple in this cité,	
2125	For it was nevere in no stede	
	In alle the storyes that men rede,	
	That wreche ne com of mannes dede	
	And so wil fallen of this in this stede."	
	"Ye," quoth Jacob, "Crist yife I may	*allow*
2130	Abide to sen that ilche day!	
	A frend of thee I hope to have."	
	"Forsothe," he seide, "Jacob, I shal thee save.	
	Whan tyme cometh thou art in nede,	
	Than oweth men fruschippe shewen in dede."	*friendship*
2135	Than onon Dame Veroyne com;	
	Thai token her leve and forth thai nom,	
	Ne listen hem stynten, withouten assoyne,	*They did not wish to linger, without delay*
	Til thai comen into Gascoyne.	
	Velosyan was of hir so gelous	*protective*
2140	That he hir ledd into his hous,	
	For there he hoped to eysen hir best	*accommodate*
	After her travaile hire to rest.	*journey*
	He went hym also swithe than	
	To his lorde Sir Vaspasyan;	
2145	"Sir," he seide, "be noughto of dred,"	*afraid*
	For I hope thine nedes ben sped;	*are successful*
	Have now gladnesse in thine herte,	

And forgete bothe sorough and smerte.   *pain*
I have a womman broughth of the best,
2150   And she is at myne hous to rest.
She hath broughth thi bote, ich understonde,   *remedy*
Fro Crist that saved alle in londe.
Also I spaak, sir, with Pilate
So that I knowe hym and his state;
2155   Fro hym I scaped; I am ful feyn,
For I had almost ben sleyn.
Sir, al is sooth, verrayment,   *true, truthfully*
That I tolde you ar I went;
For Cristes deth I have out soughth
2160   Of hem that the dede wroughth,
Biforne Jacob my gode frende
In myne in ar I wolde wende."   *inn; before I would go*
fol. 8ra   And thus he tolde hym forth arawe   *in order*
Al that he there herd or sawe.
2165   Tho the kyng his armes out cast
And enbraced hym to hym fast,   *tightly*
And kissed hym often mouthe to mothe,
And mychel thank he hym couthe;   *gave*
"For thise wordes that thou hast me broughth,
2170   Myne herte fast stiren and my thoughth,   *moves*
For swiche wonder wordes here biforne
Ne herd I nevere sithen I was borne.
And leve Y, dye Y, I most prove   *live; die; must strive*
Sumtyme that prophete for to love;
2175   A lorde he semeth ful stedfast,
That I so sone to hym am cast.
Sithen he dooth alle dedes at wille,
And that hym liketh to fulfille.
By this it semeth, Velosian,
2180   That he be pereles, that ilche man.   *peerless*
Thine wordes I have so in recorde   *memory*
That yif I be hool thorough that lorde,
I shal hem brynge to confusioun
Alle that hym duden swiche passioun."
2185   "Sir," quoth Velosian, "haveth no care,
For siker I am thou shalt wel fare,
And als I hope shal fallen tomorowghe
Thou shalt be quyte of thi sorowghe."   *free*

Amorowen com, the day sprong,
2190   Sir Vaspasyan thoughth wel long;
To coroune his son thai weren aboute,   *crown*

                For of his liif thai weren in doute.

                Of al the londe thoo that weren best

                There weren at the kynges fest;

2195   To Titus alle thai duden hem swere

                That thai shulden hym feuté bere.   *fealty*

                At that day men mightten see

                At that fest grete plenté;

                There was inough of al thing,

2200   As fel to corounyng of a kyng.   *befit*

                A stounde nedes I most dwelle,   *For a short time*

                And of Dame Veroyne I most telle,

                In hir in she stood and saie   *In her inn (lodging); saw*

                Seint Clement comen by the waie,

2205   That in that tyme was Pope of Rome

                And his clerkes with hym gonne come,

                And by his berynge thoughth she

                An holy man he mighth be,

                For wise men drawen to the wyse,

2210   And foles unto the foles gyse.   *to the fool's manner*

                She prayed hym in pes and griththe   *peace and concord*

                That he wolde come and speke hir withthe.

                He come and satte by hir stille   *quietly*

                And asked what was hir wille.

2215   "Sir," she seide, "I praye thee

                A Cristen man yif thou be;

                Seie me yif thou be or non."

fol. 8rb   "Yis, dame," he seide, "I am on.   *one*

                Swiche as I am, witterly,

2220   Seint Petres deciple was I;   *disciple*

                I siwed hym in to Rome,   *followed*

                There he suffred ful hard dome.   *fate*

                Fro Jerusalem I com with hym thider,

                He and Poule bothe togidre;

2225   Nero was emperour than,

                And yut he lyveth, that cursed man.

                He slough hem bothe upon a day,

                And siththe I have stille duelled ay   *since then*

                To seen yut yif God wolde sende

2230   That this folk hem amende.

                For longe I have praied so,

                God graunte us to seen thai comen therto.

                Forthi fro Rome hider I fley,

                And here I holde me alwey

2235   Yif Nero might sone dye

Or comen out of his heresye,
And that were now for us good,
For Vaspasian is next of blood.
And yut may it falle als I seye,

2240 For God is ny there thre or tweye   *near where; two*
Ben gadred or speken in his name,   *Are gathered*
And in his worschippe for soules frame."   *profit*
"Ye sir," seide Dame Verone,
As God wil so be it done!

2245 Sir," she seide, "now am I glad,
For I have founden that I bad.
Glad am I this ilche stounde
That I have thee here yfounde,
For Peter and Poule bothe I knew,

2250 That yeden with oure lorde Jhesu
Thorough the londe of Judé: *Judea*
There I them knew and thai me.
Forthi dere sir, I praie thee
That thou woldest my frende be."

2255 And than she told hym al the cas,   *circumstances*
Hou and whi she comen was.
"Dame," he seide, "I wil thee kithe   *tell*
That of thi comyng I am blithe.   *glad*
I hope thorough Goddes help and thine,

2260 We shullen askapen al oure pyne.
No Cristen man now dar hym shewe   *dares show himself*
Bot yif he wil ben al to-hewe;   *cut to pieces*
Therfore willen we pryvely
Speken of God, bothe thou and I."

2265 "Sir," she seide, "for this lore,
I wil be with thee evermore,
To duellen in thi compaignye,
Til my lorde wil that I dye."
Thus thai speken of holy wrytte   *scripture*

2270 Also thai togedre sytte,   *As*
That of grete whil litel hem thoughth
Fro that thai weren togedre broughth.

fol. 8va Than Vaspasyan in his paleys
Waited after hem alweys,

2275 Noo wonder thogh hym thoghte longe,   *it seemed to him*
His yvel greved hym swithe stronge.   *affliction*
He cleped Velosyan onon,
"Whan shaltou gon for Dame Verone?"
The stiward gooth hom also swithe,

2280   After hir with herte blithe;
        "Dame," he seide, "thou and thi fere   *companion*
        Beeth rigth wel yfounden here.
        Now dame, thou most comen with me,
        For my lorde hath sent for thee."
2285   "Gladly," she seide, "sir, yif this frende
        Wil with me to court wende,
        For he hath power by nighth and day
        To don and seien that I ne may,
        And yif we hym with us lede
2290   I hope the better shullen we spede."
        "Sir," seide Velosyan thoo,
        "I praie thee that thou with us goo."
        Thai risen and comen swithe than
        Biforne the kyng Sir Vaspasian;
2295   On knees uchone thai hem sette
        With mychel honoure thai hym grette.   *greeted*
        "Loo sir," seide than Velosyan,
        "Here I brynge thee this womman
        That I thee highth the bote to brynge;   *remedy*
2300   Worthschipe hire in al thinge!
        Also this clerk with hir here,
        That can thee bothe wisse and lere,   *instruct and teach*
        For Dame Verone here seith
        Bot thou conne the righth feith,   *are versed in*
2305   Thou shalt nevere be hool arighth
        Therwhiles thou lyvest, day ne nighth.
        Yut is thee better to lerne her lawghe
        Than with this yvel to ben yslawghe."   *slain*

        Sir Vaspasyan for socoure   *their aid*
2310   Welcomed hem with honoure
        And seide, "Dame, welcome mote thu be,
        And sir clerk, I praie thee,
        The righth feith that thou me kenne,   *teach*
        Here biforne alle thise menne."
2315   Seint Clement thoo was glad
        Onon to done als he hym bad.
        Pes he made onon to be
        Thorough the grete assemblé.   *assembly*
        "Lordynges," he seide, "I you praie,
2320   Listneth now that I shal saie.
        In hawe hath ben al to longe   *In an enclosure*
        Cristendom with mychel wronge,
        And God wil nough that it sprede   *now*

　　　　　　Amonges hem that hym loven and drede.
2325　　　My Lorde God of whom I spelle　　　　　　　　　　　　*tell*
　　　　　　Made hevene and erthe and ek helle,　　　　　　　　　*also*
　　　　　　And al that evere is hem withinne
fol. 8vb　　At hym bigan and at hym shal blynne.　　　　　　　　*end*
　　　　　　And this is the divisioun　　　　　　　　　　　　*separation*
2330　　　Of thre manere habitacioun:　　　　　　　　　　　*dwellings*
　　　　　　Hevene he made with joye and blis,
　　　　　　That evere shal lasten withouten mys,　　　　　　　　*sin*
　　　　　　There aungels and mannes soule shullen wone　　　　*dwell*
　　　　　　Evermore with Goddes sone.
2335　　　The erthe he made to mannes swynk,　　　　　　　　*labor*
　　　　　　To tyllen hym clooth, mete, and drynk.　　　　　　*earn his*
　　　　　　Fyve wittes he hath to man given　　　　　　　　　*senses*
　　　　　　To kepen hem while that thai lyven;
　　　　　　With eres heren, with eighen seen
2340　　　Alle that us abouten ben,
　　　　　　Nose to smelle swete and soure,
　　　　　　This is us a grete honoure;
　　　　　　Mouth to chesen with drynk and mete　　　　　　　*choose*
　　　　　　Whiche is to taken, which is to lete.　　　　　　　　*leave*
2345　　　And yut he gaf us felyng also,　　　　　　　　　　　*touch*
　　　　　　Hondes to handlen with, feet with to goo,　　　　　　*walk*
　　　　　　And non of alle thise, so we rede,
　　　　　　May stonde ne serve in others stede.
　　　　　　Yif man with thise wil hym lede,
2350　　　He shal have hevene blis to mede,　　　　　　　　　*as reward*
　　　　　　And yif he do yvel, forsothe I telle,
　　　　　　Withouten ende he gooth to helle.
　　　　　　That is the thrid habitacioun,
　　　　　　For wicked synful mannes prisoun,
2355　　　And thider went the first man,
　　　　　　For he first synny bigan,　　　　　　　　　　　　*sin*
　　　　　　And there he and his kynde lay,
　　　　　　And shulden have don til Domesday.
　　　　　　Bot God of us took pité
2360　　　And for to save us thoughth he,
　　　　　　For mannes synne was so gret
　　　　　　Bifore God and his faders feet,
　　　　　　Yif man shulde to halpe be broughth,
　　　　　　Thorough mannes deth it most be boughth.
2365　　　The synne was so foule, as we fynde,
　　　　　　That it filed al mankynde.　　　　　　　　　　　*defiled*
　　　　　　Theigh God had an aungel sent,

	He migth noughth dyen verrement.	*truly*
	Man dude the dede, man most deye,	
2370	And thorough pyté God seigh this waye:	
	God migth noughth dye bot bicom man,	
	And thus he dyed for us than.	
	With aungels and his fader the Lorde	
	Thus brougth Jhesus man to acorde.	*agreement*
2375	He defended hym with non other staf,	*staff*
	Bot his manhode to pyne he gaf;	*gave*
	For mannes love thus took he ded	
	Thorough the grace of his Godhed.	
	Of the mayden Marie he was borne,	
2380	Maiden clene sithen and ek biforne.	
	In the londe of Judé he gan duellen;	
	There fele men to hym fellen	*many*
fol. 9ra	For his wordes sothe thai founde,	*true*
	Thoo that weren seke he made sounde.	*whole*
2385	With this the Jewes hadden envie;	
	Therfore thai duden hym to dye.	
	Judas for thritty pens hym solde	
	To the Jewes felle and bolde;	
	Of his deciples he was on	
2390	That with hym was ywoned to gon.	*accustomed*
	He henge hymself, this was his ende;	
	He had no grace hym to amende,	
	For he wolde no mercy seke	
	Of his Lorde that was so meke,	
2395	That salve is to every sore.	*balm*
	Overe any synne his mercy is more.	
	Man is hym nexte of every kynde,	
	Als we in holy wrytt fynde;	
	Forthi yif any man trespase,	*trespass*
2400	He faileth noughth yif he seke grace.	
	Leve sir, loke hou this man was wood,	*Dear; crazed*
	That solde his lorde that was so good."	
	Than spaak Vaspasian so free,	
	"I hote now to that God and thee,	*promise*
2405	That yif he wil me hool make,	
	I schal be cristned for his sake.	
	And I schal slee alle that I fynde	*slay*
	Of alle the Jewes and her kynde,	
	And thritty of hem I shal selle and give	
2410	For oo peny yif that I lyve;	*one*
	For thai hym bougth for despyt, I pliighth,	

	For thritty pens with unrighth.	*injustice*
	And Jhesus, ne lete me nevere dye	
	Til I have wroken that felonye."	*avenged; treachery*
2415	Than seide Seint Clement to hym stille,	
	"Yut hope I thou shalt have thi wille,	
	For thorough this yvel, I understonde,	
	My lorde wil that thou shalt fonde	
	To wreken hym, sir, of his fon,	*foes*
2420	And that shaltou seen onon:	
	For thorough his vertu shaltou see	
	That hole shaltou sone bee.	
	Th'ensaumple I telle thee as it sytt	
	Righth evene in the holy wrytt;	
2425	He com to seken that were forlore	
	And gadred that todreved wore,	*driven away*
	To restoren that was falle,	
	Forthi he dyed for us alle,	*Therefore*
	To confermen us and oure fay	*strengthen; faith*
2430	And synful man to done away.	
	The Jewes seiden that he kem	*came*
	In destruccioun of hem,	
	Bot now ich understonde me	
	That thai seiden it by thee.	
2435	These prophecies han ben spoken	
	That yut his deth shal be wroken;	
	Muchel joy is unto us alle	
fol. 9rb	Yif it thorough thee shal bifalle.	
	Kynges worthshiped hym at his birthe,	
2440	With offryng and with mychel myrthe.	*great joy*
	Kynges weren sithen twyes in wille	*twice desirous*
	Thorough dynt of deth to don hym spylle;	*a deathblow*
	Heroudes first thoo he was borne,	
	And Heroudes efte whan his deth was sworne.	*again*
2445	The first Heroudes that the children slough —	
	I woot he suffred pyne ynough!	*know*
	Alle manere yvels, so seith the book,	
	He had er he the deth took,	
	Withouten the stronge pyne of helle	
2450	There he shal evermore duelle.	
	Withouten gylte he hated Jhesus,	
	And giltles the Jewes sloughen hym thus.	
	And kynges ben loked to wreken his ded	
	Thorough the grace of his Godhed.	
2455	Swiche knoulechyng of kynges he nam	*acknowledgment; took*

Whan he into erthe cam.

And yif thou wilt wel leve in hym,   *believe*

That he may hele thee lyf and lym,

I warante he shal helen thee,

2460   And by ensaumple thou mighth it see.

There was a knighth ded in londe,

Lazar he highth, ich understonde,   *Lazarus; was named*

That foure dayes in grave lay,

And he reised hym that many man say.   *saw*

2465   And also as we of hym rede

He dude many another dede;

Twelve desciples had he,

The best men that mightten be;

Whan he out of the erthe went,

2470   The Holy Gost he hem sent:

Sexty and ten langages, I herd,   *Seventy*

That thai of her maister lerd.

He bad hem gon into every londe

To prechen his word, ich understonde,

2475   Of alle yvels he yaf hem mighth,

To helen hem that leven arighth,   *believe rightly*

And thoo that nyllen nougth to hem wende   *those; will not*

Shullen ben lorne withouten ende.   *lost*

Swiche wondres herdestou nevere non

2480   That ever had shapp of man to gon,   *shape*

For bothe God and man he is;

There nys no God bot he, iwys.

Therfore sir, leve my sawghe,   *believe; speech*

And al thine herte to hym drawghe,

2485   For al that I seie I dar witnesse,

This is the feith, sir, more and lesse.

I was with hem that weren hym by,

And thus thai tolden me witterly,

And this lefdy that here stant   *lady; stands*

2490   I wil take here to warant,

For she sawe my lorde Jhesus.

Now dame, I praie thee, was it thus?"

fol. 9va   Than seide Veroyne at a braide,   *quickly*

"I witnesse al that he hath saide.   *attest to*

2495   Ful wel tellen I it owe   *ought*

That I have Jhesu Crist ysowe;   *seen*

Of grete yvel he heled me,

Sumtyme I shal tellen it thee.

For love and feith I hym dradde

2500	On this manere myne hele I hadde.	
	Now knele adoune with herte free;	
	This gode man shal assoile thee."	*absolve*
	Whan this was don everydel,	
	She took the vernycle fair and wel.	*cloth*
2505	"This had I of my lorde so kynde,	
	For that I shulde have hym in mynde."	
	Seint Clement was thoo revest,	*dressed in vestments*
	With riche vestement of the best,	*vestments*
	And she it took to Seint Clement,	
2510	And he it receyved with gode entent,	*good purpose*
	And thoo he and alle kneled adoune	
	For this with grete devocioune	
	Byfore the kyng Vaspasyan,	
	That lay ful sore seek than:	
2515	"Sir, this is lyk thi Saveour:	*Savior*
	With al thi mighth do hym honour.	
	Levestou that I have seide everydel?"	*Do you believe*
	"Ye," seide Vaspasian, "ful wel."	
	"Kisse this than I bidde thee,	*Kiss*
2520	In the vertu of the Trinité,	
	And hoole be thou for evermore,	
	And stonde up now us bifore,	
	And God thee blis that is most,	
	Fader and Son and Holy Gost."	
2525	Whan the gode man had thus yspeken,	
	The kyng gan out his lymes streken,	*reach out his limbs*
	And stood up biforne hem alle;	
	The yvel as a slough fro hym gan falle,	*snakeskin*
	And he bicom clene, smethe and mylde	*smooth*
2530	As the body of a childe.	
	And whan he feled hym hool and clene,	*felt himself*
	Michel joye men mightten sene	
	Of al manere of mynstralcye,	*revelry*
	And he helde up his hondes heighe	
2535	And seide, "Jhesu, now trowe I wel,	*trust*
	That I have herd of thee everydel;	
	And certes, Lorde, yif that I lyve,	
	To thi service I shal me gyve."	
	Anon he fel on knees adoun	
2540	With wel gret devocioun,	
	Byforne Seint Clement there he stood	
	And thanked hym with mylde mood,	*kind mood*
	And Dame Veroyne he dude also,	

	That from so fer com hym to.	
2545	"Praieth for me nighth and day,	
	I see that yee ben to his pay.	*liking*
	To myne herte youre wordes gon,	
fol. 9vb	And youre dedes everychon,	
	For I see by my grete nede	
2550	That thai aren of noble spede."	*good fortune*
	Thus seide his son and alle his menne,	
	"As is fallen, forsothe we kenne.	
	Thoo Nathaan com, he tolde it us;	
	Velosian witnesseth also thus."	
2555	Tho seide Vaspasyan, "Weilaway,	*Alas*
	That I ne had Jhesu Crist ysay!	*seen*
	Tybery Cesar, woo thee be,	*Tiberius Caesar*
	And that I owe to bidden thee,	
	Thoo that Pilate, the fals knighth,	
2560	Slough thus my Lord with unrighth,	
	That thou ne haddest ytaken the theef	
	And done hym dye with pynes greef.	*done him to death; grievous pains*
	It semed wel thou were no man,	
	Thou suffred hym so to taken upan;	
2565	Bot God wolde noughth it shulde bitide	*happen*
	Mowe I hym seen bot he me abide.	
	That I shal vengen hym I am ful glad,	
	For better bedes nevere I ne badd;	*orders; asked*
	Ful wel is me that I schal fighth	
2570	For swiche a lorde and for his righth.	
	Bettre enprise mighth I noughth have,	*undertaking*
	Ne no man hymself to save.	
	I thonke it God that non biforne	
	Mighth done it that yut was borne,	*yet*
2575	Bot now I woot he graunted it me:	
	Lorde, yblissed mote thou be!	*blessed*
	I praie thee Lorde, yif it be thi wille,	
	Give me liif it to fulfille,	*life*
	And I shal highe me that I may	*hurry*
2580	That it were don nighth and day.	
	Whan we have don and comen agein,	
	We shullen ben cristned alle wel feien."	*very happily*
	Thai token hym bituene her honde	
	And maden hym up biforne hem stonde.	
2585	"Dame," he seide, "yif I may spede,	*prosper*
	Of me thou getest a riche mede.	*reward*
	What thing thou wilt of me crave,	

	Sikerly, thou shalt it have."	
	"Sir," she seide, "saunz faile,	*without*
2590	I vouche saaf al this travaile	*think all this labor proper*
	That I have had hider for thee,	*until now*
	And al that thou wilt given me,	
	Thou give it to this gode man	
	And mychel thank I thee can,	
2595	For with hym wil I wone and wende,	*live and travel*
	Evere unto my lyves ende."	
	Londes and rentes he gaf hem wyde,	*property; substantial*
	Clothes and tresore, hors on to ride;	
	He made her dedes that so speken	*deeds; affirm*
2600	That thai shulde hem never breken.	*break*
	Seint Clement seide, "Sir, hereth me,	
	I rede that yee ycristned bee,	*advise; baptized*
fol. 10ra	Sone on hast, and youre men alle,	
	For alle chaunces that mowen bifalle.	
2605	Thine ost thou migth the sikerer lede,	*army; more securely*
	And there thou comest the better spede."	*prosper*
	"Nay," he seide, "that wil I noughth;	
	First here thou what I have thoughth.	
	Do me come Titus my sone,	
2610	And al my folk that non ne shone."	*that none refuse*
	Titus com his fader to,	
	And many grete lordynges also.	
	"Now son," he seide, "thou shalt me swere,	*swear*
	And also this folk that is here,	
2615	With me to wenden to Jerusalem,	
	Rigth overe the cee, the heighe strem,	*sea; great*
	To destroyen hem alle and her stede	*city*
	That duden Jhesu Crist to dede;	
	For I shal nevere be righth fayn	
2620	Until I see that kynde slayn.	*people (see note)*
	For to wende we have enchesoun,	*reason*
	Sone, namelich for this resoun:	*especially*
	Thider we moten gon this gate,	*way*
	To wreken us on Sir Pilate	
2625	For my Lordes love so fre,	
	That thus faire hath heled me,	*graciously*
	Yut dude I nevere nougth hym fore:	*Yet I never did anything for him*
	Forthi myne herte is ful sore.	
	I were to blamen and alle myne	
2630	Yif we shulde leten that wytherwyne.	*spare; enemy*
	I hote you that shal never bitide	

	Whiles that I may gon and ride;	
	This othere day ne mighth I stere,	
	And now I am bothe hoole and fere.	
2635	I thonk it God thorough whom it was.	
	I woot he heled me for this cas,	
	For his deth shulde avenged be.	
	I graunte to gon; now what seien yee?"	*say*
	"Sir," seide Titus, "So do I,	
2640	And alle that here ben, sikerly."	
	Whan this was graunted, men mightten see	*decreed*
	Song and play, gamen and glee.	
	"For leve," he seide, "wil I sende onon	*leave (i.e., permission)*
	To Sir Nero to leten us gon.	
2645	Alle I praie you dightteth you fast,	*prepare; quickly*
	That we weren redy alle on hast,	*in a hurry*
	Of men, of servauntz and vitaile,	*soldiers; food*
	So that nothing us ne faile."	
	Than sent he to the emperour,	
2650	Nero that was a cursed tretour,	
	By a lettre as yee mowe see:	
	"Vaspasian and Titus greten thee,	
	For grete nede we ben in wille	*For great need we desire*
	At Jerusalem to fulfille,	
2655	Of a grete vilenye	
	To vengen us we moten hyghe,	*go*
	Of a trespas that is us ydo	*trespass that is done to us*
fol. 10rb	We praien thee leve thider to go.	
	Graunte it us withouten feyntise;	*deceit*
2660	It mote be don in al wise.	*in every way*
	It shal thee tournen to profyt	*turn*
	And to no manere despyt."	
	The emperoure sent hem to seie,	
	"Gooth whan yee willeth in youre weie,	
2665	And on youre enemyes vengeth you,	
	So it be noughth agein my prou."	*benefit*
	Than seiden Vaspasyan and Titus,	
	"Blissed be oure lorde Jhesus!"	
	Also tyt thai maden hem yare	*Immediately; ready*
2670	In her waye for to fare.	*go*
	Seint Clement and Dame Verone	
	Weren ful glad that thai shulden gone,	
	And seiden "Sir, ar yee wennden henne,	*hence*
	Graunteth youre pes to Cristen menne.	
2675	For Goddes love dooth hem wyte	*make them know*

	That no man do hem dispyte	
	Fro that yee gon til that yee come,	*From the time that*
	Bot yif he suffre therfore dome."	
	"Now, mafay," quoth he, "and I graunte,	*by my faith*
2680	And thee, Clement, I shal waraunte,	
	Thou shalt have large commissioun	
	Fro this cuntré and fro this toun,	
	For alle that leven in God almighth	
	Myne men shullen kepen hem day and nighth,	
2685	Thou and Verone bothe tweyn	
	Dredeth noughth til I come ageyn."	
	This was cryed thorough the cuntré,	
	That it shulde yholden be.	
	"Kepe now wel thi clergye,	*clergy*
2690	Al that thou hast in thi baillye;	*control*
	Whan we comen hom at certeyn terme,	
	I schal thee and thi state conferme.	*confirm*
	I shal bidde hem that duellen here	
	That thai alle at thine honoure were.	*rule*
2695	Praye for us til we comen ageyn,	
	And whan we comen in, certeyn,	*truly*
	I wil be cristned righth onone,	*immediately*
	And myne men everychone.	
	Praieth for us that God us spede,	
2700	And haveth now no manere drede."	
	"Sir, he seide, "now am I bolde:	
	God of Hevene thi lyf holde	*preserve*
	Longe that I mote it see,	
	And namelich, til thou cristned be.	
2705	And elles were a grete reuthe,	*pity*
	For thou art in the waie of treuthe."	*way of truth (i.e., correct belief)*
	"Thorough Cristes helpe I hope to gon	
	To don this dede and comen onon;	
	Al that I may I shal me rape	*seize*
2710	So that Pilate me noughth askape."	*escape*
	Onon he dude his shippes dighth,	*prepare*
	Wel a thousande, I thee plighth,	*I promise you*
fol. 10va	With hym and with his son also,	
	An hundreth thousande men and mo.	
2715	Seint Clement and Dame Verone	
	Toward the cee with hem thai gone	
	Tyl thai weren yschipped alle	*embarked*
	And Vaspasyan to hem gan calle,	
	"Blisse us, sir, and lete us gon,	

2720	And tourneth both agein hom."	*turn*
	"Sir," he seide, "nou God you save,	
	And with his blissyng myne yee have,	
	And the water that yee inne wende	
	Til Jesu Crist ageyn you sende."	
2725	And sithen that blissyng hath don good	
	To alle men that passen the flood;	
	Thorough Goddes help and Seint Clement,	
	Sithen was there no man inne shent.	*destroyed*
	Thay droughen up sayl biforne and bihynde,	*drew; the foreward and aft sail*
2730	God hem sent ful redy wynde,	*favorable wind*
	So in sexe wekes over thai comen	*six*
	And at Acres up thai nomen.	*Acre; they arrived*
	The toun had wonder whoo thai wore	
	And weren adrad of hem ful sore.	
2735	Thai duden onon as thai sholde;	*should*
	Withouten stryf the toun thai yolde.	*fighting; surrendered*
	Vaspasian lefte there his wardeyn,	*governor*
	And on the morowen thay wenten then.	
	He went forth into the londe	
2740	And slough and brent alle that he fonde,	*slaughtered and burnt*
	And dryven beestes with grete route	*company*
	That thai prayden al aboute.	*plundered*
	From Acres thai comen the first day	
	To Japh als I you tellen may,	*Jaffa (see note)*
2745	And bicasten al the toun	*surrounded*
	With many a riche pavyloun.	*tent*
	Thay faughtten withouten and withinne;	
	There mightten men seen wondres bygynne.	
	God hem shewed swiche chaunce	
2750	Ageyn her rather vengeaunce;	*As a sign of their future*
	Rayn and hayl, frost and snowe,	*hail; snow*
	And styf wynde that loude gan blowe,	*strong*
	Hunger and thryst and grete colde,	
	And other yvels manyfolde.	*many and various*
2755	And Vaspasyan with al his ost	*host*
	Had joye with the moost,	
	Wider game and al plenté,	*Better luck (Pleasant weather)*
	Of alle caces that mightten be,	*situations*
	And so he had fro that he com	
2760	Til he tourned agein hom.	
	Vaspasyan his sege helde	
	Wel longe er thai wolden it yelde;	
	Thai withinne sworen uchon	*swore*

That thai wolden yelden her non
2765   For nothing that myghth bifalle,
Theigh thai beten doun her walle.
The kyng swoor that he ne sholde
fol. 10vb   Thennes til thai to hym yolde,
And whan thai withinne herden this ooth,   *oath*
2770   Everyche ageins other gooth,   *went*
With swerdes, speres, and knyves ydrawe,
So that uche hath othere yslawe,
That there ne lefte man ne wyve
Bot tweie knighttes thereinne alyve.   *two*
2775   Doughtty men thai weren bothe,   *Brave*
And neither ne was with other wrothe;   *angry*
Thai hadden longe felawes ben,
And neither ne wolde othere slen.
Sir Japhel I woot highth that on,
2780   Bot of that other, name have I non.
Thai yolden hem to the kynges socoure
And he hem resceyved with gret honoure.
He drough Japhel hym so neer
That he bicom his conseileer,   *adviser*
2785   And for Vaspasyan was ywar
That he was sib to Sir Cesar,   *kin; Caesar*
And also of his owen blood,
He seide hym als he understood,
And for he knew best the cuntré
2790   His lodesman he bad hym be,   *guide*
And he ful wel led hem
Til thai comen to Jerusalem.
He left at Japh kepers gode,   *defenders*
To kepen the cuntré with feeld and wode.

2795   Here may I telle you that yee knowen
Hou Jesu thanketh ay on his owen.   *always on his own*
Biforne the tyme of this wreche,
Thus he gan his folk knowleche   *acknowledge*
That cristen weren in that cuntré.
2800   Thai weren ywarned thennes to flee   *warned*
Thorough the Holy Gost fro this vengeaunce
Bot any wolde stonde to his chaunce,   *events*
As summe duden that leften stille,   *meekly remained*
Al to abiden Goddes wille.   *await (obey)*
2805   The Cristen folk fleigh and ran
Onon overe the Flum Jordan,   *Jordan River*
And there thai duelleden and cam

	Was hoten the castel of Pellam;	*called*
	There thai helden hem everychon	
2810	Til the vengeaunce were ydon.	
	The Jewes weren trapped and helden inne	
	That weren encoumbred with her synne,	
	For there nys no good dede unyolde	*unrewarded*
	Ne non wicked ne ben showe.	*revealed*
2815	Thoo Pilate wist that Japh was ytake,	*taken*
	For tene and drede he gan to quake,	*anger*
	For ay he was in mychel drede	*always*
	Sithen Velosyan from hym yede;	
	For the wordes that he had spoken	
2820	He wolde have ben in erthe loken.	*locked in earth*
	He was in so grete doute	
	That he sent al aboute,	
fol. 11ra	And bihith hem ful grete mede	*promised*
	To comen and helpen hym at his nede.	
2825	Sir Archillaus com hym to,	
	That kyng of Galilé was tho;	
	Heroudes son men hym calle,	
	He that slough the children alle,	
	With mychel dyne and grete boost	*noise*
2830	He broughth with hym a mychel ost.	*great host*
	And for drede, I woot also,	*know*
	Al the cuntré fel hem to,	
	And uche man fleigh fro home	
	And alle to Jerusalem thai come,	
2835	With wyf and children and her fee,	*property*
	There in sikernesse to be,	*security*
	For Vaspasyan and his ost	
	Sloughen and brenten by every cost.	
	Pilate sent his aspyes	*spies*
2840	Sikerlich by fele styes,	*many paths*
	For to witen hym to seie	*know*
	Where thai comen and by what waye.	
	Archillaus and Sir Pilate	
	Riden hem bothe out atte gate,	
2845	With her ost her hors to prove	*horses; test*
	Yif thai weren to her byhove.	*to their advantage*
	And yut hadde Pilate no grace,	
	For to flen out of the place,	
	The hard qued that he shulde have	*evil*
2850	And thoogh he mighth self than save.	
	For loos is better, als it is founde,	*loss*

In wood than in toun bounde;

And so ferd he by this resoun   *traveled*

Whan he fleigh agein to the toun.

2855   Bot God wolde nougth that he so askape,

Bot to his bale for to rape,   *to rush to his disaster*

For he had hym space ylent   *given*

Fourty yer to amendement.

Than comen his apsyes hom,

2860   And tolden hym wel that thai com

The moost folk that evere thai say,   *saw*

And than was Pilate in grete afray.   *fear*

Than seide the Kyng Archillaus,

"Sir, thou art most maister of us.

2865   I praie thee, sir, be bold ynow,   *enough*

For I dar make thee this avow,

That thou shalt be so wel biforne   *have the advantage*

Of men, of vitaile, and of corne,   *supplies; grain*

That nothing shal failen thee;

2870   And hereof borowe dar I be   *guarantor*

That thai ben oures every man,

So mychel I thee telle can.

Nothing bot helde thee al stille

And lete hem comen at her wille;

2875   For water fresh ner is non   *nearer*

Than is the Flum Jordan,

And yif thai willen hemselven save,

fol. 11rb   Water freshe thai mosten have.

And whan thai seen that there is non,

2880   Hom agein thai moten gon;

For thai aren noughth of that yware.   *aware*

Therfor the lesse is oure care.

And yif thai tournen us ones the bak,   *And if they once turn their backs on us*

Thai shullen ben oures, al the pak.   *all of them*

2885   I woot it is for the prophetes sake,

Al the sorough that thai make;

Thai shullen with shame tournen ageyn,

For thai wirchen al in veyn."   *work; in vain*

And whan he had his wille tolde,

2890   Over the walles thai gonnen biholde,   *look*

And al the feelde and al the fen   *marsh*

Thai seighen bicast with hors and men,   *covered*

With her baners brode yspradd   *spread*

That al the cité was adradd.

2895   In everyche wyndewe thai hem biholde,   *window*

Anon her hertes gonnen to colde   *grow cold*
And aukeward the belles runge.   *And the bells rang in reverse order*
There was outhest of many a tunge   *outcry*
With horne and mouthe thai cryen oute.
2900   The ost bicast the toun aboute
That was foure and thritty yere
After that Jesus dyed there.
Withinne thai maden sorough and care;
Withoute thai maden joye and mychel fare;   *great commotion*
2905   Withinnen thai her hondes wrongen;   *hands wrung*
And thai withouten loude songen.

On a Pask day the sege bigan,   *Passover*
Als the storye me telle can.
Vaspasyan was than ful blithe
2910   And pighth his pavylons also swithe,   *pitched*
And whan thai weren pighth uchone
He sent after Sir Japhel onone.
He seide, "Japhel, I wil thee telle
We moten nedes here duelle,
2915   Til we have wonnen this cité   *won*
And haven alle that thereinne be.
What is to don best thou woost,
For thou knowest the cuntré cost.   *the condition of the country*
Therfore sir, I thee praie
2920   That thou take onon the waye
Al aboute this ilche cité
To ordeyne for myne ost and me,   *arrange*
And loke and cast what we have nede
Of alle thinges that mowen us spede."   *prosper*
2925   Japhel rideth by every cost   *in every direction*
To ordeyne and to araye the oost;
Aboute the toun he sett engynes   *siege engines*
To destroien her witherwynes   *adversaries*
And often to the toun they cast
2930   And shetten with bowe and with arblast   *shot; crossbow*
With terbardels and wylde fyre,   *tar barrels*
With staf-slyngys and othere atyre,   *slings; equipment*
fol. 11va   Sowes to mynen men maden sleighe,   *Engines to tunnel; cleverly*
And borfreys to reisen on heighe.   *movable towers*
2935   That thai mightten seen enviroun   *all around*
What thai duden in the toun,
Men of armes thereinne to stonde
To fightten with hem honde of honde,   *hand to hand*
Ladders of lether and of corde,   *leather; rope*

2940   Fro the kirnels to the sworde   *stones*
    And maistres that weren sleighe to kest   *throw*
    To kepen the spryngales of the best,   *catapults*
    And many another queynt engyn   *crafty design*
    To slen hem that weren within.
2945   Natheles for al this woo,
    It was wel longe er it were do.
    Of all th'assaut that was withoute   *affliction*
    Thai withinne hadden no doute;
    The cité was so large withinne,
2950   That hem ne dredeth no manere gynne   *machine*
    For into hem ne raughtte no cast   *reached out*
    Bot onlich querel of arblast   *only shot of crossbows*
    Til alle the subarbes of the toun   *suburbs*
    To the grounde weren cast adoun,
2955   And swepte clene overal
    Unto the bare toun wal.
    For than bigan her woo withinne   *woe*
    And her folk fast to thinne,   *diminish*
    Yut lasted the sege seven yere,
2960   With mychel drede and grete awere,   *terror*
    For al that Goddes men mightte do
    Bot for to lengthen her paynes so.

    Whan Japhel had don, he com agein:
    "My lorde," he seide, "I wil thee seyn,
2965   Thorough thine ost by Cristes mighth,
    Thine men ben alle wel adighth.
    Bot of oo thing I have grete thoughth,   *concern*
    For fresshe water have we noughth,
    Bot I have cast by my skyl   *arranged; skill*
2970   Where to fetten it, and yee wil."   *fetch; if*
    Than seide Vapsasyan hym to
    "Als thou wilt, I wil do."
    "Sir," quoth Japhel, "this is my rede,
    Hou we shullen oure water lede;
2975   For water fresshe ner is non
    Than hennes to the Flum Jordon.   *here; Jordan River*
    Forthi we shullen slen oure praye   *prey*
    That we token by the waye,
    Hors and assen, oxen and kyne,   *cows*
2980   Mules and chamayles and grete swyne,   *camels; swine*
    Many a thousande we have broughth,
    Of hem I telle you in my thoughth
    I shal do sewen the hides fast,   *sew*

	With gode semes for to last,	*seams*
2985	And don souden every sem	*solder*
	For to leden water with hem.	
	Of some we shullen boulges make,	*water skins*
fol. 11vb	And summe skynnes we shullen take	
	And overcasten al the vale	*overturn; valley*
2990	Of Josephath, the depe dale,	*Josophat; valley*
	And thus in the valeye we shullen fonde	
	To don oure water for to stonde.	
	Foure hundreth men, yif that I may,	
	Shullen fecchen us water every day,	
2995	Alway til the valey be hylde	*covered*
	And with oure watere fulfilde."	
	Whan he had seide also sone,	
	He ne lefte noughth til was done;	
	Pepes he made many on	*Pipes*
3000	By every side out for to gon	
	The elde water that was astonde,	*standing*
	There com ay newe to her honde,	
	That thorough the ost, man and beest	
	Hadden ynough, bothe mest and lest,	*most and least (i.e., all)*
3005	This com hym of a noble wytt,	*admirable skillfulness*
	Hou water stonden withouten pytt.	*well*
	Al was don by Goddes wille,	
	For to maken the Jewes spille.	*be destroyed*
	Thoo thai withinnen the water sowe,	*saw*
3010	Stonden so ful in that lowe,	
	Michel wonder was hem among	
	Hou the water there out sprong.	*sprung out*
	Thai ronnen to Pilate and hym tolde,	*ran*
	And he went thider to byholde,	
3015	And with hym went Archillaus,	
	And the gode clerk Josephus,	
	And than seiden thai alle thre,	
	"Whennes may this water be?"	
	Than seide maister Josephus,	
3020	"Messias is ageins us.	*Messiah*
	Thai han his help, I am wel ware,	*have*
	For late was that place bare.	*empty*
	Of fresshe water ner was non	
	Than hennes to the Flum Jordon;	
3025	I ne wot from whennes it cometh, ne hou,	
	Bot thorough the prophetes vertu."	
	Than ansuered Archillaus	

Anon righttes to Sir Pilatus,
"Sir," he seide, "be noughth aferde,
3030   For noughth thou hast ysen ne herd,
Bot kepe thee in this cité stille
And thou shalt have al thi wille."
And as thai stoden and out bihelde,
Vaspasian stood in the felde
3035   And seigh hem on the walles gon   *them*
Up and doune ful gode won,   *moving*
And Sir Japhel stood hym by,
And Velosyan, witterly,   *undoubtedly*
That of Pilate was sonest ware,   *first aware*
3040   Hou that he his mace bare   *club*
Over his werkmen that wroughtten   *workmen; labored*
And the walles thorough out soughtten.
fol. 12ra   Tho seide Velosyan, "I see
Yonder Pilate, as thenketh me.
3045   Sir, speketh to hym, I you praie,
For to assaie what he wil saie."   *learn*
Vaspasian loked up to the walle,
And to Pilate he gan calle,
"Pilate," he seide, "speke with me.
3050   I am thi lorde, as thou mighth see,
And that I shal thee make aknowe   *reveal to you*
Yif that I mowe lyven a throwe.   *live a little while*
Loke out, traitour, with thine eighe,   *eye*
And be aknowe thi felonye
3055   And al the yvel that thou hast don
Ageins Jhesu and us uchon.
And also thou doost us outrage   *wickedness*
To withholden oure trowage;
And for thou art Jhesus traitour and myne,
3060   Thou shalt have the more pyne."
Yut was noughth Vaspasyan
Pilates lorde, ne he his man,
Bot so he seide to make hym adred
Yif he myghth the better have sped.
3065   Natheles I woot in that yer,   *year*
Pilate com in his daunger.   *dominion*
Pilate ansuered hym rigth noughth,
For he was greved in his thoughth;
Vaspasyan was agreved also
3070   That he ne wolde speken hym to.
And tho seide Vaspasian thus

To the Kyng Archillaus:

"Beaw sire," he seide, "thou art forsworne,   *Good; guilty of oathbreaking*

And thi fader Heroudes also biforne;

3075   Thou aughttest better have ben with me   *ought*

Than thereinne there I thee see.

Thi fader dyed in sorough ynough,

For he alle the children slough,

Whan Jesus Crist was here borne,

3080   For he wolde have hym ylorne.   *destroyed*

And thou are now ek in wille   *also*

Thiselven also for to spille;

Thi fader dyed in pynes stronge,

And so shaltou er oughth longe.

3085   Be thou and Pilate now ful bolde,

That I have seide I wil you holde."

Al that he seide thai token in veyn,

And Vaspasian went thoo ageyn.

Archillaus seide thoo to Pilate,

3090   "This kyng to us hath grete hate."

"Ye," quoth Pilate to Archillaus,

"It semeth he wil be wroken on us,   *avenged*

For to ben fel hym cometh of kynde,   *fierce; by nature*

And that I drede we shullen fynde.

3095   He was of Cesar kynde, iwis;

Of the more felonye he is,   *violent nature*

And that he hoteth, he wil holde,   *promises*

fol. 12rb   He ne wil leten hoot ne colde."   *desist on account of weather*

Quoth Archillaus, "Have no drede —

3100   Michel is bitwene word and dede.

This hoold is strong ynough aboute;   *stronghold*

Theigh he prate, yut is he withoute.   *chatters; outside*

Make he never so mychel to done,

Yut cometh he noughth in so sone.

3105   Bot go we to the wal agein,

And do now als I shal thee seyn:

Take up a floure upon the walle   *flower*

And to Vaspasyan thou calle

And seie to hym that alle it see,

3110   'Bataile, sir, I wage thee.'"

Pilate yede with herte glad   *went*

And dude as Archillaus hym bad;

Thoo he had seide that he wolde,

Vaspasyan gan hym biholde

3115   And seide, "Pilate, I it take;

This wed shal I noughth forsake,   *pledge*
And swiche shame I hote thee,
That thou shalt dye bote thou flee.   *unless*
Sorough have he that you spare!   *May he who spares you have sorrow*
3120   Myne engynes, maketh you yare!   *prepare yourselves*
And yee knighttes that ben myne,
For Jhesus love to don hem pyne,
Loketh nou that thai have no rest,   *Look*
And lete nou Pilate don his best.
3125   For so Jhesu Crist me save,
I ne shal blynne til I hym have,   *cease*
Yif God wil graunte me liif therto."
And alle his frendes seiden also,
"Ne ben yee withinne nevere so stronge,
3130   We shullen dwellen her so longe
Til we have wroken the grete wrong
That Jhesus suffred you among."
He comaundid to trumpen onon   *commanded; trumpet*
To armen his men everychon,
3135   And to the wal thai shoten and cast,   *shot; fired*
And men withinne sloughen fast.   *slew*
Thai foughtten so til it was nighth
And that hem wanted dayes lighth.   *lacked daylight*
And hapfullich a quarel drough   *by chance*
3140   And a pouver knave it slough,   *poor*
That yede and plaied in the strete;
And he was holden a prophete
Of alle the Jewes of the lawghe
For many wondres and many sawghe.   *prophecies*
3145   Vaspasian longe hem assailed,   *assaulted*
Bot litel yut it hym availed;   *helped*
Natheles many a Jew he slough
And dude withinne sorough ynough.

It was withinne the fifte yere   *fifth year (of the siege)*
3150   Fro Rome there com a messagere,
As Vaspasyan at the sege lay,
At that tyme ageins his pay.   *against his liking*
fol. 12va   He brougth word to Vaspasyan
That Nero was ded, that cursed man,
3155   That was emperour of Rome,
And her conseil there is nome.   *taken*
"Upon thee, sir, is yoven the dome,   *given the judgment*
That thou most nedes hom come;
For thai han alle chosen thee

3160	For to beren the dignité.	
	Take noughth, sir, this sonde in veyn,	*message*
	For thou mighth wenden and comen ageyn."	
	He went forth lyste hym noughth shone	*he desired not to refuse*
	And left there Titus his sone.	
3165	Swiche joye gan Titus undertake	
	That hym toke a cardiake,	*heart attack*
	For his faders gret honoure	
	That he shulde ben emperoure.	
	With overdon joye com that woo,	
3170	And with overdon sorough it most goo,	
	As yee mowen heren in that stounde	
	There Josephus sithen was yfounde.	
	Whan alle thoo that weren in Rome	
	Wisten of Vaspasianes come,	*Knew*
3175	Thai yeden and ronnen hym ageyn,	*They went and ran to meet him*
	Kyng, erl, baroun, knighth and sweyn;	*squire*
	Thai crouned hym there thaire emperoure	
	With solace, fest, and grete honoure.	*joy*
	Thai corouned hym in his paleys	*crowned*
3180	In the gyse of Sarsyneys,	*manner of Saracens (see note)*
	Bot afterward Seint Clement	
	Confermed his corounement.	
	And to gladen his frendes everychon	*cheer*
	To Jerusalem he went onon,	
3185	For hym though ful longe at Rome	
	Til that he were ageyin come.	
	And so he dude, I telle thee,	
	With hydous poeple gret plenté.	*a great many people*
	Hereth lordynges nou eft,	*again*
3190	I mote telle there I left,	
	Of the knave, the prophete,	
	That was sleyn in the strete.	
	Tho Jacob of this knave herd,	
	To Sir Pilate onon he ferd.	
3195	"Sir," he seide, "nou is it falle;	
	I wene we shullen seen it alle	
	That this Jew seide us to	
	Thritty wynter gon and mo,	
	That this cité shulde be lorne	
3200	And alle that therinne weren borne.	
	For now I woot hymself is yslawghe,	
	And wel the better I leve his sawghe.	*believe his tale*
	I rede thou do, sir, after me,	*advise*

	And yelde up swithe the cité,	*give up quickly*
3205	For evere the lenger we abide,	
	The more shame us wil bityde."	*will befall us*
	This was Jacob the gode man	
fol. 12vb	That herberewed Velosyan,	*lodged*
	Als it telleth here bifore.	
3210	Bot Pilate was agreved sore	
	And seide, "On thee I shal be wroken,	
	For the wordes that thou hast spoken;	
	For thorough the conseil of thee	
	I leve that al this sorough be!	*believe*
3215	Velosyan and thou that yere	*time*
	Casten this thoo he was here.	*Plotted*
	He spaak to me wordes smert;	
	Thai comen noughth sithen out of myne hert.	
	And yif I may, I shal thee sett	*put*
3220	There never frende ne shal thee fett."	*fetch*
	He dude fettre hym swithe fast	*arrest*
	And in swiche stede hym cast,	*such a place*
	And swore he shulde there lye	
	Withouten mete tyl that he dye	
3225	In that ilche foule dongeoun	*same foul dungeon*
	There lay he sperred in that prisoun.	*locked*
	Bot whan Marie his doughter wyst	
	That she had her fader myst,	
	Onon she seide an orisoun	*prayer*
3230	Tyl Jhesus Crist, Goddes son.	
	"Lorde," she seide, "hereth me,	
	Yif it thi swete wille be,	
	Also wys as I thee soughth	*Just as*
	With the oynement that I broughth	
3235	Unto the toumbe there thou lay.	
	Yif it were unto thi pay	*to your liking*
	That I dude that ilche dede,	
	Hereth me now at this nede!	
	Thou helpe my fader also wys	*in the manner*
3240	Out of the sorough that he inne is,	
	And also wys as he loved thee,	*as surely as*
	I praie thee that he unbounden be."	
	Whan she had seide this orisoun,	
	God sent onon an aungel doun	
3245	That com to Jacob there he satt	
	And for sorough sore gratt.	*lamented*
	"Jacob," he seide, "come with me;	

My Lorde wil that it so be.
Take to thee confort and solace,
3250   And thonke hym of his holy grace."
He took hym out of the prisoun
And led hym wel withouten the toun
And bad he shulde no man drede:
"Goo, fare wel there God thee lede."
3255   Jacob thanked God onon
That he feled hym loos so son;   *felt himself free*
Faire on knees with bothe honde   *He went out on hands and knees*
That laused hym out of his bonde.   *loosed*
Toward the ost he took his waye,
3260   So that Velosyan hym saye   *saw*
And seide to the emperour, "I see
Jacob my frende I wene it be.   *think*
fol. 13ra   Now I woot, sir, it is he righth;
Ythonked be it God almighth!"
3265   Thai welcomed hym fair and wel,
And askeden of hym hys lyf uche del.
Anon he tolde hem al the cas,
Of the Jewes hou it was,
And hou he was don in prisoun,
3270   And hou he com out of the toun.
Thai thonkeden God as the wyse
That so thenketh upon hyse.   *upon his (own)*
Tho seide Velosyan to Jacob righth,
"Jacob, wostou what I thee highth?
3275   That I at nede shulde be thi frende,
Als I shulde homward wende
Whan the Jewes her tales tolde,
Hou thai Jhesu sloughen and solde.
Als thai ben worthi, so shull thai have;
3280   No maner tresore shal hem save.   *treasure*
I owe thee evere to honoure,   *ought*
And namelich my lorde the emperoure,   *especially*
For thorough Goddes help and conseil thine
He is askaped mychel pyne.   *escaped*
3285   On my syde also I thanke thee,   *part*
For grete honoure thou dedest me;
And yif my lorde were heled, I thee highth   *promised*
To brynge hym hider with mychel mighth.
Loo, hym here as thou it bad!   *Behold*
3290   Sir, thanketh Jacob and maketh hym glad,
For yee ben gretlich holden therto."   *you are greatly obligated*

I plighth you the emperour dude so;   *promise*
He seide, "Jacob, thou getest honoure,   *will receive*
And the Jewes sorough wel soure.   *very bitter sorrow*
3295   I see hem falleth mychel shame
That be loked Goddes grame.   *are locked in God's anger*
God is with us and hem agein;   *against them*
Al that thai don, it is in veyn.
Swiche is myne hope and my trest;   *trust*
3300   Her is the travayle and oure the rest."   *Theirs*
The emperour of hym was glad,
And praied Jacob and hym bad
That he seide hym sum resoun
Hou that he mighth wynne the toun.
3305   "Forsothe," quoth Jacob, "and I shal.
Go maken a diche aboute the wal,   *ditch*
So that non mowe away flee   *might*
Bot yif al the ost hym see
And do it palicen al by the brynk,   *enclose; edge (of the wall)*
3310   Heighe and stronge upe al thing.   *against*
I wil myself therover bee
Til it be don, I hote thee.
Fyndeth me cost and men therto;   *money*
I shal noughth leven tyl it be do."   *leave*
3315   The emperour seide, "Graunt mercy,   *Thank you very much*
I graunte thee wel sykerly,
Al thing that thou wilt have,
fol. 13rb   Tymber, water, man and knave."   *Wood*
The emperour dude senden his sonde   *message*
3320   For dykers thoroughout al the londe;   *diggers*
He bad give uche man to his pay
Foure penyes upon the day   *pence*
Every maister tweie shillynges had,   *master; two shillings*
And so hymself comaunded and bad.
3325   Whan the diche was made uche del,
It liked the emperour ful wel.   *pleased*
Also Jacob dude do make
Two charnels for the ostes sake,   *mass graves*
For to hiden in that stede
3330   Alle the folk that there weren dede,
That the quyke ne dyed noughth for stynk of hem,   *living; died*
And so thai duden in Jerusalem.
Natheles there weren charnels two
In myddes of the cité also.   *In the middle of*
3335   Bot than the Jewes lokeden oute

	And seighen the diche made hem aboute	
	Michel sorough thai mightten have seen	
	Who so had withinnen ben.	
	Anon the Jewes everychone	
3340	Token her red what was to done.	*counsel*
	Thorough the conseil of Archillaus,	
	Barabas and Josephus,	
	Thai seiden to Pilate her avys,	
	"For us is fairer and more prys	*better and more worthy*
3345	To fightten with hem theroute, we gesse,	*suppose*
	Than for to lyen here in destresse.	
	Fairer is us on hem to dye	
	Than here inne as cowardes to lye."	
	Thai putten out plaunkes over the dyk,	*planks; ditch*
3350	Al by nighth ful pryvelyk.	
	Pilate onon dude hym oute	
	With thritty thousande on a route	*in a great company*
	And fifty thousande men on fote,	
	Hym to helpen the toun to-bote	*protect*
3355	With the emperour in the felde bilaste	*fulfilled*
	Fourtene thousande that he hem raste,	*fought*
	Alle thai duden hem for to fleighe	
	Agein hom to her citee.	
	Al the while that thai foughtte,	
3360	God lengthed the day, as hem thoughht.	*(see note)*
	Josephus was wounded sore,	
	That noble clerk and wiis of lore,	*wise of learning*
	He couthe more in dede and dawe	*in a day*
	Than alle that were in Jewes lawe.	
3365	Bot o thing halpe hym wel than,	*one; helped*
	That he was pryvé Cristen man;	*secretly*
	And for his kynde was noughth so,	*family*
	Therfore was hym wonder woo.	
	Thereof often he hem bisoughth,	
3370	Ac therof I woot ne sped he noughth.	*But*
	Whan the citizeins seighen this fare,	*saw*
	Than hadden thai bothe sorou and care,	
fol. 13va	That thai so overcomen were	
	And als swithe hunger gan hem dere	*hurt*
3375	So that the stronge the feble eet,	*weak ate*
	Ye, and the erthe under her feet,	
	And her owen dunge also;	*dung*
	Hors ne hounde ne leten thai go,	*Horse; dog*
	Ne othere beest, ne rote ne gres,	*root; grass*

3380	And uche by lott other ches.	*chose*
	Whan two yer weren al agoo,	
	That the sege bigan com al this woo;	
	Thorough the toun bigan to faile	
	Al manere of vitaile,	*food*
3385	So that the strengere robbed the othere,	*stronger*
	Fader the son, syster the brother,	
	Men and wymmen her children ete,	
	And uche ete othere by every strete.	
	A riche lefdy of that cuntré,	
3390	Of large londes and of fe,	*property*
	Marie she highth, sikerly,	
	A Cristen womman pryvely;	
	She had aqueyntes in Jerusalem,	*an acquaintance*
	And therfore she thider kem.	
3395	A gode lefdy that she hath knowe	
	With whom she thoughth to duelle a throwe,	*stay a while*
	Dame Clarice was hir name,	
	A womman of ful holy fame.	
	Thai lyveden there togedres longe,	
3400	Bot whan this woo bifel so stronge,	
	Othere werk couthe thai non wirche	*could*
	Bot duellen mychel in holy chirche,	
	And lyen there in afflicciouns,	*misery*
	In penaunce and in orisouns,	
3405	So bifel what more or lesse	
	Thai weren bothe in so grete destresse	
	For defaut of mete and drynk	*lack*
	That dyen thai mosten in al thing.	*That they must die*
	Hem ne was no liflode left	*food and drink*
3410	Bot al for robbed and for reft.	
	Marie had a doughtter dere,	
	That for hungere dyed there,	
	For whom she made mychel soroughe	
	Bothe on evene and ek on morowe.	*morning*
3415	Hemselven so grete hungere hadd	
	That Dame Clarice Marie badd,	
	"Ete we now this childe onon,	
	For the hungere that is us on."	
	"Nay," quoth Marie, "that wil I noughth!	
3420	I wolde dyen ar I it thoughth.	*before*
	Oure Lorde God that is so hende	*courteous*
	Of his grace may us sende;	
	Ne ben we noughth for this to sory,	*too sorry*

	It may stonde us to Purgatory.	*serve*
3425	So shal alle that wel bileve	
	That no woo ne shal hem greve."	
	In this talkyng as thai satt,	
fol. 13vb	Jhesus Crist hem noughth forgatt;	
	An aungel com from Hevene shene	*shining*
3430	As God sent hem bitwene	
	And seide to hem, "Leteth this stryf,	*Leave this disagreement*
	And als so longe as yee mowen, ledeth youre lyf.	*lead*
	Marie, loke that thou doo	
	As Clarice here seide thee to.	
3435	God wil so er than yee dye,	*God wills it so rather than that you die*
	For to fulfille the prophecye	
	That speketh of this in waye and strete,	
	That wymmen shulden her children ete.	
	Ne gruccheth noughth, bot fulfille	*grumble*
3440	Al that is Goddes wille.	
	Though that yee dyen in this nede,	
	Yee geten hevene blis to mede."	*as reward*
	Whan the aungel had seide his sawe,	
	Agein to heven he gan drawe.	*withdraw*
3445	Thai putten the childe on a spyt,	*on a spit*
	Agein the fyre to rosten it,	*roast*
	And duden as the aungel hem bad;	
	Thai eten therof and maden hem glad.	
	And as Pilate sat in his toure,	*tower*
3450	Of rost he had a grete savoure;	*roast; smell*
	Where it was onon was soughth,	
	He bad it shulde be to hym broughth.	
	Thai wenten and founden where it was,	
	And comen and tolden hym al the cas,	
3455	And whan thai hadden tolde hym al this sawe,	
	Than was Pilate nothing fawe.	*glad*
	And the Jewes that thider dede ronne,	*run*
	The womans chyld thei hem benome.	*took*
	The wymen hadde sorwe and moche woo	
3460	For her lyflode thai beren hem froo,	
	And for this sighth thai weren in drede	
	That thai duden that wicked dede.	
	Pilate had hungere non,	
	Though alle vitailes weren agon,	
3465	Ne none of the othere grete,	*nobles*
	Theigh the povere dyed for mete;	*Though; poor*
	For thai hadden the noble stones,	*virtuous stones*

Of vertu on hem for the nones,   *for that purpose*
And that made hem laste so longe,
3470   Til al the poeple them amonge
Mightten no lenger suffre ne wolde   *Could; would*
And God that had the termes tolde.   *If*
Pilate in the toun dude crye
And forbad that vilenye,
3475   That no man shulde no more ete
In that wise her owen bigete,   *manner; offspring*
Bot golde and silver eten he bad
To alle thoo that any had.
And so thai eten her tresore al,
3480   Bothe hewen and corven smal,   *chopped up; carved*
And in sum stede it is yfounde
That summe of hem her tresore grounde.

fol. 14ra   Yut there dyed many on,   *many a one*
By every strete wel good won,
3485   For it was no kyndely fode   *natural*
In no stede it hem stode,   *It stood them in no stead*
Bot hem alle to bigile.   *trick*
Whan the toun was yolden that while
For to have out of hem the tresore
3490   Men duden hem pyne wel the more.
Uche othere mighth his foo ete,
And for deynté thai helden it swete.   *a delicacy*
Wyf the housbonde, housebonde the wyf,
Everyche refte othere his lyf,   *seized*
3495   Summe with teeth other to-gnowen,   *gnaw*
And summe with hondes other to drowen.   *draw*
So thik men dyeden by strete and weye   *many*
For stynk of the men that dedun deye,
And for a commune raunsoun   *common amount*
3500   Thai beriyed the bodyes of the toun,
And whan thai faileden tresore,   *lacked*
Than weren thai beriyed no more,
Bot than thai laiden on hepes alle   *laid in heaps*
That for hunger ded gonne falle.
3505   And than the stynk the toun so fyld
Of the careynes that layen unhild,   *corpses; unburied*
That fader and moder, suster and brothere,
Dyeden that non mighth biryen othere.   *bury*
And sithen whan the toun was take,
3510   Titus mychel mone gan make,   *sorrow*
For the poeple so thik laye

On hepes dede by every waye.

Doune he fel wel sone on kne:

"Lorde, forgive my fader and me,

3515   For thorough us lyen thai noughth thus ded,

Bot for her owen feble red.   *counsel*

Hadden thai er yolden to us,   *yielded before*

Hadden thai alle noughth leyen thus."

Summe ded liggeyng he fonde,   *lying*

3520   Bitande hosen and shone in honde;   *Biting; leggings; shoes*

Therby wisten thai righth onon

For hunger thai dyeden everychon.

Dyches thai duden maken and bylde,

There thai duden the bodyes hilde.

3525   Pilate onon his conseil took,

For drede he had sore he quoke.

Thai seiden to hym, "We reden thee,

Lete yelden up swithe this cité.   *Give up*

Thus thenketh us alle that it is best;

3530   Hereinne shullen we have no rest."

"Nay," quoth Pilate, "yut is this my red: *advice*

I woot there nys no waie bot ded,   *no way but death*

Yut we shullen a while abide,

For to seen what wil bityde.   *happen*

3535   Thise lordes mowen dyen that ben withoute,   *might die*

Or we deyyen al the route;   *Before; die together*

Than thar us caren litel alle   *care*

fol. 14rb   On whether syde so it falle.   *On which side*

Or we shullen don as I shal seye,

3540   To sechen us help be another weye;

Casten we what we willen hem gyve   *Consider*

That we mowen duellen stille and lyve."

This thai graunteden everychon

And casten al hou thai wolden don.

3545   Therwhiles that thai casten so,

The emperour seide, "Jacob, goo,

And speke with summe of the cité,

And wyte what poynt thai inne be,   *find out what situation*

And for to comen out of prisoun

3550   Loke yif thai wil yelden the toun,

For thai ne have noughth her wille.

I trowe that summe for hungere spille.   *die*

Goo forth now, for I wyten wolde

Wharto we shullen us holde.   *To where*

3555   Thai dyen for defaut there in the strete;   *lack*

Thai han hunger and we han mete.
Seie hem that they comen and yelden us to,
For atte last thai shullen so."
Jacob went hym to the walle;
3560 A Jew he seigh and gan hym calle.
"Clepe me," he seide, "there Josephus;   *Summon to me*
Bidde hym comen and speken with us."
He sent and broughth hym also swithe,
And Jacob was of hym ful blithe,   *glad*
3565 And he of hym was blithe also.
Quoth Josephus, "Hou com thou us fro?"
And he tolde hym als it was,
And he seide thoo, "*Deo Gracias!*"   *Thanks be to God (Latin)*
"What," quoth Jacob, "artou Cristen?"
3570 "Yee, felaw," he seide, "Wiltou lysten?
I am pryvé Cristen man,
And my feith righth wel I can;   *know*
To loven Crist wel I owe,
And that I am to thee biknowe,
3575 This othere day thoo we out nam,   *we went out*
Whan yee us alle overcam,
I was wounded there ful sore
So that I was neigh ded therfore;   *nearly dead*
And thorough the miracles of Jhesu,
3580 I am waxen hoole ynough.   *grown*
My fader and my moder I have tolde,
To tourne hem and thai ne wolde,   *convert*
And for I may hem noughth turnen therto,
Certes, Jacob, me is ful wo."
3585 "Ye," quoth Jacob, "helde thee stille!
Thou shalt yut have al thi wille.
I shal be for thee yif that I can,   *vouch for you*
To my lorde Sir Vaspasyan,
And for alle thoo that Cristen be;
3590 Whan al is don, thou shalt it see.
Sey me hou yee faren withinne,   *Tell; fare*
And whan we shullen the toun wynne."
fol. 14va "Mafey," he seide, "I wil thee seie,   *By my faith (French)*
Ful thik oure folk bigyneth to deye,
3595 And for the stynk that cometh hem fro,
Hereinne dyen many moo.
And therfore we have don make
Amyddes the toun a wel gret lake,   *pit*
And evere as thai ded doune falle,

3600	Thereinne we don casten hem alle."	
	"Mafay," quoth Jacob, "and so don we,	
	And that was firste thorough me.	*through me (i.e., my idea)*
	The dyche with the heighe paleys	*fence*
	Thorough me was made, and the two charnels.	
3605	Me thinketh thai don a gret folye	*folly*
	To holden agein God and our partye,	
	And yut I hope atte last	
	To wynnen the toun thorou my cast,	*plot*
	As Pilate seide amyd the toun	*inside*
3610	Thoo he dude me in prisoun,	*When*
	That I and Velosyan wel gode speede	*very swiftly*
	Hadden yprocured al this dede.	*brought about*
	Forsothe, he ne gabbed noughth;	*did not lie*
	I wene therto it wil be broughth.	
3615	Forsothe, my brother Josephus,	
	I thoughth it shulde bifallen thus,	
	And Dame Verone, the gode womman,	
	Biforne the stiward Velosian,	*steward*
	I made that Dame Verone yede	
3620	To beten the emperoures nede;	*relieve*
	Forthi I am with hym pryvee,	*close*
	And so I hope yut shaltou be.	
	And so helpe me Crist as I am glad	
	That it shal fallen als I badd;	
3625	The emperoure was wonder seek	*sick*
	And wende to have ydyed eek,	*thought*
	And God heled hym thorough his grace,	
	And that hath don hym to seche this place.	*has caused him*
	He thenketh thise Jewes alle to schende	*destroy*
3630	Er than he wil hennes wende;	*go hence*
	He ne wil never letten this toun	*leave*
	Til he have al betten it doun.	*struck*
	Thou mighth seen it is Goddes wille	
	This vengeaunce to fulfille;	
3635	By many toknes men mowen ysee,	
	And thou wilt bithenken thee.	*reflect*
	Alle thoo that ben therinne	
	Ben encoumbred in foule synne,	*ensnared*
	Bot yif any Cristen wighth	*Unless; person*
3640	Be late comen to God almighth.	*recently*
	And for thei ne wollen no mercy crave,	*will not*
	I hote thee, thai shullen non have,	
	Neither of God ne of man,	

	Ne of my lorde Vaspasyan,	
3645	For he and Titus his son bothe	
	With alle the Jewes weren ful wrothe.	
	The ooth thai maden thai wil noghth breken,	
fol. 14vb	To leven the sege tyl thai ben wreken.	
	Therfore, I praie thee, seie me sone,	
3650	What thai thenken therinne to done,	
	Whether thai willen the toun thus helden	
	Oither have ydo and up it yelden."	*have done with it*
	Josephus ansuered hym ful stille,	
	"Jacob, it was nought last her wille	
3655	That thai wolden alle don so,	
	Whan I come to thee hem fro.	
	Bot forsothe, I hote thee,	
	It dureth noughth longe, as thinketh me.	*will not last; it seems*
	Me were ful leef we weren withoute,	*I would rather*
3660	For we lyven in mychel doute.	
	I wene thai casten to make youre gree	*intend to make peace with you*
	Yif thai mowen with any fee.	*price*
	Praie for us and be us fore,	
	That no Cristene man be lore!	
3665	Forsothe had Sir Vaspasian	
	Made hymself a Cristene man,	
	And his son with al his ost,	
	Er he come hider, wel thou wost,	
	For hym had ben sykernesse;	*security*
3670	Than wolden we han yelden us, more and lesse.	
	Yut is us lever to dyen hereinne	*we would rather*
	Than yelden us to a Sarasynne,	
	For we holden us worthi more	
	Tyl woo dryve us to suffre sore.	
3675	Fare wel Jacob, my leve brother,	*dear*
	For yee shullen sone wite on oither other."	*one way or another*
	"God of Hevene be with thee	
	And with alle that therinne Cristene be!"	
	The emperour he cometh than to,	
3680	And word for word he telleth hym so.	
	Than ansuered the emperoure,	
	"Sone hope I askape this erroure.	*escape*
	By thise wordes now I see	
	Hastilich thai shullen yolden be.	*Quickly*
3685	Jacob, wake we that we may;	
	It neigheth fast her terme day."	*quickly nears; day when payment is due*

Josephus com the Jewes unto,
"Lordynges," he seide, "What wil yee do?
Vaspasyan ne Titus his sone
3690   For wraththe leven thai ne conne   *Because of their wrath they cannot leave*
Til thai han wroken her tene,   *avenged their injury*
And that shal newly be sene.
So mychel I woot of hem, Sir Pilate,
As I have aspyed late,   *spied*
3695   I ne can see no waye bot on,   *one*
That we ne ben dede everychon.
Loketh what al youre folk wil seye
And do we righth as I you preye,
For thai of the communealté   *the common people*
3700   Fele this woo more than we."
A cry was made, the folk com al,
Bothe the gret and the smal.
fol. 15ra   Pilate seide, "What rede yee now?
For we don us alle upon yow."
3705   The poeple biforne hym casten a cry,
Ful reuful and ful grisely,   *piteous; frightful*
And seiden, "Fairer it were to dye   *Better*
Yerne than so longe to lye."   *Quickly*
And summe seiden hem among,
3710   "We lyen here sperred al to long!   *confined*
We dyen here in destresse,
And that is for oure wickednesse,
For we duden Messias to dye.
It is skyl that we it abye.   *reasonable; pay for it*
3715   And that seen the Romaynes wel,
For thai destroyen us and oure uche del.
Sumtyme was we seiden so
That the Romaynes shulden thus do,
Whan we and oure kynde ran
3720   For to destroyen thys gode man;
By this we mowen knowen and see
The tyme is comen that it shal be.
It semeth Messias may fulfille
And of alle to don his wille,
3725   For lenger with no manere gynne   *contrivance*
Mowen we lasten for oure synne.
He sheweth wel he is God almighth;
We duden as foles with hym to fighth.   *acted; fools*
We praiden his mercy al to late,
3730   And thou also, Sir Pilate.

	Therfore, sir, lete us alle oute gon	
	To enden al oure sorough onon."	*sorrow*
	Yut thai seiden hem among,	
	"Better is short sorough than long;	
3735	To slen uche othere fairer it is	
	Than yelden us up and faren amys."	
	Ellevene thousande there leten her lyf.	*lost their lives*
	Uche slough othere with his knyf,	
	And for the stynk that of hem came	
3740	Many on her deth there nam.	*took*
	And than thai crieden at a cry	
	To Jhesu Crist that sitteth on heigh,	
	"Agein thee, Lorde, we han mysdon,	*done wrong*
	Therfore wreche is comen us on.	*vengeance*
3745	Now mowen we seien as we er dede	
	Whan he toward the croice yede;	
	He bad us nougth wepen for his pyne,	
	Bot for us selven and for oure kyne.	*kin*
	We mowen wariyen in oure thoughth	*complain*
3750	The teres that us forth broughth,	*tears*
	We aughtten for to bidden and willen	
	That the erthe wolde us hillen,	*cover*
	That we ne seighen this vengeaunce alle	
	Yif that it so mighth bifalle.	
3755	We mowen wariyen, al oure kynde,	*complain*
	For the sorough that we fynde,	
	For we that lyven now abyen ful sore	
fol. 15rb	That thai wroughtten us bifore.	*caused*
	Withouten ende moten thai care	*grieve*
3760	That maken us thus yvel to fare,	
	For now is comen that he us higth	*told*
	Agein oure wrong he dooth us rigth.	
	Forthi, Pilate, give up the toun,	*Therefore*
	And lete us gon out of prisoun,	
3765	Or we shullen thee smertly take,	
	And alle the grettest for thi sake,	
	And yelden us selven the cité,	*ourselves*
	Hou so it evere of us be.	
	Of this avise thee, Sir Pilate,	
3770	Or thou shalt be war to late,	
	For we mowen no lengere lyven;	
	Hyghe thee the toun were up given."	*Make haste*
	Whan Pilate seigh this, and Josephus,	
	And Barabas and Archillaus,	

3775   Thai and the poeple wenten alle

And to the emperour thai gonnen calle,

"Have mercy on us, sir emperoure,

And take us nou to thi socoure;   *protection*

The tyme is comen, as we thee telle,

3780   That we ne mowen no lengere duelle.

We have don al that we may;

Of seven yer this is the last day.

And therfore sir, we thee preyen,

Whether shullen we lyven or deyen."

3785   Tho the emperour thise wordes herd,

With mychel joye therfore he ferd.

Also swithe he gan doune falle   *quickly*

On his knees biforne hem alle

And seide, "Welcome be Goddes sonde,   *by*

3790   For he is Lorde of al londe,

And now I see he wil fulfille

That I shal haven al my wille."

He roos and spaak unto hem alle   *rose*

And seide, "Hereth now what shal bifalle,

3795   That yee shullen heren, speken, and see,

Yee shullen no mercy fynde in me!

For yee sloughen in this stede

Jhesu Crist in his manhede.   *humanity*

Withouten al manere gylte

3800   Yee demed hym to ben yspilte,   *killed*

And evermore riwen I it owe;   *regret*

Ne hadden yee ben, I had hym sowe.   *seen*

Yee han failed of his grace,

So shulle yee don of myn in uche place.   *in every place*

3805   Al my wille ich have you tolde

And wharto that yee shulle you holde."

Now seide the Kyng Archillaus,

"Sir emperour, shal it ben thus?"

He gan to renden a gappe wyde   *tear*

3810   Doun of hym after his syde,

And onon his swerd out drough

And therwith hymself he slough;

fol. 15va   He fel doune biforne hem alle

Into the dyche under the walle.

3815   "Forsothe," seide the emperoure,

"Archillaus was treytoure;

Forthi on swiche deth he sterved,   *died*

Righth as he hath arst deserved.   *first*

Gooth beryye hym," he seide, "upe al thing

3820   With honoure, for he was a kyng."

Pilate and alle wenten adoune

To a gate of the toune,

And out atte gate he wonde

With the keyes in his honde.

3825   The gate was upon that ilche cost   *coast*

There Titus lay with al his host,

Whan the toun shulde be yolden and take

In the pres he gan out shake   *army (host)*

Josephus with many a man

3830   Into the cité of Joneperham,   *Joneperam (see note)*

For to askapen al the woo

That the Jewes shulden to.

The emperour wyst this on hast,

And sone I woot he was bycast,   *surrounded*

3835   Wel armed men with many a wepen

Nighth and day the toun to kepen,

And Josephus strongely withstood

And arst wolde sheden his blood   *first*

Than to yelden hym to Vaspasyan,

3840   For he was nougth a Cristene man,

Bot I am syker he dude atte last.   *certain*

The emperoure soughth on hym so fast

That the sege he lete be,   *gave up*

And with ellevene felawes he gan flee

3845   Under the erthe into a kave,   *cave*

Hem to socouren and to save.

Whan her vitailes weren alle gone,   *victuals*

Hise felawes seiden everychon,

"Sire, thus mowe we noughth lye.   *lie*

3850   Ful wel we witen here shullen we dye;

Uche of us shal other ete

At the last for nede of mete.

Maister, at thee we willen bygynne,

For thou art most maister hereinne.

3855   Than shullen we han the lesse reward

Of hem that duellen afterward."

Josephus ansuerd als a man

Ful queyntlich, as nede was than,   *craftily*

And seide, "It wolde noughth ben wel so.

3860   Casteth lott bitwene two and two,   *Draw lots between each other*

Whiche of us shal other ete

And whiche we shullen alyve lete.   *leave alive*

Holde yee alle," he seide, "to this?"

"Ye sir," thai seiden, "I wys."

3865   Thus uche of hem ate otherr than,

Tyl it to Josephus cam;

Thoo the loth fal hym upon,   *lot*

fol. 15vb   Deyen he shulde righth onon.

Bot God wolde noughth he dyed than,

3870   For his wytt halpe many a man.

His fere gan his swerd out drawe,   *fellow*

And Josephus he wolde have slawe,

Bot Josephus, that sotyle was,   *crafty*

Seigh that he was in that cas,

3875   And leepe on hym als he cam,   *leapt*

And his swerde hym bynam,   *he took from him*

And that same dome he hym gave   *fate*

That he shulde hymselven have.

And hym bileved he there alone,

3880   So that he com out onone,

With his swerd in his honde,

And to the emperoure he wonde.

And thoo the emperour to hym drough,

And seide, "Felawe, wo artou?"   *who*

3885   "Sir," he seide, "I am Josephus,

That wroot the storye amonges us

Of al that yee here writen yfynde

Amonge the Jewes of oure kynde."

"Forsothe," he seide, "thou seist amys!   *wrongly*

3890   For yif thou haddest ben so wys,

Why naddestoun warned hem to save   *didn't you*

Fro the armes that thai shullen have?"   *harm*

"Sire," seide Josoephus hym to,

"On thoo that lyven, Y it do

3895   That I warned hem of this cas,

Fele yeres er it was.   *Many years ago*

And of her bokes I take witnesse,

That I have writen, so I gesse."

And men that lyveden many on

3900   Witnessed it everychon,

And alle thai witnessed in that stede

That Josephus had writen and sede.

Than seide Jacob for hym thore,

"Al that he seith I wil be fore."

3905   Than seide Sir Vaspasian,

"Josephus, artou a Cristen man?"

	"Ye sir," he seide, "Sikerly,	*Certainly*
	Bot I have borne it prively."	*endured; secretly*
	And righth onon he was unbounde,	*untied*
3910	And he thanked hym that ilche stounde	
	And seide, "Sir, yif thou loke,	
	Yut shaltou fynde in the boke	*book*
	That I seide thine was the honoure	
	Of Rome to ben emperoure	
3915	Fourty dayes er it fel,	*before it happened*
	And hou Titus foryede his hele,	*gave up*
	And thorough the conseil of me,	
	I hope yut hole shal he be."	
	Than was the emperour ful glad,	
3920	And seide, "Than have I that I bad,"	
	And seide, "Maister Josephus,	
	I nolde forgon my son Tytus,	*will not forsake*
fol. 16ra	And I wist hou his lyf to save	
	For nothing that I mighth have.	
3925	Michel honoure thee shal ben give	
	Yif thou helpe that he lyve."	
	"Sir," he seide, "have thou no drede.	
	I hope ful wel shul we spede."	*prosper*
	He broughth hym to Titus also swithe,	
3930	That of his comyng was glad and blithe.	
	Whan Titus herd his fadirs sawghe,	
	To Josephus he gan hym drawghe,	*turn to*
	And loved and leved hym sithen moost	
	Save his fader of al the oost.	
3935	"Whan shal be don thou highttest us,	
	That my fader tolde us?"	
	"Sir," he seide, "tomorowe day	
	It shal be don, yif that I may."	
	"Come tomorowe and ete with us than."	
3940	"I shal be redy yif that I can,	
	On a forward that thou ne wraththe thee	*promise; do not become angry*
	For what man that I brynge with me.	
	I shal come by this covenaunt."	*agreement*
	"Perfay," quoth Titus, "and I graunt."	*By my faith*
3945	Josephus in thoughth gan cast	
	And bithoughth hym atte last:	
	"With a joye com this yvel, perfay,	
	And with a sorough it most away."	
	Onon he dude to aspien than	*search out*
3950	Yif there were evere any man	

	That Titus had hated stronge	*fiercely*
	And the wraththe had lasted longe,	
	And hym was tolde there was swiche on.	
	He dude hym comen forth onon,	
3955	And righth onon he lete calle	
	The stiward of the kynges halle.	
	Thoo seide Josephus, "Gode felawghe,	
	Wiltou don after my sawghe?	
	Loke thou assente to me now	*consent*
3960	For Titus love and for his prow."	*benefit*
	"Sir, I sey thee sikerlich,	
	I graunte to don wel blethelich."	*gladly*
	"Wel," seide Josephus also sone,	
	"As mete tyme is atte none,	*meal; noon*
3965	Do me setten a litel borde	*table*
	Righth biforne Titus thi lorde,	
	And there at shal this man be sette,	
	And loke that hym be mete fette	
	Wel grete plenté and riche drynk,	
3970	Righth as shal comen bifore the kyng.	
	And yif I rehete hym, do thou also."	*make much of*
	"Sir," quoth the stiward, "it shal be do."	
	Al this was don word for word;	
	Josephus satt at the kyngis bord.	
3975	Titus was agreved and thoughth	
	How was this man hider broughth;	
	Thus he satt agreved longe	
fol. 16rb	That mete ne drynk nolde he non fonge.	*take*
	For tene he chaunged al his mood,	*anger*
3980	And sithen an hete com in his blood	*heat (see note)*
	That his yvel than hym forsook	
	And nevere after hym ne took.	
	Josephus bihelde this man	
	And reheten hym bigan,	*make much of*
3985	And the stiward dude also	
	With faire semblant as fel therto.	*hospitality*
	Titus tourned hym ful smert,	*sharply*
	"Josephus, I thanke thee in myne herte!	
	I bad thee brynge a man with thee;	
3990	I wende noughth it had ben he.	
	Thou bad I shulde me wraththe noughth	
	With no man that thou hider broughth,	
	And I graunted thee sikerly.	
	It shal ben holden treuly,	*be kept*

3995   For thou dude it for myne hele,

    I thanke it thee I have it wele.   *nobly*

    Thou shalt be me dere while I lyve,

    And hym my wraththe I forgyve."

    Thoo his fader wyst hou it was,   *knew*

4000   I woot he made gret solas,   *joy*

    And after this over alle thinges,

    Josephus was next the kynges.

    Go we now to Pilate ageyn,

    For of hym I have to seyn.

4005   Hereth hou he gan his profre make   *offer*

    For the toun and for his sake,

    To witen yif thai mighth saved be

    With golde or silver or other fee.   *payment*

    Titus seigh Pilate and was ful glad;

4010   No better tydynges he ne bad.   *tidings*

    Pilate seide, "I praie thee,

    Sir Titus, that thou here me.

    For to ben stille I wil thee give   *remain here*

    Every yere while that I lyve,

4015   So that thi fader wil me save,

    And my baily stille to have,   *office*

    I wil given hym this trowage:

    An hundreth sparehaukes ramage,   *wild sparrowhawks*

    An hundreth gentyl faukons also,   *falcons*

4020   And houndes thritty mute therto,   *packs*

    An hundreth palles of sylk and golde,   *fine cloths*

    The richest that ben boughth or solde,

    And ten leopardes and lyons ten,

    And ten beres fro the den,   *bears*

4025   And fyve mules charged wel,   *loaded*

    With golde and sylver everydel,

    And with alle the best stones,

    That mowen ben founden for the nones.   *for the moment*

    Wite at thi lorde yif he wil so,   *Find out*

4030   And seie me swithe what I shal do."

    Titus was glad that ilk tyde   *time*

    For he the gate opened wyde,

fol. 16va   And for he seigh Sire Pilate

    Redy to yelden hym atte gate.

4035   He com and tolde his fader this,

    And he onon gan wepe for blis.

    The fader seide mekely this tale: *humbly*

    "Forsothe, son, I am his bale;   *destruction*

	Though he wolde give me al this worlde,	
4040	He ne shal nevere the better ben herd.	
	And though he migth thelen als myche shame	*suffer as much shame*
	As alle the men that beren name,	
	Fro man was made to the werldes ende,	
	He were more worthi, my leve frende.	
4045	Take thi folk and goo hym to,	
	And telle hym that I seide so.	
	Take hym son upe my blissyng,	*with*
	And loke thou do hym in good kepyng,	*secure keeping*
	And do thee forth in to the toun,	
4050	And I shal kepen enviroun	*surrounded*
	That non askape bot I it see.	*escape*
	And Jacob here take with thee,	
	For he knoweth the Cristen men,	
	And ek the wymmen, whiche there ben,	
4055	For thou woost wel I have sworne	
	That non of hem ne shal be lorne.	*lost*
	And alle thoo that yee shullen selle	
	As thai ben sleyn lete hem telle."	
	Titus onon than forth sprong	
4060	With his oost gret and long,	
	Thai ne wolden no lengere abide	
	Bot fylden the dyche in every side.	*filled*
	Thai casten the gates open wyde,	
	Sir Titus onon gan in ride	
4065	With thritty thousande armed wel,	
	Bothe in yrne and in steel.	*iron*
	He took Pilate there he stode,	
	Thritty knighttes hym keped gode.	*guarded*
	I woot that he ful sore quook	
4070	Whan the knighttes hym undertook!	*took into custody*
	Titus lett take all that he mett,	
	And thoo that hidden hem, he dude hem fett.	*fetch*
	He comaunded his men als blyve	
	To kepen that thai token alyve;	
4075	He dude bynde hem everychon	*bind*
	That hem ne askaped lyves non,	*alive*
	Bot yif any braak his nek	*were to break*
	Or drenched hem in any bek.	*drown; stream*
	The Jewes weren leide on hepes grete,	
4080	Fast ybounden, honde and fete.	
	Als Titus rood up and doune	
	And felde the walles of the toune,	

	On the wal he found a plas,	*place*
	Wel thicker than that other was.	
4085	He had wel mychel ferlyk	*great wonder*
	Whi it was there so thikke.	
	Tyl it was open nolde he blynne	*cease*
fol. 16vb	For to wyten what was therinne;	
	And at the last in he wan	
4090	And fonde therinne an olde hore man,	*gray-haired*
	Al glad and wel hiwed of the best,	*of good complexion*
	As on that were comen fro the fest.	*feast*
	He asked hym hou he there cam,	
	And what tyme and thorough wham,	
4095	And what he highth wonderly.	*marvelously*
	And he seide, "Joseph of Aramathy.	
	First I was in prisoun as men herd,	
	For Jhesus love wel fast ysperd,	*locked up*
	And that was don for his berying,	*burying*
4100	And here was I don for my prechyng.	
	Righth now I woot seven yere ben gon,	
	Thai shetten me in this wal of ston.	*shut*
	Atte first Jhesus fette me oute	
	And bad me have righth no doute,	
4105	To kithe me love was his thoughth,	*reveal*
	Sithen he me hath forgeten noughth.	*Since*
	My lorde me hath fed and kepte to now,	
	For I shulde be delivered thorough yow;	
	To thi fader and to thee and to youres alle,	
4110	This honourable grace be ordeyned to falle,	
	That men shulden therof longe yelpe	*speak*
	And after tourne youre soules to helpe.	
	Jhesus Crist wil that it be so;	
	He ordeyned this dede for you two."	
4115	Titus thanked oure heven kyng	
	Of Joseps wordes and his fyndyng.	*discovery*
	To his fader onon he hym sent,	
	That honoured hym with gode entent;	
	With hym and Titus he was pryvé,	
4120	And honoured with her bothers meignee,	*both of their armies*
	For he was most honourable man	
	After Titus and Vaspasyan,	
	And than Japhel and Josephus,	
	And Jacob that loved Jhesus.	
4125	While Titus alle the Jewes soughth,	
	Jacob other men togedre broughth,	

	Alle that leveden on Jhesu Crist,	*believed*
	Feble thai weren for hunger and threst.	*Weak; thirst*
	He led hem softe with honoure	*gently*
4130	Righth biforne the emperour.	
	The emperour gret hem everychon	
	And dude hem eten wel gode won,	*according to good custom*
	And thanked God that thai were save,	
	And that he mighth hem lyves have.	*alive*
4135	He dude hem bathen and clothen uchon	
	With white clothes that faire shoon,	*shone beautifully*
	So that his oost shulde hem knowe	
	And honouren hem whan thai hem sowe.	*saw*
	Of the Jewes thai hym tolde	
4140	Al that evere he witen wolde,	
	And that he shulde no tresoure gete,	
	For uche a Jew hath his y-ete,	*each Jew had eaten his*
fol. 17ra	Bothe clothes, palles and baudekyn,	*Eastern silks (brocade)*
	And athere of wolle and of lyn,	*wool; linen*
4145	And vessel mychel of riche prys	
	Of al manere metal that is,	
	And fele beestes wilde and tame,	
	And hordes of hous al same,	*household stores together*
	Bot thai han oughth in erthe hyd	*ought to have*
4150	Ellas nothing is thee her bityd.	*So that nothing would have happened to them*
	"Now," seide the emperour, "is it so?	
	I wolde non othere thai hadden do.	
	Her tresore coveite I noughth to wynne,	*desire*
	For it is ful of falshede and synne.	*falsehood*
4155	Al that is left is myne uche del,	
	And that thai han eten paieth me wel,	*rewards me well*
	For now shal I fulfillen my sale	
	And everyche bygger haven his tale.	*buyer; total*
	For I thenk to avaunce myne	*benefit*
4160	And the more shal be her pyne.	
	A fair grace is us bityd	
	That thai han eten is noughth hyd;	
	For the biyete and for the prow,	*profit; benefit*
	Myne men shullen don hem sorough ynow,	
4165	And alle othere that willen hem bye.	
	In al this londe I shal don crye	*announce*
	That al manere Cristene wighth	*person*
	That of the Jewes han despyt yplighth	*sworn disdain*
	Shullen comen and bye my ware	*goods*
4170	And evermore the better fare.	

That is my joye and my game;

Thai mowen noughth have to mychel shame."

Rigth onon than sent he

Thorough the londe of Judé,

4175   And comaunded every Cristene man

Comen to Sir Vaspasyan,

Upon lyf and upon lyme,

Her avauncement for to nyme.   *reward; take*

Non withstood that he ne kem

4180   To the cité of Jerusalem.

Than dude he cryen thorough his oost

That alle shulden come, lest and most.

He seide to hem, "Yee han herd tolde

For thritty pens Jhesus was solde,

4185   In despyt of Cristene lawghe,

And sithen the Jewes han hym slawghe.

Yee that ben comen into this stede,

Cometh forth and awreketh his dede!   *avenge*

I seie you, who so wil bygge any,   *buy*

4190   I selle hym thritty for a peny

Of alle the Jewes and her kynde,

And loketh what yee in hem fynde;

For I dar you wel warraunte,   *guarantee*

Yee shullen ben riche of the remenaunte.   *remainder*

4195   Whan thai ben opened everychon,

Yee shullen fynde tresore gode won.

Uche man take his part of alle

fol. 17rb   Of uche heved as wil bifalle;

In her wombes thai han it broughth,   *stomachs*

4200   It ne thar nevere ben ferther soughth.   *need never*

And whan yee han out the tresore,

That yee seen there nys no more,

Loke yee don hem al the peyne

That any man can wyte or seyne.

4205   Honge hem, bren hem, dooth hem drawe,   *burn; torn apart (drawn and quartered)*

Flee hem, bore hem, dooth hem sawe   *Flay; pierce; cut them*

Roste hem, scolde hem, bete hem, and putte,   *scald; smite*

And al on peces her body cutte,

And thus fordooth hem, liif and lyme: *destroy*

4210   So shullen men quyten hem her venyme.   *reward them for their corruption*

And Goddes blissyng have thay ay

That serven hem so tyl Domesday!   *treat*

Cometh now and byggeth fast

Evere while the route wil last."   *crowd*

4215	Thai comen and boughtten up everychon,	
	And uche opponed his folk onon,	
	And after duden her enemyes	
	As hem was boden the same wyse.	*commanded*
	There mightten men seen, sikerly,	
4220	Gronyng, gruntyng, sorough and cry.	*Groaning, grunting*
	While al this sorough was ywroughth,	*made*
	I hote thee, Titus sleep righth noughth;	*I assure you*
	He rood overal thorough the toun,	
	And al that there was he felde adoun.	*knocked*
4225	With pycoys and mattok many a knighth	*pickax; mattock (see note)*
	Felden the walles doune righth,	
	And al the toun sikerlyk,	
	And filden there with the grete dyk.	*filled; ditch*
	Thai swepten al clene al that thai fonde,	*swept*
4230	So that after hem ne lete thai nawght stonde,	
	Bot the temple Salamon sikerly,	*temple of Solomon*
	And the castel with the toure Davy.	*tower of David*
	For love of hem thai leften stille	
	The prophecies to fulfille:	
4235	"There schal no ston on othere dwelle,	
	Bot men shullen it doune felle."	
	Thai fulfilled the prophecye	
	In alle thinges that thai mightte aspye.	
	Thai duden beryye the bodyes alle	*bury*
4240	In dunge hepes withouten the walle;	*dung heaps outside*
	Thai boughtten and solden by hem one	
	On that othere syde the other uchone.	
	The summe of Jewes boughth and solde	*number*
	As thai weren sleyn thai weren tolde;	*counted*
4245	The noumbre was, as yee mowen lithe,	*hear*
	An hundreth thousande elleven sithe,	*111,000*
	And the summe of alle that les her liif,	*lost*
	With hunger or with swerd or kniif,	
	Withouten thoo that weren solde, I understande,	*Excluding*
4250	Was foure hundreth and seventene thousande.	*417,000*
	And this wreche shal lasten ay	*vengeance*
	And evermore tyl Domesday,	
fol. 17va	Upon al the Jewes kynde	
	In what londe so men hem fynde.	*land*
4255	Evere thai shullen ben, I plighth,	
	In despyt with gode skil and righth;	*reason*
	Thai shullen nevere duellen in no londe	
	Bot for raunsoun, Ich understonde.	*payment*

This was, I wene, grete vengeaunce
4260 Thorough Goddes owen ordinaunce.
There may no mannes slaughth ben hyd   *manslaughter*
That it ne shal sumtyme be kyd;   *revealed*
Loke than yif Goddes sones sholde
That alle thinges had in holde.   *grasp*

4265 Thoo al the cité was doune cast,
Titus toke Pilate atte last
And broughth hym bifore his faders kne.
"Fader," he seide, "loo, here is he
That slough Jhesu that was thi leche,   *physician*
4270 And this traitour I thee biteche."
Than ansuered Sir Vaspasyan,
"Me thinketh I mighth noughth haten this man."
Twies or thries thus he seide,   *thrice*
"Hou shulde my wraththe ben on hym leide?
4275 Me thenketh I ne can see non other,
I mighth loven hym as my brother.
Helpe, sum man, I mighth hym knowe,
That he lede us thus no throwe."   *not lead us a while*
Forth there com than a wel olde man,
4280 "Sir emperour, I thee telle can,
Hereth me and yee shullen wyte;
I shal telle you as it is wryte.
Whan Jhesus dyed, so seith oure book,
Pilates knighttes from hym took
4285 His clothes and deled amonges hem,
And there was a kirtel that had no sem   *garment that had no seam*
That thai leten ben and parted it noughth,
Bot hom to Pilate it was broughth.
He woot ful wel that I ne lyye,   *that I do not lie*
4290 He hath it kepte sithen in tresorye.
Seint Marie the kirtel waaf,   *wove*
And Jhesu Crist hir son it gaf.   *gave*
Sir, he dude it on hym than   *he (Pilate)*
Whan the gret hunger bigan;
4295 Gode stones and that clooth
Made that he feled no looth.   *felt; harm*
While he it hath, he mighth gon
Among his frendes, among his fon.   *enemies*
Longe it is gon he was a fyle;   *He has been a wretch for a long time*
4300 I knowe hym wel and al his gyle.   *treachery*
Take the kirtel fro the traitour,
And were it thiself, sir emperour;

	It fel noughth hym therewith be clad	*is not fitting*
	After hym that first it had.	
4305	Also wel to hym it falles	
	As a donge heep ben spredde with palles!	*A dung heap spread with fine cloth*
	Upon hym thou mighth it fynde:	
fol. 17vb	Whiles he it hath on, thou beest al blynde,	
	So tourne it of hym bifore thi kne.	*knee*
4310	On hym I woot that I it see."	
	Whan the kirtel was fro hym ytake,	
	Michel sorough he gan make.	
	The emperour on hym gan loke,	
	And on hym his heved he shoke	*head*
4315	And seide, "Stronge theef, thu shalt be shent,	*Vile thief; destroyed*
	For thou hast us so longe ablent!	*blinded*
	Fy on thee, theef! For longe while	
	Thou hast us led al with gile.	*guile*
	Yif I may, theef, thou schalt abye,	
4320	And in stronge tourment thou shalt dye,	
	Elles had I lorne al my journé	*Or else; lost; travel*
	That I made to this cité.	
	For thou art worthi more shame alone	
	Than the Jewes everychone."	
4325	As the story witnesseth and seith,	
	A barel of steel was for hym greith,	*barrel; arranged*
	And al quyk he was thereinne ydo.	*alive; put*
	Hereth now what thai duden also.	
	Thai thoughtten han caste hym in the cee,	*sea*
4330	Bot for this resoun thai leten be,	
	His paynes to lengthen, verreyment.	*truly*
	Unto Vyenne he was sent,	*Viene*
	That tyme there was the heighe prisoun	
	That longed to Rome and to the croun.	*belonged; crown*
4335	The barel was seled with his seal,	*sealed*
	So that he were kepte wel,	
	And evermore he shulde there ybe	
	In pyne and woo tyl that he dye.	
	Out of the barel he was ydo	
4340	Whan he com the prisoun to,	
	And he was in agein done	
	Whan he was ded also sone.	*After he was dead*
	He was tyed with a cheyne	*chain*
	To a stake with fettres tweyne,	*stake; shackles*
4345	And gynes on his handes tway,	*ropes*
	Bot it were the heigher day.	*Unless; holy*

	There he lay two yer er he was ded,	
	And lyved with water and barly bred,	*barley*
	Bot on every heighe day	
4350	Than he was served to his pay,	*to his liking*
	Of gode mete and of drynk,	
	And a man it to hym brynge.	
	So fer the devel was hym withinne	
	That ones ne rewed hym his synne,	*he did not once regret*
4355	Bot lay there as an hethen hounde	*heathen hound*
	Upon the bare swepen grounde.	*swept*
	Ay he lay righth as he yede,	
	Ne was hym chaunged no manere wede,	*clothing*
	In wel mychel unclennesse	*filth (uncleanness)*
4360	And wel mychel and gret destresse.	
	The story telleth also he lay	
	So longe hym thoughth that on a day,	
fol. 18ra	He wex al ful of his lyf,	*grew tired*
	And of on he borowed a kniif	*from someone; knife*
4365	For to paren a pere, he drough,	*pare a pear; drew*
	And therwith hymselven he slough.	
	The sept sages thus willen you telle,	*Seven Sages (see note)*
	As men in the jestes spelle,	*stories tell*
	Hou he dyed thai senten to seie than	
4370	To the emperoure Sir Vaspasyan	
	And the emperoure seide onon,	
	"To fouler deth mighth he nougth gon	
	Than slee hymself with his owen honde,	
	For wers was non, ich understonde,	*none was worse*
4375	Whiles he lyved, ne more forlorne	
	That evere was of moder borne,	
	For he assented by dome and red	*judgment and advice*
	To don Jhesu Crist to ded.	
	He ne migth noughth, I understonde,	
4380	Have ben sleyn with a fouler honde.	
	I vouche wel saaf he ended so,	*think it proper*
	Als he dude, so lete hym go."	
	Out of the prisoun thai hym drough,	
	Wel vileynlich ich hote yow,	*disrespectfully*
4385	And sperred hym in the barel ageyn,	*locked*
	As biforne yee herd me seyen.	
	Thai beriyed hym by a watres syde	*buried*
	There no man shulde go ne ride,	
	In a stede that was al wast.	*waste*
4390	There fele men weren siththe sore agast;	*many*

	For stynk and cry thai hadden doute	*fear*
	Of fendes that walked hym aboute	*around*
	Wharthorough many on took there the deth,	*Through which place*
	What of stynk and of his breth.	*stench*
4395	Fro that syde the folk hym drough	
	For the men that it slough,	
	And than thai token hem to rede	*upon advice*
	To remeven hym to another stede,	*remove*
	And so thai duden atte last,	
4400	And in a water thai hym cast.	*threw*
	There he fleet longe up and doune	*floated*
	To many mannes confusioune	*ruin*
	Now in the myddes, now by the brynk,	*middle; edge*
	That doun to grounde migth it noughth synk,	
4405	So the devels gonnen hym posse and bere	*began; move*
	That he ne mighth resten no where.	
	I trowe the soule had litel rest	
	Whan the body was so forkest,	*tossed about*
	And yif the fendes shewed hem mychel byfore,	*shoved*
4410	Than they shewed hem wel more.	
	With derknesse, stynk and hidous cries,	*darkness; horrible*
	Men thoughtten it dyned into the skies;	*resounded*
	By the water mighth no man wende	
	Into no londe fer ne hende,	*no land far or near*
4415	And theigh the cuntré wenden and seyn	
	That the water had borne hym agein.	
	Tyl on a day a shipp com glide	*sail*

fol. 18rb
	For by fast in a nones tyde,	*midday*
	Alle thai weren in grete afray	
4420	Whan that thai the barel say.	*saw*
	With mychel woo londe thai nam,	
	And into Vyenne thoo thai cam	
	And tolden the folk of that cité	
	Hou thai hadden the barel ysee,	*seen*
4425	Up and doun floterande fast,	*floating*
	Wharfore thai weren sore agast	
	For derknesse and for devels cry	
	And for stynk thai felten hem by.	
	Than the clergie of the toun	*clergy*
4430	Amonge the poeple with resoun,	
	With holy bedes and with penaunce,	*prayers*
	That God delyvered hem of that chaunce	
	Leyen fast in orisoune,	*Lay down; prayer*
	Tyl God sent his grace adoune.	

4435	A voice there com that bad hem gon	
	To the watres side onon,	
	And there thai shulden sone seen	
	Hou it shulde of that barel ben.	
	Alle that mightten gon and ride	
4440	Wenten hem to the watres syde.	
	A roche bigan to oppen wyde	rock
	As thai alle seighen that ilche tyde,	
	And aboven hem roos a wyndes blast	gust of wind
	That made hem alle sore agast;	
4445	Therwith com both lighth and thonder	light and thunder
	Als the werlde shulde gon asonder.	go to pieces
	This weder forth the barel blew,	
	And into the roche wel righth it threw.	
	Whan it was in, it loke agein,	
4450	That roche that thai alle it seyn.	
	Thai thankeden God in that stede;	
	Thereafter ne hadden thai no drede.	
	And evere sithen into this day,	
	The hole is open there he lay.	
4455	With ston ne erthe ne may it ben dytt,	closed
	In tokne of that foule pytt,	
	For he ne was worthi, ich understonde	
	To have rest in water ne londe	
	He that demed Jhesu to ben yspylt	put to death
4460	To shameles deth withouten gylt.	
	Now wil I telle an aventoure	
	Of Judas, Goddes traytoure.	
	First yhereth hou he was borne	
	And sithen thorough falshede forlorne.	
4465	His owen fader highth Ruben,	
	And woned in Jerusalem;	lived
	Sabaria his wyf highth,	
	And was Judas moder righth.	
	Upon that nigth that he was geten,	conceived
4470	Ful the hous of devels seten;	The house was full of devils
	On slep Sabaria mette a wonder cas	dreamed
	In that ilche nighth of her son Judas,	
fol. 18va	Hou that the devels tolde alle this tale,	
	This childe shal be the Jewen bale;	the Jews' destruction
4475	Thorough hym shullen thai sorough yfynde	
	Alle thoo that ben of the Jewes kynde.	
	Of hire sweven she upbrayde,	dream; started up
	And to Ruben this tale she sayde,	

"We have don this nighth a ded   *deed*
4480   That al oure kynde may evermore drede;
        A childe is geten bitwene us two
        That shal brynge us alle to wo.
        Ruben, ich wil be siker biforne,
        Yif the childe of me be borne,
4485   Hou so evere I with hym spede,
        I kepe hym never fostre ne fede."   *foster nor feed*
        "Dame," quoth Ruben, "Artow wood?   *Are you crazy*
        Thou hast a spirit other than good.
        What lyst thee, dame, for to telle?   *What do you want*
4490   Sweven nys bot a foles spelle."   *A dream is but a fool's tale*
        "Sir," she seide, "this is myne afray;   *fear*
        It was me tolde thus as I lay.
        Yif I have conceyved as I wene,
        It schal tourne many on to tene."   *to grief*
4495   Ruben gan this al forgete,
        Tyl that his wyf was al grete.   *great (with child)*
        The childe was borne whan tyme cam;
        Michel sorough for hym thai nam.
        To kepen hym forth thai hadden care,
4500   And thai wolden hym nougth forfare.   *destroy*
        Anon thai ordeyned and hem bithougth,
        A nywe boot for hym was wrougth   *new boat; made*
        In to the cee he was ydighth,   *sea; put*
        And leten hym goo where he mighth.   *cast adrift*
4505   This boot was to and fro ycast,
        To londe it com atte last
        In an ylde that Caryoth highth,   *island; Iscariot*
        And there he took his name arighth.
        The quene com pleyeande of the londe   *amusing herself*
4510   With her maydens by the stronde   *shore*
        Of this boot she was wel yware
        And onon therto gan fare.
        "Maydens," she seide, "cometh with me;
        A boot cometh seilande on the cee.   *sailing*
4515   Sum wonder I hope it be, iwys,
        Go we and sen what it is."
        The boot in the sonde gan fast   *sand began to stick*
        As the water wawghes it cast,   *waves*
        Drye foot upon the gravel   *sand*
4520   Thai wenten therto fair and wel.
        A childe in riche clothes wounde
        In this boot thai han yfounde.

	Thai seighen it was a knave, I wys;	*boy*
	Than made the lefdy mychel blis.	
4525	She seide to hir maidens ilchone,	
	"Childe ne had I nevere non.	
	I shal done it kepen and save,	
fol. 18vb	Oure heritage yut may he have.	*inheritance*
	This chaunce is for us ful faire:	
4530	Now hath my lorde and I an haire."	*heir*
	Homwardes onon thai wolde,	
	And to hir lorde this tale she tolde.	
	Thorough her bothers red, therfore,	*both of their advice*
	She made as she with childe wore,	*pretended*
4535	And so was don to understonde	
	To alle the lordes of the londe.	
	Thai maden hym borne, and forth it tolde	
	Thorough the londe to yonge and olde.	
	For hym was made joye and game;	
4540	Judas Carioth thai gaven hym name.	
	Thai duden hym yeme as thai cone,	*cared for him; could*
	Righth als he were the kynges sone.	
	Sone afterward tyme byfel,	
	As God wolde, faire and wel,	
4545	A knave childe conceyved the quene,	
	That Judas mordred sithen, I wene.	*murdered*
	Whan he was borne thai weren glad,	
	For it was the first that thai had.	
	Thoo thai weren waxen and thryven	*When; grown; matured*
4550	In play often thai foughtten and stryven;	
	Judas often mysseide that other	*spoke ill of*
	That he wende had ben his brother.	*thought*
	Sone croketh that wil be wrong;	*becomes crooked*
	In eelde mote biten that yonge stong.	*must bite; stung*
4555	So gan Judas wyk to be,	
	Bothe thorough blood and destynee.	
	The nettle greveth the swete rose,	
	By thise two children we mowen suppose,	
	For Judas often that childe smoot	*smote*
4560	And made hym wepen teres hoot,	*weep hot tears*
	And thoo the quene it understood,	
	Hire thoughth the gamme nothing good.	
	She took it swithe sore to hert	
	And dude Judas to skoure smert	*beat*
4565	And tolde hym he nas nothing hem sybbe	*related*
	By flessh ne blood, bon ne rybbe,	*bone*

	Bot that he was a fundelyng	*foundling*
	Bothe to hir and to the kyng.	
	"And therfore smyte noughth my sone,	
4570	Yif thou wilt with us wone."	
	For this leten hym ne lyst	*he did not desire to cease*
	The kynges son to beten and byst.	*beat and strike*
	Thoo Judas wyst and understood	
	That he com thider by the flood,	*water*
4575	He wende noughth it were so,	*He did not believe*
	Bot that for wraththe it had ben do;	
	He was so cherilich with kyng and quene,	*lovingly treated*
	Forthi he wende it mighth noughth bene.	
	Ac the maydens witnessed that thing	*But*
4580	That weren at his fyndyng,	
	And than he herd of hem this fame,	*report*
	He took to hym ful mychel shame	

fol. 19ra — For he wende ever and oo
He were the kynges son til thoo.

4585	Wel pryvely that childe he slough,	
	And rigth onon he hym withdrough;	
	He was aferde to lesen his hede	*afraid; lose his head*
	Oither to han suffred sum othere dede,	
	And so he shulde had he abyde.	*remained*
4590	And therfore on his feet he hym dude	
	With messagers of that londe	
	That beren trowage, I understonde,	*carried truage*
	That wenten to Jerusalem,	
	In her compaignye thider he kem.	
4595	To Pilates court he hym drough,	
	And there he wexe sone couth ynough	*grew; renowned*
	With sotilté and with queyntise	*trickery; guile*
	And with giftes to hym and hise	
	As in the proverbes ben ytolde,	
4600	Bothe of yonge and of olde,	
	That gode men togedres drawe,	
	And everyche fole to his felawe,	
	So ferden Pilate and Judas,	
	So glad oither of othere was.	
4605	Her maners acorded everydel,	*manners agreed*
	Forthi oither loved othere wel.	*each*
	Yif Pilate to yvel redy was,	
	Yut redyer was Judas;	
	Fro that thai weren togedres yknowe	*known*
4610	Thai weren togedres a gret throwe.	*a long time*

It bifel that Pilate went on a daye
Into the cité hym for to playe,
And for to avisen hym up and doun   *observe*
To the kepyng of the toun.
4615   And als he loked on every side,
He seigh a tree that spred wyde
In an orchard there it stood.
That sighth menged al his blood   *provoked him*
For hym thoughth he was war
4620   That tre the fairest appels baar   *apples*
That evere he seigh in his lyve.
His herte stood on hem so blyve
That he ne wist what to done;
Bote he had of hem sone   *Unless*
4625   He thoughth his herte wolde to-brest,   *burst*
Ne wolde he never have no rest
Tyl he mighth at his wille
Of that fruyt have his fille.
And of this foule temptacioun
4630   Com sithen gret confusioun;
This orchard was, wel I woot,
Judas faders Carioth,
Man that was most pryvee
With Pilate of al his meignee.   *company*
4635   Pilate on this fruyt so thoughth,
Til he hem had ne lefte he noughth,
And forth onon he cleped Judas,
fol. 19rb And seide, "Thou most me helpen in this cas,
For I woot thu nylt leve for no greef   *will not cease for any trouble*
4640   To don that thing that me is leef.   *dear*
This othere day I went adoun
And seigh here withouten the toun
In an orchard upon a tre
The fairest apples that mightten be.
4645   Now as thou wilt myn hele save,
Helpe me of that fruyt to have,
I praie thee, Judas my derlyng,
Hastilich upon al thing."   *Quickly*
Judas seide, "Sir, I thee plighth,   *promise*
4650   Thou shalt have therof tonighth,
I hote thee er we slepen bothe
Who so be therof glad or wrothe."
Judas dude hym thider onon   *there*
As hym was taughtte for to gon;

4655	An hard hap than was hym biforne	*bad fate*
	That evere was he geten or borne.	
	He stirte in as hym ne roughth,	*jumped; cared*
	There Ruben woned that wist he noughth.	*dwelled*
	He understood nevere biforne	
4660	That he was there yborne,	
	Ne his kynde ne couthe hym knowe,	
	Though thai every day hym sowe.	*saw*
	Thai wenden noughth that it were he	
	That with Pilate was so pryvé;	*close*
4665	Thai wenden the cee had hym forfare	
	And fordon her alder care.	*destroyed; previous*
	Bot his destynee so ne wolde,	*destiny*
	For it most nedes be as it scholde.	
	Theigh men wenden stoppen Goddes cast,	*try to stop; intention*
4670	It wil forth gon atte last.	
	Whan he into the orchard cam,	
	Of the apples fast he nam;	*took*
	He loked aboute hym and helde hym trest,	*secure*
	And the fruyt in his bosome threst.	
4675	And therwith come Ruben thoo,	
	And seigh hym hou he plucked so,	*pulled (i.e., picked apples)*
	And wexe onon ful of yre	*anger*
	And seide, "Whi doostou so, beau sire?	*good sir*
	What hastou in my cloos to done?	*garden*
4680	Highe thee out, I rede thee sone,	*Get out*
	And yelde up the fruyt that thou hast,	
	And make amendes for the wast,	*waste*
	And yut thou shalt ful dere abye	*pay for*
	This apert vilenye."	*overt villainy*
4685	Judas ansuerd hym with pride	
	And seide, "I nyl leve, theigh thou chide,	*will not; scold*
	And bot thou sone goo by this day,	
	Thou shalt abyen, yif that I may."	*pay for it*
	"Yee," quoth Ruben, "Is it so?"	
4690	And onon he stirte hym to,	*leapt*
	And by the throte uche othere laughtte	*throat; grabbed*
	And togedres longe thai faughtte,	
fol. 19va	So that Judas atte last	
	Fro Ruben his fader brast,	*broke apart*
4695	And laughtte a ston that he fonde,	*grabbed*
	And hente his fader by the honde,	*seized*
	And bete hym bihynde on the hede,	
	That he fel doun under hym dede.	

	Out of the orchard blyve he fleye,	*quickly; flew*
4700	And hom to Pilate he took his weye.	
	Pilate had sone the fruyt ynome	*taken*
	And mychel thank he hym cone.	*could*
	Al his cas he tolde hym sone	
	That was for the apples done.	
4705	"Ye," quoth Pilate, "recche thee noughth.	*don't worry*
	There woot no man who it wroughth.	
	Bere thee wel and holde thee stille,	
	And thou shalt have al thi wille.	
	Alle the godes that hise wore	*goods; were*
4710	I graunte thee for evermore,	
	And the wyf that was his	
	Shal ben at thi wille, iwys."	
	Whan it toward evene cam,	*evening*
	The wyf into hir orchard nam,	*went*
4715	After hir housbonde she soughth fast,	
	And com and fonde hym atte last,	
	Stark ded ful sikerly.	*Utterly dead*
	She wende it had ben sodeynly,	*sudden*
	For she wyst noughth of that cas,	*knew*
4720	Whanne ne thorough whom it was.	
	Erly amorowe whan it was day,	*Early in the morning*
	She yede to Pilate for this affray.	*disturbance*
	"This nighth I fonde myne hosebonde ded;	
	I ne woot hou ne thorough whas red.	*whose bidding*
4725	Leve sir, helpe me at this res,	*Dear; emergency*
	For I am now al helples."	
	"Dame," quoth Pilate, "Drede thee no del,	
	Thou shalt ben holpen swithe wel.	
	Do beriye hym swithe and have no care,	
4730	For I have ordeyned al thi fare.	
	Dame, I thenke to given thee	
	The man that is pryvyest with me;	*closest*
	Take hym here by the honde,	
	For he shal be thine housebonde."	*(see note)*
4735	She ne durst ones seien naye	*dared not once say no*
	Bot Pilate and Judas for to paye.	*please*
	Thoo thai weren ywedded, Judas and she,	
	And hadden a while togedres be,	
	Upon a nighth she hire biwent,	*turned pale*
4740	And weep and sore hire byment.	*mourned*
	Judas asked, "What is this fare?	
	Whi makestou, dame, thus mychel care?	

	Is there oughth that agreveth thee?	*anything*
	Telle on, thou shalt avenged be."	
4745	"Sir," she seide, "I may wel sorowe,	
	Bothe on even and on morowe.	*evening; morning*
	I may be ever careful wyf	*sorrowful*
fol. 19vb	Whan I thenk upon my lyf;	
	Ruben and I a childe we had,	
4750	For hym ne be I nevere glad,	
	For in the cee we hym cast,	
	And there we seighen oure son last.	
	I woot he is ded sikerlich,	
	And his fader sodeynlich,	
4755	And now Pilate with bote yare	*zealous relief*
	Hath ynewed al my care.	*made new*
	Agein my wille he wedded me	*Against*
	To lede my lyf, Judas, with thee."	
	Thoo Judas understood this cas,	
4760	He seide that he hir son was.	
	"Allas," she seide, "artou so?	
	For now is woo upon woo,	
	Here is sorough upon sorough,	
	Hou shulde we evere ben borough?"	*saved*
4765	Thoo Judas wyst his moder his wyf	*knew his mother was his wife*
	And had bireft his fader his lyf,	*robbed*
	Of thise synnes he gan hym repent.	
	His moder redde hym that he went	*advised*
	To seken Jhesu the prophete,	
4770	His synnes foule for to bete.	*atone for*
	To Jhesu com this Judas,	
	And cried hym mercy for his trespas;	
	Jhesus graunted hym ful sone	
	And gaf hym penaunce for to done.	
4775	So wel he dude that he hym bade	
	That his deciple he hym made,	*disciple*
	He plesed so wel Jhesu hymselve,	
	He made hym on of th'apostles twelve,	
	And though he were to Jhesu leef,	*dear*
4780	Yut he was pryvelich his theef.	
	For Jhesus dude hym that honoure	
	That he made hym his procuratoure,	*steward*
	To beren the purs for queynt and wys	*carry; prudence; certainly*
	Of that was geven hym and hys.	
4785	And as men reden, the tenth part	
	He helde hym self to hym ward.	

	And to hasten his confusioun	*hasten his destruction*
	As telleth in the Passioun,	
	Thoo Marie with the oynement	
4790	Alithed Jhesu with gode entent,	*Anointed*
	That was riche, he understood,	*That (the ointment); costly*
	And therfore he was wel neigh wood	
	And wex wrooth with Marie	
	For it com noughth to his bailye.	*keeping*
4795	Worth thre hundreth pens cast it he	*estimated*
	Redy to sellen of her monee.	
	And for to restoren thatt oynement,	*compensate for*
	Thorough the fendes procurement,	
	For the tenthe peny his lorde he sold	
4800	Thritty pens, it wolde ben told.	
	Sorough and shame, wanhope and woo	*despair*
	Undertook Judas thoo,	
fol. 20ra	That he nolde God no mercy crye,	*he would not cry for mercy to God*
	For his falshede ne for his felonye.	*betrayal*
4805	And sithen he knew hym and his fame,	*him (Jesus); reputation*
	He was the more for to blame,	
	For he seigh hym evere curteis,	
	To hem that bisoughtten hym alweys,	*entreated*
	That weren seek or in trespas	*sick*
4810	Merciable and meke he was.	*Merciful and meek*
	Bot he most nedes ben lorne,	*lost*
	As it was loked hym biforne.	*ordained to him*
	Than to the Jewes agein he cam,	
	With her monee that he nam	*took*
4815	And seide, "Loketh there youre monee;	
	I have synned and so duden yee."	
	The Jewes seiden, "Thine is the synne —	
	Thou us bede Jhesu to wynne.	*offered; take*
	Thorough thee we comen hym to;	
4820	Forthi thenk what thou haste ydo."	*what you have done*
	Whan he seigh no better bote,	*remedy*
	He dude hym smertly on his fote.	*went quickly on foot*
	Into a wast pryvé stede	*secret waste place (i.e., a waste land)*
	A wicked maister gan hym lede,	*master*
4825	And there upon an hildre tree,	*elder*
	He henge hymself in pryveté.	
	His wombe cleef in two and rente,	*stomach split; tore*
	His guttes to his feet wente;	
	He ne mighth noughth flee that foule wreche,	*vengeance*
4830	For he ne wolde God knowleche.	

Up in the eir he most dye,   *air*
For he dude aungels vilenye,
And to us he dude also,
Therfore he most dyen so,
4835   For he solde Jhesu oure aller frende,   *the friend of us all*
For to dyen in Jewes kynde.
Thus suffred he his penaunce
To fulfillen the grete vengeaunce.
Bitwene Holy Thursday and Pentecost,
4840   Tho Jhesus sent the Holy Gost,
Peter stood among hem alle
And seide, "Yee witen what is bifalle;
On is lore that was oure brother.   *lost*
Amonge us we moten chese another.   *choose*
4845   We moten alle ben hole twelve,   *must all be a full twelve*
As oure maister bad hym selve,
For to prechen in every londe,
And thus he bad us, I understonde.
Of oure deciples chese we
4850   Of alle thoo that under us be,
Sexty and twelve under alle;
Loketh to whom it wil bifalle."
Thai casten loth by and by;   *cast lots*
Alweys it fel on Seynt Mathy.   *Matthias*
4855   Thus thai fulfilden her tale   *completed; total*
That Judas had broken with bale.   *evil*
Thus com Judas to his ende,
fol. 20rb   To dampnacioun withouten ende.   *damnation*

Now let we Judas and Pilate dwelle,
4860   Of the emperour I wil you telle.
At Jerusalem while that he lay,
His men wenten nighth and day
Into the cuntré abouten hem
Many a myle fro Jerusalem,   *mile*
4865   For al manere of vitaile   *kind of victuals*
Whan that any gan hem fayle.   *lack*
Tounes, castels, and cité,
Thai token thoroughout al Judé,
And duden Goddes lawghe to take
4870   And her fals bileve forsake,   *belief*
Also wide as thai went
Thorough the emperours comaundement;
And hem that wolden noughth, thai slough
With sorough and pyne ynough.

4875	Thai token into her baundoun	*control*
	The keyes of citees, castels, and toun,	
	And duden hem all, lesse and more,	
	Sweren hem feuté that there wore,	*fealty*
	And to his eyres withouten ende,	*heirs*
4880	Where so thai duelleden, fer or hende.	*far or near*
	Of lawghes he made amendement,	
	After his manere with gode entent;	
	He stabled alle thinges that he on thougth	*confirmed*
	So that there failed righth noughth,	
4885	And thus wroughth Sir Vaspasian	*did*
	That he had thank of God and man,	
	And Sir Titus dude also,	
	For he halpe wel therto.	
	Than bithoughth hym the emperour,	
4890	"Now mote I do myne men honoure	*must*
	That han duelled here with me,	
	In grete travaile for this cité.	
	For deth ne lyf ne for woo,	
	Ne for no wantyng from me goo,	*inadequacy*
4895	On no manere wise thai nolde,	
	Bot alway stifly with me holde."	*strongly*
	"Nou graunt mercy," he seide, "lordynges,	*many thanks*
	That yee me have holpen to ende thise thynges."	
	The riche he gaf londes and rentes,	*lands and income*
4900	The mene men grete avauncementz,	*common; promotions*
	And the povere men that litel wonnen	*poor; won little*
	And kepten inward and noughth out ronnen,	
	Hem he feffed fair and wel	*endowed*
	With the citezeinus loos catel.	*citizens'; forfeited property*
4905	Of al that evere there was founde,	
	I woot thai leften al bare grounde;	
	There hous and wal wel fast stood,	*house and wall*
	Thai swepten al clene away the good.	*possessions*
	Than took he leve of the londe	
4910	And toward shippes he gan fonde;	*proceed*
	Thai setten her wardeyns, his son and he,	*governors*
	In tounes and in the cuntré,	
fol. 20va	And thai and al her compaignye,	
	With song and mychel melodye,	
4915	Whan al was don unto the ende,	
	Homward thai gonnen for to wende.	
	Thai saileden so til that thai come	
	Hool and sounde agein to Rome.	*Whole*

	Ageins hym com Seint Clement,	*Towards*
4920	And al the clergie with hym went,	
	With song and faire processioun	
	The belles rongen thorough the toun.	
	Dame Verone with Seint Clement cam,	
	And the emperoures honde thai nam,	*took*
4925	And he kissed hem bothe two	
	With wepyng, and Titus also.	
	Anon whan Verone Jacob sawe,	
	To hym swithe she gan drawe;	
	She kyssed hym and clipte many a sithe	*embraced many times*
4930	And seide, "Jacob, ay be thou blithe!"	
	To Japhel and Josephus she dude also,	
	And to alle the othere that comen there tho,	
	And namelich to Josep of Aramathie,	*especially*
	For he was noblest of that compaygnye.	
4935	Seint Clement and Dame Verone than	
	Blissede thoo Sir Vaspasyan,	*Blessed*
	That had the Holy Gost wonne and soughth,	
	And alle the Cristene saved and broughth	
	Out of travaile into rest,	*toil*
4940	To lyven in Goddes servise best.	
	Evermore while thay lyve,	
	Uche man his warison is yyive,	*reward; given*
	That thai mightten faire lyve by,	
	Thai and her heires sykerly.	
4945	Seynt Clement seide to Vaspasyan,	
	"Me liketh that thou art lyves, man,	*alive*
	And that thou shalt Cristen be,	
	As thou and thine byhightten me.	*promised*
	Sir, I praie thee highe sone	*hurry*
4950	That yt were in dede done,	
	And bot thou do withouten ooth,	*unless; oath*
	God wil sone be with thee wrooth.	
	He hath broughth thee to thine above	
	His laghghe to undertake and love."	*law*
4955	Than seide the emperour ful sone,	
	"Dightte thee, sir, that thing were done."	*Prepare*
	Seint Clement of this was glad	
	And made redy als he hym bad;	
	He dude hem shaven more and lesse	
4960	Her hevedes in tokne of clennesse,	*heads*
	And clothen hem in white wede	*clothing*
	Alle that to Cristendom yede,	

	And for to maken solempnité	*ceremony*
	That thai alle alyves be.	
4965	Als holelich righth as thai went	*together*
	To resceiven the sacrement;	*sacrament*
	It semed that God wolde hem save,	
fol. 20vb	That made hem mychel joye to have.	
	And than weren thai alle shryven	*confessed*
4970	And absolucioun he has hem given,	*absolution*
	He cristned the emperour onon	*baptized*
	And his men everychon.	
	Seint Clement song hem a masse,	
	Thai offreden bothe more and lasse,	
4975	Her righth feith he hem taughtte	
	That weren wrothe he made saughtte;	*troubled; harmony*
	Thai lerned of hym so the laghghe,	*law*
	Thai lyveden sithen after his saghghe.	*teaching*
	The emperour made many a kyrke	*church*
4980	Of the temples that weren derk;	*dark*
	There maumetries hadden ben,	*idols*
	Riche atyre men mightten sen.	*Rich apparel*
	Wel richely he dude to wirche	
	Al that shulde to Holy Chirche,	
4985	Of golde and silver and riche stones,	
	With crafty werk for the nones,	
	And riche fee he yaf hem to	
	Of londes and rentes also.	
	He lete conferme the Cristen lawghe	
4990	Thorough everyche londe with strengthe and awghe.	
	He lete sperre the vernycle wel,	*enclose*
	In golde and cristal everydel,	*crystal*
	In crystal he dude it couche,	
	Men to seen and noughtt to touche,	
4995	And to Petres mynster gaf it righth:	*Peter's church*
	Of Dame Verone vernycle it highth.	
	Seint Clement took the coroune than	*crown*
	And sete it on Sir Vaspasian	
	And oyned hym with an oynement	*anointed*
5000	As falleth to kynges corounement.	*coronation*
	Vaspasyan thoughth God to queme	*serve*
	And took a riche dyademe,	*diadem*
	That is a mytre with coroune,	*head covering with a crown*
	This falleth the Pope with resoune.	*befits*
5005	He sacred the Pope Seint Clement	*consecrated*
	And sett on hym this with gode entent	

And bitook hym the Popes staf, *gave*
That was his croice that he hym gaf,
And seide, "Pope I conferme thee,
5010 Of alle clerkes most thou be
That is thorough everyche londe,
I wil that thai ben under thine honde
And thorough thee her lawghes be ladd
As Peter and other biforne thee hadd.
5015 And al the power that Pope shal have,
In alle poyntes I vouche save; *In every part*
Oure gostly fader I holde thee, *spiritual father*
Under God Almightty in Trinité."
Whan this was don in joye and pes,
5020 The emperour anon hym ches *chose*
Thorough every londe for to sende
Pes to make, lawghes to amende,
fol. 21ra And so it was holde upe lyf and lyme,
For hym and for his sones tyme,
5025 And lyved in swiche devocioun
That of hym com sithen gret renoun,
For God shewed sithen in that stede
Biforne his tumbe there he was dede, *tomb*
As we in his story fynde,
5030 There heled the croked and the blynde.
After hym regned Titus his sone,
Emperoure of curteys wone, *gracious conduct*
That evere yut was of tolde;
In gestes he is so holde *tales*
5035 That witnesseth he was alweys
Of godenesse and giftes so curteys.
Communelich he had seide and sworne, *Commonly*
"This day I have foul forlorne *lost*
Whan I ne have none giftes given.
5040 Hou shulde ich thusgates lyven, *therefore*
I that so mychel tresore have,
Bot I sum man therof gave?
For God sent me this richesse
To parten with hem that han lesse." *share*
5045 Now I hope seien fewe so *think*
As Titus was ywoned to do. *accustomed*
Now bothe Vaspasian and Titus,
Biteche you swete Jhesus! *Commend*

A merveile I may you telle
5050 Yif yee willeth a stounde duelle, *a while*

	What wonder toknes God sent	
	Siththe the emperour was hom went,	
	In tokne of that destruccioun.	
	Thai that ne dyed in that synful toun	*Those that did not die*
5055	And weren assentaund to his ded,	*compliant; death*
	In word, in werk, and in red,	
	Fro that thai toughtten it til it were don	*thought*
	Rest ne was with hem non,	
	Theigh thai aboden longe her penaunce	*Though; delayed*
5060	Or he sent them this vengeaunce.	*Before*
	Summe of the grettest that leften alyve	*remained*
	Of the Jewes comen ful blyve,	
	There the toun stood of Jerusalem	*Where*
	Her merkes on the ground thai nem,	*measurements; took*
5065	For to have bilded the toun ageyn.	*built*
	Bot I hope thai wroughtten in veyn,	*worked in vain*
	For God wolde ther kynde no more	
	Shulde lyven to dwellen thore.	*Should live to dwell there*
	Thai loked doune a litell stounde:	
5070	Croices hem thoughtten leien on the grounde,	*Crosses; lying*
	Of dew blood red unto her sighth,	*wet, bloody red*
	That made hem flen ful swithe, iplighth.	*flee; I promise*
	The rede croices bitokned onon	*red crosses*
	That her vengeaunce was noughth gon.	
5075	Another day agein thai comen,	
	And her merkes there thai nomen,	
	For thai wenden to speden bett;	*fare better*
fol. 21rb	Than fonden thai her clothes bysett	*covered*
	Ful of swiche croices as thai say	*saw*
5080	Bifore hem on that othere day.	
	Of this sighth hem thoughth no play;	*they thought it no game*
	Righth onon thennes thai fley.	
	The thrid day thai comen efte —	*again*
	Them hadden ben better thai hadden lefte!	
5085	Two warnynges thai hadden at wille	
	Yif thai wolden have holden hem stille.	
	Thai auntreden hem for to see	*ventured*
	Yif hym mightten have founded that cité.	
	Looth hem was that place forgoo,	*Loath (reluctant)*
5090	Yif thai mightten have comen therto.	
	And als thai stouped her merkes to take,	
	Thai hadden no mighth thennes to shake	
	For to tellen no carpentere	
	What mesure thai token there.[1]	

---

[1]   Lines 5092–94: *They had no power to run from there and tell a carpenter what measurements they took*

5095	Out of the erthe spronge a fer,	*fire*
	With sparcles hote and glowede cler,	*hot sparks; shining embers*
	That forbrent hem alle there,	*burnt*
	That body and bones askes were.	*ashes*
	Thus ended thoo foles with that fyre,	
5100	Ne hadden thai non othere hyre,	*payment*
	For thai duden withouten skyll	*good judgment*
	And alweys ageynus Goddes will.	*always*
	Thai mosten nedes alle forfare:	*be destroyed*
	Helpeth it nought for hem to care.	
5105	Thus the Jewes destroied wore	
	Als the prophetes seiden bifore,	
	Bot yut is nought the vengeaunce gon,	
	Tyl Goddes grete dome be don.	*last judgment*
	Loke what man wolde so han bede	
5110	As Jhesus Crist hymself dede;	
	He that is God and Lorde of alle	
	A meke God we mowe hym calle,	
	That so longe his wreche withdrough	*withheld*
	For the Jewes that hym slough,	
5115	For the toknes he dude hem sende,	
	Yif thai wolde hem oughth amende,	
	And so longe it forth glood	*passed*
	That fourty yer he abood.	
	Sithen he is so meke, loke hym to:	
5120	Lere we of hym to suffre so.	*Learn*
	Josephus the gode clerk,	
	He witnesseth al this werk;	
	He mighth the better the sothe writen,	*truth*
	For he sawe the vengeaunce smyten,	*saw; struck*
5125	Also he wroot al the story	
	Of al that fel into the Jewery.	*all that befell*
	And so witnesseth yonge Seynt Jame,	
	That suffred than so mychel shame,	
	And the knave, the prophete,	
5130	That was sleyn in the strete,	
	Why Jacob was agreved sore	
	As yee han herd here bifore.	
fol. 21va	Nichodemus bereth witnesse	
	Of thise thinges, more and lesse,	
5135	And of this thinges maketh mencyoun	
	In Nichodemes Passioun,	*the Gospel of Nicodemus*
	And in the gestes of emperoures	*tales*
	Of thise wonder aventours.	*events*

	In the Godspel also it sytt,	*Gospel*
5140	And fele prophetes witnesseth it,	*many*
	And the foure Godspellers uchon	*Gospellers (i.e., Evangelists)*
	To this wreche acorden in on.	*vengeance agree*
	Of al this werk that was wroughth,	
	Out of her bokes it is broughth.	
5145	Honoured be Oure Lorde so hende,	*courteous*
	Now is this story broughth to ende!	
	Yblissed moten thai alle be	
	Of Jhesu Crist in Trinité,	
	That thusgate his deth han wroken,	*in this way*
5150	As I have biforne spoken.	
	I hope that thai have, I wys,	
	To her mede Hevene blys;	*reward*
	God graunte us alle ther to be,	
	Amen, amen, par charité!	

Here endeth the vengeaunce of Goddes deth.

9   *Nichodeme.* The Gospel of Nicodemus, one of the major sources for the poem. The Middle English version of *GN* has been dated to the early to mid-fourteenth century, and it was also an influence on the York Cycle Plays (p. xxi).

11   *gestes of emperours.* The word *gestes* comes from Latin *gestae*, as in *res gestae* (things done) a Latin phrase meaning "history" (the manuscripts of the fourth-century CE historian Ammianus Marcellinus are entitled *Res Gestae*, for example). From Augustus on, emperors inevitably became the focal point of histories, such as Tacitus's *Annales and Histories.* Tacitus would have covered the Jewish war in the fifth book of the *Histories*, now largely lost. In Middle English, the term refers to stories, songs, and poems (*MED geste*).

32   *no leve.* Compare Matthew 21:23–27, Mark 11:27–33, and Luke 20:1–8, in which Jewish officials ask by whose authority Jesus is preaching. This matter would have particular resonance in medieval England: though canon law dictated that ordained priests could (and indeed were obliged to) preach, there was debate about this point. At the Blackfriars Council of 1382, it was declared incorrect that priests and deacons had authority to preach simply on the authority of their holy orders (Spencer, *English Preaching*, pp. 50–51). Canon law gave parish priests the right to preach in their own churches, but friars had to be given consent to preach in parish churches, and bishops were often required to adjudicate disagreements between friars and other clergy (Spencer, *English Preaching*, pp. 59–60).

40   *That thei ypocrites were.* Compare, for example, Matthew 23:14.

61–86   *As Nichodemus hath witnessed . . . And prively held.* The story of Nicodemus's conversation with Jesus appears in the canonical Gospels in John 3:1–17. Much of Nicodemus's role in this poem, however, expands on that account using *GN* as its primary source.

94   *unbynt and byndeth agayn.* Compare Matthew 16:19.

97–110   *Ones thei asked . . . to God almight.* This episode appears in three of the Gospels: Matthew 22:15–21; Mark 12:13-17; and Luke 20:19–26.

108   *kyng Cesar.* The first Roman emperor, born Gaius Octavius, was adopted by Julius Caesar to become Gaius Julius Caesar Octavianus (better known as Augustus). This phrase appears in all the synoptic gospels (Matthew 22:15–22; Mark 12:13–17; and Luke 20:20–26).

113–36   *By a womman . . . kep thee forthward fro syn.* The story of the woman taken in adultery occurs in
             John 8:2–11, but is also common in medieval cycle drama, with the episode appearing in the
             York (Play 24), N-Town (Play 24), and Chester (Play 12) plays. It is often paired (as in York
             and N-Town) with the raising of Lazarus, an episode to which *Destruction* refers. Thus, this
             episode was likely a familiar one for *Destruction's* audience.

158   *Moises and Abraham I seigh also.* Compare John 8:57–58, in which Jesus claims to have existed
             before Moses and Abraham.

181   *I com the lawghe to fulfille.* Compare Matthew 5:17.

186–87   *Youre michel temple I may felle / And areisen agein the thrid day.* Compare John 2:19–22.

209   *he held noght her Sabath day.* Sabbath-breaking episodes appear in all four Gospels; compare
             Matthew 12:1–14; Mark 2:23–27; Mark 3:1–6; Luke 6:1–11; and John 5:16–18.

247–49   *He hight to fordon . . . stronge and heighe.* Compare Luke 21:20–26.

286   *Forgeven hem that it scholde be.* Compare Luke 23:34.

305–16   *Whan schull we us wreke . . . have hym schent.* This episode in which Jewish leaders plot against
             Jesus most closely follows John 11:47–53. This conspiracy appears frequently in cycle plays as
             well: see Chester Play 14, York Play 26, Towneley Play 20, and N-Town Play 26.

309   *Romeins and other schull comen us on.* Roman foreign policy in the empire was predicated on
             maintenance, not expansion. The optimal state was for peace in the provinces and the flow of
             taxes to Rome. Given the extent of the imperial borders and the urgency of the northern bor-
             ders in particular, it would take a spectacular offense against the empire, such as the ambush
             of Gallus's men in the Beit-Horon pass, to earn Roman attention.

331–32   *atte Flum Jurdon . . . baptized Seint Jon.* Jesus is baptized by John in three of the canonical gos-
             pels (Matthew 3:13–17; Mark 1:9–11; Luke 3:21–22); the language of this Middle English
             construction seems to imply that Jesus baptized John, but that is not the case.

351   *Caiphas prophecied there.* Compare John 11:49–51. Caiphas, in his role as high priest, will
             oversee Jesus's trial later in the Gospels, particularly as recounted in Matthew 26 and John 18;
             he is a frequently-occurring character in Cycle plays (see N-Town Passion Play 1 and 2; York
             Play 29). Caiphas was appointed in 18 CE by Pontius Pilate's predecessor, Valerius Gratus,
             according to Josephus, *Jewish Antiquities*, 18.36.

377–78   *Whan men hem seen the more thai synne; / Tif thai ben fer the more thai blynne.* Though not a
             direct reference, the sentiment here seems to echo that of Whiting S333, that one sin leads to
             another. See also Whiting S340 and M591.

383   *Effroem.* This location appears as Ephraim in John 11:54, while Eusebius calls it Ephron. This is likely the same site as Ophrah (Josue [Joshua] 18:23), possibly modern al-Tayyiba (Avi-Yonan, "Ophrah," *Encyclopedia Judaica*, 15:439).

404   *wrightes son.* Matthew 13:55 is the only place where Joseph's trade as a carpenter is mentioned in the Gospels, though Jesus is also identified as the son of a wright in *GN* (lines 25–28).

407–16   *The tuelve namis . . . Jewes weren wrothe.* These figures are challenging whether or not Jesus is legitimate, born to married parents. In *GN*, a group of Jews swear before Pilate and Caiaphas that Mary and Joseph were indeed married (lines 243–48); they are not named in the Middle English account. However, a group of ten Jews assert some lines earlier that Jesus is the son of Mary and Joseph rather than the son of God; conflation of these two moments of *GN* may be the source for the list of names here. They are identified in *GN* as Simon, Zayrus, Caiphas, Datan, Gamaliel, Neptalim, Levi, Judas, Alexander, and Annas (lines 14–16).

445–46   *Centurio biheld . . . Goddus son Jesus.* Compare Mark 15:39 and Matthew 27:54, where the centurion identifies Jesus as God's son. In Luke 23:47, in contrast, Jesus is called simply "a just man." See also *GN*, lines 673–76, and York Play 36, lines 322–25 and Chester Play 16, lines 360–367.

447   *Longens the knyght.* Longinus is Biblical; at least, there is a figure who pierces Jesus in John 19:34. (He is often conflated with the centurion who identifies Jesus as the son of God: see Luke 23:47, Matthew 27:54, and Mark 15:39.) This figure is unnamed in the Gospels, though named as Longinus in *GN*, lines 625–28; he also appears in York Play 36, lines 691–99 and in Chester Play 16, where he is presented as distinct from the centurion (pp. 322–23). *LA* provides a description of the piercing of Jesus's side by Longinus that extends to include Longinus's conversion, twenty-eight years of monastic life, and eventual martyrdom (1:184).

449–54   *The gret temple atwo aclef . . . of her kyn.* Matthew 27:50–53 similarly recounts that tombs open and dead people are resurrected at the moment of Jesus's death. The temple curtain tears in two at Jesus's death in three of the canonical Gospels: Matthew 27:51, Mark 15:38, and Luke 23:45.

469   *Adam bigan first the game.* This is a reference to the "original sin" in Genesis; Adam is often juxtaposed to Jesus in particular by theologians; see for example Augustine, *City of God*, book 14 on original sin; and book 13, chapter 23, trans. Walsh and Monahan, pp. 335–38, on the juxtaposition of Adam and Jesus.

474   *thai hadden sought his mercy.* The theological point that Jesus's mercy applies even to Judas, his betrayer, likely originates in Augustine, who discusses Judas in *City of God* (book 1, chapter 17, trans. Zema and Walsh, pp. 46–47). As Leydon notes in his reading of Augustine, "Augustine isolates despair — the failure to believe in (or pray for) God's mercy — as the reason that the remorseful Judas was unable to be fully repentant, and consequently the cause of his suicide" ("Insular Iscariot," p. 14).

483–84   *Aggeus, Phinees, and Escandas . . . hou it was.* These witnesses are not named either in Biblical accounts or in *GN*.

487   *Carianus and Elyntheus.* Munro identifies this material as referring to *GN* (p. 350). In that account, the two men are raised from the dead at Jesus's resurrection and recount the Harrowing of Hell (*GN*, lines 1095–1636).

492   *Seynt Mighel.* Saint Michael, whose feast is observed on September 29, was an archangel often associated with intercession for the souls of the dead. He appears in both the Book of Daniel and the Book of Revelation. See Farmer, *Dictionary of Saints*, pp. 348–49.

497   *Tho spak Nichodemus onon.* Nicodemus and Joseph of Arimathea both condemn the Jews for the death of Jesus; this material draws on *GN*, lines 739–768.

508   *That he was to Jhesu sworne.* Joseph of Arimathea denounces his Jewish identity and claims to be Christian. This is a moment when the poem diverges from *GN*, in which Joseph is arrested for burying Jesus and not directly accused of following Jesus.

519–20   *He is nought my frende, ye han herd told, / That seith as myne hert wold.* Though this is not directly attested in Whiting, it seems to be functioning proverbially; see for example Whiting F664.

523   *in a strong prisoun.* The imprisonment of Joseph of Arimathea draws heavily on *GN*, lines 769–792.

539   *Body for body.* That is, they guaranteed Joseph's imprisonment at the cost of their own lives.

555   *wymmen there comen thre.* Though accounts of women coming to the tomb appear in all four gospels, only Mark's identifies three women (Mark 16:1). The so-called "three Maries" — Mary Magdalene, Mary Salome, and Mary Jacobi — also feature in cycle drama, for example N-Town Play 36 and Chester Play 18.

559   *blake.* In using color symbolism, the poem engages in discourses of whiteness developing during this period; that is, the poem uses "black" here as a shorthand for sin and wickedness. For a careful detailing of the use of blackness as signifying foreignness — though not always unequivocal evil — see Heng, *Invention of Race*, chapter 4.

565   *Pilate.* The historical Pontius Pilate was prefect of Judea under Tiberius from 26/27 CE to 36/37 CE. The Roman *gens* Pontii is well attested in inscriptions, as is Pilate himself in an inscription on the so-called "Pilate stone" discovered in 1961 in Caesarea Maritima, as well as accounts of Josephus and Philo. This is all we know about the man beyond what is in the New Testament.

583   *Al halp nought that thai ne tolde.* Compare *GN*, lines 853–64, in which the knights are bribed to lie and claim that Jesus was stolen by his disciples, which the people believe.

590   *Letres of pes.* That is, letters granting the bearer safe passage through the territory they control. These letters have literary analogues in a variety of texts, especially medieval travel texts: compare, for example, Marco Polo's *Divisement du Monde*, in which Polo's father and uncle (Niccolo and Maffeo) are given "a golden tablet on which was contained that the . . . envoys, in all the places they might go, should be given all the lodgings they needed and horses and men to escort them from one land to another" (ed. Kinoshita, p. 6), or several pages later where Marco is given similar privileges (p. 13). Similarly, in the *Book of John Mandeville*, while the Muslims of Jerusalem limit Jewish and Christian access to the Dome of the Rock, a major holy site, the Mandeville narrator is given access to this and other holy sites "on the strength of letters from the Sultan" (ed. Higgins, p. 50); the narrator then describes a system of seals and letters that grant their bearers access to controlled spaces.

597–656 *"Sires," he seide . . . yee hadden sente.* The rescue of Joseph of Arimathea, and the circumstances in which he explains it to the assembled Jews, follows *GN*, lines 1033–80.

629   *Mount of Olyvete.* The Mount of Olives, located east of Jerusalem on the road from Jericho to Jerusalem, is mentioned in all four Gospels and identified in Acts 1:12 as the site of the Ascension. Shrines existed on the site from before 400 CE, when the early pilgrim traveler Egeria mentions their presence. See Musholt, "Mount of Olives," *New Catholic Encyclopedia*, 10:33–34. The site is mentioned as the site of the Ascension in *LA*, as well, which calculates its distance from the city (1:291, 293).

639   *And summe that arisen thoo he aroos.* The poem here refers not only to the Gospel of Matthew, but to the events that occur previously in the text, at lines 449–54. These references to events that have occurred or will occur are very frequent in the poem, creating a network of inter- and intratextual references.

649   *drede for no Jew.* This adjustment from *GN* emphasizes Joseph of Arimathea's Christian status and reinforces the strong Jewish/Christian binary present in the poem.

671   *In her toun wal thai shetten hym.* Joseph of Arimathea is imprisoned inside the town wall as a punishment for his preaching; he stays there for seven years, until he is freed by Titus (lines 4090–4114). There does not seem to be an analogue for this second imprisonment, which extends the Joseph of Arimathea story even from its expansion in *GN*. For more on early expansions of Joseph of Arimathea, see William John Lyons, *Joseph of Arimathea*, especially chapter 3.

681   *Listneth you, ich wil you rede.* Formulae like this one appear frequently in Middle English romance, invoking some sense of oral reception, but this instance is particularly interesting in the context of L. In this manuscript, the first 680 lines have been bound at the end of the book, and thus this formula appears at the start of the codex's opening folio. Thus, though it is meant to indicate a transition in the poem, it seems to have indicated a beginning to some reader.

700   *And spaak thus toward the citee.* Many passages in the Gospels were imagined as prefiguring the destruction of Jerusalem by medieval Christian theologians; passages of particular interest

included Luke 13:34; Luke 19:41–44; Luke 21:5–6; Luke 23:27–31; Mark 13:5–37; Matthew 23:37–39; and Matthew 24:1–36. This material was of interest in preaching and performance well into the early modern period, as Beatrice Groves attests; see Groves, *Destruction of Jerusalem in Early Modern English Literature*, especially pp. 18–20.

716   *Hosie and Jeremye.* References to violence and destruction in Jerusalem are frequent in these books of the Bible; see for example Jeremias 9:11, Jeremias 19, Osee [Hosea] 3:4, Isaias 1, and Isaias 2. Many of these verses are used in present-day theological defenses of Christian Zionism.

724   *And seide to hem.* For this description of sufferings at the end of time (or at the destruction of Jerusalem), compare especially Luke 21:20–26.

761–92   *In the temple . . . ne lenge to duelle.* This episode of Jesus overturning tables in the temple origi-nates, of course, in the Gospel, particularly Matthew 21:12–13; Mark 11:15–18; Luke 19:45–46; and John 2:13–22. The whip of cords referenced here is unique to John's version. The de-scription here is nonetheless noteworthy for its references to "Fraunce" and "pilgrimes". The poem engages in temporal blurring; "France" would not be a useful geographical designation for the historical Jesus. This blurring emphasizes the extent to which the poem is more closely aligned with Crusades romance than with the historical events of the Temple's destruction by Roman forces.

804–06   *For his word so sore thai quook . . . As ded men oither men in swoughne.* Compare John 18:6, where those who have come to capture Jesus fall to the ground when he identifies himself.

831   *Dispersioun.* That is, the Diaspora, or the displacement of Jewish communities after the 587 BCE capture of Jerusalem by the Babylonians, led by Nebuchadnezzar. As Denise Eileen McCoskey notes, historians differ in identifying the Babylonian or the Roman capture of Jerusalem as primarily central to ideas of diaspora and dispersal ("Diaspora in the Reading of Jewish History," p. 390). For a rich and complex study of diaspora's impact on Jewish identity and community, see also Erich Gruen, *Diaspora: Jews amid Greeks and Romans.* See also lines 867–78, where diaspora in the aftermath of the Temple's fall is further described.

833   *pilrynage.* Pilgrimage is here associated with the book of Exodus, in which the Jewish people traveled through the wilderness after escaping captivity in Egypt.

855   *servage.* While this seems to refer to the Babylonian diaspora and captivity (see note to line 831, above), it also invokes the recurrent emphasis on the lack of a sovereign Jewish homeland in medieval texts. Compare, for example, the *Book of John Mandeville*, where the Jews living enclosed in the mountains pay rent to the Queen of the Amazons (ed. Higgins, pp. 158–59). See also Akbari, *Idols in the East*, pp. 115–16.

866   *yer of gret perdoun.* This seems to refer to a Jubilee year, or a year in which special indulgences were granted to pilgrims to Rome. As Gary Dixon describes the Jubilee in the year 1300, "the Jubilee was unlike any other pilgrimage. First of all, it was authorized solely by the Pope.

Secondly, the only acceptable destination was Rome. Thirdly, the Jubilee was limited to a pre-scribed calendrical period . . . Finally, as a supreme inducement,the Pope granted a religious reward to Jubilee pilgrims which was unprecedented for non-crusaders, a plenary indulgence" ("The Crowd at the Feet," p. 285). He further notes that crusades and jubilees were closely linked (p. 285), so the invocation of jubilee here adds to the crusading ethos of the poem. It is worth noting that the idea of the Jubilee is Biblical in origin and comes from Jewish tradition: see Leviticus 25:10–16. Further, the tradition of the Jubilee year continues: 2000 was also a Jubilee year.

888   *Amonge the Jewes seide thus.* This appears to be a reference to the so-called *"Testimonium Flavium,"* a passage in *Jewish Antiquities* 18.63–64, where Josephus appears to offer testimo-ny about the divinity of Jesus. In addition, there is also the scene in *JW* (3.399–408) where Josephus, captured by the Romans, prophesizes to Vespasian that he will soon become emper-or. It appears to be some combination of Christian witness and oracular reputation.

913–82   *Sithen thai slough the yonge Seint Jame . . . his good dede.* This account of St. James the Less draws heavily on *LA* (1:269–77). A short version of the account also appears in the *South English Legendary* (ed. D'Evelyn and Mills, 1:165–67). The *LA* account, which in turn draws on Josephus, Hegesippus, and Jerome, sets James's martyrdom in the temple for his outspoken support of Jesus. Munro suggests Eusebius as the ultimate source for this anecdote (pp. 351–52): Eusebius also describes James's devotion and martrydom, attributing to Hegesippus the details that James did not bathe; did not drink wine or eat meat; wore linen; and had knees hardened like camel's horn due to constant prayer (*EH* 2.23).

938   *bisshop of the toun.* According to Eusebius (*EH* 2.23), James was bishop of Jerusalem after Peter left the region; this claim originates in James's role in the book of Acts (Acts 12, 15). *LA* identifies him as bishop, claiming to follow Hegesippus (1:271). See also Jerome, *On Illustrious Men*, chapter 2 (trans. Halton, pp. 7–10).

950   *As chamailes knees that ben of horne.* See *MED kne* (n.), sense 2a which cites this line. The im-plication here is that James's knees have become hard, like horn, due to consistent prayer and kneeling on unforgiving surfaces.

955   *Paske Day.* The *MED* lists "Paske" as both Passover and Easter. This potential confusion indi-cates the extent to which supersessionist thought is at work here; it also creates confusion in terms of when, precisely, these events are happening. *LA* claims this martyrdom occurred on Passover in the thirtieth year of James's tenure as bishop (1:272), and *Siege* likewise sets the events at "Paske-tyme" (*SJ*, line 320).

977   *fullyng staf.* Fulling is the process of beating wool cloth; thus, a fulling staff is a heavy stick one would use to beat the damp cloth. According to *LA*, this detail of James's death by fulling staff originates in Hegesippus (1:272).

1001–1122 *Listneth now . . . meynted forth her fals lawghe.* The poem lists ten signs given as warnings of the city's looming destruction. The first is the witness of James before his martyrdom (lines

999–1000); the second is a feast at which the Jews spontaneously begin to attack and kill each other (lines 1005–18); the third is when a cow meant for sacrifice gives birth to a lamb in the temple (lines 1019–28); the fourth is a bright light that appears in the middle of the night at the temple, as though it were 3 PM (lines 1029–35); the fifth is when the gates of Jerusalem are blown open by a great wind (lines 1036–44); the sixth is when a mysterious voice is heard by the Jewish priests in the temple (lines 1045–56); the seventh is when stars appear in the sky above the city in the shape of a sword (lines 1057–64); the eighth is when stars in the shape of armed men fighting on horseback appear (lines 1065–76); the ninth is when chariots appear in the air (lines 1077–82); and the tenth is when James, Ananias's son, has a vision of the city's destruction (lines 1083–1114).

These warnings of the pending fall of Jerusalem seem to come from Eusebius, who attributes them to Josephus. Eusebius lists them as follows: first, the appearance of the star hanging over the city like a sword; second, a comet; third, a light on the altar for an hour during Passover (which he calls the "Feast of Unleavened Bread"); fourth, the cow giving birth to the lamb; fifth, the gate of the city having opened itself (rather than being blown open by a great wind, as in *Destruction*); sixth, the chariots in the air; seventh, the priests who hear the cry "we go hence"; and lastly, the prophet named Jesus son of Ananias, who laments the fate of Jerusalem despite being beaten and punished (*EH* 3.8). Many of these warnings also appear in *LA*, which likewise attributes them to Josephus. *LA* includes the death of James, the sword in the sky, the bright light in the Temple (there at the ninth hour of the night), the heifer giving birth to a lamb, the chariots and armed men in the sky, the mysterious voice in the temple, and the prophesy of Jesus son of Ananias. However, it omits the comet and the gates opening on their own (1:273). The signs of Jerusalem's impending fall occur considerably later in *Siege*, and they are less extensive: *Siege* mentions a sword hanging over the town, as well as armed men in the air, a calf giving birth to a lamb, and the prophet (nameless in *Siege*) who is killed by a slung rock (*SJ*, lines 1221–36). Though *Siege* recounts them, it does not make much of these signs, perhaps because they appear so late in the poem; by placing them much earlier, they become another means by which *Destruction* can cast blame on the Jews for their failure to repent the death of Jesus.

1049   *Witsoneeday.* Whitsunday, or Pentecost, is the day the Christian church celebrates the Holy Spirit descending on Jesus's apostles after his death, causing them to speak in tongues and preach the Gospel. See Acts 2 for the Biblical account. Pentecost remains a liturgical season in many Christian traditions.

1127–28   *Natheles her lawghe gan blynne / And the niwe lawghe to bigynne.* The distinction made here between the Old Law and the New Law follows a distinction in Christian theology between Judaism and Christianity; that is, after Jesus's death and resurrection, Christianity posits that Jesus's teachings as reflected in the canonical Gospels serve as a new law that supercedes Jewish teaching. The distinction is made in Thomas Aquinas's *Summa Theologiae*, ed. Gilby, particularly questions 90–97.

1130   *And "consummatum est" seide.* Jesus's words from the cross, "It is finished", appear in John 19:30.

1135   *Her owen bokes.* This is likely a reference to the works of Josephus.

1141   *Whan Seint Eleyne the croice fonde.* Helen's discovery of the true cross appears in *LA*, 1:278–83. Helen, the mother of Constantine, comes to Jerusalem and orders the Jews of the region to tell her where the cross is hidden, locates it, and brings it to Rome along with the nails that held Jesus to the wood. The story, which claims the Jews themselves hid the cross, is often used as justification for antisemitism; compare the episode's appearance twice in the *Book of John Mandeville* (ed. Higgins, pp. 10, 47).

1153–54 *The erthen vessel . . . of metal is wrought.* Proverbial: compare Whiting P319; Munro notes this reference (p. 353).

1157   *Lete we now the Jewes duelle.* This type of formula is typical of Middle English romances, appearing, for example, in *Bevis of Hampton* ("Let we now ben is em Saber / And speke of Beves, the maseger!", ed. Herzman, Drake, and Salisbury, lines 1345–46) or in Chaucer's Knight's Tale ("Lete I this noble duc to Atthenes ryde," *CT* I [A] 873). On these romance tags more generally, see Susan Wittig, *Stylistic and Narrative Structures*. This line also marks the end of the preliminary material in *Destruction*, after which the poem moves into Vespasian's healing and the siege of the city.

1161   *kyng, Sir Vaspasian.* The text has Vespasian as king in Gaul, which is unhistorical. Before his appointment to replace Cestus in Judea, Vespasian had a fairly standard, if not illustrious, career in the government, achieving the consulate in 51 CE. His retirement subsequently may be due to earning the emnity of Claudius's last and fatal wife, Agrippina. For a comprehensive account of Vespasian's life, see Barbara Levick's biography, *Vespasian*.

1163   *meselrie.* "Meselrie," or leprosy, was understood in the Middle Ages as a mark of sinfulness or uncleanness. As R. I. Moore notes, in England, lepers could not inherit property (p. 59); for Christians, leprosy was often associated with sexual misconduct or even heresy. As Moore further suggests, "For all imaginative purposes heretics, Jews and lepers were interchangeable" (p. 65). (See Moore, *Formation*, pp. 45–65 for an overview of the view and treatment of lepers.) In literary representations, leprosy as punishment is central to *Amis and Amiloun*, where Amiloun is struck with leprosy for prioritizing his sworn oath to Amis over upholding truth (ed. Foster, lines 1255–82). In Vespasian's case, then, his leprosy may be interpreted as a sign of his status outside Christian doctrine, though Pope Clement will suggest later in the poem that Vespasian's suffering, which comes from God, is designed to give God a chance to show his power.

1174   *righth name Vaspasianus.* According to Suetonius (*Divine Vespasian* 1, trans. Rolfe), Vespasian derived his name from his mother's (Vespasia Pollio) family. The Vespasii were a family of some standing at Nursia (modern Norcia) in Umbria.

1177   *Of thise waspes his name he took.* This passage seeks to explain Vespasian's name, which purportedly comes from the "waspes" (Latin *vespa*) living in his nose. In *LA*, Vespasian suffers from worms, rather than wasps, living in his nose (1:274).

1215   *With a viis.* Vespasian's men use a winch, a mechanical device using a pulley system, to deliver
            his meals. This allows them to feed him without touching him or indeed coming too close
            to him, emphasizing the smell of his body as well as the fear of contagion that was especially
            strong where leprosy was concerned. For more on leprosy, see note to line 1163, above.

1221–22   *Alle yvels comen of Goddes sonde . . . ich understonde.* The implication here is that illnesses come
            from God and thus can be alleviated by God. See *MED ivel* (n.), sense 5a.

1223   *sept sages.* This is the first of two references in the text to the "Seven Sages," likely a reference
            to *Seven Sages of Rome*, a popular frame tale. These references are particularly notable because
            neither this story nor the later reference to Herod (line 4367) appears in the *Seven Sages of
            Rome*. As Moe notes, "The only similarity found between *Titus and Vespasian* and any ver-
            sion of the *Seven Sages* is in the Old French *Romans des Sept Sages*, which has the leprous
            Vaspasianus, emperor of Rome, healed by Cilofida" ("A Study of Two Manuscripts," p. 35).

1226   *Sir Thiberius.* Tiberus was emperor from 14–37 CE. He was the natural son of Augustus's
            third wife, Livia, and her first husband, T. Claudius Nero, and he was adopted as Augustus's
            last choice heir in 4 CE. This merger of the Julian gens (represented by Augustus, via adoption
            by Julius Caesar) and the Claudian gens (represented by Tiberius via Livia) led to what mod-
            ern historians refer to as the Julio-Claudian dynasty, beginning around 30 BCE with Augustus
            and concluding in 68 CE with the death of Nero.

1231   *the tyme of his eighttende yere.* That is, the eighteenth year of Tiberius's reign, putting the cruci-
            fixion around 35 CE.

1236   *A lettre endited by on assent.* This letter is referenced in *LA* (1:213), which cites Peter Comestor's
            Historia Scholastica as its source. However, Comestor reports that Pilate was exiled for the ac-
            tions described here, which contradicts the narrative provided earlier in *LA* and in this poem
            (*PL* 198.1053–1722, especially columns 1585 and 1680). Eusebius likewise claims that Pilate
            tormented the Jews after the death of Jesus: "in Judaea Pilate, under whom the crime against
            the Saviour was perpetrated, made an attempt on the temple, still standing in Jerusalem, con-
            trary to the privileges granted to the Jews, and harassed them to the utmost" (*EH* 2.5).

1244   *To slen the childer giltles.* This seems to attribute the Slaughter of the Innocents to Pilate
            rather than Herod, which contradicts line 2445 later in the poem, where Herod is blamed.
            However, *LA* notes that in the *Historia Scholastica*, the Jews accuse Pilate of the Slaughter of
            the Innocents as well as the abuse of temple funds (1:213–14).

1246   *Of fals goddes set up ymages.* While we have no evidence Pilate himself did this, Caligula
            (reigned 37–41 CE) attempted towards the end of his reign to have a statue of himself set up
            in the temple in Jerusalem and to have the temple rededicated to the Roman imperial cult. The
            Roman legate in Syria, P. Petronius, was able to delay the execution of this plan, and it became
            moot once Caligula was assassinated. See *JW* 2.184–203 and *Jewish Antiquities* 18.261–309.

1251   *conduyt merveillous.* Eusebius describes Pilate's use of temple money to build an aqueduct (*EH* 2.6).

1265–67   *After hym regned Sir Gayus . . . And sithen Nero.* This lineage is not quite accurate — or, rather, it is incomplete. Tiberius was emperor from 14–37, followed by Caligula (37–41 CE); Claudius (41–54 CE); Nero (54–68 CE); and finally Vespasian (69–79 CE) and his son Titus (79–81 CE). Eusebius includes Galba and Otho (both of whom were involved in the Roman civil war) after Nero's reign (*EH* 3.5). In addition, Vitellius also made a claim to the throne after Otho, though his forces were defeated by Vespasian's in 69 CE (the infamous "year of the four emperors").

1268   *That slough bothe Peter and Poule.* The legend of Nero's slaughter of Peter and Paul on the same day appears in *LA*, 1:344–48. Orosius also recounts this detail (*Seven Books of History*, ed. Fear, 7.7.10, pp. 334–35).

1273   *Galice and Gascoyne.* "Galice" here is somewhat confusing. It may refer to Galicia, in northwestern Spain, a region that was under Roman control from 411 to 585. The area gained prominence as part of the pilgrimage route to Santiago de Compostela after the twelfth century (D'Emilio, "Galicia," *Oxford Dictionary of the Middle Ages*, p. 683). However, both *Siege* and *LA* give Galatia, which is a region of Asia Minor. Galatia would be a particularly interesting choice since Paul's letters to the Galatians emphasize correct faith and works over the law (Brooks, "Galatia, Galatians," *Encyclopedia of Early Christianity*, p. 447). "Gascoyne" is somewhat more straightforward, presumably suggesting Gascony: Munro, however, suggests that it may be a term for Aquitaine (p. 31). We have no records that Vespasian had any service in these areas (though he did participate in the invasion of Britain under Claudius). See Levick, *Vespasian*, pp. 4–27.

1276   *a son that highth Titus.* Titus Flavius Vespasianus was born in 39, and reigned from 79–81 CE. He was the elder son of his father; his younger brother Domitian reigned from 81–96 CE. For more on his life, see Brian Jones, *The Emperor Titus*.

1277   *cité of Burdeux.* Bordeaux, a trading port on the Garonne River in France, had links to both Spain (perhaps explaining "Galice" in line 1273) and to Britain (Hsy, "Bordeaux," *Oxford Dictionary of the Middle Ages*, p. 279). The city was also a port of call for English Christian pilgrims traveling to Rome or Jerusalem: see Nicholson, "Haunted Itineraries," p. 453. A. Boyarin notes that the route from Jerusalem to Bordeaux was a known crusader route (*Siege of Jerusalem*, p. 34n1).

1285   *The maister com bifore his kne.* These events unfold differently in *Siege*. In that version, Nathan departs for Nero, bringing word that the tribute from the Jews is behind, considerably earlier in *Siege* (*SJ*, lines 45–54). After being blown off-course, he is similarly questioned by Titus, king of Bordeaux, who suffers from a cancer (that is, a growth) on his face. Nathan provides a description of the Trinity and the life of Jesus in which he explicitly mentions the Vernicle of Veronica and its healing powers (lines 57–172). Most importantly, Nathan's account leads to Titus's immediate baptism: he is healed through his belief in Nathan's words. He cries out in anger at Rome's complicity in Jesus's death and is immediately healed, after which he declares that he will avenge Christ's death (lines 185–88). The poem claims Titus's baptism, immediately after this vow, "[m]ade hym Cristen kyng that for Crist werred" (line 194).

1300   *A wynde me hath dryven another gate.* Nathan is blown off course by a storm. Storms at sea that redirect travelers are often taken as a sign of God's providence in medieval romance, as the popularity of Constance cycle romances like Chaucer's Man of Law's Tale and others can attest; see Cooper, *The English Romance in Time*, especially chapter 2. This is also a common feature of hagiography, particularly notable in narratives of St. Brendan.

1329   *arered Lazar the knighth.* The raising of Lazarus occurs in John 11:1–45 and features in many medieval dramatic works: see the Digby Magdalen play (lines 869–924); Towneley Play 31; York Play 24; N-Town Play 25; and Chester Play 13.

1337–38   *Ten and sexty langages I herd / That thai of her maister lerd.* Acts 2 recounts the coming of the Holy Spirit and the disciples' ability to speak in tongues, commemorated in the feast of Pentecost. The number of languages, however, is not referenced in the account in Acts.

1340   *To prechen his name thorough his sonde.* The roots of Jesus sending out the disciples are Biblical: compare Matthew 28:18–19 and Mark 16:14–18.

1357–58   *Sir Nero . . . slough hymselven sone than.* Nero, when it was clear his reign was over, did prepare himself for suicide, but couldn't go through with it, getting a slave Epaphroditus to strike the killing blow. "What an artist dies with me!" the fatuous prince exclaimed. See Suetonius, *Nero* 49, trans. Rolfe.

1361   *Onon thai chosen Vaspasian.* When Vitellius's forces were defeated by Vespasian's forces at Cremona, Vespasian himself was still in Egypt. At the defeat of Vitellius, the Senate acclaimed Vespasian emperor on December 21, 69 CE. He had left Titus in command at Judea as he tried for the throne.

1378   *Pilates letter.* References to a letter from Pilate to Tiberius that recounts the events of Jesus's death and resurrection also appears in Eusebius (*EH* 2.2), Orosius (*Seven Books of History*, ed. Fear, 7.4.5, p. 325), and Gregory of Tours, *The History of the Franks*, where, according to Arnold Williams, it is "Christian in tone" (*Characterization*, p. 2).

1407   *I sat as justise in domes sted.* Pilate's insistence here that he is not guilty of Jesus's death parallels line 1434 and note, below. While this has its origins in Matthew 27:24, in which Pilate washes his hands and disavows guilt in Jesus's death, this moment is strongly reflected in cycle plays: see for example Chester Play 16, lines 235–44 (p. 308). Pilate, as a procurator, was more of a bureaucrat than a military governor; the real military power in the region lay with the governor of Syria who commanded legions.

1434   *It was her dede and her thoughth.* Continued blaming of Jews for Christ's death was, of course, a common problem in the theology of the Middle Ages and indeed to the present day; the emphasis on Jewish culpability is especially noteworthy in the Gospel of John. Rubin notes this imagined guilt for the crucifixion became increasingly more central to Christian theology alongside the proliferation of host desecration narratives: "Jews were increasingly being associated with vicious and wilful attacks against the host, just as the theological interpretation of their culpability in the crucifixion was being rethought by mendicant theologians" (*Corpus Christi*, p. 122). See also Rubin, *Gentile Tales*, p. 141.

1444   *To saien that he was stolen hem froo.* This order given to the knights repeats Matthew 28:11–15, in which the chief priests pay the guards to report that Jesus's body was stolen by his disciples. The guards also spread this false information in *GN* (lines 853–64).

1471   *He was warned also by his wyf.* In Matthew 27:19, on the basis of a dream, Pilate's wife warns him that he should not condemn Jesus. Pilate receives a similar warning in *GN*, lines 193–200.

1484   *Hou Pilate com into this word.* This is the beginning of a lengthy digression on the life of Pilate, one of two major episodes not present in the short version of *Destruction*. On the surface level, it seems to echo Cain's fratricide of Abel, though in Pilate's case it is only his half-brother. *LA* recounts essentially this narrative (1:211). A similar version appears in the *South English Legendary*, where the poem also recounts Vespasian's victory and the imprisonment and death of Pilate (ed. D'Evelyn and Mills, 2:697–706). This account of Pilate's origins also has clear echoes with the poem's later, longer digression about the life of Judas Iscariot.

1485–88   *It was a kyng that highth Tyrus . . . He knouleched, ich understonde.* This history — and life — of Pilate was a common legend in the medieval period. Arnold Williams identifies similar accounts in the *Stanzaic Life of Christ*, *LA*, Higden's *Polychronicon*, and Mirk's *Festial* (*Characterization*, p. 9). For more on the historical Pilate, see the note to line 565, above.

1512   *for trowage the kyng of Fraunce.* It is unclear why Pilate would owe Vespasian tribute. Even when Vespasian is emperor, it is the procurator's role to ensure that tax revenue flows to the imperial purse from the provincials; that is, the people of Judea would owe tribute to Rome, not the procurator himself.

1533   *Pounthes.* Nothing is known of Pilate's geographical origins from before his arrival in Judea in 26 CE, and "Pontius" is in fact a family name. See note to line 565, above.

1551   *Heroudes.* Herod the Great was an Idumaean, the son of Antipater the Idumean, a high ranking official under Hyrcanus II. While Herod and his father were Jewish, they were converts (Jews had conquered Idumaea first in 163 BCE, and around 125 BCE they forcibly converted the population). Herod owed his position to the skill he and his father possessed in gaining power and authority by dealing with the Romans (in this case, Julius Caesar). His nearly 40 year rule of Judea found the region stable, but Herod's undermining of the high priesthood as a rival power base, as well as his murderous failure to ensure a stable succession, resulted in intermittent tensions between Rome and the Jews culminating in the first Jewish war, due to the lack of a stable client ruler (frequently necessitating direct Roman management in the form of procurators like Pilate), as well as a class of elites who could be intermediaries for

Roman rule with the people of Judea. On these issues, see Martin Goodman, *Ruling Class of Judea.* Josephus records the rise and fall of Herod in *JW* 1.203–673 and *Jewish Antiquities* 14.158–17.192.

1570   *As yee mowen in the Passioun here.* Pilate sends Jesus to Herod in Luke 23:4–12. Whereas Luke's Gospel suggests that the two have been enemies, *Destruction* details their early friendship (lines 1551–70). Pilate's sending of Jesus to Herod is another moment popular in cycle plays (Chester Play 16, lines 151–57, p. 291; N-Town Play 30; York Play 30).

1581   *A floure of blood cometh hem on.* The idea that male Jews experienced menstruation is a common and troubling stereotype of the period, one that served to promote notions of Jewish uncleanliness. (Menstruating women were also considered unclean.) This myth was part of a larger trend of systematically imagining Jewish bodies as animal-like and physically inferior to Christian bodies. See Kruger, "Bodies of Jews," pp. 303–04.

1595   *Sir Pilate.* In reality, Pilate's tenure in Judea ended in 36/37 CE. According to Josephus (*Jewish Antiquities* 18.85–89), Pilate had soldiers slaughter a number of Samaritans in the village of Tirathana near Mt. Gerizim. Pilate claimed the Samaritans were armed, although the Samaritans themselves (complaining to L. Vitellius, the governor of Syria and father of Vespasian's rival for the throne) claimed they were unarmed. Vitellius sent Pilate to Rome to be judged by Tiberius, who passed away while Pilate was en route. We hear no more of Pilate in the ancient sources.

1601   *Lucifer first.* Lucifer's position as a fallen angel was well-established in Biblical drama (Chester Play 1, York Play 1, Towneley Play 1). This idea has its origins in the Apocalypse of St. John (12:7–10), and developed considerably from the brief link there.

1615–16   *helle brast / And his owen out he cast.* A reference to the "harrowing of hell" (compare Dante, trans. Singleton, *Inferno* 4.52–63), where Christ (between his death and resurrection) descended into hell and rescued his Hebrew ancestors. While it is only hinted at in the canonical gospels, the event forms a major part of the *GN*, a major source for our text, and appears frequently in English cycle drama.

1620   *And thai that duden hym to dede.* In this poem's context, "thai" are literally Jews.

1656   *Cesars tyme bifelle.* Since Jesus's death took place during the reign of Tiberius, the use here shows how *Caesar* quickly shifted from personal family name to a title.

1663   *His oo deciple his traitour was.* This is the start of the first account of Judas's life and death, a theme that will later be expanded considerably.

1666   *thritty pens.* Matthew 27:1–8 recounts Judas returning the pieces of silver and hanging himself. The thirty pieces of silver are strongly picked up in the Judas plays of the York Cycle; see in particular Play 32, "The Remorse of Judas."

1687   *me met a drem.* Velosian dreams of going to Jerusalem, arriving at the temple of King David, where he finds a solution to Vespasian's suffering. This dream and Velosian's plan are a key difference between *Destruction* and *Siege*. In *Siege*, Velosian does not appear as a named character, nor does this dream scene happen; rather, Vespasian is inspired by Titus's miraculous healing to send for Peter, currently Pope, who tells him about the vernicle; the knights of Rome then go to Jerusalem in search of Veronica and the vernicle specifically (*SJ*, lines 213–220). Here, the dream functions instead as a prophetic revelation.

1701   *For he is shirreve and longe hath ybe.* Eusebius claims that Pilate was given the administration of Judaea in twelfth year of Tiberius's reign and governed for 10 years (*EH* 1.9).

1705–06 *Vaspasyan that hath power . . . is Neroes viker.* In fact, Vespasian was out of favor with Nero: while accompanying the emperor on a tour of Greece, Vespasian had dozed off during one of Nero's theatrical performances (Suetonius, *Divine Vespasian* 4, trans. Rolfe). His appointment in 66 to suppress the Jewish revolt was precisely because of his political exile. Even if he won a signal victory against the rebels, it would hardly make him a threat to Nero's power.

1718   *he dooth you no profit.* This argument would be more properly aimed at Nero rather than Vespasian, but in a Roman context, it is an effective one; if no revenue reaches Rome from the province, then the procurator (Pilate) is failing to do his job.

1749   *He was a pryvé Cristen man.* Jacob is one of several secret Christians living in and around Jerusalem in the poem; the presence of Jacob and figures like him is a key part of how *Destruction* in particular erases Jewish identity and amplifies the antisemitic elements of its counterpart text *Siege*.

1770   *Yif any thing be left of his.* Velosian explicitly asks for objects belonging to Jesus, invoking the practice of contact relics for healing. Bodily relics were pieces of the saints — fingers, bones, blood, or other body parts — while contact relics, or objects that had been touched by the saints during their lives, were also believed to have healing power. As Carolyn Walker Bynum notes, "The faithful revered not only bodies and body parts but also pieces of cloth, dust, water, flowers, or herbs that had touched the saints or their tombs" (*Christian Materiality*, p. 136). These relics were especially important in the cases of Jesus and Mary since their bodies had been taken directly to heaven according to theology, making bodily relics incredibly rare (p. 137).

1797   *Als I seigh it with myne eighen.* Jacob identifies himself as a witness at the death of Christ and links himself to one of the three Marys in Mark 16:1 who went to Jesus's tomb and discovered he was not there. (It is likely that Mary Jacobi is interpreted as the daughter of Jacob; see note to line 555, above.) Jacob's first-hand witness has a similar kind of "proximity power" as the object Velosian asks for; Jacob's closeness to Jesus thus authenticates his account for Velosian.

1838   *To fecchen of hym Neroes rent.* Tribute from the provinces could be paid in coin or in kind (e.g. grain).

1847–48   *Sir Pilate thai founden there . . . for to here.* Finding Pilate in a synagogue is perhaps surprising, as he identifies himself as markedly not Jewish in the Gospels (see John 18:35); the poem's interest in making him a Jew fits into its attempts to create a strong binary, much as the figures who help Titus and Vespasian are often secret Christians. Standing to hear a service occurs in many Middle English romances; compare, for example, *Sir Gawain and the Green Knight*, in which Gawain hears mass while armed before setting off in search of the Green Knight (ed. Andrew and Waldron, Fitt 2, line 592).

1863   *Al the trowage is byhynde.* While this is a failure for a procurator, properly this would be an issue with Nero, not Vespasian. It is characteristic of the poem's incuriosity about temporal order to treat Vespasian as if he has already become emperor.

1888   *Failen his visage for to knowe.* Velosian makes the journey to be sure he recognizes Pilate's face. This allows Velosian to be the first of Vespasian's men to recognize Pilate upon their arrival in Jerusalem; see lines 3038–46. The implication here is that Velosian, at least, is already planning vengeance against those responsible for the death of Jesus, as he told Vespasian in lines 1713–16.

1899   *a knighth that highth Barabas.* Barabbas is the figure released from prison by Pilate instead of Jesus in the Gospels (named in Mark 15:7–15, Luke 23:17–25, and John 18:39–40). He receives an upgrade here to knightly status, while he is often described as a thief. Robert Eisenman notes that the Greek word used to describe Barabbas, *lēstēs*, often translated as "bandit," is the word that Josephus uses to refer to those involved in uprisings and to revolutionaries (*James*, p. 178).

1977   *With a flixa I was ysmyten.* By tradition, Veronica is healed of dysentery by Jesus; she has come to be conflated with the woman healed of a blood issue in Matthew 9:20–22. In *LA*, she tells Volusian (here Velosian) that she sought to have Jesus's picture painted while he was going about and preaching; when Jesus heard her request, he pressed the cloth to his face and left an image of his face there (1:212). The account in *Destruction* places Veronica and the cloth much closer to the moment of Jesus's crucifixion, following after Mary and Jesus on his way to be crucified. *LA* is likely the source of the episode as recounted here. Veronica's role is considerably larger in *Destruction* than in *Siege*. In *Siege*, Nathan and Peter both describe the vernicle, which is directly sent for (*SJ*, lines 165–72, 215), and Veronica relinquishes it to Peter, the Pope, on her return to Rome. She speaks only one line in *Siege*, committing herself and the vernicle to Peter's keeping (*SJ*, line 224). Her much more central role in *Destruction* suggests a different understanding of the role of holy women is at work in the poem. Eusebius likewise describes the woman with an issue of blood found in the Gospels, identifying her home as a site with memorials of her healing (*EH* 7.18).

2019   *In my cofre I have it sperd.* Veronica keeps the vernicle in a "cofre," a term for a trunk or chest for storing valuables that can also refer to a shrine (*MED cofre* [n.]). This treatment is very much in keeping with the actual treatment of relics in the later Middle Ages; they were often kept in reliquaries that obscured the objects themselves, and access to these holy objects was highly mediated for pilgrims and others who traveled to visit them. For more on relic discourse, see Malo, *Relics and Writing*, pp. 3–6.

2054   *That was at Jhesuses Passioun.* Velosian asks for witnesses of the passion, a request in line with his earlier request for contact relics that conveys his desire for material connections and proximity to Jesus. However, he also seems to be asking for the culprits, those responsible for putting Christ to death, given that these people come and boast of their role in the deed when Jacob invites them to the inn.

2094–95   *he mighth oure temple felle / And raisen it on the thridde day.* These lines reference John 2:19–21, but they also refer back to lines 189–94 of the poem itself.

2133–34   *Whan tyme cometh thou art in nede, / Than oweth men fruschipp shewen in dede.* Proverbial: compare Whiting F634, which identifies variants of this sentiment as early as 1025. The modern equivalent, "a friend in need is a friend indeed," remains in use.

2167   *And kissed hym often mouthe to mothe.* This is an enthusiastic, warm greeting, meant to emphasize Vespasian's gratitude to Velosian for his travels. Kisses between men are not necessarily unusual as a greeting or goodbye in medieval romance; see Carolyn Dinshaw, "A Kiss is Just a Kiss," for an extensive analysis.

2183–84   *I shal hem brynge to confusioun / Alle that hym duden swiche passioun.* Vespasian's first instinct is revenge, much as Titus's is in *Siege* (*SJ*, lines 185–88).

2191–92   *To coroune his son / For of his liif thai weren in doute.* Vespasian's move to crown Titus before he is healed may be taken as a sign of Vespasian's responsible kingship, ensuring continuity and stability in the event of his death; this trend occurs in medieval romances such as *Sir Orfeo*, where Orfeo entrusts his kingdom to his steward before departing in search of his wife, designing a method of choosing a successor in the case of his death (ed. Laskaya and Salisbury, lines 201–18). Concern about continuity of rulership is also key to the crisis and plot in other narratives, such as Chaucer's Clerk's Tale (*CT* IV [E] 85–140). Vespasian's other son, Domitian, seems to play no role in the poem (as he was a teenager at the time of the events).

2204   *Seint Clement.* Clement, a first century pope, was reportedly martyred "for the skill and extent of his apostolic activities in Rome" (Farmer, *Dictionary of Saints*, p. 105). Interestingly for this narrative, his miracles and death are both associated with water: this makes the miracle of his blessing the sea (lines 2721–28), so none are lost on the oversea journey, particularly appropriate. Clement's presence and papacy is also a key difference from *Siege*, where Peter is Pope when Vespasian is healed (*SJ*, line 205).

2209–10   *For wise men drawen to the wyse, / And foles unto the foles gyse.* Proverbial: see Whiting, M344, which cites only this reference. However, Whiting links this phrase to the more general "like to like," L272, which is very frequently attested.

2227   *He slough hem bothe upon a day.* See note to line 1268, above. Tacitus, *Annales* 15.44 (trans. Jackson) records Nero's persecutions of Christians (without specifically naming Peter or Paul) in the context of finding scapegoats for the great fire of 64 CE.

2238   *For Vaspasian is next of blood.* Nero left no issue upon his demise, ending the Julio-Claudian dynasty. Vespasian may have initially found an "in" at court via his relationship with Antonia Caenis, a freedwoman of Antonia Minor, great-grandmother of Nero (Suetonius, *Divine Vespasian* 3, trans. Rolfe).

2240–41 *For God is ny there thre or tweye / Ben gadred or speken in his name.* These lines echo Matthew 18:20.

2287–88 *For he hath power . . . that I ne may.* By deferring authority to Clement, Veronica reinforces gendered religious hierarchies regarding who may convert and preach. The moment echoes similar instances where holy women can only convert others to a particular point; while they may be the source of healing power or authority, they often send or bring clerics with them to do the actual converting. Compare Digby *Mary Magdalene*, lines 1675–83, in which Mary Magdalene sends the newly converted King of Marseilles to Peter in Jerusalem for baptism and further Christian instruction. Likewise, Cecilia of Chaucer's Second Nun's Tale sends her husband Valerian to be converted by Urban (*CT* VIII [G] 169–89).

2337   *Fyve wittes.* The five senses were imagined as key tools in humanity's ability to perceive God's presence in the world. See for example Bonaventure, *The Mind's Road to God*, in which he describes the senses as doors through which the world enters the soul (ed. Boas, pp. 14–15).

2368   *He migth noughth dyen verrement.* The notion of Jesus as fully human and fully divine — thus both God and able to die as sacrifice for humankind — preoccupied many early Christian theologians. See especially Augustine, *The Trinity*, book 4, chapter 2 (trans. McKenna, pp. 133–34). For an explanation of this theory in the work of Athanasius, see Khaled Anatolios, "Athanasius's Christology Today," especially pp. 45–46.

2397   *Man is hym nexte of every kynde.* On the theology of humankind's proximity to God, see for example St. Bonaventure, *The Mind's Road to God*: "the soul itself is the image of God and His likeness" (ed. Boas, p. 23).

2410   *For oo peny.* This is the first reference to this inversion, which will be repeated throughout: Vespasian proposes to sell Jews thirty for a penny, in retaliation for their purchase of Jesus for thirty pieces of silver. Selling slaves was a typical way Romans got rich from war and imperial expansion.

2419   *To wreken hym.* In Clement's view, Vespasian's illness is a sign of God's hand; that is, Vespasian is ill entirely so he can be cured and then wreak vengeance on the Jews.

2445   *The first Heroudes that the children slough.* This line references Herod's Slaughter of the Innocents, a narrative that appears in Matthew 2:16 as well as in medieval drama (Chester Play

10, York Play 19, N-Town Play 20). There are two Herods referred to in this poem, though *LA* identifies three: Herod of Ascalon, who was king at the time of Jesus's birth and ordered the Slaughter of the Innocents; Herod Antipas, who killed John the Baptist; and Herod Agrippa, who killed St. James and imprisoned St. Peter (1:56).

2462   *Lazar he highth.* This is not the first reference in the poem to Lazarus: see note to line 1329, above.

2504   *the vernycle.* The word "vernicle" describes the cloth used to wipe Jesus's face on the cross that, according to legend, carried the imprint of Jesus's face. See *MED vernicle* (n.). For the retelling of this episode in the poem, see lines 1986–2024.

2507   *Seint Clement was thoo revest.* Clement puts on vestments, markers of his clerical office, before accepting the vernicle. The moment emphasizes concern about the proper treatment of relics as well as the special authority of the ordained to handle and control access to them. Relics here thus engage in sacramentality that is deeply imbricated with clerical authority; as Miri Rubin has demonstrated, medieval Christianity functioned as a cultural system: "The whole structure of the church, the approval of secular authorities, the very naturalness of the only place of worship and of a comprehensive worldview preached and taught frequently, was empowered in the claim of sacramentality and in the practice of an exclusive right of mediation" (*Corpus Christi*, pp. 8–9). This mediating power is especially noteworthy in the case of relics; by the fourteenth century, access to relics was incredibly mediated spatially, through both reliquaries and church spaces; see Malo, *Relics and Writing*, p. 31. In *Siege*, the vernicle is given a procession through a Roman temple, and idols crumble as the cloth is carried through the space (*SJ*, lines 235–40).

2528   *a slough fro hym gan falle. MED slough* (n.2) refers to this line in sense 1b. The idea here is that the skin falls from Vespasian like a snakeskin — an appropriate remedy for someone experiencing leprosy, a disease primarily of the skin.

2569–70   *I schal fighth / For swiche a lorde and for his righth.* Questions of just warfare and the idea of the just war circulated throughout the later Middle Ages. Writers such as Honoré Bovet's and Christine de Pisan's works drew on codes established by Vegetius's *De re militari*, which itself survived in over 260 Latin manuscripts; as Yeager notes, "it was 'just war' theory which authorized Christians to undertake crusading on all of its fronts; condoning wars which satisfied such requirements as just cause, right intention, and right authority or divine sanction" ("Captivity and Execution," p. 86). These debates extended beyond guidelines for warfare, influencing literary production of the period; John Gower includes a passage that advocates against crusading in book 3 of the *Confessio Amantis* (*CA* 3.2485–2638), while many medieval romances, such as *Richard Coer de Lion*, champion holy war. For a more detailed account of just war theory at work in medieval England, see *SJ*, pp. 24–30.

2581–82   *Whan we have don and comen agein, / We shullen ben cristned.* This insistence upon completing deeds before baptism also occurs in Malory's *Morte d'Arthur* in the famous case of Palomides, who believes in Jesus and Mary but vows not to be baptized until he has achieved the Questing

Beast and completed seven battles (*Works*, ed. Vinaver, p. 436). This is also a major deviation from *Siege*, in which Titus is baptized immediately upon hearing the story of Jesus's death and resurrection.

2597   *Londes and rentes he gaf hem wyde.* Vespasian in effect enfeoffs Clement and Veronica, rewarding them with land in his kingdom. The episode thus reads as a precursor of sorts to the Donation of Constantine, the (apocryphal) document that gave the Bishop of Rome property and worldly wealth in Rome (Montero, "Donation of Constantine," *Encyclopedia of Ancient Christianity*). Here, though, the land is meant to secure Clement and Veronica's immediate welfare, and giving land to the Church is presented as uncontroversial throughout this poem. These grants also reflect similar ones given to Josephus after the war (see Josephus, *Life*, ed. Mason, 422–23).

2602   *I rede that yee ycristned bee.* Clement's concern is that baptism will protect them in the fight to come. Medieval Christian theology considered baptism the point of entry into Christian community, as baptism purged the newly baptized of their pre-existing sins; thus, baptism played a crucial role in marking conversion. As Siobhan Bly Calkin puts it, "For late medieval theologians, what makes a Christian is the pronunciation of a specific verbal formula over the body of the candidate as that body is washed with water . . . The words of baptism translate the candidate from a state of sin into one of grace, and from outsider to Christian insider and member of the body of Christ" ("Romance Baptisms," pp. 106–07). Eamon Duffy notes that the baptismal liturgy included some of the same readings as those used at exorcisms (*Stripping of the Altars*, pp. 280–81). Vespasian's response, that he wants to avenge Jesus first, seems to echo that of knights such as Palomides, who set tasks for themselves in order to "earn" baptism; see note to lines 2581–82, above. Vespasian's reluctance here might mirror that of Constantine, who was not baptized until his deathbed (Eusebius, *Life of Constantine*, trans. Cameron and Hall, 4.61–63).

2620   *that kynde.* When used to refer to a group of people, *kynde* in Middle English tends to mean tribe or even race, as in a class of people. See *MED*, *kinde* (n.), sense 10a. In imagining Jews as a race, the poem engages in the same biopolitical and theological race-making that the Church developed throughout the period; England was particularly notable for the earliness of its racialized thinking against Jews. See most recently Heng, *Invention of Race*, chapters 1 and 2.

2644   *To Sir Nero to leten us gon.* Vespasian writes for leave, since Nero has jurisdiction over Jerusalem at this point. Since Vespasian technically holds his lands through Nero's authority, he seeks permission to wage war on another part of the empire. While in *Destruction*, Nero is oblivious until Vespasian and Titus send for leave, in *Siege*, he is already angry that his tribute has been withheld. As a result, it is the senators of Rome, not Nero alone, who collectively determine that Titus and Vespasian are the appropriate parties to go and punish the Jews, though Titus and Vespasian are motivated by keeping the vows they made upon being healed rather than by Rome's economic concerns (*SJ*, lines 265–80). In reality it was Gallus's shocking defeat at Beth Horon that led Nero to appoint Vespasian (at the time out of favor with the emperor) to suppress the revolt (Josephus *JW* 3.1–8). According to Orosius, Vespasian was sent by

Nero to quell Jewish rebellions in the regions (*Seven Books of History*, ed. Fear, 7.9.2–3, pp. 337–38).

2657   *that is us ydo*. Vespasian adopts the death of Jesus as a trespass done against him and Titus, making the vengeance both holy and personal and identifying himself as Christian despite his pre-baptismal state. Nero's identification of those in Jerusalem as Vespasian and Titus's enemies at line 2665 reinforces their association with Christianity, since it makes the wrong done to Jesus into a wrong done to them.

2674   *Graunteth youre pes to Cristen menne*. Clement and Veronica ask Vespasian to put the Christians in his land under his protection while he is away, reversing their status as persecuted earlier in the poem. (Compare Clement's claims at lines 2261–62 that no Christians dare show themselves for fear of being chopped to pieces.) Vespasian agrees, but also gives Clement authority over all the Christians in his land in his absence.

2714   *An hundreth thousande men*. The exact numbers of men in a Roman legion varied, but a Roman legion on paper had about 5,400 men, subdivided into cohorts. Vespasian began his campaign with four legions, the legio V Macedonica, X Fretensis, XII Fulminata (already in Syria, weakened after fighting at Beth Horon), and XV Apollinaris. Even including auxiliaries, this would give Vespasian and Titus about 25,000 men (representing about 1/7th of the total military strength of the empire — 28 legions — at the time). Even with allied contributions, at most Vespasian could count on half of this number, and likely far less. See Mason, *HJW*, pp. 139–53, for a good primer on the Roman army. As Susanne Yeager notes in her "Captivity and Execution," many late medieval English readers would have no sense of the scale of such a number of people or the size of such a group, as "the population of London alone numbered less than 20,000 people" (p. 93).

2732   *Acres*. Acre (or Akko) was a major target for Crusaders; Boas identifies it as "the most important port city on the Palestinian coast" (*Crusader Archaeology*, p. 32). A central administrative center during the thirteenth century while under Christian control, it was a walled city in the fourteenth century, with several gates of entry on land as well as a substantial harbor (Boas, *Crusader Archaeology*, pp. 32–35). The city was known in antiquity (and to Josephus) as Ptolemais. While here it is given up without a fight, battles for control of Acre feature in many Crusades romances; see for example *Richard Coer de Lyon*, ed. Larkin, lines 2891–2956, in which Richard burst through chains designed to limit access to the harbor using bees as a form of biological warfare.

2740   *slough and brent alle that he fonde*. Vespasian is enacting what would come to be known as a scorched-earth policy, destroying the area around the city despite their surrender. This is an occasional ancient strategy, but not always wise because it was more efficient for the invading army to use the produce of the land for themselves, which both aided them and hurt the enemy. Josephus records (*JW* 3.29ff.) in his account of Vespasian's early offensive that he torched the first several towns in his methodical march around Galilee.

2744   *Japh.* Jaffa "was the main port of the kingdom south of Acre and served as the port of Jerusalem" (Boas, *Crusader Archaeology*, p. 49). As a result, the city was the site of considerable violence from 1099 onward (Boas, *Crusader Archaeology*, pp. 49–51).

2751–52   *Rayn and hayl, frost and snowe, / And styf wynde that loude gan blowe.* Bad weather is a common feature of Crusades romances; in *Richard Coer de Lyon* (ed. Larkin, lines 2837–46), for example, it impairs Richard's forces and kills a considerable number of soldiers. Here, in contrast, the weather serves as a type of divine intervention that gives Vespasian the advantage, as this weather only impacts Jaffa; his own host enjoys good weather throughout their journey (lines 2755–60).

2779   *Sir Japhel.* Japhel is not an historical figure. He functions as a kind of native guide to the area, positioned to give Vespasian crucial information about the terrain. Japhel is related to Caesar, which makes him (in this poem's genealogy) also related to Vespasian, who is "next of blood" to inherit the empire.

2808   *Pellam.* Eusebius explains that the Christians in Jerusalem were commanded by revelation "to depart and dwell in one of the cities of Perea which they called Pella" (*EH* 3.5). *LA* likewise gives Pella (1:274) — which is a city in the upper Jordan valley where the early Christian church of Jerusalem did indeed settle after the fall of the city (MacCulloch, *Christianity*, p. 107).

2826   *kyng of Galilé.* Archelaus, referenced here, is identified as one of Herod's six sons in the *LA* (1:56); according to this account, which cites Macrobius as its source, Herod lost two sons to treason, fell ill at age 70 with itching, pain, a horrible smell, and worms in his testicles. He was seized by a coughing fit while peeling an apple and moved to stab himself. Herod was unpopular with his subjects, who were pleased at his close brush with death, though Herod was stopped from stabbing himself. His son Antipater tried to bribe the guards to free him from prison to assume Herod's place. In a rage, Herod named Archelaus his heir and died five days later (*LA*, 1:58–59). Archelaus plays a minor role in Josephus. One of Herod's many sons by several different wives, Archelaus was not much involved in the lethal intrigues between Herod's eldest sons that takes up so much of the first book of the *Jewish War*. After coming to the throne, Archelaus quickly faced a small popular uprising, and worried that it would spread, authorized a lethal suppression, which led to the deaths of a few thousand people within Jerusalem (*JW* 2.5–15). This augured ill for Archelaus's reign, and made Augustus reluctant to confirm him as Herod's full heir. Instead, Archelaus became ethnarch of Judea, Samaritis and Idumaea. In fact, his full brother, Antipas, was appointed by Augustus as Tetrarch of Galilee, when Antipas was disputing the succession with his brother (*JW* 2.20–38). Archelaus failed in the main task of a Roman client ruler, regional stability, and so was removed in 6 CE and banished to Vienne, in Gaul (*JW* 2.111–117). It is interesting to note that this is where, according to the present poem, Pilate will be exiled.

2828   *slough the children alle.* See note to line 2445, above.

2834   *And alle to Jerusalem thai come.* The people of the country here come to Jerusalem for safety as Vespasian's armies approach, seeking refuge behind the city walls, in a moment parallel to events in *Siege* (*SJ*, lines 313–14). This is, indeed, the point of city walls, which were designed to withstand sieges. Medieval fortifications were incredibly thick: Boas notes most substantial castles had three or four meter-thick walls (*Crusader Archaeology*, p. 120).

2851–52 *For loos is better, als it is founde, / In wood than in toun bounde.* See Whiting W558, which cites only this instance of this proverb. Munro also notes this in her commentary (p. 355).

2858   *Fourty yer to amendement.* Eusebius claims that the inhabitants of Jerusalem had forty years to repent their deeds after the death of Jesus (*EH* 3.7), and the poem uses this same number elsewhere (see line 5118). This math, however, does not quite work historically: while forty years after the death of Jesus would have been roughly 74 CE, the historical war began in 66 CE, as Mason notes (*HJW*, p. 3).

2870   *And hereof borowe dar I be.* The borowe, or guarantor, is a common figure in both financial transactions and knightly duels: the idea here is that Archilaus is vouching for the truth of Pilate's statement. The term is used both literally, in legal situations or to refer to a sponsor or witness, and more figuratively, as here. See *MED borgh* (n.), especially senses 2a and 2b.

2875–78 *For water fresh . . . thai mosten have.* Archelaus's plan is for them to shut themselves up inside Jerusalem, since there is no source of fresh water for Vespasian's armies near the city. Thus, he expects that they will be able to easily outlast Vespasian's armies inside Jerusalem by providing themselves with ample food and other supplies. Adrian Boas notes that Jerusalem had four major methods of supplying itself with water, including aqueducts that carried water from Bethlehem, its own spring, public and private cisterns, and "large open reservoirs both within and outside the city walls" (*Crusader Archaeology*, p. 31).

2907   *Pask day.* The siege of Jerusalem begins on Passover, though this term is also used occasionally in Middle English to designate Easter. See also the note to line 955, above.

2927   *engynes.* That is, siege engines, or large military weaponry. These could include catapults, ballistae, large circumvallations, earthworks, and sapping operations. Modern sites (like Masada) can provide archaeological remains from the level of earthworks, like the enormous ramp at Masada, or ammunition and traps, like on the fields of Gaul.

2931   *With terbardels and wylde fyre.* The barrel of tar here is being used as an incendiary material, in conjunction with Greek fire. Greek fire, an oil-based mixture, is similarly notable for burning easily. In effect, these are flaming projectiles being hurled at and over the walls of Jerusalem by Vespasian's army. It is still not entirely clear how Greek fire was produced; it was in use well before the First Crusade, when it was likely brought to Europe by the French, though it was not commonly used there (Norris, *Siege Warfare*, pp. 172–73).

2933–34 *Sowes to mynen men maden sleighe, / And borfreys to reysen on heighe.* Sow was another name for a battering ram, used to pound against walls and gates (Norris, *Siege Warfare*, figure 118 and

p. 215). Borfreys, or towers, were crucial to siege warfare, as they provided a platform from which soldiers could fight soldiers on the walls (Norris, *Siege Warfare*, p. 211).

2949   *so large withinne*. The city of Jerusalem during the second temple period was built up surrounding the enormous Temple plaza on the mount. (The archaeological remains are most often from Herod's reign, unsurprising given his dedication to public works.) A series of three city walls of increasing size protected the city within, and separated the Temple precinct from the residential districts (*JW* 5.142–59).

2959   *seven yere*. The war has historically been dated from 66 to 73 or 74 CE, for a total of seven or eight years; however, Mason notes that from the Roman perspective, the war lasted from 67–70 CE (*HJW*, p. 3). The idea of a seven-year siege has symbolic significance from the Christian perspective, however, as seven is a powerful number in Christian imagination: consider, for example, the seven deadly sins or seven Acts of Corporal Mercy. For further consideration of the numerology of seven, see Peck, "Number as Cosmic Language", pp. 18–19.

2974   *Hou we shullen oure water lede*. Japhel's plan is for an aqueduct made from the skins of animals, stitched together to transport water from the Jordan river to Jerusalem, a distance of roughly 21 miles east. Aqueducts, of course, were commonly built and used by Romans. Inhabitants of medieval England would be well aware of them, as remains of Roman aqueducts at sites like Bath and Dorchester make clear. Maintenance of water supplies was a key element in withstanding a siege by an enemy force.

2989–96   *And overcasten al the vale . . . with oure watere fulfilde*. The plan here is to pipe in water and literally fill in the valley, so that it is covered in water: in essence, to create an artificial lake that will allow Vespasian's army to have water even though there is none in the immediate region. This is done through the "pepes" or pipes in line 2999.

2990   *Josephath*. The Valley of Josaphat is Biblical in origin, mentioned in Joel 3:2 and 3:12, identified by early Christian writers such as Eusebius and Jerome as a part of the Kidron Valley. As Jerome Murphy-O'Connor describes, "The prophets speculated on where God would finally judge the world. Joel declared for a valley called Jehoshaphat (3:2, 12), whereas Zechariah opted for the Mount of Olives (14:4). The Bordeaux pilgrim (333 [CE]) recorded the obvious harmonizing solution as a well-established identification; the Kidron valley is the Valley of Jehoshaphat ('Yahweh judges')" (*The Holy Land*, p. 133).

3019   *maister Josephus*. Appropriately, since he is a character in his own history that is the ultimate source of this account, Josephus appears as a character here in the narrative. (This is true in other adaptations as well, like Pseudo-Hegesippus). The historical Josephus was one of the commanders of the rebellion in its early days, responsible for the defense of Galilee. This put him directly in the path of Vespasian's initial offensive, and he was captured after the fall of Jotapata in 67 CE. Josephus is somewhat cagey about the exact circumstances that led to his acceptance by the Romans — his account of surviving a suicide pact (*JW* 3.340–91), and his timely prophecy of Vespasian's imperial accession (*JW* 3.399–408) are too obviously self-serving in his narrative to be entirely true.

3073   *"Beaw sire," he seide, "thou art forsworne."* Archelaus had failed in his basic role of keeping the peace, since according to Josephus (*JW* 2.111–13) he had antagonized the Jews and Samaritans equally so that both groups had sent embassies to Rome to complain. The failures of Herod's heirs to fulfill the role of Roman client ruler had led to the imposition of direct Roman rule and the attendant cross-cultural tensions that came along with it. Vespasian's taunt here, in its own oblique way, recognizes local failures that contributed to the war. See Goodman, *Ruling Class of Judea*, pp. 27–134.

3095   *He was of Cesar kynde.* Vespasian's familial relationship to Nero is well known in the world of the poem, and here his ferocity is attributed in part to it. Nero's reputation is blackened by both Roman sources and Christian ones. Nevertheless, Nero's reputation amongst the common people was such that prophecies of his return were current for *centuries* after his death. Suetonius (*Nero* 40, trans. Rolfe) records a prophecy that Nero's return would start in the east, from Jerusalem!

3100   *Michel is bitwene word and dede.* Proverbial: compare Whiting W642. For other literary uses, see Gower *CA* Prol.450–51: "Betwen the word and that thei werche / There is a full gret difference."

3110   *Bataile, sir, I wage thee.* Archilaus is encouraging Pilate to issue Vespasian a challenge — essentially, to egg Vespasian on. The insult will anger Vespasian several lines later.

3149   *It was withinne the fifte yere.* This is another example of the poem's loose relationship with time. The Jewish War properly began in 66; Vespasian arrived in 67; and the siege began on April 14, 70 CE (three days before Passover, *JW* 5.99). Vespasian had left for Egypt before Titus invested Jerusalem with siege works.

3159–60 *For thai han alle chosen thee / For to beren the dignité.* Vespasian became emperor with his decisive victory in the Roman Civil War, late in 69 CE, at the battles of Cremona. See Mason, *HJW*, pp. 7, 13–14.

3166   *cardiake.* Titus "becomes ill with joy." This illness in *LA* is paralysis in the leg, caused by an imbalance in humors that Josephus later heals (1:275). The episode also appears in *Siege* (*SJ*, 1027–36), where the illness more closely matches that described in *LA*. The "cardiake" referred to here suggests pain not in the leg, but in the heart: see *MED cardiake* (n.1): "a malady characterized by pain in the heart and palpitation," which cites this appearance of the word.

3169–70 *With overdon joye com that woo, / And with overdon sorough it most goo.* These lines foreshadow Titus's later healing by Josephus; see note to line 3980, below.

3172   *There Josephus sithen was yfounde.* At this point, Josephus had become a *de facto* advisor to Titus. In his own text, this is likely meant to echo the role of Croesus as a captured *de facto* advisor to Cyrus of Persia in Herodotus's *Histories*, book 1.

3180   *Sarsyneys*. This is the first reference to the Romans as "Saracens," here seemingly used as a
            catch-all term for non-Christians. However, it has strong associations with Muslims during
            this period; see Tolan, *Saracens*, p. xv and Akbari, *Idols in the East*, pp. 2–5 for a brief discus-
            sion of this terminology. (Both studies are foundational for understanding medieval Latin
            Christian representations of Islam.) In identifying Romans as Saracens, the poem simulta-
            neously invokes the idea of Muslims/Saracens as pagan idol worshippers and identifies the
            Romans as firmly non-Christian. As Tolan observes, "Ecclesiastical writers schooled in the
            Latin classics had a vivid image of pagan worship, an image they transposed to create a portrait
            of the religious error of the 'pagan' Saracens. The chroniclers of the first Crusade used this
            image to glorify and justify the crusaders' exploits" (p. xx).

3181–82   *Bot afterward Seint Clement / Confermed his corounement.* Vespasian is essentially crowned
            twice. The "Sarsyneys" here seem to be Roman pagans, who crown Vespasian first accord-
            ing to their rituals; but he will later be crowned by the Christian Pope Clement. See note to
            line 3180, above. Such a scene recalls more the coronation of Holy Roman Emperors, like
            Charlemagne.

3191   *of the knave, the prophete.* This is the man mentioned in lines 3140–41.

3199   *That this cité shulde be lorne.* This prophesy appears at lines 1085–1117 as the last of the ten
            signs warning of the fall of Jerusalem.

3227   *Marie his doughter.* Jacob's daughter Mary is identified earlier as one of the three Marys who
            goes to the tomb to anoint Jesus's body (lines 1805–10); her prayer here invokes that service
            to Jesus as she seeks help for her father. Mary's role here, like Veronica's enhanced role from
            Siege, creates another moment where women are central to the poem's action.

3306   *a diche.* The ditch here will serve to make it impossible for those in the city to escape unno-
            ticed, creating an obstacle something like a reverse moat. The ditch here also parallels the mass
            graves that will be used to bury the dead; see note to line 3328, below.

3322–23   *Foure penyes upon the day / Every maister tweie shillynges had.* For comparison's sake, unskilled
            labor by the 1390s in England received a daily rate of about three pence, with skilled building
            workers receiving about five pence (Penn and Dyer, " Wages and Earnings,"p. 356). Penn and
            Dyer also cite an example from Essex in 1380, in which a man was paid two shillings and
            six pence for ten days of digging and collecting stones (p. 357). See Simon A. C. Penn and
            Christopher Dyer, "Wages and earnings." The wages Vespasian offers for most workers, then,
            are on par with those they might receive in England, but the master builders are here given an
            excessively high rate, presumably to encourage diligent work.

3328   *Two charnels.* Channels, or mass graves, are made to bury the dead as a means to protect the
            living against contagion. Eusebius, citing Josephus on this detail, declares that "At first orders
            were given to bury the dead at the public expense because of the unbearable stench; then
            afterwards when this was impracticable they were thrown from the walls into the trenches.
            When Titus, going round the trenches, saw them full of the dead and the thick gore oozing

from the rotting bodies, he groaned, and raising his hands called God to witness that this was not his doing" (*EH* 3.6). A similar detail occurs in *Siege*, where the citizens throw corpses into ditches when the death toll overwhelms the ability of the citizens to bury the dead (*SJ*, lines 1151–54). The recounting of massive death tolls and the complete lack of normal social mechanisms to handle corpses — namely, religious burials — is reminiscent of accounts of the carnage left by the Black Death. See in particular Boccaccio's *Decameron*, the introduction to the First Day of which describes Florence in eerily similar terms, from the abandonment of family members to the eventual disposal of plague victims in large trenches (trans. McWilliam, pp. 9–12, especially p. 12). A similar moment in crusades romance occurs in *Richard Coer de Lyon*, where Richard and his men behead their enemies and throw them into a ditch on an angel's orders (ed. Larkin, lines 3745–56).

3342   *Barabas and Josephus.* Though Josephus was helping the Romans by the time Titus's army besieged Jerusalem, here the poem recalls Josephus's initial allegiance on the rebels' side. The fullest account of Josephus's activities (though with curious differences from his account in the *JW*) in Galilee in support of his people is *Life*, 17–417.

3360   *God lengthed the day.* This miracle seems to parallel that in the book of Josue (10:12–15), in which God lengthens a day at Joshua's request until the Israelites have defeated their enemies.

3366   *That he was pryvé Cristen man.* In the poem, Josephus's eventual allegiance to Titus and Vespasian is foreshadowed by his secret Christian identity. The "Testimonium Flavium," where Josephus appears to offer testimony about the divinity of Jesus, offered evidence to medieval readers of Josephus's possible Christian identity. However, the origin of this passage remains controversial today. Eusebius is the first author to quote this in his *Proof of the Gospel* and *On Divine Manifestation.* It is probably via Eusebius, or Pseudo-Hegesippus, that the author of our poem came across the Testimonium. For more on this curious text, see Alice Whealey, "The *Testimonium Falvianum*," and the note to line 888, above.

3374–88   *hunger gan hem dere . . . And uche ete othere.* Cannibalism in the Vengeance of Our Lord tradition has been extensively discussed, and this famine is recounted in a range of materials: most of these, however, focus on the famine and the abuse of power, the strong stealing resources from those weaker, rather than describing mass, indiscriminate cannibalism, as these lines suggest. See also the note to line 3391.

3380   *uche by lott other ches.* Drawing lots is a means of using chance to quickly make a random decision: for example, drawing straws (one means of drawing lots) involves everyone involved selecting a straw, and the person who winds up with the shortest straw being selected for a particular fate — in this case, being eaten. Casting lots occurs with some frequency in the Bible; see for example Acts 1:26, where Matthias is selected as an apostle, or famously, the soldiers who crucify Jesus casting lots for his clothing as in Matthew 27:35 and John 19:24.

3391–3462   *Marie she highth . . . that wicked dede.* This episode is what A. Boyarin calls a "set-piece" in this version of events, though there are considerable variations in its presentation across works (*Siege of Jerusalem*, p. 23). The episode is most similar in *Siege* and Eusebius, as well as *LA*: in those three versions, a woman named Mary kills her child, a son, in a fit of madness, hunger, and/or rage: she roasts the child and eats a portion. When she is discovered, she offers a portion of the cooked child to those who have found her, and they react with horror and sorrow. See *SJ*, lines 1069–1100; *LA*, 1:276; and Eusebius, *EH* 3.6: versions also appear in Josephus's *JW* and Higden's *Polychronicon*. As A. Boyarin (among others) notes, a Jewish Mary who consumes her son has clear Eucharistic overtones (*Siege of Jerusalem*, p. 26). However, the version which appears here in *Destruction* is distinct in several critical ways: to begin with, Mary's child is a daughter, already dead from the famine in the city. Likewise, it is the idea of her friend Clarice — a new addition to the account — to eat the child, and Mary resists until persuaded by an angel. These variations serve to approve of this episode of maternal cannibalism as divinely ordained, a horrifying act that is nonetheless necessary as part of the city's fall. As a result, the horror of the Jews who discover Mary and carry away the cooked child suggests another failure of Jewish understanding from the poem's point of view, somewhat shifting the valences of the episode's potential eucharistic overtones. Josephus probably adopted the bare form of this story from 4 Kings 6:24 ff., where the consumption of a child occurs during the siege of Samaria. Josephus retells this very story in *Jewish Antiquities* 9.66–68 — though *JA* is composed after *JW*. For the most comprehensive reading of this episode and its sources, see Merrall Llewelyn Price, "Imperial Violence." For a reading of the original passage in Josephus, see Honora Chapman, "Josephus and the Cannibalism of Mary."

3424   *It may stonde us to Purgatory.* Purgatory, which developed as a concept through the twelfth century, was a place of suffering where punishments were similar to those in hell; however, it was a temporary, transitional space in which one was purified and prepared for salvation. The living might facilitate the movement of dead loved ones through this time of suffering through prayer and intercession. See Eileen Gardiner, "Hell, Purgatory, and Heaven." Mary's hope here, then, is that their time of suffering in Jerusalem will reduce the time she and Clarice will spend in purgatory after death.

3436   *For to fulfille the prophecye.* Mothers consuming their children is a frequent image in prophecy in the Hebrew Testament. See, for example, Leviticus 26:28–29: "I will also go against you with opposite fury, and I will chastise you with seven plagues for your sins, so that you shall eat the flesh of your sons and of your daughters." Similar images appear in Deuteronomy 28:54–57; Jeremias 19.8–9; Lamentations 2:20; and Ezechiel 5:9–10.

3467   *the noble stones.* "Noble stones," or gems and rocks with healing or magical properties, are common in medieval English lore; collected descriptions of such stones, known as lapidaries, are extant. (Indeed, parts of Hildegard von Bingen's *Physica* read much like a lapidary.) However, while lapidaries include cures for drunkenness, childbirth pains, and other ailments, no particular stone is identified as preventing hunger and thirst.

3477   *Bot golde and silver eten he bad.* As here, the Jews in *Siege* eat their gold (*SJ*, lines 1167–68) as a means of staving off hunger; this has devastating repercussions once the city falls to Vespasian (see lines 4195–4200). This scene derives from an episode in Josephus (*JW* 5.550–52), where Arabs and Syrians discover that Jewish deserters swallowed gold before they left the city (after they see one deserter picking the coins out of his excrement), and begin tearing apart the

Jews to discover their swallowed treasure. Eating gold and silver is used as a punishment in several medieval travel texts: both the *Book of John Mandeville* (ed. Higgins, pp. 138–39) and Polo's *Divisement du Monde* (ed. Kinoshita, pp. 20–21) retell the account of the Mongolian lord Mongke Chan who, upon capturing the Caliph of Baghdad, imprisoned him with only his gold and silver to eat, as a punishment for the Caliph's failure to spend his money attempting to protect the city from capture.

3515–16   *For thorough us lyen thai noughth thus ded, / Bot for her owen feble red.* Titus denies responsibility, blaming instead a sense of fate and perhaps even the Jewish law for the death of Jerusalem's inhabitants. At the same time, his moment of pity suggests the extent to which Titus is moved by compassion. Thus, it is in keeping with Maija Birenbaum's reading of the poem as using pity and Christ's love for the Jews as a means to present their suffering and destruction as their own fault ("Affective Vengeance," pp. 338–39). This detail is also present in Eusebius (*EH* 3.7).

3520   *Bitande hosen and shone.* The detail of citizens gnawing on shoes seems to come from *LA* (1:276) and is also in *Siege* (*SJ*, line 1075).

3542   *That we mowen duellen stille and lyve.* Pilate is essentially asking for terms for a truce, that is, a ransom that the city can pay to end the siege and continue to occupy Jerusalem.

3566   *Quoth Josephus.* Josephus's presence in Jerusalem here reflects his participation as a military leader earlier in the revolt. See Josephus, *Life* for exhaustive details of his activities, in addition to *JW* book 3.

3569   *artou Cristen.* Josephus the historical figure remained Jewish and not Christian. However, as Yeager notes, Josephus's writings were considered incredibly authoritative by Christian thinkers: "Writings about Josephus from the later medieval period suggest that his work had become fully integrated into the fabric of western Christianity. For instance, Guy N. Deutsch has shown that Peter Comestor, author of the *Historia scholastica*, considered Josephus to be 'on par with the highest religious authority.' Josephus contributed to the writing about the fall of Jerusalem in medieval biblical commentary by providing information not offered by the Bible, and which was received as the exegetical counterpart to the Old Testament: just as the New Testament was thought to complement the Old, the Josephan account was received as part of the new covenant in biblical history" ("Biblical Exegesis," p. 79). It is possible, then, that Josephus himself is made Christian in *Destruction* partly to validate his work, which was highly regarded. In addition, several manuscripts (Eusebius is the earliest testimony to this), contain the "*Testimonium Flavium*" in *Jewish Antiquities* 18.63, where "Josephus" claims that Jesus was in fact the messiah. See notes to lines 888 and 3366, above.

3672   *Than yelden us to a Sarasynne.* Josephus's objection to yielding the city originates in Vespasian's lack of baptism; despite Vespasian's avowed belief in Jesus, he has not undergone the Christian sacrament of baptism. Thus, Josephus claims, the city will not yield to him. This is a problematic view for the Jews to hold, as it suggests that they are deeply concerned about the religious state of their besiegers, seeing themselves as superior to a "Saracen" but apparently not to a

Christian. The use of the term "Saracen" to describe a first-century Roman is unusual: the term normally refers to Muslims by the late-fourteenth and early-fifteenth centuries. On this last point, see Akbari, *Idols in the East*, p. 2 and Rajabzadeh, "The Depoliticized Saracen," pp. 2–3. This "Freudian slip" shows how various siege stories involving Jerusalem (Roman, crusade, etc.) have common themes and features that begin to merge together.

3687   *Josephus com the Jewes unto.* Though at this point in the poem Josephus is still on the side of the Jews in Jerusalem, this speech advising the surrender of the city likely adapts *JW* 5.362–419, where Josephus (as an official envoy of Titus) allows himself a lengthy, historically minded speech before the walls of Jerusalem to convince the inhabitants to surrender to the Romans.

3713–20   *we duden Messias to dye . . . thys gode man.* In these lines, the Jewish community claims their overthrow is justified because of their role in Jesus's death. This unquestionably antisemitic statement is aligned with medieval Christian theology, even that of figures such as Augustine who preached what some scholars have called a doctrine of toleration; that is, Augustine thought living Jews provided an important witness to the truth of Christian doctrine, despite their clear guilt, which in his view justifies their punishment. See Jeremy Cohen, *Living Letters*, Part 1, especially pp. 20–47, for a detailed account of Augustine's theology on Jews and its impact on later medieval Christian thinkers.

3737   *Ellevene thousande there leten her lyf.* This bloodletting resembles the mass suicides at Masada in 73–74 CE, where the Romans found a deserted fortress once they had scaled the heights. This siege closes Josephus's account in the *JW* (7.252ff.).

3739   *for the stynk that of hem came.* Non-Christians are notable on several occasions in Middle English literature for their posthumous odors. Compare, for example, Palomides's killing of the pagan Sir Corsabryne in Malory's *Morte*; when Corsabryne is killed, "therewithall cam a stynke of his body, whan the soule departed, that there myght nobody abyde the savoure" (*Works*, ed. Vinaver, p. 407).

3752   *That the erthe wolde us hillen.* Compare both Apocalypse 6:16 and Osee [Hosea] 10:8, in which the people ask that the mountains will cover them.

3782   *Of seven yer this is the last day.* Though sometimes dated from 66 to 73 CE, Mason suggests that from the Roman perspective, the siege truly ended in September 70 with the fall of the temple. See Mason, *HJW*, p. 3.

3809–11   *He gan to renden . . . onon his swerd out drough.* In these lines, Archilaus rips his clothing to draw out a sword, presumably one he has concealed, and kills himself with it before falling into the ditch around the city walls.

3830   *Joneperham.* This seems to refer to the historical Jotapata: see Josephus, *JW* 3.158–408, which describes the siege, Josephus's escape, his parley with Vespasian and his well timed imperial prophecy. While in Josephus, Vespasian's siege of Jotapata occurred a few years before the siege of Jerusalem (for the latter part of which Titus was in charge, as Vespasian had already gone to Alexandria to begin making his moves for the imperial throne), here our poet makes it a side story, adapting Josephus's rather unbelievable tale of survival at *JW* 3.340–91 and his prophecy at 3.399–408.

3840   *For he was nougth a Cristene man.* There may be a reflection here on cultural differences between observant Jews and Gentiles, like Romans. For more, see note to 3672, above.

3844   *with ellevene felawes he gan flee.* Josephus did indeed flee the city after it was clear Jotapata was lost; see *JW* 3.340ff. This group of twelve (including Josephus) echoes Jesus's twelve disciples.

3851   *Uche of us shal other ete.* This comment is thematically appropriate to the poem, since at this point cannibalism has become a default response of Jews under siege. However, in Josephus (*JW* 3.340–91), the men undertake a suicide pact. Josephus suggested the men draw lots and begin killing each other to avoid capture. Somehow, Josephus ended up being one of the last two left, and was able to talk the other man out of finishing the suicide pact. This later became an example story in mathematics — the Josephus problem — where one needs to figure out the best place to stand in a circle to avoid execution. Like in *JW*, the character Josephus here has the other men cast lots to see who gets eaten first. Unlike in *JW*, God himself is the agent of the secret Christian's salvation, for, as the poet says, "his wytt halpe many a man" (line 3870).

3886   *That wroot the storye amonges us.* That is, Josephus is the author of *The Jewish War*, making this comment an interesting meta-poetic and meta-historical moment.

3909   *righth onon he was unbounde.* Christianity was still nascent when Josephus wrote the *JW* and so plays no role in it. In fact, it was Josephus's imperial prophecy that later secured his release, after Vespasian had ascended to the throne (which was still in the future when Josephus was captured in Jotapata). (Though, with Eusebius — see note to 3915, below — modern readers of the poem and of *JW* are right to show skepticism of this prophecy and Josephus's escape from the cave.) In other words, Josephus spent significant time in chains before his eventual release and acceptance by Titus as a useful ally. As often, the poet has changed and altered the narrative chronology of *JW* to suit his own needs.

3915   *Fourty dayes er it fel.* Josephus does recount Vespasian's ascent to the imperial seat. Eusebius mentions the prophetic element to this with some skepticism: "The same writer has a still more remarkable account in which he alleges that an oracle was found in 'sacred script' to the effect that at that time one from their country should rule the world and he himself considered that this was fulfilled by Vespasian" (*EH* 3.8). Orosius likewise recounts this prophetic claim of Josephus's (*Seven Books of History*, ed. Fear, 7.9.3, p. 338). The "fourty dayes" may also reference the fact that Josephus predicted the fall of Jotapata would take 47 days (*JW* 3.406), a secondary prophecy he offers to bolster his credibility concerning the more important imperial prophecy.

3980   *And sithen an hete com in his blood.* Josephus's healing of Titus appears in many other versions of the story; see *Siege* (*SJ*, lines 1039–60) and *LA* (1:275). As A. Boyarin notes, Josephus's cure relies on his ability to balance the humors: "the four chief bodily fluids that, in medieval medical theories, determine physical and mental health. Titus's joy caused too much phlegm, or cold . . . and Josephus manipulates Titus's anger to produce a hot, or choleric, response" (*Siege of Jerusalem*, p. 76n4). While frequently told in contexts like *Siege* or *LA*, this account does not appear in Josephus's own texts.

3997   *Thou shalt be me dere while I lyve.* In his *Life*, Josephus exhaustively lists the honors granted him by the Flavians, though all these combined still put him closer to the fringes of imperial favor than the center (he was certainly not "next the kynges" as our text has it). At *Life* 363, Josephus notes Titus's particular approval and publication of the *JW*, while *Life* 423–29 details the grants of land, a house in Rome, and other honors given to him by Vespasian, Titus, and Domitian.

4018–19   *sparehaukes . . . faukons.* Hawks and falcons are both hunting birds; Pilate is offering courtly animals to Vespasian in an attempt to preserve his own status.

4023   *leopardes and lyons.* The leopards and lions here invoke both exotic and extreme wealth. Pilate's offer is meant to appeal to Vespasian's status and nobility. Lions in particular had religious symbolism in medieval bestiaries, where they are described as having associations with Jesus (*Physiologus*, trans. Curley, pp. 3–4); in courtly romance, they often serve as judges of chivalric character, responding innately to nobility, as in Chrétien de Troyes's *Knight With the Lion*.

4073–74   *He comaunded his men als blyve / To kepen that thai token alyve.* Josephus is cagey about this — those refugees from the city that are not outright killed (that is, most of them) are sequestered away separately from the others by Titus. Josephus gives no further information — the Jews of Jerusalem would not all have been as fortunate as him! There is plenty of epigraphical evidence in the form of tombstones around Rome testifying to the enslavement of Jews.

4079   *The Jewes weren leide on hepes grete.* This moment parallels the description earlier in the poem when Jewish corpses lie in massive piles inside the city, but here the Jews are alive — and bound. In its focus on piles of bodies, the poem draws on discourses of crusades warfare and also the suffering at times of plague. (See note to line 3328, above.)

4082   *felde the walls of the toune.* It took the Romans a significant amount of time to break through the three walls of the city, a process that takes up the bulk of *JW* 5 and 6.

4090   *an olde hore man.* Joseph of Arimathea was secured in the wall at lines 669–80; upon his reappearance, his happy and well-fed state emphasizes that he is protected by God. This account of Joseph of Arimathea seems to follow *LA* (1:276).

4139–50   *Of the Jewes thai hym tolde . . . her bityd.* The Christians here detail what wealth the Jews have, the material possessions. Though Vespasian claims material wealth does not motivate him, this depiction of the Jewish community as uniformly wealthy plays into stereotypes associating Jews with financial success that were present in medieval Europe, especially England. Geraldine Heng notes that Jews were closely associated with wealth in the context of England, where they were essential to the credit market; this endangered them due to Christian views on wealth as dangerous (*Invention of Race*, pp. 58–59). In *Siege* as in *Destruction*, the Jews eat their gold (*SJ*, lines 1167–68); however, while this is Vespasian's idea in *Destruction*, *Siege* makes it clear that this was done without Titus's leave (*SJ*, lines 1168–72). *Siege* spends considerable time describing the wealth found in the Jewish temple and its extravagance, and how the Romans tear down the temple and bring this considerable wealth with them to Rome (*SJ*, lines 1265–80).

4157   *For now shal I fulfillen my sale.* Vespasian had earlier threatened to sell the Jews at the rate of thirty for a penny (lines 2409–10). Sale of slaves after conquest was the easiest way for Roman generals and their men to realize profit. Though clearly meant to invert Judas's betrayal of Jesus for thirty pieces of silver, this could also be a form of sacrifice on Vespasian's part to forgo the profit (as he had said he was not warring for profit, line 4153), while still taking vengeance upon the Jews.

4195   *Whan thai ben opened everychon.* See note to line 3477, above.

4205–12   *Honge hem . . . tyl Domesday.* Vespasian's lengthy list of possible tortures, ending with the reference that doing these deeds will "bless" Christians, reads as justification for continued and continuous abuse of the Jews. While many accounts of the violence enacted on Jews after the capture of the city suggests that Titus and Vespasian did not know what was happening, *Destruction* instead makes this torture Vespasian's direct order (compare, for example the *Book of John Mandeville*, ed. Higgins, p. 50 and *SJ*, lines 1317–21, where Titus leads the Roman forces at this point in the war). Mason argues that Josephus's description of Titus's helplessness before his own soldiers' atrocities may be a subtly damning portrait of Titus's would-be imperial patron (*HJW*, pp. 402–65). The emphasis on dismembering and wounding Jewish bodies is itself not unusual among antisemitic works in Middle English; as Steven Kruger notes in his reading of Chaucer's Prioress's Tale and the Croxton *Play of the Sacrament*, the injured Jewish body makes a direct point of contrast with notions of the ecumenically and physically whole Christian body: "The Christian body resists disintegration, and Jewish violence is finally visited back upon the Jews themselves, demonstrating simultaneously the corruptibility of their unholy bodies and the miraculous vitality of the sanctified body of Christ . . . Corruption of body attends disbelief, attacking those who presume to attack the fabric of Christianity; wholeness of body, on the other hand, comes with true belief" ("Bodies of Jews," p. 312, p. 317). As Akbari puts it, "The dismemberment of Jewish bodies . . . symbolically represents the fragmentary, partial nature of Judaism itself" (*Idols in the East*, p. 123).

4225   *mattok.* A mattock is, according to the *MED*, "an agricultural tool used for breaking up hard ground, gravel, etc."

4231   *Bot the temple Salamon.* The temple was not left standing: see Goldhill, *Temple*, pp. 1–3. The temple on this site was not Solomon's original temple, but one reconstructed first by Zerubbabel and then by Herod (Goldhill, *Temple*, p. 9). Orosius similarly notes that Titus destroyed the temple (*Seven Books of History*, ed. Fear, 7.9.5–6, pp. 338–39). Compare also *SJ*, lines 1265–80. There is some controversy about whether the destruction of the temple was deliberately ordered or was accidental. T.D. Barnes provides a great discussion of the evidence; see Barnes, "The Sack of the Temple."

4235–36   *There schal no ston on othere dwelle, / Bot men shullen it doune felle.* Compare Matthew 24:2 and Mark 13:2.

4243–50   *The summe of Jewes . . . Was foure hundreth and seventene thousande.* This is an unlikely number, particularly given that Paris and Cairo, numbering about 300,000, were two of the world's largest cities (Nichols, "Paris," 1:21). *LA* claims that 97,000 people were sold and another 110,000 died in the destruction, numbers it draws from Josephus (1:276). As Yeager notes, between 2700 and 3000 were killed at Acre by Richard I's crusading forces, and this was considered a brutal slaughter by contemporary chroniclers ("Captivity and Execution," p. 92). Eusebius's estimates do not match these, but they are likewise extreme: he claims that 1,100,000 perished by famine and war; those under seventeen were enslaved, and he estimates their numbers at 90,000 (*EH* 3.7). *Siege* gives 110,000 Jews killed (*SJ*, line 1175). As Mason notes, not all the Jews were killed: "After Jerusalem's fall, Titus allowed his soldiers to kill and plunder for several days. Only when they were 'tired of slaughtering' did he order thousands of enemy survivors to be corralled in the temple's Court of Women. The soldiers were now instructed to kill only those who resisted, while carefully preserving the youngest and fittest for Roman use" (*HJW*, pp. 26–27). Orosius attributes a total count of 600,000 Jews killed to Cornelius and Suetonius, while his own estimate of 111,000 is closer to that of Josephus (*Seven Books of History*, ed. Fear, 7.9.7, p. 339).

4258   *Bot for raunsoun.* The Jews without homeland and paying tribute to others is also a feature of the *Book of John Mandeville*, where the narrator explains that "the Jews do not have their own land… in the whole world except this land between the mountains [Gog and Magog]; and in addition, they pay tribute from this land to the Queen of the Amazonia" (ed. Higgins, p. 158). The Jews are imagined as elsewhere, in the mythical enclave of Gog and Magog, but also wandering and without home. (On Gog and Magog, see Scott D. Westrem, "Against Gog and Magog"). See also the note to line 831, above, on Jewish diaspora.

4286   *a kirtel that had no sem.* This item of Jesus's clothing is referenced in John 19:23–24, where the soldiers at the crucifixion cast lots for the seamless garment. Pilate is similarly captured while wearing this kirtle in *LA* (1:212–13), the likely source for its appearance here; the kirtle is also referenced in cycle plays (Chester Play 16, line 133).

4326   *A barel of steel.* A version of these posthumous adventures of Pilate appears in *LA*; in that account, Pilate's corpse is weighed down and thrown into the Tiber, where it is tossed around by demons; it is then removed from the river and sent to Vienne, where it is tossed in the Rhone and the spirits reappear. It is only when the body is sent to Lausanne that the residents are able to sink it into a pit (1:213). In the initial impulse to toss the barrel into the sea (line 4329), there is some resemblance here to the Roman method of execution for parricide — being sown up in a sack with animals (typically a dog, snake, monkey, and a rooster) and tossed into the Tiber.

4332   *Vyenne.* Vienne was an "[e]arly centre of Gallo-Roman Christianity on the Rhone south of Lyons. After the Carolingian decline it became part of the kingdom of Provence before being absorbed into the empire. The Council of Vienne (1311–12) resulted in the condemnation of the Knights Templar. Vienne was not included in the sale of the Dauphiné to France in 1349, but was ceded to the crown in 1449" (Johnson, "Vienne," *Oxford Dictionary of the Middle Ages*, p. 1697). Eusebius mentions Vienne, claiming that Herodias, wife of Herod, was "condemned to live in Vienne, a city of Gaul" (*EH* 1.11). Josephus too says that Archelaus, one of Herod's sons, was exiled to Vienne in 6 CE (*JW* 2.111–17).

4349   *on every heighe day.* A "heighe day" here is, essentially, a holy day. Pilate is fed good food only on these days as a sort of Christian charity.

4355   *hethen hounde.* This epithet is often applied to Muslims in crusades romance. *King of Tars*, for example, is especially noteworthy for the repetition of this comparison (ed. Chandler, lines 93, 169, 740, 1170), where it serves to dehumanize non-Christian characters throughout. Likewise, Muslim characters are called "dogges" in *Richard Coer de Lyon* (ed. Larkin, line 3721).

4365   *to paren a pere.* Pilate kills himself using a knife he has borrowed to cut a pear. *Siege* similarly includes his suicide by paring knife (*SJ*, lines 1329–34), while Eusebius comments only that Pilate "was forced to become his own slayer" (*EH* 2.7).

4367   *sept sages.* On the Seven Sages, see note to 1223, above. This account, like the previous one, does not appear in *Seven Sages of Rome*.

4372–73 *To fouler deth mighth he nougth gon / Than slee hymself with his owen honde.* The implication here is that since no person is more morally depraved or worse than Pilate, it is appropriate that he kills himself. However, this might be read also as a reference to the damnation of those who commit suicide in Christian theology. For a comprehensive treatment of this theological matter, see Alexander Murray, *Suicide in the Middle Ages*.

4391–92 *For stynk and cry thai hadden doute / Of fendes that walked hym aboute.* The stench from Pilate's body is mark of his sinfulness and of the presence of the fiends, and it also parallels the earlier stink of the dead in Jerusalem. Julian of Norwich associates stink with the presence of the devil in her visions (ed. Crampton, lines 2781–86). See also the note to line 3739, above, on the stink of non-Christian corpses.

4405   *the devels gonnen hym posse and bere.* This line begins an account of the posthumous travels of Pilate's corpse, which has been returned to its barrel and tossed in the water, where it is tormented by devils. Though the *South English Legendary* includes the storms and tempests where Pilate's corpse sits, the barrel is absent (ed. D'Evelyn and Mills, 2:706). The moral, that Pilate is denied rest after death due to his part in the death of Jesus, is present in source texts: see for example *LA* 1:213, a likely source for the *South English Legendary*. Williams notes that a similar ending appears in the *Stanzaic Life of Christ* (*Characterization*, p. 9).

4462   *Of Judas.* This account of the life of Judas Iscariot is the second major digression unique to
            the long version of *Destruction.* Versions of this narrative appear in a wide range of languages,
            though the most likely source for this version is *LA.* The *LA* version includes Cyborea's dream,
            Judas's discovery by the queen of Scariot, the murders of his adopted sibling and his father,
            and the death of Judas with this interpretation of its meaning (1:168–69); it attributes this
            life of Judas to "an apocryphal history" (1:168). For more discussion of the medieval Judas
            legend, see Paull Franklin Baum, "Mediæval Legend of Judas Iscariot" and Mariah Junglan
            Min, "Damned If You Do: Judas Iscariot and the Invention of Medieval Literary Character."
            The *South English Legendary* gives a similar account to the one here (ed. D'Evelyn and Mills,
            2:692–97).

4490   *Sweven nys bot a foles spelle.* Proverbial: see Whiting S952.

4502   *nywe boot.* Setting the newborn Judas in a new boat and setting him adrift parallels Exodus 2,
            where Moses is put into a basket, set adrift, and eventually discovered and saved. The *South
            English Legendary* gives "barel" (ed. D'Evelyn and Mills, 2:693, line 23).

4553   *Sone croketh that wil be wrong.* Munro identifies Whiting T470 as the proverbial referent (p.
            359), and the Whiting entry does indeed list this quotation as an example.

4554   *In eelde mote biten that yonge stong.* Proverbial: see Whiting E62, which links it to T222.

4557   *The nettle greveth the swete rose.* Munro connects this line to Whiting G478 (p. 359); the entry
            cites Trevisa's translation of Higden's *Polychronicon* as a similar variant, which is suggestive
            since *Polychronicon* has been cited as one potential source for the poem's content. On Higden
            as a possible source for *Siege* and for *Destruction,* see Millar, *Siege and Contexts,* p. 104. Millar
            sees *Siege* as drawing more strongly on *Polychronicon* than *Destruction* does.

4601–02   *That gode men togedres drawe, / And everyche fole to his felawe.* Whiting M93 cites this quotation
            as proverbial, also referring to L272 ("like to like"), as at lines 2209–10.

4620   *fairest appels.* The use of an apple as the fruit that here tempts Pilate may have its origins in
            the legend that the forbidden fruit consumed by Adam and Eve in the Garden of Eden was
            an apple. Robert Appelbaum notes that tradition comes from a translational pun in Jerome's
            Vulgate Bible: while the Hebrew Bible refers to the fruit as simply a fruit, the Vulgate uses the
            Latin word *malus.* Appelbaum explains that "A *malum* in Latin was any of three things: either it
            was any fleshy tree-born fruit, and thus close in meaning to *tappuach* [the word in the Hebrew
            Bible]; or it was the genus of a variety of fleshy tree-born fruits, including the *Pyrus malus* or
            pomum (the 'apple' in the usual modern sense of the word, growing from the rosaceous tree),
            the *malum Punicum* — the 'apple of Punic,' or pomegranate—and the *malum Persicum,* that
            is, the 'Persian apple,' or peach; or, finally, the *malum* was simply the apple in our sense, the
            Pyrus malus" (p. 194). See Appelbaum, *Aguecheek's Beef, Belch's Hiccup, and Other Gastronomic
            Interjections,* pp. 192–200. The *South English Legendary* also gives "applen" (ed. D'Evelyn and
            Mills, 2:694, line 71).

4734   *For he shal be thine housebonde.* The Oedipal overtones of this episode are a common part of the lore of Judas's early life; they are present in Latin materials from the twelfth century and were disseminated "in almost every language and country of mediæval Europe" (Baum, "Mediæval Legend of Judas Iscariot," p. 481). These overtones most likely entered narratives about Judas via Statius's *Thebaid* and its vernacularizations like the *Roman de Thebes*, rather than through Sophocles, who was unknown to medieval audiences; for a more comprehensive discussion of its origins, see Leydon, "Insular Iscariot," pp. 30–40.

4783   *To beren the purs.* It is generally tradition that Judas was the one who kept the purse (John 12:1–8), and his stealing from the common purse is also a feature of cycle plays (particularly the York cycle, Play 26). Indeed, as scholars have noted, Judas's concern with and about money, though present throughout Judas legends, is especially marked in the *York Cycle*; see Mariah Junglan Min, "Damned If You Do" and Margaret Aziza Pappano, "Judas in York."

4788   *As telleth in the Passioun.* The narrative that follows, of the woman anointing Jesus's feet and the disciples' response, is found in all four Gospel accounts (Matthew 26:6–13; Mark 14:3–10; Luke 7:37–50; John 12:3–8). Judas is only specifically mentioned in John's account.

4800   *Thritty pens, it wolde ben told.* This emphasis on the precise cost in the Judas digression parallels its appearance throughout the poem; see for example lines 1666 and 2409–10.

4813   *to the Jewes agein he cam.* Judas returns to the chief priests in Matthew 27:3–5. The moment is greatly expanded in the York: see Play 32, "The Remorse of Judas."

4825   *an hildre tree.* In Matthew's Gospel, the only one that recounts Judas's hanging, the variety of tree is not identified, nor is it in the *South English Legendary*. However, the tree is identified as an elder tree in *Piers Plowman*'s C-Text (Langland, ed. Schmidt, 1.64), suggesting that the association was already well-established by the fourteenth century in England.

4835   *oure aller frende.* "Aller" here seems to be derived from *MED allen* (v.): to recognize God as "the one and all," but the word is very infrequently attested.

4854   *Seynt Mathy.* Matthias's selection by casting lots is retold in Acts 1:15–26. *LA* recounts multiple legends of Matthias's origins and eventual death (1:170–77).

4873   *And hem that wolden noughth, thai slough.* Conversion at swordpoint, though not uncommon, was theologically suspect. It was repudiated as a practice both in the Fourth Council of Toledo in 633 and in the Decretum of Gratian; by the thirteenth century, Jews could be required to listen to evangelizing sermons, but forcible conversion was still not permitted (Weed, "Forced Conversion," pp. 129–30). Thomas Aquinas in particular spoke against forced conversion, even as he insisted that Jews who did convert must keep to that conversion (Weed, "Forced Conversion," p. 131). Accounts of conversion (or refusal to convert) on pain of death are also present in Hebrew chronicles of the First and Second Crusades; see Eidelberg, *The Jews and the Crusaders*, especially pp. 60, 67. Examples also abound in other Middle English romances; see for example *King of Tars*, ed. Chandler, lines 1045–50.

4878   *Sweren hem feuté.* In requiring oaths of loyalty from those they have conquered, Vespasian and Titus are securing their control of the region. This process imagines a Christianized kingdom that swears loyalty to Rome and operates politically in ways recognizable to the poem's readership.

4899–4904   *The riche he gaf . . . loos catel.* Vespasian's acts of rewarding those who have helped him conquer fulfill a model of good kingship familiar from Middle English romance: compare, for example, *Bevis of Hampton* (ed. Herzman, Drake, and Salisbury, lines 4575–76) or *King Horn* (ed. Herzman, Drake, and Salisbury, lines 1507–10). For a brief discussion of gift-giving as idealized kingship, see the Introduction to *Havelok the Dane* (ed. Herzman, Drake, and Salisbury, pp. 75–76). In Vespasian's case, of course, his deeds also completely redistribute the land and resources of the Holy Land, placing them in Christian hands. Historically, Vespasian would have advanced his leading men and others into imperial administrative positions, replacing previous bureaucrats and administrators of the earlier regime's and brief *juntas* of 69 CE.

4909   *Than took he leve of the londe.* Though Titus and Vespasian depart from Jerusalem back to Rome at this point, the war was not entirely over. Pockets of resistance still endured, most notably at Masada, and Josephus details the "mopping up" operations in *JW* 7.163–453.

4922   *The belles rongen thorough the toun.* These bells ring as an announcement and public celebration at Vespasian's homecoming, a civic celebration. This ringing of bells may also mark a public procession, an imperial triumph of the sort that was indeed a Roman custom upon the return of conquerors to the city; see Mason, *HJW*, pp. 10–13. It was a way to reintegrate a victorious army and general back into the body politic, by allowing them to cross Rome's pomerium, a sacred religious boundary designed to keep military matters out and governmental or civilian matters within. Only Roman generals who had successfully expanded Roman territories were allowed within the pomerium, ritually expanding its boundaries. In the Republic at least, it was height of glory for a man's career (and for this very reason, highly restricted in the empire to the ruling family alone). Our poet has replaced one ancient religious ceremony (the triumph), with a Christian one (baptismal mass). Josephus's account of the triumph at *JW* 7.123–57 is, in fact, our best ancient account of this Roman ceremony. For more on the Roman triumph, see Mary Beard, *The Roman Triumph.* For such public use of bells in Middle English, compare *St. Erkenwald*, ed. Morse, lines 351–52.

4961   *in white wede.* White clothing serves as an outward sign of purity. Margery Kempe, for example, reports a vision from God in which she was told to wear white clothing (ed. Staley, book 1, lines 732–33); likewise, white armor suggesting spiritual improvement or excellence appears in a range of romances, including *Richard Coer de Lyon* (ed. Larkin, lines 386–96) and *Sir Gowther* (ed. Laskaya and Salisbury, lines 563–64). Further, this white clothing that Clement makes the converts wear parallels the white garments given to Jerusalem's Christians by Vespasian at lines 4135–36.

4979–80   *The emperour made many a kyrke / Of the temples that weren derk.* The building of churches is a common activity for romance heroes; *King Horn*'s title character builds churches (ed. Herzman, Drake, and Salisbury, lines 1393–94), and Sir Gowther builds an abbey as recompense for his earlier habit of burning them down (ed. Laskaya and Salisbury, *Sir Gowther*, lines 703–08). Vespasian's work is slightly different, as he transitions pagan temples into churches, but it is not unique in Middle English romance; for example, this transition is the impetus for the narrative in *Saint Erkenwald*. While this does reflect a historical process in Rome (where today the best preserved temples are the ones that became churches, such as the Pantheon), it was accomplished over centuries and not truly begun until the reign of Constantine, the first historically attested emperor to favor Christianity (as opposed to the legendary attestations of Marcus Aurelius, or as here, Titus and Vespasian).

4987   *riche fee.* On giving property to the Church, see note to line 2597, above.

4992–94   *In golde and cristal . . . noughth to touche.* This is where the vernicle officially becomes a relic, secured in recognizable context as one. Its placement in St. Peter's Church (line 4995) further confirms its sacred position. See Chaganti, *Poetics of the Reliquary* and Malo, *Relics and Writing* on the status and positions of relics more broadly.

4997–5017   *Seint Clement took the coroune . . . Oure gostly fader I holde thee.* In an interesting twist on the concept of Caesaro-Papism, though Vespasian is already the crowned emperor (see lines 3179–82), here Clement re-crowns him as a Christian king. In turn, Vespasian confirms Clement as pope. The poem thus neatly circumvents ongoing struggles in the fourteenth century about papal supremacy: evidenced by Adam Easton's 1376 writings in support of papal supremacy against John Wyclif (Gibson and Coletti, "Lynn, Walsingham, Norwich," 1:313) and earlier writings by Dante and Jean de Jandun in support of limiting the pope's temporal power (Nichols, "Paris," 1:14).

5030   *There heled the croked and the blynde.* These miracles associated with Vespasian's tomb are signs of his holiness, common in hagiographical texts. However, these signs of holiness are not unique to saints: Bynum describes the tomb of Isabelle of France, sister of Louis IX of France and the founder of an abbey at Longchamp; while Isabelle was not canonized, she was venerated after her death, and "[e]arth from around her tomb was said to heal; not only her hair but also her pillow, a goblet she drank from, and even a nightcap she knitted were treated as relics" (*Christian Materiality*, p. 136). These healings at Vespasian's tomb, then, authenticate his holiness and religious devotion.

5049   *A merveile I may you telle.* After wrapping up Vespasian and Titus's lives, the poem ends with a miracle story that keeps the Jews as the focus of the poem's conclusion. This is a marked difference between *Destruction* and *Siege*. The three attempts the Jews make to rebuild the city here draw on *LA* (1:276–77); however, Vespasian and Titus's Christian deeds seem to be unique to the *Destruction* poet (Munro, pp. 105–06).

5067–68   *For God wolde ther kynde no more / Shulde lyven to dwellen thore.* This removal of Jews from Jerusalem is typical of much Middle English literature. As Suzanne Conklin Akbari notes, Jews are uniquely conceptualized as being without a homeland in much literature of the period: see *Idols in the East*, pp. 115–35.

5070–71   *Croices . . . Of dew blood red.* The appearance of these crosses is the most explicit connection the poem makes to the Crusades. As Giles Constable notes, evidence suggests that crusaders were told by Pope Urban II to wear crosses (*Crusaders and Crusading*, p. 63), and red crosses in particular were associated with the Knights Templar: "On banners, a red cross on a white ground was generally accepted in the thirteenth century" (*Crusaders and Crusading*, p. 77). The appearance of these crosses on the clothing of the returning Jews seems to mark them for God's vengeance, which occurs quickly — in the following lines.

5095–98   *sprenge a fer . . . askes were.* Upon their third return to the site of the city, the Jews are burned when fire suddenly springs up. This last sign serves as the ultimate destruction of the Jewish community in the poem. In Nicholson's reading of *Siege*, he suggests that the end is crucial in presenting Jerusalem as a blank slate, a necessary precursor to Christian endeavors there ("Haunted Itineraries," p. 471).

5121–44   *Josephus the gode clerk . . . it is broughth.* The poem gives one last list of its sources that echoes the opening list at lines 7–14. While many of these sources do seem to have influenced the poem, these are not likely the sources that the poet most heavily or directly used, as Munro has observed (p. 12). For more on the actual sources, see the Introduction, pp. 12–18.

5151–54   *I hope that . . . par charité.* This ending prayer is typical of the ends of medieval English romances as a way of wrapping up the work: compare, for example, *King Horn*, lines 1539–44, ed. Herzman, Drake, and Salisbury, or *Havelok the Dane*, lines 2994–3001, ed. Herzman, Drake, and Salisbury, in which the scribe asks for prayer for himself as part of this closing.

Textual Notes

Title	*The bataile of Jerusalem.* So MS, A. O: *The vengeance of god taken upon the Jewys for Chrystus deathe.* Cov: *Here biginnith the sege of Jerusalem bi Vaspasian.*
1	*Listneth.* So MS. Addit: *Herkneth.*
	alyve. So MS, O, C, D, Addit. A, Herbert: *in live.*
2	*men.* So MS, C. O, A, Herbert, D, Addit: *man.*
3	*wil.* So MS, A. O: *wul.* Addit: *wolle.* C: *shal.* Cov: *shalle.*
4	*Hou.* So MS. O, A, C, Addit, Cov: *how.* D: *howe.*
	bihated. So MS. O, D: *byhated.* A: *byhatede.* Addit: *Hatyd.* C: *yhated.*
5	*felle.* So MS. Addit: *fell.* C, D: *fel.*
7	*Gospelles I drawe to witnesse.* So MS. C: *þe holy gospel y tak to wytnesse.*
8	*more and lesse.* So MS, A, C, D, O. Addit: *more ne lasse.*
9	*Passioun and Nichodeme.* So MS, C, Addit. A: *passioun of nichodeme.* O: *passion of nycodeme.* D: *passioun of nicodeme.* Cov: *passioun of Nichodeme also.*
10	*taketh.* So MS, A. D, Cov: *takith.* O: *nymeþ.* Addit: *nume.*
	good yeme. So MS. Cov: *goode heede þereto.*
12	*Of thise wonder aventours.* So MS, C, O. D: *that tellen of these aventour.* A: *That tellen of þese aventures.* Addit: *Of þese wondyr anen to crie.*
15	*gret despyt.* So MS, C, O. A: *grete.* D: *greet.* Addit: *mikyll.*
18	*thai dere it boght.* So MS. Addit: *þay hyt dere abozt.* O: *þey hit dere abouzte.* A: *they hit dere aboght.* D: *that thei it dere abouzt.* C: *sithen þei have yt ful dere abought.*
22–26	*That many on . . . her schame, iwis.* So MS. Cov includes additional lines: *For our trespas it was and nat for his / Suffrid he here shame I wys /As many oone gilteles yhongid ys / And so bifelle of Ihesu Crist / As us sheweth the evaungelist.*
33	Paraph mark in left margin.
	hem in. So O, A, C, D. Addit: *ham.* MS: *telde in his.*
35	*that in fele manere.* So MS. A: *þei deden in fele manere.* D: *that thei diden in fele manere.* C: *þat right in fel manere.*

36	*rought never.* So MS. A: *chargeth noght.* C: *þei shulden yt weel.*
39	*telde hem everywhore.* So MS. O, D: *tolde hem everywhere.* A: *tolde everywhere.* Addit: *told hym far and nere.* C: *tolde among hem þere.*
41	*maden.* So MS. C: *shewed.* O: line absent.
42	*As thai liveden.* So MS. O: *as ȝyf þey lyfed.* A: *as þei lyveden.* Addit: *þat þey levyd.* C: *as þough þei lyvede.* D: *as they leveden.* Cov: *And yif thei lived.*
46	*Her wrong with hem noght ne slepeth.* So MS. C: *þerfore þe veniaunce þerof not longe slept.*
53–54	*Altheigh thai hym in manhode sowe / His godhede might thai noght knowe.* So MS. Addit: *All þow he hym saw in his manhed / þey myȝt not know his god hed.*
55	*schewed after.* So MS. C: *used forþer here.* O: *sued after.* Cov: *sewed after.*
57	*wonders.* So MS. O, C, D: *wondres.* Addit: *wondyrs.* A: *wordes.*
58	*thai.* MS: *i* inserted above line.
59	*For no man migth swich maistré kithe.* So MS. Addit: *for nevir soche maystrie be þe.* D: *for no man ne myȝte suche maistries kiþe.*
61	Paraph mark in left margin.
64	*That thu art maister.* So MS, O, D. Addit: *þew art þe most maystyr.* A: *Thou art moost mayster.* C: *þu art most mayster.*
66	*merveiles.* So MS. Addit: *merakyllis.*
67	*coude.* So O, D. MS: *muþe.* A: *couthe.* Addit: *chowde.* C: *can.*
70	*in his werk.* So MS, A, Cov. Addit: *and his werke.* C: *and hys werk.* O, D: *in his werke.*
71	*Therfore, we wolde.* So MS. O: *forþy we wolden.* D: *forthy we wolde.* A: *forthy wolde.* Addit: *for why we wolde.* C: *Wherfore we wolden.*
72	*God almightty.* So MS. A: *Goddes sone.* Cov: *allemyghti God.*
77	*gon.* So MS. O: *gode.*
79	*Forthi of Heven.* MS: *Forthi of of heven.* O: *forthy of heven.* D: *forthy of hevene.* A: *for thogh I of heven.* Addit: *forwhy of hevyn.* C: *and þerfore yf y of hevene.* Cov: *For thouȝ of heven.*
82	*Whan ye trowen me therof nought.* So MS. A: *Whan ȝe þat other troweth nouȝt.* Addit: *Wan þou trowist þat oþer noȝt.*
88	*The Jewes hym tempted oft.* So MS, Cov. A: *The jewes curst Crist temptede oft.* Addit: *þe iewis hym temptis oft.* C: *þe jewys tempted ihu ful often.* D: *the jewes crist tempted eft.*
89	*wonder.* So MS, O, A, D. Addit: *wondyr.* C: *wondre.*
90	*For to ateint.* So MS. O: *for to ateynt.* A: *And ofte opposede.* Addit: *For to temptyn.* C: *For to have atteynte.* D: *For to ateinten.*
92	*In sum manere.* So MS. C: *Yn ony wyse.*

94   *That al unbynt.* So D, MS. O: *þat al onbynt.* A: *þat al unbyndeth.* Addit: *þat alle unbynt.*

96   *gret.* So MS. O, A, Addit, D: *grete.* C: *owene.*

101   *youre.* So MS, O, A, Addit, C. D: *oure.*

102   *name.* So MS, O, A, C, D. Addit: *man.*

103   *asked.* MS: *ked* inserted above line.

105   *was a Jewes kyng.* So MS. O: *was god and jewes kynge.* A, D: *was god and Jewes kyng.* C: *was god a and jewes kynge.* C: *was god and jewys kyng.* Cov: *was god and jewes kinge.*

106   *Tho ansuered thai to this thing.* So MS. A: *in hym þei had noo trewe levyng.*

107   *Oure moné, we maken the war.* So MS. O: *Oure money sire we maken þe war.* A: *Oure money sire we make þe war.* Addit: *Oure mone sire we makyþ þe ware.* C: *Oure money þei seyde we maketh yare.* D: *oure moneye sir we make the war.*

110   *that is Goddes.* So MS. Addit: *And þat is to god ys to god all myȝt.*

111   *confounded.* So MS, O. A: *confoundet.* Addit, Cov: *confoundid.* C: *confunded.* D: *answered.*

116   *tolde hym.* So MS, C. O, D: *tolden hym.* Addit: *told hym.* A: *accusede hir to hym.*

117   *onon.* So MS, D. O: *ryȝt onon.* A: *right anoon.* Addit: *riȝt anone.* C: *and þat right anon.*

118   *the erth.* So O, Addit. MS: *there.* A, C: *þe erthe.* D: *þe erþe.*

121   *writen.* So MS. A: *unswared.*

122   *Hy gon the hens to biholde.* So MS. Cov: *Gothe the lettris he saide and beholde.*

124   *Sore thai weren all adrad.* So MS. O: *I plyȝt ȝou þei were adradde.* A: *I seye to ȝou þei were adradde.* C: *As y yow telle þei were adrad.* D: *I bihote ȝow þei were alle adrad.*

129   *the.* MS: *the the.*

130   *he.* So MS. O, A, Addit, C, D: *Jesus.*

133   *not, sikerli.* So MS. O: *not never sikerly.* A: *not noght sikerly.* Addit: *notȝ never sikirly.* C: *not sykerly.* D: *not nevere sekerly.* Cov: *wote never sikirly.*

135   *forth.* So MS. O, Addit, C, D: *dame.* A: *þou dame.*

137   *thus on.* So O, A, C, D. MS: *þer ȝ.* Addit: *on.*

141   *Than.* MS: decorated initial capital.

144   *to bryng hym doun.* So O. MS: illegible here. Addit: *bryng hym adoun.* C: *to bryngen hym adoun.*

147   *Sith.* So MS, O, A, Addit: *sire.* D: *sir.* C: *also.*

149   *Messias took.* So MS, O, C, Addit: *messias toke.* D: *messias goodliche took.* A: *messias godelich toke.*

150   *by.* So MS, O, Addit. A, D: *in.* C: *yn.*

153   *brake hit nought.* MS: *brake noughth.* O: *braken hit nouȝth.* A: *breke it noght.* Addit: *brekyþ hit noȝt.* C: *breke yt nought.* D: *breken it nouȝt.* Cov: *breke it nought.*

162   *glad.* So MS. O: *jolyf.* A: *joiefull.* Addit: *yoyfuul.* C: *joyeful.* D: *joieful.* Cov: *ioiefulle.*

166   *knewe.* So MS. O: *seyȝen.* A: *segh.* Addit: *seyn.* C: *seyen.* D: *syȝe.*

        wist what I wasse. So A, Cov. MS: illegible here. O: *west what I wasse.* Addit: *wyst what y was.* C: *wyste what y wasse.* D: *wist what i was.*

167   *lynde.* So C, D, O, A. MS: illegible here.

168   Paraph mark in left margin.

        mankynde. So MS, O, Addit, C. A, D: *mannes kynde.*

170   *fyfty wynter olde.* So O, A, C. MS: *xl wynter elde.* Addit: *fifte ȝere olde.* D: *fifty wynter oolde.*

171   *nast.* So MS. O, A, D: *hast.*

172   *in no wise ben.* So A, C. MS illegible here. O: *in none wyse been.* Addit: *yn none wise bene.* C: *nought yn no wyse ben.*

173   *but.* So O, A, C, D. Addit: *bot.* MS: *for.*

174   *seyen hem than.* So O. C: *seyen hem.* A: *seen hem.* Addit: *sey ham.* D: *han seen hem þan.* MS: *seie ham.*

183   *prophetes.* So MS. C: *profettes.* O, A, Addit, D: *prophecies.*

184   *other ben.* So O. MS: *oither hem.* A: *or shull.* Addit: *oþer be.* C: *or ben.* D: *or shal.*

187   *areisen agein.* So MS. O: *areys hit uppe.* A: *reisen hit up.* Addit: *rere hyn up.* C: *arered yt up.* D: *reisen it up.*

197   *six and fourty.* So Addit. MS: *vi and xl.* A, C: *sex and fourty.* D: *sixti and fourty.* O: *syxsty and forty.* Cov: *sixtie and fourtie.*

199   *Right.* So MS, Addit, C, D. O: *ryȝth.*

        men. So O, A, Addit, D. C: *me.* MS: *he.*

201   *he.* So MS. O, Addit, D: *Jesus.* A: *Jhesus.* C has extra lines here: *þei wolde not leven on hym be no wey / But evere dured forth yn here false lay.*

203   *loked.* So MS. Addit: *lokid.* O, A: *ordeyned.* D, Cov: *ordeined.* C: *holpen hym.*

205   *bileve.* So MS. C: *vylene.*

207   *such.* So O. D, A, C: *suche.* Addit: *swich.* MS: *suich.*

213   *Fendes.* So MS. O, A, D: *worldes.* Addit: *worldys.* Cov: *Worldis.* C: *suche.* C has extra lines here: *þerfore þei nolde hym a lyve y here / And yut worldes werks wrought he none.*

215   *areden.* So MS. O, C: *asked.* A, D: *askede.* Addit: *axid.*

216   *as God and man.* So O, A, C, D. MS: *als a good man.* Addit: *as god and god and man.*

217   *any.* So MS. O, C: *non.* A, D: *noon.* Addit: *none.*

218   *youre beest.* So A. MS: *youre o beest.* O: *ʒoure best.* Addit: *youre beste.* C: *þe best hys beste.* D: *oone of ʒoure bestis.*

219   *in*₁. So O, A, D. Addit, C: *yn.* MS: *and.*

226   *wolden.* So MS. O: *wold.* A, Addit: *wolde.* C: *shulde.* D: *myʒte.*

234   *wel.* So MS. O, A, C, D: *ful.*

237   *But.* So O, A, C, D. MS: *Ac.* Addit: *Bot.*

241   *That thei despyt.* So A, C. O: *þat þey despyt.* Addit: *þat þay despise.* D: *that dispit.* MS: *For thai no spyt.*

246   *sende.* MS: inserted above line.

251   *had.* So MS, A, Addit, D. O: *ne hadden.* C: *hadde.*

254   *michel.* So MS. C: *ful grete.*

262   *Bothe in toun and in strete.* So MS. O, Cov: *where he walked in toune or strete.* C: *where he walked yn toun oþer strete.* A, D: *where he walkede in toun or strete.* Addit: *whare so þay walkyd toun of strete.*

264   *be.* So MS. A, D: *goon.*

267   *thousand.* So O, C, D. MS: *man.* A: *thousandes.* Addit: *þusoond.*

270   *faren.* So MS. A: *pynede.*

278   *What manere men.* So A, D, Cov. MS: *Whan men.* O: *what maner men.* Addit: *what maner hy.* C: *what manere of men.*

282   *any other had.* So MS. O: *eny oþer so had.* A: *any oþur nacioun.* D: *ony othir nacioun.*

285   *He.* So O, A, C, D. MS: *þe.* Addit: *ʒet.*

288   *in eny envye brenne.* So O. MS: *in envie ne brenne.* A: *in any envye ben.* Addit: *yn eny brenne.* C: *yn envye bren.* D: *in any envie ben.*

294   *hymself.* So O, C. MS: *hym.* A: *hymselfe.* Addit: *hamself.* D: *hymsilfe.*

296   *vileynous.* So MS. A: *grevose and grete.*

302–03   *There thai wore gadered . . . / . . . thai spaken his ded.* So MS. Lines absent in O, Cov.

307   *leten.* So O, A, Addit, C, D. MS: *lete.*

309   *Romeins and other schull comen us on.* Line absent from C.

310   *fordon.* So MS, O, Addit, C. A: *fordoon.* D: *fodoon.*

320   *withoute skill.* So MS. O: *with skylle.* A: *by her skyll.* Addit: *wiþ will.* C: *ful stylle.* D: *by here wille.*

322   *quyt.* So O, A, Addit. MS: *crist.* C: *quyte.* D: *quite.*

325   *hym.* So MS. O, A: *hymself.* Addit: *hem.* D: *hymsilfe.*

326   *a man.* So O, A, Addit, C, D. MS: *no man.*

327   *thai.* So MS. C: *þay.* O, A: *her boyes.* C: *here here boyes.* D: *here boyes.*

336   *lither.* So MS. A: *evell.*

338   *felony.* So MS. O, C, D: *felonye.* A: *vileny.*

340   *That is Jesus on oure tunge leide.* So MS. C: *þat ihu on hem þe wronge wolde ley.*

342   *also.* MS: *al* inserted above line.

348   *Thei.* So A, C. MS, O: *that.* Addit: *þay.* D: *they.*

351   *Caiphas.* MS: decorated initial capital.

352   *we.* So MS. O, A, Addit, D: *men.* C: *me.* Cov: *ye.*

354   *ne were.* So O, A, Addit, D. C: *were.* MS: *nere.*

356   *the.* So O, A, Addit, C, D. MS: *tho.*

363   *blynde.* So A, C. MS: *holden.* O: *heled.* D: *blinde.* Addit: *brynd.* Cov: *hillid.*

373   *To prelates and to other men.* So O. MS: *Tuo prelates and tuo other men.* A: *two prelates and two
             other men.* Addit: *A preletis an oþer mene.* C: *Boþe to prelates and to oþer men.* D: *to prelates and
             to oþere men.*

373, 377   In the MS, there is a connection drawn between these two lines.

379   *Thus.* MS: decorated initial capital.

382   *citee.* So MS, A, D. O: *cyte.* Addit, C: *cite.*

383   *Effroem.* So MS. O, D: *Effreem.* A: *Eifraym.* Addit: *Effrem.* C: *Effraym.* Cov: *Effraem.*

384   *A.* So O, D, A, Addit, C. MS: *At.*

390   *That.* So MS. D: *they.* O: *þey.* A, C: *þei.* Addit: *þay.*

394   *That thoughtten alday don hym despitte.* So MS. Addit has an extra couplet after this line:
             Byhynd hys bak þay on hym liede / Afur hys ~~slyn~~ kyn þan þay aspide. Cov contains two extra
             lines: *Behynde his bak thei on hym lyed / After his kynde than thei aspied.*

399   *with sawe.* So MS, O. A: *with oon sawe.* Addit: *all bi on saw.* C: *with one sawe.* D: *with oone sawe.*

404   *iplight.* So MS, D. A: *yplyght.* O: *yplyȝth.* Addit: *ypliȝt.*

410   *Cripus.* So MS. Addit, C, D, Cov: *crispus.* O: *cryspus.*

411   *Jacob.* So O, A, Addit, C, D. MS: *joab.*

415   *dedes.* So O, A, C, D. Addit: *dedis.* MS: *bodes.*

422   *every.* So O, A, C, D. MS: *uche a.* Addit: *everch.*

426   *his₁.* So MS. O, A, C, D, Addit: *þat.*

427   *Joseph.* So O, A, Addit, C, D. MS: *Josep.*

429	Paraph mark in left margin.
434	*cursyng.* So MS. O, A, D: *skornynges.* Addit, C: *scornynge.*
442	*hende.* So O, A, C, D. MS: *ende.*
447	*Longens.* So A, Addit, C, D. MS, Cov: *Longius.*
449	Paraph mark in left margin.
454	*of₂.* So MS. O, A, D: *with.* Addit: *wiþ.* C: *wheche manere.*
471	*Bot Oure Lorde.* So MS. O: *but god lor.* A: *But god lorde.* Addit: *Bot god oure lorde.* C: *But yut oure lord god.* D: *but goode lorde.* Cov: *But god þe lorde.*
481	*Tho.* MS: decorated initial capital.
483	*Aggeus.* So MS O, A, Addit. C: *And ages.* D: *augeus.*
486	*Mychel.* So O. A: *michell.* Addit, D: *michel.* C: *myghel.* MS: *miȝhel.* Cov: *michelle.*
487	*Carianus.* So MS. O, Cov: *Caricius.* D: *Carisius.* Addit: *Carrasius.* C: *and þat was carrianne.* A: *Caryne.*
488	*Doumbe thai weren til swete Jhesus.* MS: *doumbe thai weren / til swete ihu.* O: *dombe þey were til swete ihs.* A: *Both þese in certeyn / Doumbe þei were til swete Jesus.* Addit: *Som þay were to suete ihus.* C: *Dombe þei were tyle swete ihus.* D: *doumbe þei were til swete jesus.*
492	*Of the lore.* So O, A, D. Addit: *þruȝ þe lore.* C: *þrow þe lore.* MS: *þe lore.*
495	*Also it witnesseth.* So A. O: *also wyttenesseþ.* Addit: *Also hit wittened.* C: *As yt ys wytnessed.* MS: *hise witnesseth.* D: *Also it witnessith.*
499	*wycked.* So O. A: *wickede.* Addit: *wickid.* C: *wykked.* D: *wicked.* MS: *wicken.*
531	*Jhesus.* So MS. O, A, C, D: *crist.* Addit: *cryst.*
536	*They sought and cleped thai hadden hym lor.* MS: *and soughtten in clepeden thai hadden hym lor.* O: *þey souȝt & cleped þey han hym lore.* A: *þei clepede and soght and haveth hym lore.* Addit: *þay soȝt & clepid þay had hym lore.* C: *þe soughte & cleped & hadde hym lore.* D: *they souȝten him cleped him þei han hym lore.*
541	*And also thai hadden.* So A: *And as þei stode in.* O: *And als þay stoden in.* Addit: *And as þey stode yn.* C: *And so þei stoden yn.* D: *And als þei stoode in.* MS: *also thai hadden.*
550	*they.* So O, Addit. A, C, D: *þei.* MS: *hy.*
554	*mad.* MS: inserted above line.
557	*taught.* So MS. O: *telde.* A, Addit, C, D: *tolde.*
561	*swythe.* So O, C. A: *swith.* Addit: *swiþ.* D: *swithe.* MS: *sinþe.*
564	*myght hem.* So C, A. Addit: *miȝt ham.* MS: *might.* O, D: *myȝt.*
	brought. MS: inserted above line.
569	*pay.* So MS. O, A, C, D: *pray.* Addit: *prey.*

571   *Joseph*. So O, A, Addit, C, D. MS: *josep*.

586   *be*. MS: inserted above line.

587   *Than*. MS: decorated initial capital.

           Secheth ye. So MS, O. A: *Seerche ʒe*. Addit: *seke ʒe*.

594   *socour*. So MS, A, D. O: *socoure*. Addit: *onoure*.

601   *Up in to the eir*. So MS. Cov: *Upon hiʒe ayens*.

608   *by hym stond*. So O. D: *by hym stonde*. A: *up stande*. C: *be hym stond*. MS: illegible here.

609   *face*. So O, A, C, D. MS: *nebbe*.

622   *let*. So MS, Addit. O, A, C, D: *lette*.

624   *more*. So MS, O, A, C, D. Addit: *mare*.

625   *fourti*. So MS. O: *forty*. Addit, C, D: *fourty*. A: *sexty*. Cov: *XL*.

626   *drede you non*. MS: *drede youre non*.

627   *And at the fourty dayes ende*. This line appears at the beginning of the MS, fol. 1r. MS is bound non-sequentially, with the first 626 lines appearing at the end of the MS, fols. 71v–72v, in compressed columns (two lines of text per MS line).

640   *biforne his foos*. So MS. O: *byforn his foos*. Addit: *he hem chose*.

644   *his*. So MS, O. D, A: *myn*. Addit: *my*.

669   *laughtten*. So MS. O: *laughten*. Addit: *caught*. D: *cauʒte*. C: *kaughte*. A: *toke*.

681   *Listneth*. MS: decorated initial capital.

693   *bereth*. So MS. O, Addit: *haþ*. A, C, D: *hath*.

712   *thee*. So MS. Addit, C: *all*.

716   *Hosie*. So MS. O: *Helye*. A: *Ely*. Addit: *Hely*. C, D: *Elye*. Cov: *Helie*.

731   *Qualme*. So MS, D. O: *on alive*. A: *Moreyne*. Addit: *Qualm*. C: *and eken moren*.

737   *plen*. So MS, O, Cov: *fleen*. Addit: *flee*. A, D: *sleen*. C: *slen*.

752   *theef*. So MS. Addit: *barning brynstone*.

759   *Whan*. MS: *a* inserted above the line.

775   *thei*. So A, D. MS: *hy*. Addit: *þey*.

781   *And*. So MS. O, A, Addit, C, D: *He*.

789–90   *Bestes for hym . . . boordes with monee*. So MS. These lines in Cov have an important adjustment and read: *The jewes gunne from hym to flee / and leften her boordes with monee*.

790   *felden boordes with monee.* So MS. O: *felden bordes with monee.* A: *fallede doun boordes with her monee.* Addit: *fell doun bordys wiþ mone.* C: *fellen a down the bordys with the mone.* D: *felden doun burdes with here mone.*

791   *to selle.* So MS, O, A. Addit, D: *to felle.* C: *to fyll.*

796   *deth with felonye.* So MS, O, C. D: *dethe with felonye.* Addit: *deþ wiþ felony.* A: *deth with vilenye.*

811   *Gode.* MS: decorated initial capital.

812   *how.* So O, A, Addit. D: *howe.* MS: *bow.*

826   *hereth.* So MS, O, A, D. Addit: *hireþ.*

830–34 *That other thraldom . . . with his lynage.* So MS. Lines absent in Cov.

836   *mychel.* So MS, O. Addit: *mochil.* A: *grete.* C: *gret.* D: *greet.*

846   *withouten.* So MS, C. A, Addit: *without.* O, D: *withoute.*

855   *Nou.* MS: decorated initial capital.

880   *barnetem.* MS: *tem* inserted above line. Cov: *children bidene.*

884   *he shulde.* So MS, D, Cov, Addit. O: *sche shulde.* A: *she shulde.* C: *he shold.*

885   *Of.* So O, A, D. Addit: *Oof.* C: *And of.* MS: *Er.*

899   *her werkes.* So MS. C: *heore cursyd werkys.*

900   *Taken thai nevere so wel her merkes.* So MS. Line absent in Cov.

911   *After.* MS: decorated initial capital.

917   *whiche.* MS: *whice.*

921   *hem that.* So O, A, C, D. MS: *hem of that.*

942   *brede.* So MS, O, D. Addit, A: *bred.*

963   *law.* So O, Addit. A, C, D: *lawe.* MS: *laghghe.*

965   *folk.* So MS. O, A, Addit, D: *folke.* C: *pepull.*

973   *also.* So MS, O. A, Addit, C, D: *as.*

989   *they were ylich.* So O. A: *þei were ylike.* Addit: *þay were ilich.* D: *þei were yliche.* MS: *thai yliche.* C: line absent.

1001   *Listneth.* MS: decorated initial capital.

1008   *fele.* So O, A, Addit, D, Cov. MS: *fole.*

1012   *thai.* So MS. O, D: *they.* A: *þei.* Addit: *þay.*

1014   *of.* MS: inserted above line.

1039   *of yren ysperred fast.* So O. MS: *of yrne.* A: *of iren ysperede faste.* Addit: *of yre sparrid fast.* C: *with yren ibarryd ful fast.* D: *of iren yspered fast.* Cov: *or iren isperred fast.*

1040   *suche.* So O, D. Addit: *such.* MS: *swice.*

1056   *wore.* So O, A, Addit, D. MS: *were.*

1060   *strenge.* So MS, O. A: *strynge.* Addit, D: *streng.* C: *stryng.*

1064   *yliche nere.* So MS, A. O: *ylych nere.* Addit: *hliche nere.* C: *ilich nere.* D: *iliche neer.*

1087   *On James, Ananias sone.* So O. A: *His name was hoten Ananus sone.* Addit: *Of ierusalem amayus sone.* C: *They callyd hym ihu anamas sone.* D: *His name was hoten ihu amaunes sone.* MS: *On ihus yat was godys sone.* Cov: *One James Ananias sone.*

1095   *worlde.* So O, D. MS: *werd.*

1097   *a voys.* So O, Addit, D. A: *a voice.* C: *a blast.* MS: illegible here.

1107   *hym.* So O, A, Addit, C, D. MS: *hem.*

1119   *For they ne might hym noght at holde.* MS: *For he ne might hym noȝt at holde.* O: *For they ne myght hym naght at holde.* A: *For þey ne might hym not at holde.* Addit: *For hy ne myȝt hym noȝt holde.* D: *for þei myȝte hym nouȝt with holde.*

1144   *Til she overcom hem by her book.* So MS. A: *þey levede neither woorde ny booke.*

1148   *For that thai hym to deth broughth.* So MS. Several manuscripts have an additional couplet after this line, as follows. O: *but al his wraþ had in veyn / for alle þe toknes þat þey had seyn.* A: *But all his wrath turnede to vayn / For all þe tokenes þat þei sayn.* Addit: *Bot all his wraþ torned in vayne / For all þe tokenes þay þay sayne.* C: *but all togedur they turned to veyn / for all the tokenus þat þey had seyn.* Cov: *But alle his wrath hadde in veine / For alle the tokenes that thei had seine.*

1151   *hurtlen.* So MS. O: *hurtel.* A: *hurtle.* Addit: *horle.* C: *hortyll.* D, Cov: *strive.*

1157   *Lete.* MS: decorated initial capital.

1166   *al to.* So O, A, Addit, D. C: *all to.* MS: *also.*

1167   *bye.* So MS. O, A: *laye.* Addit, C: *ley.* D: *leye.*

1209   *so.* MS: inserted above line.

1223   *Also.* MS: decorated initial capital.

1241   *mysberyng.* So O, D. A: *misberynge.* Addit: *misbering.* MS: *onys beryng.*

1265   *After.* MS: decorated initial capital.

1267   *the.* So MS, O, Addit, D. A, C: *þat.*

1273   *Galice.* So A, Addit, D. C: *Galis.* MS, Cov: *Galile.* O: *Galilee.*

1331   *of Jhesus dede.* So MS. Cov: *of þe jewes deedis.*

1363   *worlde.* So O, A, D. MS: *werd.*

1364   *heighest.* So MS. O: *heyest.* A, D: *nexte.* Addit, C: *next.*

1375   *emperoure.* So MS. C: *Syre Vaspasian.*

1379   *Sire.* MS: decorated initial capital.

1392   *barnetem.* So MS. Cov: *childre bigooten.*

1409   *povere.* So MS. O, A, Addit, C, D: *pore.* MS: *poile.*

1420   *wordes.* So MS, O, D. A, Addit: *wondres.* C: *wondyrs.*

1427   *by no resoun.* So MS, O, D. A: *by noo resoun.* Addit: *for no resoun.* C: *for no maner of reson.*

1428   *suspecioun.* So MS, O, Addit, D. A: *suspectioun.* C: *suspeccion.*

1429   *othere waye.* So MS. O: *other waye.* A: *oþer way.* Addit: *oþer wey.* C, D: *other way.*

1432   *put this werke on me.* So MS, O. A: *pytte þe work on me.* Addit: *pot þes worke on me.* C: *put thys werk on me.* D: *putte þis werke on me.*

1436   *kyn.* So MS, A, D. O, Addit: *kynne.*

1443   *mede thoo.* So MS, O, A. Addit: *knitis mede.* D: *mede tho.*

1444   *was.* MS: inserted above line.

        stolen. So O, A, C, D. MS: *stolne.* Addit: *stole.*

1483   *And.* MS: decorated initial capital.

        hath. So O, A, Addit, D. MS: *har.*

1502   *hym therfore.* So MS, O, D. C: *the child therefore.*

1533   *Pounthes.* So MS. O: *ponithos.* A: *peyntes.* Addit: *pnthos.* C: *pounce.* D: *pouns.* Cov: *Pouns.*

1534   *wilde.* So MS. Cov: *vile.*

1563   *thai ne parted.* So MS. O: *they ne perted.* A: *they ne partede.* Addit: *þe ne partid.* D: *þei ne parted.*

1587   *Cristes.* So MS. Cov: *cristen.*

1601   *Lucifer.* MS: decorated initial capital.

1623   *Tho.* MS: decorated initial capital.

1628   *That I noot.* MS: *I that I noot.* Emended for sense.

1639   *Sithen.* MS: decorated initial capital.

1644   *tolde.* So MS, A, Addit, D. C: *told.* O: *telde.*

1671   *falonus.* So MS. O: *feloun.* Addit: *felonus.* C: *heore fals.* D: *felynous.*

1684   *hym giltles.* So MS. Cov: *hym.*

1696   *Any thing heren of that man.* So MS. O: *ȝif y may auȝt heren of þat man.* A: *If I may heren oght of þat man.* Addit: *If y miȝt hire oȝt of þat man.* C: *ȝif I may here ouȝt of that man.* D: *ȝif i may heren of þat man.*

1698   *sounde.* So O, A, Addit, C, D. MS: *sonde.*

1729   *Than.* MS: decorated initial capital.

1731   *with al thi mayne.* So MS. O, D, Cov: *and come ageyn.* A: *and come agayn.* Addit: *and come agayne.* C: *with all þyn mayn.*

1737   *And more tresore than I can telle.* So MS. O: *ȝe more þan y þe can telle.* A: *ȝe more þan I can of telle.* Addit: *ȝe more þan y þe can tell.* C: *ȝe much more than I can tell.* D: *ȝe wel more thanne I can of telle.* Cov: *ȝe more than I can telle.*

1741   *hende.* So O, A, Addit, D. C: *hend.* MS: *hurde.*

1745   *fast by.* So O, A, Addit, C. D: *faste by.* MS: *sikerly.*

1762   *in this contré.* So D, C. MS: *in in this cite.* O: *in þys cyte.* A: *in þis citee.* Addit: *yn þes cite.*

1821   *gode.* So MS, O, Addit. A, D: *kynde.* C: *kynd.*

1830   *thar.* So MS. O: *þere.* Addit: *dare.* D: *darst.* C: *shalt.*

1881–82   *And asken yif . . . / . . . shuldest hym owe.* So MS. Lines absent from A, D.

1885   *tharwhile.* So MS. O: *ther while.* A: *the while.* Addit: *þat while.* C: *for a wyle.* D: *there þat while.*

1887   *anothere.* So MS, O, A, Addit, C, D: *another.*

1906   *thee.* So MS, O, A. D: *yow.*

1908   *his.* So O, A, Addit, C, D. Gap in MS.

1909   *thou.* So MS, A, D. O, Addit, C: *thu.*

1911   *thu no thyng.* So MS, O, C. Addit: *þu noþing.* D: *the nothing.* Line absent in A.

1913   *lette.* So O, Addit, D. A: *lete.* C: *lett.* MS: *bette.*

1926   *passed.* So MS, O. Addit: *passid.* A, D: *ascaped.* C: *scapyd.*

1935   *Ac sir.* So MS. O, A, Addit: *Sire.* D: *Sir.* C: *And syre.*

1946   *And I wende.* So MS, A. O: *And Y wende.* Addit: *And y wend.* C: *and when I am grevyd I goo.* D: *And ofte I wende.*

1948   *long.* So MS. O, C: *boþ.* D: *boþe.*

1968   *That thou graunte.* So MS. O: *Thu wilt.* A: *þat þou wilt.* Addit: *þat þu.* C: *That thu woll.* D: *that thou.*

1973   *conne.* So MS. D: *konne.* O: *kunne.* A: *coon.* Addit: *cone.* C: *con.*

1974   *Goddes.* So MS, A, D. O: *godes.* Addit: *Mari.* C: *goddus.*

1977   *a flixa.* So MS. O: *a flyxe.* A: *þe flux.* Addit: *þe flix.* C, D: *the flux.*

2010   *And handled a litel upon his wede.* So MS. C: *and hopyd of hym to have goode mede.*

2018   *Left.* So O, Addit. A: *Lefte.* C: *Laft.* D: *bilefte.* MS: *lefce.*

2027   *Natheles I wel thee now telle.* So MS. O: *Naþeles y wul þe now telle.* A: *Nevertheles sire I the telle.* Addit: *Naþeles siþ y will þe tell.* C: *Natheles syre as y the tell.* D: *Natheles sir as I the telle.*

2033   *Velosyan.* MS: decorated initial capital.

2036 *Oo tidyng I wil telle thee.* So MS. Line absent in Cov.

2040 *I.* So MS. O: *y.* A, Addit, C, D: *he.*

2063 *so.* MS: inserted above line.

2074 *he hem.* So MS, O, D. A: *unto hem.* Addit: *he ham.* C: *hem he.*

2090 *And seiden Listneth.* So MS. O: *whiltou heren.* A: *wilt þou heere.* Addit: *wyll þow here.* C: *And wylt thu here.* D: *Sir wele ʒe heren.* Cov: *Wolt thou hire.*

2132 *Forsothe.* So MS, O. A: *Per fay.* Addit: *maffay.* C: *ʒis hardely.* D: *mafreye.*

2135 *Than.* MS: decorated initial capital.

2154 *and.* So MS, O, Addit. A, C, D: *by.*

2166 *And enbraced hym to hym fast.* So MS, O. Addit: *And enbracyd to hym faste.* A: *And byclipte Velocian faste.* C: *A lord he semeth full syker & faste.* D: *and byklipte velosian ful faste.*

2173 *And leve Y, dye Y.* So C. MS: *Lyve I dye I.* O: *Lyf y dye.* A: *Wheþer I live or dye.* Addit: *Love y dye.* D: *Lyve i dyne.*

2175–76 *A lorde he semeth ful stedfast / That I so sone to hym am cast.* So MS. O: *a lorde he semeþ ful stedefast.* These lines are inverted in A, Addit, C, D. Addit: *þatt i so sone to hym am caste / A lorde he semyd full stedefste.* C: *that þus sone on hym myn hert is cast / a lord he semeth full syker & stodefast.* A: *That I to hym þus am cast / A lorde he bysemeth ful studefast.* D: *that i to hym thus sone am cast / he semede a lorde ful stidefast.*

2187 *shal fallen.* So O. Addit: *schall falle.* A: *shall be.* C: *y by tymes.* MS: *forsoþe.*

2189 *Amorowen.* MS: decorated initial capital.

2198 *At that fest.* So MS, O. A: *Of myrthe and game.* Addit: *Fest & game.* C: *Revell & game.* D: *of murthe and gamen.*

2199 *inough.* So Addit, C, D. O: *ynow.* A: *ynogh.* MS: *a feste.* Cov: *ynowgh.*

2201 *A.* MS: decorated initial capital.

2202 Addit: a passage of approximately 182 lines appears in the wrong place. Lines 2201–382 are inverted with lines 3820–4002.

2205 *Pope.* So MS. Cov has an erasure over this word.

2206 *gonne come.* So MS. O, A, C, D: *come.*

2256 *Hou and whi.* So MS, O. C: *how and whi.* A, D: *why and wherfore.*

2267 *thi.* So MS, D. O, A, C: *thy.*

2275 *Noo wonder thogh hym thoghte longe.* So A. O: *No wonder þon hym þouʒt longe.* C: *And no wondur theygh hym thouʒt long.* D: *no wonder they hym þouʒte ful longe.* MS: *No wonder þeiʒ hym longe.*

2296 *mychel.* So O. MS: *mmychel.* A: *mikell.* C: *mykell.* D: *mochel.*

2297   *Velosyan.* So MS. O, D: *Velosian.* A: *Velocian.* C: *Velosyan.*

2309   *Sir.* MS: decorated initial capital.

2336   *tyllen.* So C. D: *telen.* A: *husband.* MS: *tiliyen.* O: illegible here. Cov: *tilien.*

2341   *smelle swete.* So O, Cov. A: *smellen swete.* C: *smellen bothe swete.* D: *smellen þe swete.* MS: *smelle with swete.*

2350   *Hevene blis.* So MS. O: *Heven blis.* A: *heven blisse.* C: *hevyn all.* D: *blisse.*

2352   *ende.* MS: *ennde.*

2354   *wicked.* So MS, D. O: *wycked.* A: *wickede.* C: *wykked.*

2383   Addit: At this point, the manuscript aligns with other manuscripts.

2394   *Lorde.* So MS, O, Addit. A, D: *Maister.* C: *mayster.*

2403   *Than.* MS: decorated initial capital.

2404   *hote.* So MS. Cov: *promice.*

2428   *Forthi.* So MS, D. O, A: *Forthy.* Addit: *For why.* C: *Therefore.*

2431   *The.* So MS, O, A, Addit, D. C: *But the.*

2432   *In.* So MS, O. A, D: *In the.* Addit, C: *Into.*

2433   *Bot.* So MS. O, A, Addit, C, D: *But.*

2435   *These.* So MS. O, Addit: *Thes.* A, D: *The.* C: *For the.*

2472   *her.* So O, A, Addit. C: *heore.* D: *here.* MS: *þair.*

2474   *ich understonde.* So MS, O. Addit: *i undyrstone.* A: *þurgh his sonde.* D: *þoruʒ his sonde.* C: *all throuʒ his sonde.*

2480   *shapp.* So O. D, Cov: *shape.* Addit: *schape.* A: *ʒifte.* MS: *shaft.*

2491   *sawe.* So O. MS: *saghʒe.* A: *segh.* Addit: *say.* C: *sygh.* D: *seiʒ.*

2552   *As is fallen, forsothe we kenne.* So MS. C: *iblessyd be ihu oure lord amen.*

2555   *Tho.* MS: decorated initial capital.

2609   *Do me come.* So O, Addit, D, Cov. A: *Doo me come.* C: *and make com hydur.* MS: *Do me to come.*

2630   *wytherwyne.* So MS. Cov: *þat cursid lyne.*

2647   *servauntz.* So MS. O: *servaunt.* A, D: *armes.* Addit: *servauntys.* C: *armus.*

2676   *man do hem.* So O, A, Addit, C. MS: *man ne do hem.* D: *to hem they do.*

2711   Addit: marginal note reading *de ingressione Vespasiani ad nauem cum omni populo versus Ierusalem* [about the entrance of Vespasian onto the ship with all the people against Jerusalem] before this line.

2729   *Thay.* MS: decorated initial capital.

2733   *whoo.* So MS. O, A, Addit, C, D, Cov: *what.*

2740   *he.* So A, Addit, C, D. O: *þey.* MS: *thre.*

2762   *it.* So MS. O, A, Addit, C, D: *hem.*

2789   *best.* MS: inserted above line.

2795   *Here.* MS: decorated initial capital.

2814   Addit: heading reading *de tristicia pilati* [about the sadness of Pilate].

2815   *Thoo.* MS: decorated initial capital.

2847   *hadde Pilate no grace.* So D. O: *had pilate no grace.* A: *had Pilate noo grace.* Addit: *hadde pilat no grace.* MS: *and ȝut pilate no grace hadde.*

        In the MS, *hadde* is circled in the margin and inserted with a caret to preserve rhyme and what passes for meter.

2849   *qued.* So MS. Cov: *dethe.*

2865   *praie.* So MS. O, Addit: *pray.* A, C, D: *rede.*

2885   *I woot it is.* So MS. O, A: *hit is.* Addit: *it ys.* C: *and hit is.* D: *it is.*

2898   *outhest.* So O, C. D: *outeheste.* A: *houthest.* Addit: *ontys.* MS: *oticheste.*

2907   *On.* MS: decorated initial capital.

2914   *nedes.* So MS, O, A, D. Addit, C: *nedys.*

2929   *they.* So Addit, C, D. O: *þay.* A: *þei.* MS: *thare.*

2932   *staf-slyngys.* So MS, Addit. C, D: *staf slynges.* O: *staffe slynges.*

2934   *reisen.* So MS. O, C: *reysen.* A, Addit, D: *risen.*

2959   *yere.* So MS, O. A, Addit, C: *ȝere.* D: *ȝeere.*

2963   *Whan.* MS: decorated initial capital.

2987   *some.* So O. A, D: *somme.* Addit: *som.* C: *sum.* MS: *summe.*

3006   *Hou.* So O. MS: *oon.* A: *to do.* Addit: *done.* C: *to make.* D: *to done.*

3020   *ageins us.* So MS. O: *aȝeyns us.* Addit: *Aȝens ous.* A: *wroth with us.* C: *now wroth with us.* D: *wrothe with us.*

3025   *I ne wot from whennes.* MS: *wot from* circled in margin and inserted after *ne* with a caret.

3044   *Yonder.* So MS. O, A: *þat is.* Addit: *þat ys.* C: *that ȝondur is.* D: *that is.*

3073   *Beaw sire.* So MS. O: *Beau sire.* Addit: *Bele sir.* C: *Now beau syre.* A: *By all þinges.* D: *By al thyng.*

3080   *For he wolde have hym ylorne.* So MS. Cov has an extra couplet after this line: *Therefor the children he slouȝ alle / For he wende þat god shulde in þat lotte have falle.*

3102   *prate.* So MS. Addit: *prete.* O, A, C, D, Cov: *threte.*

3118   *bote.* So MS. O, Addit, C: *or.* A, D: *er.*

3119–20   *Sorough have he . . . maketh you yare.* Lines inverted in O.

3140   *pouver.* MS: *ppouver.*

3149   *It.* MS: decorated initial capital.

3152   *ageins his pay.* After this line, Cov includes a Latin note: *hic vaspasianus electus est in Imperatorem* [here Vespasian is elected to the imperial throne].

3158   *hom.* So MS. O, C: *home.* A: *þider.* Addit: *þedyr.* D: *thedir.*

3166   *That hym toke a cardiake.* So A, D. MS: *Þat hym took þe cardiacle.* O: *That hym toke a cardiacke.* Addit: *þat hym toke a cordyake.* C: *that hym then toke a cardyake.*

3189   *Hereth.* MS: decorated initial capital.

3229   *an.* So MS. O, A, D: *this.* Addit: *þes.* C: *thys.*

3247   *he.* MS: inserted above line.

3256   *That.* So O, A, Addit, C, D. MS: *of that.*

3266   *hys lyf.* MS: a caret appears after *hys*, which is written *hy* with a macron over the *y*. *hys lyf* appears in a box at the end of the line.

3306   *Go.* So MS, O. Addit, D: *do.* A: *doo.* C: *leteth.*

3316   *I graunte thee wel sykerly.* MS: *i graunte thee ~~al~~ wel sykerly.*

3329   *For to hiden in that stede.* MS: *forto hiden ~~hem~~ in that stede.*

3348   *cowardes to.* MS: *to* inserted after *cowardes* above line with a caret.

3370   *Ac.* So O. MS: *At.* A, Cov: *But.* Addit: *As.* C: *Natheles.* D: *And.*

3396   *duelle a throwe.* So Addit. MS: *duelle throwe.* O: *dwellen a þrow.* A: *dwell a throwe.* C: *dwell a throw.* D: *dwellen a þrowe.*

3432   *so longe as.* MS: inserted above line.

3457   *dede.* MS: added in right margin.

3474   *forbad.* So MS, O, C. Addit, A: *forbede.* D: *forbed.*

3482   *summe.* So MS. O: *some.* A: *þei.* Addit: *som.* C: *sum.* D: *they.*

3525   *Pilate.* MS: decorated initial capital.

3526   *he quoke.* So MS, O, Addit, C, D. A: *he qwoke.*

3536   *Or we deyyen al the route.* So MS. O: *or we amyddes al þe doute.* A: *or elles we in myddes her route.* Addit: *as do we wiþeoute doute.* C: *and that happeli or we amyddus all heore rout.* D: *or elles we amiddes the route.* Cov: *or we amyddis alle the rout.*

3540   *help be.* MS: *be* inserted after *help* above line with a caret.

3546   *goo.* So MS, A, D. O, Addit: *go.* C: *tho.*

3557   *they.* So O, Addit, D. A: *þei.* MS: *hy.*

3602   *firste.* So D. MS: *frst.* O: *furst.* Addit: *fyrst.*

3611   *Velosyan.* So MS. O: *Velosian.* A: *Veroigne.* Addit, Cov: *Verone.* D: *Veroyne.*

3648   *ben.* MS: *ben ben.* Emended for sense.

3673   *For.* So MS, O. A, D: *But.* Addit: *Butt.* C: *And.*

3687   *Josephus.* MS: decorated initial capital.

3690   *conne.* So MS, O. A: *cone.* Addit: *come.* D: *konne.*

3697   *youre.* So MS. O, A, C, D: *oure.* Addit: *our.*

3708   *to.* MS: inserted above line.

3720   There is a lacuna in O beginning after this line; the text picks up again at line 3775.

3723   *It.* So MS, D. A, Addit: *Hit.* C: *And hit.*

3743   *mysdon.* So MS, C. A, D: *mysdoon.* Addit: *mysdone.*

3757   *For we that lyven now abyen ful sore.* MS: rough sketches of stylized faces drawn in same ink as the text appear in the margin below this column.

3778   *thi.* So MS, A, Addit, D. O, C: *thy.*

3785   *Tho.* MS: decorated initial capital. Cov: *Whan.*

3810   *Doun of hym after his syde.* So MS. Cov: *And gnewe of hym alle his hide.*

3821   *Pilate.* MS: decorated initial capital. Addit: the 182-line inversion begins again here: the lines that are properly lines 2201–382 appear here, lines 3820–4002.

3900   *Witnessed it everychon.* So MS. Line absent from A, C, D.

3914   Douce, a partial manuscript, begins here and continues to the end of the poem.

3918   *hole.* So MS. Douce: *holpyn.*

3919   *was.* So MS, O. A: *wex.* C: *waxith.* D, Douce: *wax.*

3945   *Josephus.* MS: decorated initial capital.

3961   *sey.* So O, A. MS: *see.* D: *seie.*

3973   *Al.* So MS, O, D, A, C: *all.*

3995   *for myne hele.* So Cov. MS: *for nyme hele.* O, A, D, Douce: *for myn hele.* C: *for my hele.*

4003   *Go.* MS: decorated initial capital. Addit: the manuscript realigns with other manuscripts from here to the end of the poem.

4020   *And houndes thritty mute therto.* So MS. O: *& houndes þrytty mute þerto.* A: *Of houndes xxxti medes þerto.* Addit: *Of houndys þtretty hundred þerto.* C: *And of houndus þrytty innotus eken therto.* D: *and an hundred hondes þat be mete þerto.* Douce: *Of houndis þritty muȝt and mo.*

4037	*mekely.* So MS, O. A, D: *me liketh.* Addit: *me likeþe.* C: *me lyketh.* Douce: *me lykyþ.* Cov: *me likith.*
4039	*worlde.* So O, A, Addit. C: *werld.* D: *werde.* MS: *werd.* Douce: *word.* Cov: *world.*
4053	*the.* MS: inserted above line.
4070	*the knighttes.* So MS. O, A, D: *the knyghtes.* Addit, Douce: *þe knyȝtys.* C: *the knyȝtus.*
4110	*be ordeyned to.* So MS. O: *he wul hit.* A, D: *he wil it.* Addit: *he wyll yt.* C: *he wol hit.* Douce: *it shal be.* Cov: *he wolle it fall.*
4118	*That honoured hym with gode entent.* So O. A: *þat honoured hym with mychel entent.* Addit: *þat honoured hym with grete entent.* C: *þat wurship hym with good entent.* D: *that honoured hym wiþ mochel entent.* MS: *Hat honoured hym with god entent.* Douce: *þat turned hym to good entente.*
4120	*bothers.* So MS, O. A, Addit, D, Douce: *bothe.* C: *both.*
4132	*won.* So MS, O, C, A, D: *woon.* Addit: *wone.*
4133	*save.* So O, A, C, D, Douce. Addit: *saffe.* MS: *alive.*
4134	*lyves have.* MS: illegible addition above the line between these words.
4172	*shame.* MS: *me* inserted above line.
4200	*ferther.* So O, Addit, D. A: *forther.* C: *ferthere.* Douce: *feþere.* MS: *feirer.*
4225	*and.* MS: inserted above line.
4230	*nawght.* MS: *nawȝt* added in margin.
4247	*summe.* So MS, C, D. A, Addit: *somme.* O: *sume.* Douce: *noumbre.*
4265	*Thoo.* MS: decorated initial capital.
4271	*Sir.* MS: inserted above line.
4285	*and.* MS: inserted above line.
4303	*clad.* So MS, A, C, D, Douce. O: *cladde.* Addit: *clas.*
4345	*gynes.* So MS. Cov: *manaclis.*
4368	*jestes.* So O, A. Addit, D: *gest.* C: *gestys.* MS: *goste.* Douce: *geste.*
4375	*forlorne.* So MS, O. A, D, Douce: *lorn.* Addit: *forlore.*
4380	*fouler.* So MS, O, Addit. Douce: *foulere.*
4409	*byfore.* MS: *fore* inserted above line.
4410	*they.* So O, C, Douce. A: *þei.* Addit: *þay.* D: *thei.* MS: *hy.*
4461	*Now.* MS: decorated initial capital.
4532	*tale.* So MS. O: *case.* A, D: *caas.* Addit, Douce: *cas.*
4554	*biten.* So MS, O. Douce: *bytyn.*

4608	*was Judas.* So A, Addit, C, D, Douce. MS: *was liþer Judas.* O: *was lyþer Judas.*
4610	*a gret.* MS: added at end of line with a box around it.
4638	*helpen.* So O. MS, A, D: *helpe.* Addit, C: *help.* Douce: *helpyn.*
4657	*hym ne.* So MS, A, D. Addit, C: *he ne.*
4686	*leve.* So O, A, Addit, C, D. MS: *lete.* Douce: *letyn.*
4703	*Al his cas he tolde hym sone.* So MS. C: there is a gap of 28 lines here; the poem picks up again at line 4730.
4750	*be.* So O, A, Addit. C: *shall.* D: *shal.* MS: *worþe.*
4785	*tenth.* So Addit, C. D: *tenþe.* A: *tethe.* O: *tende.* MS: *tiende.*
4799	*tenthe.* So A, Douce. Addit: *ten.* C: *tennth.* D: *tiþe.* O: *tende.* MS: *tiende.*
4804	*his.* MS: inserted above line.
4807	*evere.* So MS. O, C: *ever.* A, D: *ay.* Addit: *evyr.*
4820	*what.* So O, A, Addit, C, D, Douce. MS: *whhat.*
4859	*Now.* MS: decorated initial capital.
4872	*Thorough the.* MS: *the* inserted after *Thorough* above line with a caret.
4876	*The keyes of citees, castels, and toun.* So MS. O ends here.
4887	*dude.* So MS, Addit. A: *yhad.* C: *eken.* D: *it hadde.* Douce: *so hadde.*
4909	*Than.* MS: decorated initial capital.
4928	*gan.* So A, Addit, D, Douce. C: *can.* MS: *ga.*
4932	*And.* So A, Addit, C, D, Douce. MS: *ant.*
4935	*Seint.* So MS, D. Addit, C, Douce: *Seynt.* A: *Sire.*
4937	*Gost.* So MS, Addit. A, D: *lande.* C, Douce: *lond.*
4960	*hevedes.* So MS. Cov: *beerdis.*
4972	*And his men everychon.* So MS, Addit. A: *And Titus his sone and everychon.* C: *And tytus his son also & sethen everychon.* D: *And Titus his sone and everychoon.* Douce: *and titus his sone & everychon.*
4995	*Petres mynster.* So A. Addit: *Petyrys mayster.* C: *seynt petrus mynstre.* D: *petres maister.* MS: *name hem.* Douce: *petris menstre.* Cov: *Petir his maister.*
4997	*Seint.* MS: decorated initial capital.
5005	*Pope.* MS: *pope.*
5007	*Popes.* MS: *popes.*
5009	*Pope.* MS: *pope.*

5015   *Pope.* MS: *pope.*

5049   *A.* MS: decorated initial capital.

5054   *Thai that ne dyed in that synful toun.* So MS. A: *þat God wolde of þat synfull toun.* Addit: *þat ded wold of þat senfull toune.* C: *That God wold han of that synfull town.* D: *that God wolde of that synful toun.* Douce: *þat God wolde of þat synful toun.*

5055   *assentaund.* So MS. A, C: *assentant.* Addit, D: *assentaunt.* Douce: *assentid.*

5068   *Shulde lyven to dwellen thore.* So MS. Cov has two additional lines following this one: *But thei shulden her wonynge wide / Ordeine aboute in eche a side.*

5069   *a litell.* So A, Addit. C: *a lytyll.* D: *a litel.* MS: *þat ilche.*

5096   *glowede.* MS: *de* inserted above line.

5102   *alweys.* So MS. A: *allweyes.* Addit: *allwey.* C: *allgatys.* D: *alweies.* Douce: *alwey.*

5118   *That fourty yer he abood.* So MS. Cov ends here.

5124   *sawe.* So A. Addit: *sey.* C: *syȝ.* D: *siȝe.* MS: *saghȝe.* Douce: *seyȝ.*

5138   *aventours.* So A, D, Douce. Addit: *aventourys.* C: *aventourus.* MS: *aventoutoures.*

Explicit   *Here endeth the vengeaunce of Goddes deth.* So MS. A: *Thus endeth þe seege of Jerusalem / Rede hit for trewe and for noo dreme.* Addit: *Here endiþ þe vengaunce of godys deþe / mercy lady help.* C: *liber joannis blandi / explicit hit sedes uf obsidium de / civitate jerusalem / ihs est amor meus* [the book of charming John / this place ends the siege of / the city of Jerusalem / in this sign is my love]. D: *Here endith the sege of jerusalem.* Douce: *Here hendiþ þe sege of jerusalem.*

✤ BIBLIOGRAPHY

MANUSCRIPTS AND DOCUMENTS

New Haven, Beinecke Library, MS Osborn A.11, fols. 1r–38v.
　　Online at https://brbl-dl.library.yale.edu/vufind/Record/4161295.
Oxford, Bodleian, MS Digby 230, fols. 195r–223v.
Oxford, Bodleian, MS Douce 78, fols. 19r–76v.
Oxford, Bodleian, MS Douce 126.
Oxford, Bodleian, MS Laud Misc. 622, fols. 1r–21v, 71v–72v.
London, British Library, MS Additional 10036, fols. 2r–61v.
London, British Library, MS Additional 36523, fols. 1r–71r.
London, British Library, MS Additional 36983, fols. 216r–255r.
London, British Library, MS Harley 4733, fols. 40v–127r .
Coventry, City Records Office MS 325/1, fols. 98r–129v.
Cambridge, Magdalene College, Cambridge, MS Pepys 2014 (formerly Pepys 37.)
New York, Pierpont Morgan, MS M.898, fols. 1r–100r.

PRIMARY SOURCES

Alighieri, Dante. *The Divine Comedy: Inferno*. Trans. Charles S. Singleton. Vol. 1. Princeton: Princeton University Press, 1977.
Ammianus Marcellinus. *History: Books 27–31. Excerpta Valensiana*. Trans. John C. Rolfe. Cambridge, MA: Harvard University Press, 1939.
———. *History: Books 20–26*. Trans. John C. Rolfe. Cambridge, MA: Harvard University Press, 1940.
———. *History: Books 14–19*. Trans. John C. Rolfe. Cambridge, MA: Harvard University Press, 1950.
Andrew, Malcolm, and Ronald Waldron, eds. *Sir Gawain and the Green Knight*. In *The Poems of the Pearl Manuscript: Pearl, Cleanness, Patience, Sir Gawain and the Green Knight*. Exeter: University of Exeter Press, 1978. Rpt. 2007. Pp. 207–300.
Appian. *The Iberian War*. In *Roman History*. Ed. and trans. Brian McGing. Vol. 1. Cambridge, MA: Harvard University Press, 2019. Pp. 136–307.
———. *The Mithridatic War*. In *Roman History*. Ed. and trans. Brian McGing. Vol. 3. Cambridge, MA: Harvard University Press, 2019. Pp. 146–393.
Aquinas, Thomas. *Summa Theologica*. Vol. 28: Law and Political Theory (Ia2æ. 90–97). Ed. Thomas Gilby. Cambridge: Cambridge University Press, 2006.
Augustine, Saint. *The City of God*. Trans. Demetrius B. Zema, Gerald G. Walsh, Grace Monahan, and Daniel J. Honan. 3 vols. Washington D. C.: The Catholic University of America Press, 1950–54.

————. *The Trinity*. Trans. Stephen McKenna. Washington, D.C.: The Catholic University of America Press, 2002.

Boccaccio, Giovanni. T*he Decameron*. Trans. G. H. McWilliam. 2nd edition. London: Penguin Books, 2003.

Bonaventure, Saint. *The Mind's Road to God*. Trans. George Boas. Upper Saddle River, NJ: Prentice-Hall, 1953.

Boyarin, Adrienne Williams, ed. and trans. *The Siege of Jerusalem*. Toronto: Broadview Press, 2014.

Caesar. *The Gallic War*. Trans. H. J. Edwards. Cambridge, MA: Harvard University Press, 1917.

Cassiodorus. *Institutions of Divine and Secular Learning and On the Soul*. Trans. James W. Halporn. Liverpool: Liverpool University Press, 2004.

Chandler, John H., ed. *The King of Tars*. Kalamazoo, MI: Medieval Institute Publications, 2015.

Chaucer, Geoffrey. *The Riverside Chaucer*. Gen. Ed. Larry D. Benson. 3rd edition. Boston: Houghton Mifflin, 1987.

Cicero. *Pro Flacco*. In *In Catilinam 1–4. Pro Murena. Pro Sulla. Pro Flacco*. Trans. C. Macdonald. Cambridge, MA: Harvard University Press, 1976. Pp. 413–557.

Coletti, Theresa, ed. *The Digby Mary Magdalene Play*. Kalamazoo, MI: Medieval Institute Publications, 2018.

Comestor, Peter. *Historia Scholastica*. In *Patrologia Latina*. Vol. 198. Ed. J. P. Migne. Paris, Petit-Montrouge,1853. Columns 1053–1722.

Curley, Michael J., trans. *Physiologus*. Austin: University of Texas Press, 1979.

Davidson, Clifford, ed. *The York Corpus Christi Plays*. Kalamazoo, MI: Medieval Institute Publications, 2011.

D'Evelyn, Charlotte, and Anna J. Mill, eds. *The South English Legendary: Edited from Corpus Christi College Cambridge MS. 145 and British Museum MS. Harley 2277 with Variants from Bodley MS. Ashmole 43 and British Museum MS. Cotton Julius D. IX*. 3 vols. EETS o.s. 235, 236, 244. London: Oxford Univeristy Press, 1956–59.

Ehrman, Bart D., and Zlatko Pleše, eds. and trans. *The Apocryphal Gospels: Texts and Translations*. Oxford: Oxford University Press, 2011.

Eidelberg, Shlomo, ed. and trans. *The Jews and the Crusaders: The Hebrew Chronicles of the First and Second Crusades*. Hoboken, NJ: KTAV Publishing House, 1996.

Eusebius. *The Ecclesiastical History*. Vol. 1. Trans. Kirsopp Lake. Vol. 2. Trans. J. E. L. Oulton and H. J. Lawlor. Cambridge, MA: Harvard University Press, 1975.

————. *Life of Constantine*. Trans. Averil Cameron and Stuart G. Hall. Oxford: Oxford University Press, 1999.

Fischer, Rudolf, ed. "*Vindicta Salvatoris.*" *Archiv für das Studium der neueren Sprachen und Literaturen* 111 (1903), 285–98 and 112 (1904), 25–45.

Florus. *Epitome of Roman History*. Trans. E. S. Forster. Cambridge, MA: Harvard University Press, 1929.

Ford, Alvin E, ed. *La Vengeance de Nostre-Seigneur: The Old and Middle French Prose Versions: The Version of Japheth*. Toronto: Pontifical Institute for Medieval Studies, 1984.

Foster, Edward E., ed. *Amis and Amiloun*. In *Amis and Amiloun, Robert of Cisyle, and Sir Amadace*. Kalamazoo, MI: Medieval Institute Publications,1997. Pp. 1–88.

Gower, John. *Confessio Amantis*. Ed. Russell A. Peck, with Latin translations by Andrew Galloway. 3 vols. 2nd edition. Kalamazoo, MI: Medieval Institute Publications, 2006–13.

Gryting, Loyal A. T., ed. *The Oldest Version of the Twelfth Century Poem La Venjance Nostre Seigneur*. Ann Arbor: University of Michigan Press, 1952.

Hanna, Ralph, and David Lawton, eds. *The Siege of Jerusalem*. EETS o.s. 320. Oxford: Oxford University Press, 2003.

Herbert, J. A., ed. *Titus and Vespasian, or The Destruction of Jerusalem in Rhymed Couplets: Edited from the London and Oxford MSS*. London: Roxburghe Club, 1905.

Herzman, Ronald B., Graham Drake, and Eve Salisbury, eds. *Four Romances of England: King Horn, Havelok the Dane, Bevis of Hampton, Athelston*. Kalamazoo, MI: Medieval Institute Publications, 1999.

———. *Bevis of Hampton*. In *Four Romances of England*. Pp. 187–340.

———. *Havelock the Dane*. In *Four Romances of England*. Pp. 73–185.

———. *King Horn*. In *Four Romances of England*. Pp. 11–70.

Herodotus. *The Persian Wars: Books 1–2*. Trans. A. D. Godley. Cambridge, MA: Harvard University Press, 1920.

———. *The Persian Wars: Books 3–4*. Trans. A. D. Godley. Cambridge, MA: Harvard University Press, 1921.

———. *The Persian Wars: Books 5–7*. Trans. A. D. Godley. Cambridge, MA: Harvard University Press, 1922.

———. *The Persian Wars: Books 8–9*. Trans. A. D. Godley. Cambridge, MA: Harvard University Press, 1925.

Higgins, Iain Macleod, ed. and trans. *The Book of John Mandeville with Related Texts*. Indianapolis, IN: Hackett Publishing, 2011.

The Holy Bible: Douay-Rheims Version. Rockford, IL: Tan Books and Publishers, 1899. Online at http://www.drbo.org/.

Hulme, William Henry, ed. "Gospel of Nicodemus." In *The Middle-English Harrowing of Hell and Gospel of Nicodemus*. EETS e.s. 100. London: Oxford University Press, 1907. Rpt. 1961. Pp. 22–136.

Jacobus de Voragine. *The Golden Legend: Readings on the Saints*. Trans. William Granger Ryan. 2 vols. Princeton, NJ: Princeton University Press, 1993.

Jerome, Saint. *Sancti Eusebii Hieronymi Epistulae*. Ed. Isidorus Hilberg. 3 vols. Vienna: F. Tempsky, 1910–18.

———. *On Illustrious Men*. Trans. Thomas P. Halton. Washington, D. C.: The Catholic University of America Press, 1999.

Josephus. *The Jewish War*. Trans. H. St. J. Thackeray. 3 vols. Cambridge, MA: Harvard University Press, 1927–28. Rpt. 1997.

———. *Jewish Antiquities*. Trans. H. St. J. Thackeray, Ralph Marcus, Allen Wikgren, and Louis H. Feldman. 9 vols. Cambridge, MA: Harvard University Press, 1930–65. Rpt. 1998.

———. *Flavius Josephus: Translation and Commentary*. Vol. 9: *Life of Josephus*. Ed. and trans. Steve Mason. Leiden: Brill, 2001.

———. *Against Apion*. Trans. John M. G. Barclay. Leiden: Brill, 2007.

———. *The Jewish War*. Trans. Martin Hammond and Martin Goodman. Oxford: Oxford University Press, 2017.

Julian of Norwich. *The Shewings of Julian of Norwich*. Ed. Georgia Roman Crampton. Kalamazoo, MI: Medieval Institute Publications, 1994.

Kempe, Margery. *The Book of Margery Kempe*. Ed. Lynn Staley. Kalamazoo, MI: Medieval Institute Publications, 1996.

Langland, William. *Piers Plowman: A Parallel-Text Edition of the A, B, C and Z Versions*. Ed. A. V. C. Schmidt. 2 vols. 2nd Edition. Kalamazoo, MI: Medieval Institute Publications, 2011.

Larkin, Peter, ed. *Richard Coer de Lyon*. Kalamazoo, MI: Medieval Institute Publications, 2015.

Laskaya, Anne, and Eve Salisbury, eds. *The Middle English Breton Lays*. Kalamazoo, MI: Medieval Institute Publications, 1995.

———. *Sir Gowther*. In *The Middle English Breton Lays*. Pp. 263–307.

———. *Sir Orfeo*. In *The Middle English Breton Lays*. Pp. 15–59.

Livingston, Michael, ed. *Siege of Jerusalem*. Kalamazoo, MI: Medieval Institute Publications, 2004.

Lumiansky, R. M, and David Mills, eds. *The Chester Mystery Cycle*. 2 vols. EETS s.s. 3, 9. London: Oxford University Press, 1974.

Malory, Thomas. *Works*. Ed. Eugène Vinaver. 2nd edition. Oxford: Clarendon Press, 1971.

Moe, Phyllis, ed. *The ME Prose Translation of Roger d'Argenteuil's Bible en françois: edited from Cleveland Public Library, MS W q 091.92 – C 468*. Heidelberg: Carl Winter, 1977.

Morse, Ruth. *St. Erkenwald*. Cambridge: D. S. Brewer, 1975.

Munro, Diane A., ed. "An Edition and Study of Portions of MS Laud Misc. 622 of the Bodleian Library." Ph.D. Dissertation: Aberdeen University, 1977.

Orosius. *Seven Books of History against the Pagans*. Trans. A. T. Fear. Liverpool: Liverpool University Press, 2010.

Plutarchus. *Vitae Parallelae*. Ed. Konrat Ziegler and Hans Gärtner. 5th edition. Volume 1, Fascicle 1. Munich and Leipzig: K. G. Saur, 2000.

Polo, Marco. *The Description of the World [Divisement du Monde]*. Ed. and trans. Sharon Kinoshita. Cambridge: Hackett Publishing, 2016.

Pseudo-Hegesippus. *Hegesippi Qui Dicitur Historiae Libri V*. Ed. Vincente Ussani. New York: Hoelder-Pichler-Tempsky A. G., 1932.

———. *On the Ruin of the City of Jerusalem*. Trans. Wade Blocker. 2005. Online at http://www.tertullian.org/fathers/hegesippus_00_eintro.htm.

Sallust. *Histories*. In *Fragments of the Histories; Letters to Caesar*. Ed. and trans. John T. Ramsey. Cambridge, MA: Harvard University Press, 2015. Pp. 2–471.

Stevens, Martin, and A. C. Cawley. *The Towneley Plays*. 2 vols. EETS s.s. 13, 14. Oxford: Oxford University Press, 1994.

Suetonius. *Lives of the Caesars, Volume 2: Claudius. Nero. Galba. Otho, and Vitellius. Vespasian. Titus, Domitian. Lives of Illustrious Men: Grammarians and Rhetoricians. Poets (Terence. Virgil. Horace. Tibullus. Persius. Lucan). Lives of Pliny the Elder and Passienus Crispus*. Trans. John C. Rolfe. Cambridge, MA: Harvard University Press, 1914.

Sugano, Douglas, ed. *The N-Town Plays*. Kalamazoo, MI: Medieval Institute Publications, 2007.

Tacitus. *Histories: Books 4–5. Annals: Books 1–3*. Trans. Clifford H. Moore and John Jackson. Cambridge, MA: Harvard University Press, 1931.

———. *The Annals: Books 13–16*. Trans. John Jackson. Cambridge, MA: Harvard University Press, 1937. Rpt. 1981.

Terrell, Katherine H., ed. and trans. *Richard Coeur de Lion*. Ontario: Broadview Editions, 2019.

Thucydides. *History of the Peloponnesian War, Volume 1: Books 1–2*. Trans. C. F. Smith. Cambridge, MA: Harvard University Press, 1919.

———. *History of the Peloponnesian War, Volume 2: Books 3–4*. Trans. C. F. Smith. Cambridge, MA: Harvard University Press, 1920.

———. *History of the Peloponnesian War, Volume 3: Books 5–6*. Trans. C. F. Smith. Cambridge, MA: Harvard University Press, 1921.

———. *History of the Peloponnesian War, Volume 4: Books 7–8*. Trans. C. F. Smith. Cambridge, MA: Harvard University Press, 1923.

Valerius Maximus. *Memorable Doings and Sayings, Volume 1: Books 1–5*. Ed. and trans. D. R. Shackleton Bailey. Cambridge, MA: Harvard University Press, 2000.

———. *Memorable Doings and Sayings, Volume 2: Books 6–9*. Ed. and trans. D. R. Shackleton Bailey. Cambridge, MA: Harvard University Press, 2000.

Wilson, John Holmes, ed. "Titus and Vespasian: A Trial Edition of the Osborne Manuscript." Ph.D. Dissertation: Yale University, 1967.

SECONDARY SOURCES

Akbari, Suzanne Conklin. *Idols in the East: European Representations of Islam and the Orient, 1100–1450*. Ithaca, NY: Cornell University Press, 2009.

Anatolios, Khaled. "Athanasius's Christology Today: The Life, Death, and Resurrection of Christ in *On the Incarnation*." In *In the Shadow of the Incarnation: Essays on Jesus Christ in the Early Church in Honor of Brian E. Daley, S. J.* Ed. Peter W. Martens. Notre Dame, IN: University of Notre Dame Press, 2008. Pp. 29–49.

Appelbaum, Robert. *Aguecheek's Beef, Belch's Hiccup, and Other Gastronomic Interjections: Literature, Culture, and Food Among the Early Moderns*. Chicago: University of Chicago Press, 2006.

Ash, Rhiannon. "The Great Escape: Tacitus on the Mutiny of the Usipi (*Agricola* 28)." In *Ancient Historiography and its Contexts: Studies in Honour of A. J. Woodman*. Ed. Christina S. Kraus, John Marincola, and Christopher Pelling. Oxford: Oxford University Press, 2010. Pp. 275–93.

Avi-Yonah, Michael. "Ophrah." In *Encyclopeaedia Judaica*. Ed. Fred Skolnik and Michael Berenbaum. 2nd ed. Vol. 15. Detroit, MI: MacMillan Reference USA in association with Keter Publishing House, 2007. p. 439.

Bale, Anthony. *The Jew in the Medieval Book: English Antisemitisms, 1350–1500*. Cambridge: Cambridge University Press, 2006.

———. *Feeling Persecuted: Christians, Jews and Images of Violence in the Middle Ages*. London: Reaktion Books, 2010.

Barlow, Jonathan. "Noble Gauls and Their Other in Caesar's Propaganda." In *Julius Caesar as Artful Reporter: The War Commentaries as Political Instruments*. Ed. Kathryn Welch and Anton Powell. London: Duckworth Press, 1998. Pp. 139–70.

Barnes, T. D. "The Sack of the Temple in Josephus and Tacitus." In Edmondson, Mason, and Rives, *Flavius Josephus and Flavian Rome*. Pp. 129–44.

Baum, Paull Franklin. "The Mediæval Legend of Judas Iscariot." *PMLA* 31 (1916), 481–632.

Beard, Mary. *The Roman Triumph*. Cambridge, MA: The Belknap Press of Harvard University Press, 2007.

Bhabha, Homi K. *The Location of Culture*. London: Routledge Classics, 1994.

Biddick, Kathleen. *The Typological Imaginary: Circumcision, Technology, History*. Philadelphia: University of Pennsylvania Press, 2003.

Birenbaum, Maija. "Affective Vengeance in *Titus and Vespasian*." *Chaucer Review* 43.3 (2009), 330–44.

———. "Communal Purity and Jewish "Filþe" in *Cleanness*." *Philological Quarterly* 91.3 (2012), 339–59.

Blurton, Heather. "'His right hond he liet of-smite': Judas/Quiriac and the Representation of Jewish Identity in the *South English Legendaries*." In *Rethinking the South English Legendaries*. Ed. Heather Blurton and Jocelyn Wogan-Browne. Manchester: Manchester University Press, 2011. Pp. 313–28.

Boas, Adrian J. *Crusader Archaeology: The Material Culture of the Latin East*. 2nd edition. London: Routledge, 2017.

Boyarin, Daniel. *A Radical Jew: Paul and the Politics of Identity*. Berkeley: University of California Press, 1994.

Boyle, A. J., and W. J. Dominik, eds. *Flavian Rome: Culture, Image, Text*. Leiden: Brill, 2003.

Brooks, James A. "Galatia, Galatians." In *Encyclopedia of Early Christianity*. Ed. Everett Ferguson. 2 vols. 2nd edition. New York: Garland Publishing, 1997. Pp. 446–47.

Brown, Carleton, and Rossell Hope Robbins. *The Index of Middle English Verse*. New York: Columbia University Press, 1943.

Bynum, Caroline Walker. *Christian Materiality: An Essay on Religion in Late Medieval Europe*. New York: Zone Books, 2011.

Calkin, Siobhain Bly. "Romance Baptisms and Theological Contexts in *The King of Tars* and *Sir Ferumbras*." In *Medieval Romance, Medieval Contexts*. Ed. Rhiannon Purdie and Michael Cichon. Cambridge: D. S. Brewer, 2011. Pp. 105–19.

Chaganti, Seeta. *The Medieval Poetics of the Reliquary: Enshrinement, Inscription, Performance*. New York: Palgrave Macmillan, 2008.

Chapman, Honora Howell. "Josephus and the Cannibalism of Mary (*BJ* 6.199–219)." In *A Companion to Greek and Roman Historiography*. Vol. 2. Ed. John Marincola. Malden, MA: Wiley-Blackwell, 2007. Pp. 419–26.

———. "Josephus." In *The Cambridge Companion to the Roman Historians*. Ed. Andrew Feldherr. Cambridge: Cambridge University Press, 2009. Pp. 319–31.

Chapman, Honora Howell, and Zuleika Rodgers, eds. *A Companion to Josephus*. Malden, MA: Wiley-Blackwell, 2016.

Chemers, Michael Mark. "Anti-Semitism, Surrogacy, and the Invocation of Mohammed in the *Play of the Sacrament*." *Comparative Drama* 41 (2007), 25–55.

Clark, Eleanor Grace. "Titus and Vespasian." *Modern Language Notes* 41.8 (1926), 523–27.

Clifton, Nicole. "*Kyng Alisaunder* and Oxford, Bodleian Library, MS Laud Misc. 622." *Journal of the Early Book Society for the Study of Manuscripts and Printing History* 18 (2015), 29–49.

Cohen, Jeffrey Jerome, ed. *The Postcolonial Middle Ages*. New York: Palgrave, 2001.

Cohen, Jeremy. *Living Letters of the Law: Ideas of the Jew in Medieval Christianity*. Berkeley: University of California Press, 1999.

Collins, John J. *Seers, Sibyls, and Sages in Hellenistic-Roman Judaism*. Leiden: Brill Academic Publishers, 2001.

Constable, Giles. *Crusaders and Crusading in the Twelfth Century*. Burlington, VT: Ashgate, 2008.

Cooper, Helen. *The English Romance in Time: Transforming Motifs from Geoffrey of Monmouth to the Death of Shakespeare*. Oxford: Oxford University Press, 2004.

Cotton, Hannah M., and Werner Eck. "Josephus' Roman Audience: Josephus and the Roman Elites" In Edmondson, Mason, and Rives, *Flavius Josephus and Flavian Rome*. Pp. 37–52.

Cutts, Cecilia. "The Croxton Play: An Anti-Lollard Piece." *MLQ* 5 (1944), 45–60.

Czarnowus, Anna. "Judas, A Medieval Other? Religion, Ethnicity, and Gender in the Thirteenth-Century Middle English *Judas*." *Terminus* 13 (2011), 15–30.

D'Emilio, James. "Galicia." In *Oxford Dictionary of the Middle Ages*. Pp. 682–83.

Delany, Sheila, ed. *Chaucer and the Jews: Sources, Contexts, Meanings*. New York: Routledge, 2002.

———. "Chaucer's Prioress, the Jews, and the Muslims." In Delany, *Chaucer and the Jews*. Pp. 43–57.

DeMarco, Patricia A. "Cultural Trauma and Christian Identity in the Late Medieval Heroic Epic, *The Siege of Jerusalem*." *Literature and Medicine* 33 (2015), 279–301.

DeVries, Kelly, and Robert Douglas Smith. *Medieval Military Technology*. 2nd edition. Toronto: University of Toronto Press, 2012.

Dinshaw, Carolyn. "A Kiss is Just a Kiss: Heterosexuality and Its Consolations in Sir Gawain and the Green Knight." *Diacritics* 24, no. 2/3 (1994), 205–26.

Dixon, Gary. "The Crowd at the Feet of Pope Boniface VIII: Pilgrimage, Crusade and the First Roman Jubilee (1300)." *Journal of Medieval History* 25 (1999), 279–307.

Dönitz, Saskia. "Sefer Yosippon (Josippon)." In Chapman and Rodgers, *A Companion to Josephus*. Pp. 382–89.

Duffy, Eamon. *The Stripping of the Altars: Traditional Religion in England c.1400–c.1580*. 2nd Edition. New Haven: Yale University Press, 2005.

Edmondson, Jonathan, Steve Mason, and James Rives, eds. *Flavius Josephus and Flavian Rome*. Oxford: Oxford University Press, 2005.

Ehrman, Bart D. *Forged: Writing in the Name of God — Why the Bible's Authors are not who we think they are*. New York: Harper Collins Publishers, 2011.

Eisenman, Robert. *James the Brother of Jesus: The Key to Unlocking the Secrets of Early Christianity and the Dead Sea Scrolls*. New York: Viking, 1997.

Endelman, Todd M. *The Jews of Britain, 1656–2000*. Berkeley: University of California Press, 2002.

Farmer, David Hugh. *The Oxford Dictionary of Saints*. 4th edition. Oxford: Oxford University Press, 1997.

Feeney, Denis. *Beyond Greek: The Beginnings of Latin Literature*. Cambridge, MA: Harvard University Press, 2016.

Frassetto, Michael, ed. *Christian Attitudes Toward the Jews in the Middle Ages: A Casebook*. New York: Routledge, 2007.

Gardiner, Eileen. "Hell, Purgatory, and Heaven." In *Handbook of Medieval Culture: Fundamental Aspects and Conditions of the European Middle Ages*. Vol. 1. Ed. Albrecht Classen. Berlin: De Gruyter, 2015. Pp. 653–73.

Gasse, Rosanne. "The Dry Tree Legend in Medieval Literature." *Fifteenth-Century Studies* 38 (2013), 65–96.

Gatewood, Brian. "The Narrative Characterization of Pontius Pilate in Early Gospel Literature." Ph.D. Dissertation: University of Denver, 2005.

Gibson, Gail McMurray, and Theresa Coletti. "Lynn, Walsingham, Norwich." In Wallace, David, ed. *Europe: Literary History, 1348–1418*. 1:298–321

Goldhill, Simon. *The Temple of Jerusalem*. Cambridge, MA: Harvard University Press, 2005.

Goodman, Martin. *The Ruling Class of Judaea: The Origins of the Jewish Revolt Against Rome A.D. 66–70*. Cambridge: Cambridge University Press, 1987.

———. *Rome and Jerusalem: The Clash of Ancient Civilizations*. New York: Alfred A. Knopf, 2007.

———. *Josephus's Jewish War: A Biography*. Princeton: Princeton University Press, 2019.

Groves, Beatrice. *The Destruction of Jerusalem in Early Modern English Literature*. Cambridge: Cambridge University Press, 2015.

Gruen, Erich S. *Diaspora: Jews Amidst Greeks and Romans*. Cambridge, MA: Harvard University Press, 2002.

Guddat-Figge, Gisela. *Catalogue of Manuscripts Containing Middle English Romances*. München: Wilhelm Fink, 1976.

Hamel, Mary. "*The Siege of Jerusalem* as a Crusading Poem." In *Journeys Toward God: Pilgrimage and Crusade*. Ed. Barbara N. Sargent-Baur. Kalamazoo, MI: Medieval Institute Publications, 1992. Pp. 177–94.

Hebron, Malcolm. *The Medieval Siege: Theme and Image in Middle English Romance*. Oxford: Clarendon Press, 1997.

Heng, Geraldine. "The Romance of England: *Richard Coer de Lyon*, Saracens, Jews, and the Politics of Race and Nation." In Cohen, *Postcolonial Middle Ages*. Pp. 135–71.

———. *Empire of Magic: Medieval Romance and the Politics of Cultural Fantasy*. New York: Columbia University Press, 2003.

———. *The Invention of Race in the European Middle Ages*. Cambridge: Cambridge University Press, 2018.

Hudson, Anne. *Lollards and Their Books*. London: Hambledon Press, 1985.

———. *The Premature Reformation: Wycliffite Texts and Lollard History*. Oxford: Clarendon Press, 1988. Rpt. 2002.

Hsy, Jonathan H. "Bordeaux." In *Oxford Dictionary of the Middle Ages*. P. 279.

Izydorczyk, Zbigniew, ed. *The Medieval Gospel of Nicodemus: Texts, Intertexts, and Contexts in Western Europe*. Tempe, AZ: Medieval and Renaissance Texts and Studies, 1997.

Johnson, Eric F. "Vienne." In *Oxford Dictionary of the Middle Ages*. P. 1697.

Johnston, Andrew C. "*Nostri* and 'The Other(s).'" In *The Cambridge Companion to the Writings of Julius Caesar*. Ed. Luca Grillo and Christopher B. Krebs. Cambridge: Cambridge University Press, 2017. Pp. 81–94.

Jones, Brian W. *The Emperor Titus*. New York: St. Martin's Press, 1984.

Jones, Kenneth R. *Jewish Reactions to the Destruction of Jerusalem in A.D. 70: Apocalypses and Related Pseudepigrapha*. Leiden: Brill, 2011.

Judd, Jr., Frank F. "Pontius Pilate in Early Christian Literature." Ph.D. Dissertation: University of North Carolina at Chapel Hill, 2003.

Kaplan, M. Lindsay. "The Jewish Body in Black and White in Medieval and Early Modern England." *Philological Quarterly* 92 (2013), 41–65.

Kissane, Alan. *Civic Community in Late Medieval Lincoln: Urban Society and Economy in the Age of the Black Death, 1289–1409*. Woodbridge: The Boydell Press, 2017.

Kleiman, Irit. "The Life and Times of Judas Iscariot: Form and Function." In *Beyond the Literary Ambit*. Ed. Paul Maurice Clogan. Lanham, MD: Rowman and Littlefield Publishers, 2007. Pp. 15–40.

Kletter, Karen M. "The Christian Reception of Josephus in Late Antiquity and the Middle Ages." In Chapman and Rodgers, *A Companion to Josephus*. Pp. 368–81.

Kruger, Steven F. "The Bodies of Jews in the Late Middle Ages." In *The Idea of Medieval Literature: New Essays on Chaucer and Medieval Culture in Honor of Donald R. Howard*. Ed. James M. Dean and Christian K. Zacher. Newark: University of Delaware Press, 1992. Pp. 301–23.

———. *The Spectral Jew: Conversion and Embodiment in Medieval Europe*. Minneapolis: University of Minnesota Press, 2006.

———. "The Times of Conversion." *Philological Quarterly* 92 (2013), 19–39.

Krummel, Miriamne Ara. *Crafting Jewishness in Medieval England: Legally Absent, Virtually Present*. New York: Palgrave Macmillan, 2011.

———. "Staging Encounters: The Touch of the Medieval Other." *postmedieval* 7 (2016), 147–60.

Krummel, Miriamne Ara, and Tison Pugh, eds. *Jews in Medieval England: Teaching Representations of the Other*. Cham: Palgrave Macmillan, 2017.

Lapina, Elizabeth, and Nicholas Morton, eds. *The Uses of the Bible in Crusader Sources*. Leiden: Brill, 2017.

Lavezzo, Kathy. "Introduction: Jews in Britain—Medieval to Modern." *Philological Quarterly* 92 (2013), 1–18.

———. *The Accommodated Jew: English Antisemitism from Bede to Milton.* Ithaca, NY: Cornell University Press, 2016.

Leoni, Tommaso. "The Text of the Josephan Corpus: Principal Greek Manuscripts, Ancient Latin Translations, and the Indirect Tradition." In Chapman and Rodgers, *A Companion to Josephus.* Pp. 307–21.

Levenson, David B., and Thomas R. Martin. "The Ancient Latin Translations of Josephus." In Chapman and Rodgers, *A Companion to Josephus.* Pp. 322–44.

Levick, Barbara. *Vespasian.* 2nd edition. London: Routledge, 2017.

Leydon, Christopher. "The Insular Iscariot: Judas in Medieval British and Irish Literary Traditions." Ph.D. Dissertation: City University of New York, 2010.

Liszka, Thomas R. "The Dragon in the 'South English Legendary': Judas, Pilate, and the 'A(1)' Redaction." *Modern Philology* 100 (2002), 50–59.

Lyons, William John. *Joseph of Arimathea: A Study in Reception History.* Oxford: Oxford University Press, 2014.

MacCulloch, Diarmaid. *Christianity: the First Three Thousand Years.* New York: Penguin Books, 2011.

Mackley, J. S. "Kissing Heaven's Door: the Medieval Legend of Judas Iscariot." Paper presented to: York Medieval Religion Research Group Meeting, King's Manor, University of York, February 2007. Online at http://nectar.northampton.ac.uk/5008/.

Mader, Gottfried. *Josephus and the Politics of Historiography: Apologetic and Impression Management in the Bellum Judaicum.* Leiden: Brill, 2000.

Malo, Robyn. *Relics and Writing in Late Medieval England.* Toronto: University of Toronto Press, 2013.

Mannetter, Drew A. "Narratology in Caesar." Ph.D. Dissertation: University of Wisconsin-Madison, 1995.

Mason, Steve, ed. *Understanding Josephus: Seven Perspectives.* Sheffield: Sheffield Academic Press, 1998.

———. *A History of the Jewish War A.D. 66–74.* Cambridge: Cambridge University Press, 2016.

McCoskey, Denise Eileen. "Diaspora in the Reading of Jewish History, Identity, and Difference." *Diaspora* 3 (2003), 387–418.

McLaren, James S. *Turbulent Times? Josephus and Scholarship on Judaea in the First Century CE.* Sheffield: Sheffield Academic Press, 1998.

Mellinkoff, Ruth. *Outcasts: Signs of Otherness in Northern European Art of the Late Middle Ages.* 2 vols. Berkeley: University of California Press, 1993.

Middle English Dictionary. Ann Arbor: University of Michigan Press, 2001–. Online at http://quod.lib.umich.edu/m/med/.

Millar, Bonnie. "The Role of Prophecy in the *Siege of Jerusalem* and its Analogues." *The Yearbook of Langland Studies* 13 (1999), 153–78.

———. *The Siege of Jerusalem in its Physical, Literary, and Historical Contexts.* Dublin: Four Courts Press, 2000.

Min, Mariah Junglan. "Damned If You Do: Judas Iscariot and the Invention of Medieval Literary Character." Ph.D. Dissertation: University of Pennsylvania, 2019.

Mize, Britt. "Working with the Enemy: The Harmonizing Tradition and the New Utility of Judas Iscariot in Thirteenth-Century England." *Journal of Medieval Religious Cultures* 36 (2010), 68–110.

Moe, Phyllis Gainfort. "Titus and Vespasian: A Study of Two Manuscripts." Ph.D. Dissertation: New York University, 1963.

Montero, J. A. Cabrera. "Donation of Constantine." In *Encyclopedia of Ancient Christianity*. Ed. Angelo Di Berardino. Downers Grove, IL: InterVarsity Press, 2014. Pp. 734–35.

Moore, R. I. *The Formation of a Persecuting Society: Power and Deviance in Western Europe, 950–1250*. Cambridge, MA: Blackwell Publishing, 1990.

Morey, James H. *Book and Verse: A Guide to Middle English Biblical Literature*. Urbana: University of Illinois Press, 2000.

Mueller, Alex. "Corporal Terror: Critiques of Imperialism in *The Siege of Jerusalem*." *Philological Quarterly* 84 (2005), 287–310.

Murphy-O'Connor, Jerome. *The Holy Land : An Oxford Archaeological Guide From Earliest Times to 1700*. 5th ed. Oxford: Oxford University Press, 2008.

Murray, Alexander. *Suicide in the Middle Ages, vol. 2: The Curse on Self-Murder*. Oxford: Oxford University Press, 2000.

Musholt, S. "Mount of Olives." In *New Catholic Encyclopedia*. 2nd edition. Vol. 10. Detroit, MI: Gale Group in association with the Catholic University of America, 2003. Pp. 33–34.

Narin van Court, Elisa. "'The Siege of Jerusalem' and Augustinian Historians: Writing about Jews in Fourteenth-Century England." *The Chaucer Review* 29 (1995), 227–48.

A New Index of Middle English Verse. Ed. Julia Boffey and A. S. G. Edwards. London: The British Library, 2005.

Nichols, Stephen G. "Paris." In Wallace, David, ed. *Europe: Literary History, 1348–1418*. 1:11–42

Nicholson, Roger. "Haunted Itineraries: Reading the Siege of Jerusalem." *Exemplaria* 14 (2002), 447–84.

Nievergelt, Marco. "The *Sege of Melayne* and the *Siege of Jerusalem*: National Identity, Beleaguered Christendom, and Holy War during the Great Papal Schism." *The Chaucer Review* 49 (2015), 402–26.

Nisse, Ruth. *Jacob's Shipwreck: Diaspora, Translation, and Jewish-Christian Relations in Medieval England*. Ithaca, NY: Cornell University Press, 2017.

Norris, John. *Medieval Siege Warfare*. Stroud: Tempus, 2007.

Oxford Dictionary of the Middle Ages. Ed. Robert E. Bjork. 4 vols. Oxford: Oxford University Press, 2010.

Pappano, Margaret Aziza. "Judas in York: Masters and Servants in the Late Medieval Cycle Drama." *Exemplaria* 14 (2002), 317–50.

Parke, H. W. *Sibyls and Sibylline Prophecy in Classical Antiquity*. Ed. B. C. McGing. London: Routledge, 1988.

Paul, Nicholas, and Suzanne Yeager, eds. *Remembering the Crusades: Myth, Image, and Identity*. Baltimore, MD: The Johns Hopkins University Press, 2012.

Peck, Russell A. "Number as Cosmic Language." In *Essays in the Numerical Criticism of Medieval Literature*. Ed. Caroline D. Eckhardt. London: Bucknell University Press, 1980. Pp. 15–64.

Penn, Simon A. C., and Christopher Dyer. "Wages and Earnings in Late Medieval England: Evidence from the Enforcement of the Labour Laws." *Economic History Review* 43.3 (1990), 356–76.

Price, Merrall Llewelyn. "Imperial Violence and the Monstrous Mother: Cannibalism at the Siege of Jerusalem." In *Domestic Violence in Medieval Texts*. Ed. Eve Salisbury, Georgiana Donavin, and Merral Llewelyn Price. Gainesville: University Press of Florida, 2002. Pp. 272–98.

Rajabzadeh, Shokoofeh. "The Depoliticized Saracen and Muslim Erasure." *Literature Compass* 16 (2019), 1–8.

Rajak, Tessa. *Josephus: The Historian and His Society*. 2nd edition. London: Duckworth, 2002.

Rouse, Robert Allen. "Emplaced Reading, or Towards a Spatial Hermeneutic for Medieval Romance." In *Medieval Romance and Material Culture*. Ed. Nicholas Perkins. Cambridge: D. S. Brewer, 2015. Pp. 41–57.

Rubenstein, Jay. "Cannibals and Crusaders." *French Historical Studies* 31.4 (2008), 525–52.

Rubin, Miri. *Corpus Christi: The Eucharist in Late Medieval Culture*. Oxford: Cambridge University Press, 1991.

———. *Gentile Tales: The Narrative Assault on Late Medieval Jews*. Philadelphia: University of Pennsylvania Press, 2004.

Rudnytzky, Kateryna A. "'Behold the Man': Portraits of Pontius Pilate in Medieval English Literature." Ph.D. Dissertation: University of North Carolina at Chapel Hill, 1997.

Schadee, Hester. "Caesar the Ethnographer." In *The Landmark Julius Caesar: Web Essays for the Complete Works*. Ed. and trans. Kurt A. Raaflaub. New York: Pantheon Books, 2018. Pp. 223–28. Online at http://www.thelandmarkcaesar.com/.

Schreckenberg, Heinz. *Rezeptionsgeschichtliche und textkritische Untersuchungen zu Flavius Josephus*. Leiden: Brill, 1977.

Spencer, H. Leith. *English Preaching in the Late Middle Ages*. Oxford: Clarendon Press, 1993.

Stinson, Timothy L. "Makeres of the Mind: Authorial Intention, Editorial Practice, and *The Siege of Jerusalem*." *The Yearbook of Langland Studies* 24 (2010), 39–62.

Stone, Charles Russell. "'Many Man He Shal Do Woo': Portents and the End of an Empire in 'Kyng Alisaunder.'" *Medium Ævum* 81 (2012), 18–40.

Tattersall, Jill. "Anthropophagi and Eaters of Raw Flesh in French Literature of the Crusade Period: Myth, Tradition, and Reality." *Medium Ævum* 57.2 (1998), 240–53.

Throop, Susanna A. *Crusading as an Act of Vengeance, 1095–1216*. Surrey: Ashgate, 2011.

Timmermann, Achim. *Memory and Redemption: Public Monuments and the Making of Late Medieval Landscape*. Turnhout: Brepols, 2017.

Tolan, John V. *Saracens: Islam in the Medieval European Imagination*. New York: Columbia University, 2002.

Tomasch, Sylvia. "Postcolonial Chaucer and the Virtual Jew." In Cohen, *Postcolonial Middle Ages*. Pp. 243–60.

van Anrooij, Wim. "Nine Worthies." In *The Encyclopedia of the Medieval Chronicle*. Ed. R. Graeme Dunphy. 2 vols. Leiden: Brill, 2010. 2:1150–52.

Wallace, David, ed. *Europe: A Literary History, 1348–1418*. Volume 1. Oxford: Oxford University Press, 2016.

Weed, Jennifer Hart. "Aquinas on the Forced Conversion of Jews: Belief, Will, and Toleration." In *Jews in Medieval Christendom: 'Slay Them Not.'* Ed. Kristine T. Utterback and Merral Llewelyn Price. Leiden: Brill, 2013. Pp. 129–46.

Weitbrecht, Julia. "The Vera Icon (Veronica) in the Verse Legend *Veronica II*: Medializing Salvation in the Late Middle Ages." *Seminar: A Journal of German Studies* 52 (2016), 173–92.

Westrem, Scott D. "Against Gog and Magog." In *Text and Territory: Geographical Imagination in the European Middle Ages*. Ed. Sylvia Tomasch and Sealy Gilles. Philadelphia: University of Pennsylvania Press, 1998. Pp. 54–75.

Whealey, Alice. "The *Testimonium Flavianum*." In Chapman and Rodgers, *A Companion to Josephus*. Pp. 345–55.

Wheatley, Edward. "'Blind' Jews and Blind Christians: Metaphorics of Marginalization in Medieval Europe." *Exemplaria* 14 (2002): 351–82.

Whitaker, Cord J. "Ambivalent Violence: Josephus, Rationalist Evangelism, and Defining the Human in the *Siege of Jerusalem.*" *The Yearbook of Langland Studies* 28 (2014), 137–72.

Whiting, Bartlet Jere, and Helen Wescott Whiting. *Proverbs, Sentences, and Proverbial Phrases from English Writings Mainly before 1500.* Cambridge, MA: Belknap Press of Harvard University Press, 1968.

Williams, Arnold. *The Characterization of Pilate in the Towneley Plays.* East Lansing: Michigan State College Press, 1950.

Wittig, Susan. *Stylistic and Narrative Structures in the Middle English Romances.* Austin: University of Texas Press, 1978.

Wright, Stephen K. *The Vengeance of Our Lord: Medieval Dramatizations of the Destruction of Jerusalem.* Toronto: Pontifical Institute of Mediæval Studies, 1989.

Yeager, Suzanne M. "The Siege of Jerusalem and Biblical Exegesis: Writing about Romans in Fourteenth-Century England." *The Chaucer Review* 39 (2004), 70–102.

———. *Jerusalem in Medieval Narrative.* Cambridge: Cambridge University Press, 2008.

———. "Jewish Identity in 'The Siege of Jerusalem' and Homiletic Texts: Models of Penance and Victims of Vengeance for the Urban Apocalypse." *Medium Ævum* 80 (2011), 56–84.

———. "Racial Imagination and the Theater of War: Captivity and Execution in *Richard, Coer de Lion.*" In *A Companion to British Literature, Volume I: Medieval Literature 700–1450.* Ed. Robert DeMaria, Jr., Heesok Chang, and Samantha Zacher. Chichester: John Wiley & Sons, 2014. Pp. 81–96.

Zissos, Andrew, ed. *A Companion to the Flavian Age of Imperial Rome.* Malden, MA: Wiley Blackwell, 2016.

❧ GLOSSARY

ABBREVIATIONS: **adj.**: adjective; **adv.**: adverb; **art.**: article; **aux.**: auxiliary; **conj.**: conjunction; **def.**: definite; **interj.**: interjection; **n.**: noun; **p.**: participle; **pa.**: past; **pref.**: prefix; **prep.**: preposition; **pron.**: pronoun; **v.**: verb

abaten (v.) *to abate*
abiden (v.) *to bide [one's time]; to abide*
abougth (pa.) see **abye(n)**
abye(n) (v.) *to pay for*
adoun(e) (adv.) *down*
adrad(d), adred (adj.) *afraid; crazed*
affray (n.) *attack*
agayn (adv.) *again*
agrisen (v.) *to terrify*
agros (v.) *tremble*
aknowe (v.) *know*
alighth (v.) *descend*
alithed (pa.) *soothed; anointed*
aller (adj.) *best, highest*
alwey(s) (adv.) *always*
amende (v.) *to amend*
amys (adv. or adj.) *wrong*
anon (adv.) *at once*
apeire (v.) *diminish*
apert(e) (adj.) *clear, apparent*
aplig(h)th (adv.) *in faith*
aquiten (v.) *to repay*
arblast (n.) *crossbow*
areden (v.) *to guess; to advise*
arst (adv.) *first*
aspye (v.) *discover, spy;* **aspyed** (pa.)
aspyes (n.) *spies*
assaien (v.) *to test, attempt*
assent(e) (v.) *consent; comply;* **assented** (pa.), **assentaund** (p.)
assoile (v.) *to absolve*
astonde (p.) *to be standing*
ateynt (pa.) *convicted*

atte (prep.) *at*
atyre (n.) *attire*
aungel(s) (n.) *angel*
avoutre (n.) *adultery*
avys (n.) *information; advice*

---

baillye, baily(e) (n.) *control; office*
bak(e) (n.) *back*
bale (n.) *misfortune; destruction; evil*
barnetem (n.) *offspring*
baudekyn (n.) *silk*
baundoun (n.) *control*
bede(s) (n.) *prayers; orders*
beden (v.) *to pray*
berande (p.) *carrying*
bete (n.) *misfortune*
beten (v.) *to beat, to atone for*
be(e)th (v.) *be*
betide (v.) *happen*
bett (adj.) *better*
bicast(en) (v.) *to surround; cover*
bicomen (v.) *to come about, to happen; to be fitting*
biforne (adv.) *before*
bigan (pa.) *began*
bigete (n.) *offspring*
bigile (v.) *trick*
bihated (pa.) *hated*
bihigth (v.) *promise*
bihote (pa.) see **bihigth**
bileve (n.) *beliefs*

221

bileven, bileveth (v.) *to believe;* **beleved** (pa.)
bilowen (pa.) *loved*
birefte (pa.) *robbed*
bisoug(h)th, bisoughte (pa.) *entreated*
biteche (v.) *deliver; commend*
bitought (pa.) *taught;* see **biteche**
bithenken, bithougth (v.) *to think, reflect*
biwrayed (pa.) *accused*
blent(en) (pa.) *blind, blindfolded, befuddled*
blithe (adj.) *glad; gracious*
blynne (n.) *end*
blynne(n) (v.) *to cease, fail*
boght (v.) *bought*
borfreys (n.) *movable towers*
borowe (n.) *guarantor*
bote (n.) *remedy; relief; protection*
boulges (n.) *water skins*
braide (adv.) *quickly*
brast (pa.) *broke*
bren(ne) (v.) *burn*
brent (adj.) *burnt*
brynk (n.) *edge, brink*
buffeted (pa.) *hit*
byggeth (v.) *make amends*
byhightten (pa.) see **bihigth**
byhove (n.) *advantage*
byment (pa.) *lament; mourn*
bynam (pa.) *took away*
byst (v.) *strike*

———

cardiake (n.) *heart attack*
careynes (n.) *corpses*
chaffare (n.) *goods for trade*
chepyng (p.) *trading*
chere (n.) *manner*
chese(n) (v.) *to choose*
cleef (pa.) *split*
clepen, clepeth (v.) *to call, name, summon;* **cleped, clepeden** (pa.) *called, named, summoned*
clippen (v.) *to embrace*
cloos (n.) *garden*
coffre (n.) *trunk, chest*

communeliche (adv.) *commonly*
comyng (n.) *coming*
confounded (pa.) *baffled*
couth(e) (pa.) *could*
couth(e) (pa.) *gave*
crave (v.) *desire*
cristal (n.) *crystal*
curteys (adj.) *courteous, gracious, benevolent*

———

dampned (pa.) *condemned*
dar (v.) *dare*
dawe(s) (n.) *days, period of time*
deden (pa.) *did*
dedes (n.) *deeds, actions*
defaut, defautes (n.) *lack, defect*
dele (n.) *part*
delen (v.) *to give; to part; to act or behave*
dere (adj.) *dear, fierce* (adv.) *dearly*
deren (v.) *to hurt*
despyt(t) (n.) *disdain*
deynté (n.) *a delicacy*
dightten, dightteth (v.) *to make; prepare;* **dight(te)** (pa.) *made, prepared*
dispersioun (n.) *dispersion; diaspora*
dome (n.) *doom, judgment; end*
doughttynesse (n.) *braveness*
doumbe (adj.) *mute*
drowen, drough(en) (v.) *to draw, pull;* **drawen** (pa.) *brought; drawn*
dykers (n.) *diggers*
dytt (pa.) *prepared;* see **dightten**

———

efte (adv.) *again*
enchesoun (n.) *reason*
encombraunce (n.) *ensnarement*
encombred (pa.) *encumbered*
ende (n.) *end*
endited (pa.) *written*
enviroun (adv.) *all around*
er (prep.) *before*

everychon(e) (n.) *everyone*
everydel (n.) *everything; (adv.) everywhere*

————————

fadres (n.) *forefathers*
faire (adj.) *good; (adv.) graciously*
fallen (v.) *to happen, to occur*
fare (n.) *condition; fare*
faren (v.) *to go out*
fast (adv.) *quickly*
fawe (adj.) *happy*
fay (n.) *faith*
fayn (adv.) *gladly; (adj.) glad*
fecchen (v.) *to fetch*
feffed (pa.) *invested*
fel (pa.) *came about*
fel, felle (v.) *fell; destroy;* **felde** (pa.) *fell*
felde (n.) *field*
fele (adj.) *worthy; many*
felle (adj.) *bitter, cruel, evil*
felle (n.) *bodily appearance, skin*
felony(e) (n.) *treachery*
fer (adj.) *fierce*
ferd (pa.) *fared*
fere (adj.) *healthy, strong*
fere (n.) *companion*
ferlyk (n.) *wonder*
fest (n.) *feast, festivities; joy*
fet (pa.) *fetched;* see **fecchen**
fett(e) (pa.) see **fecchen**
feuté (n.) *fealty*
feyntise (n.) *deceit*
filden (pa.) *filled*
fleen (pa.) see **fleghe**
fleghe, fleigh(e), fley (v.) *flee, flew*
flesshe, flesch (n.) *meat; skin; a living creature*
floterande (p.) *floating*
flum (n.) *river*
fole (adj.) *many*
fole, foles (n.) *fool*
fonde (v.) *found; seized*
fonge (v.) *take*
foos (n.) *foes*

fordon (v. and pa.) *destroy*
fore (prep.) *for*
forfare (v.) *destroy*
forgete(n) (v. and pa.) *forget*
forferd (pa.) *terrified*
forlore (pa.) *lost*
forthy (adv.) *therefore, consequently*
fram (prep.) *from*
frame (n.) *profit*
frende (n.) *friend*
fyle (n.) *wretch*

————————

gabbed (pa.) *lied*
gadered (pa.) *gathered*
gaf (pa.) *gave*
gate (n.) *gate; way*
gate (pa.) *gained; begat;* see **geten**
gelous (adj.) *protective*
geste(s) (n.) *story, poem, song*
geten, gete, getest (v.) *to get, receive; conceive*
geven (pa.) *given;* see **gaf**
glade (adj.) *glad; (adv.) gladly*
glade (v.) *cheer*
grame (n.) *hatred; anger*
gree (n.) *good will, favor;* **in ~** *in agreement*
gres (n.) *grass*
grete (adj.) *great*
greve(n) (v.) *to grieve*
grisely (adj.) *frightful*
grith (n.) *mercy*
gruccheth (v.) *grumble*
gunne (pa.) *made; done*
gyle (n.) *treachery*
gynne (n.) *machine; contrivance*
gynneth (v.) *begins;* see **gunne**

————————

han (v.) *have*
hap (n.) *fate*
hast (v.) *has, have;* see **han**
heer (n.) *hair*

heighe (adj.) *high*
hele (n.) *protection*
hele (v.) *heal;* **heled** (pa.) *healed*
hende (adj.) *gentle, courteous*
hende (adv.) *near*
henne(s) (adv.) *hence*
hent(e) (pa.) *seized*
here (adv.) *here*
here (v.) *hear*
hethen (adv.) see **henne(s)**
heved(e), heveden, hevedes (n.) *head*
hiderward (adv.) *until that time; in this direction; to this place*
highe (v.) *hurry*
hight, highth (pa.) *to be named; promised;* see **hote, hoteth**
hilde (pa.) *piled, buried*
hise (pron.) *his*
hit (pron.) *it*
holden (v.) *to hold; to keep; to consider, believe*
hond(e) (n.) *hand; control*
hool (adj.) *whole, spiritually sound*
hoot (adj.) *hot*
hore (adj.) *gray, white (as in hair)*
hosen (n.) *leggings*
hote (adj.) *hot*
hote, hoteth (v.) *assure, promise;* **hoten** (pa.) *called*
hou (conj. adv.) *how*
hurtlen (v.) *to fight*
hy (pron.) *they*

———

ilk (adj.) *same*

———

kem (pa.) *came*
kene (adj.) *cruel*
kenne (v.) *teach, proclaim*
kepeth (v.) *keep, guard*
kest (pa.) *cast, threw; knew*
knouleched (pa.) *had intercourse with*
knoulechyng (n.) *acknowledgement*

kyd (pa.) *made; reveal;* see **kithe**
kynde (n.) *kind; nature; rank*
kithe (v.) *show, reveal*

———

lacchen (v.) *to catch, to capture*
laghghe (n.) *law*
lasse (adv.) *less*
laused (pa.) *loosed*
leche (n.) *physician; leech*
lede (v.) *lead*
leef (adj.) *dear*
leef (adv.) *rather*
lefdy (n.) *lady*
leide (pa.) *laid;* ~ **on** *called*
lere (v.) *learn; teach;* **lered** (pa.) *taught*
lesse (adv.) *less*
lest (adj.) *least*
let(e) (v.) *let, allow*
lette(d) (pa.) *hindered*
leve (adj.) *dear*
leven, leve (v.) *to stop, leave; believe;* **leved, leveden** (pa.) *believed*
lever (adv.) *rather, prefer*
lewed (adj.) *unlearned*
liggeyng (p.) *lying*
lith (n.) *joint*
lodesman (n.) *guide*
lordhed (n.) *lordship*
lore (n.) *story, knowledge; learning*
lore, lorne (pa.) *lost*
loos (adj.) *free; forfeited*
loos (n.) *loss*
looth (n.) *harm*
looth (v.) *despise; be loath to, reluctant to*
loth (n.) *lot*
loud(e) (adj.) *loud*
lough (adj.) *low*
lowe (adj.) *low*
lowe (n.) *well*
lyme (n.) *limb*
lyst(e) (v.) *desire*
lyven (v.) *to live*

manqualme (n.) *death from plague*
maumetries (n.) *idols*
mayn (n.) *strength*
mede (n.) *reward*
mede(n) (v.) *to reward*
merk(es) (n.) *boundaries, place; measurement;*
    taken ~ *taken note (of)*
meschaunce (n.) *misfortune*
meselrie (n.) *leprosy*
mete halle (n.) *dining hall*
meten (v.) *to dream*
meyn (n.) *followers*
michel (adj.) *great*
might (n.) *miraculous power, might*
mistolde (pa.) *misspoke*
moo (adj.) *more*
mowen (v.) *to move*
mowen, mowe (v.) *to be able to, might*
mychel (adj.) *much*
mykel (adj.) see **michel**
myne (pron.) *mine, my*
mys (n.) *sin, wrong*
mysberyng (n.) *misconduct*
mysseide (pa.) *spoke ill of; spoke wrongly*
myst (pa.) *missed*

namelich (adv.) *especially*
nolde(n) (pa.) *would not; cease;* see **nyllen**
nome (adv.) *none*
nomen (v.) *to name*
nomen (v.) *to take*
nones (n.) **for the ~** *for the particular occasion,*
    purpose
nones (n.) *noon, midday*
ny (adv.) *not*
nyllen, nyl, nylt (v.; negative of **willen**) *will not*
nyme (pa.) *taken;* see **nomen** (v.) *to take*
nys (v.) *is not*

onde (n.) *spite*
orisoun (n.) *prayer*
other(e) (adj.) *other*
oures (pron.) *ours*
outtake (prep.) *except*
owe (aux. v.) *ought*

paieth (v.) *rewards*
paleys (n.) *palace*
palles (n.) *silk*
paren (v.) *to pare, cut*
pask(e) (n.) *Passover*
pay (n.) *satisfaction, pleasure; reward*
pere (n.) *pear*
pereles (adj.) *peerless*
perfay (interj.) *by my faith*
perre (n.) *jewels*
perted (pa.) *divided*
peyntour (n.) *painter*
pigth (pa.) *pitched*
plighth (v.) *promise*
praie (v.) *pray;* **praied** (pa.) *prayed*
privé (n.) *secret*
prively, privelich (adv.) *secretly*
profre (v.) *offer*
prow (n.) *benefit*
pryck (n.) *point of vengeance*
prys (adj.) *worthy*
prys (n.) *value*
pycoys (n.) *pickaxes*
pyne(s) (n.) *pain*
pytt (n.) *pit, well*

qued (n.) *evil*
queintise, queyntise (n.) *trickery; craftiness*
queme (v.) *serve*
querel (n.) *shot (as for a bow)*

queyntelich (adv.) *slyly*
quyk(e) (adj.) *alive*
quyt (adj.) *free;* (adv.) *freely*
quyt (pa.) *freed*

———

ramage (adj.) *wild*
rape (v.) *rush to*
rape (v.) *seize*
raught(te) (pa.) *stretched out*
recche (v.) *care, worry*
rede (n.) *advice, counsel*
reden, redeth (v.) *to read*
rehete(n) (v.) *to make much of*
reised (pa.) *raised*
remenaunte (n.) *remainder*
rent, rentes (n.) *income, property*
rente(n) (v.) *to tear*
resoun (n.) *reason*
reuthe (n.) *pity*
reuthe (v.) *feel pity;* see **rewe**
reve (v.) *plunder*
revest (pa.) *dressed in vestments*
rewe (v.) *regret;* **rewed** (pa.)
roche (n.) *rock*
rode (n.) *rood, the cross*
roos(e) (pa.) *rose*
route (n.) *numbers, company*

———

saghghe (n.) *words, speech; teaching*
sake (n.) *strife*
samplaire (n.) *example*
saughtte (n.) *harmony*
sawe (n.) *harm*
sawe (n.) *speech;* see **saghghe** (n.)
sawe (v.) *cut*
sawe (pa.) *saw*
sege (n.) *siege*
seien (v.) *to say*
sembla(u)nt (n.) *image; welcome, hospitality*
semed(en) (pa.) *seemed*

servage (n.) *servitude, bondage*
sewen (v.) *to sew*
seyen, sey(e) (v.) *say;* **seyden, seyne** (pa.) *said*
shent (pa.) *destroyed*
shrewe(s) (n.) *villain*
shulde (pa.) *should*
siker, sikerer (adj.) *certain;* **sikerli, sikerlich, sikerly, sikerlyk** (adv.) *truly*
sikernesse (n.) *security*
skere (adj.) *safe, blameless*
skil(l), skyl (n.) *skill*
slee (v.) *slay;* see **slough(en)**
sleigh(e) (adj.) *wise, clever*
slough (n.) *skin; snakeskin*
slough(en) (pa.) *slayed, slew*
smert(e) (adj.) *sharp; painful;* **smertly** (adv.) *sharply; quickly*
smert(e) (n.) *pain*
smerteth (v.) *suffer; injure*
smyten (pa.) *struck*
socour(e) (n.) *protection; aid*
socouren (v.) *protect*
sodeynlich (adv.) *suddenly*
sonde (n.) *message*
sonde (n.) *sand*
sonde (v.) *send*
sone (adv.) *soon; immediately*
sone (n.) *son*
sooth (adj.) *true;* (adv.) *truly*
sore (adj.) *sore;* (adv.) *sorely*
sorwe (n.) *sorrow*
soth(e) (adj.) *true*
soth(e) (n.) *truth*
sotilté (n.) *trickery*
sparehaukes (n.) *sparrow hawks*
sped(e) (n.) *fortune*
sped(e) (v.) *prosper, fulfill; fare*
spele (v.) *save*
sperre(n) (v.) *to lock;* **sperred** (pa.) *locked, confined*
spillen (v.) *to kill; to invalidate*
sprad (pa.) *dispersed*
spryngales (n.) *catapults*
spylt (pa.) *killed*

staf-slyngys (n.) *slings*
stede (n.) *place*
stede (n.) *horse*
stedfast (adj.) *steadfast*
stere (v.) *proceed; steer, go*
sterved (pa.) *died*
stien (v.) *to ascend*
stille (adv.) *quietly; still*
stole (v.) *stolen*
stounde (n.) *place, time*
stouped (pa.) *stooped*
styes (n.) *paths*
stynte (pa.) *stopped*
swet(e) (adj.) *holy; beloved; gracious*
swetande (p.) *sweating*
sweven (n.) *dream*
sweyn (n.) *squire*
swithe (adj.) *great; (adv.) very; swiftly*
swoun (n.) *a faint*
swynk (n.) *labor*
swythe (adj. or adv.) see **swithe**
sybbe (adj.) *related*

---

tene (n.) *insult, injury; suffering; anger*
terbardel(s) (n.) *a barrel filled with wildfire used in war*
thank(e) (v.) *thank*
thar (adv.) *immediately, right then*
thennes (adv.) *then*
theigh (conj.) *though*
thewes (n.) *manners*
thider (adv.) *thither*
thirled (pa.) *pierced*
tho (adv.) *then*
tho (def. art.) *the*
tho (pron.) *which, that*
thoghte (pa.) *thought*
tholed (pa.) *executed*
thore (adv.) *there*
thraldam (n.) *subjection*
thre (adj.) *three*
throwe (n.) *time, while*

to- (pref.) *a prefix that intensifies verbs of motion, either verbs indicating direction, extension, or addition; or verbs indicating separation, division, or destruction*
to-bote (v.) *protect*
to-brast (v.) *burst*
to-dreve (v.) *pursue;* **to-drevyng** (p.) *scattering;* **to-dreved** (pa.) *driven*
to-gnowen (pa.) *gnaw*
to-hewe (v.) *cut to pieces*
token (n.) *sign*
token (pa.) *took*
tournen, tourne, tourneth (v.) *convert; turn;* **tourned** (pa.)
travaile, travile (n.) *affliction; labor, toil; journey*
trew(e) (adj.) *honest*
trowe (v.) *trust; think*
trowage (n.) *tribute, payment*
tweye (n.) *two*
twyes (adv.) *two times*
tyrauntes (n.) *villains*

---

unfawe (adj.) *joyless*
unhild (adj.) *unburied*
unnethe (adv.) *with difficulty*
unrigth (n.) *injustice*
upbrast (pa.) *burst open*
usages (n.) *practices*

---

vernicle (n.) *cloth belonging to Veronica upon which an image of the face of Christ has been impressed*
verrayment, verrement (adv.) *truly*
vertu (n.) *virtue, power*
viis (n.) *winch*
vileny(e) (n.) *villainy; harm*
vitaile(s) (n.) *food*

---

waie (n.) *way*

wan (pa.) *went*

wan (pa.) *won*

wanhope (n.) *lack of faith in God*

war(e) (adj.) *aware*

war(e) (n.) *goods*

warison (n.) *reward, payment*

warraunte (v.) *guarantee*

wasse (v.) *to wash; see* **wesshe**

wed (n.) *pledge*

wed (pa.) *married*

wem (n.) *flaw*

wende(n) (v.) *go; turn*

wende (v.) *know;* **wenden** (pa.) *knew*

wene(th) (v.) *hope, hopes; think*

wepen (n.) *weapons*

wepen (v.) *to weep*

weren (v.) *were*

werst (adv.) *worst*

wesshe (v.) *wash*

wex(e) (v.) *grew*

wham (pron.) *whom*

wirche (v.) *accomplish; work*

wist(en) (pa.) *knew; see* **witen**

witen, wite (v.) *to know; understand; find out*

withseie (v.) *oppose; deny*

witterly (adv.) *clearly, undoubtedly; cleverly*

wode (n.) *madness;* (adj.) *mad, insane*

wode (n.) *wood*

wold(e) (pa.) *would*

wone (n.) *manner*

wone (v.) *go; live*

woned (adj.) *accustomed*

woo (n.) *woe*

word(e) (n.) *word*

worne (pa.) see **weren**

wot (v.) *know;* see **witen**

wrecched (adj.) *wretched*

wrec(c)he (n.) *vengeance; calamity*

wreken (v.) *to avenge;* **wroken** (pa.) *avenged*

wroght (pa.) *done*

wynne (n.) *bliss*

wynne(n) (v.) *to take*

wys (adv.) *just as; certainly*

wyten (v.) see **witen**

---

ybe (v.) *be;* see **be(e)th**

ycome (pa.) *coming*

ydighth (pa.) *put;* see **dightten**

ydo (pa.) *done; put*

yeelden, yelde (v.) *to give; give up; to punish*

yfalle (pa.) *to fall down;* see **fel, felle**

yholden (pa.) *held;* see **holden**

ylde (n.) *isle*

ylich(e) (adv.) *constantly*

ynough (adv.) *enough*

ynome (pa.) *taken;* see **nomen** (v.) *to take*

yplighth (adj.) *in danger*

ypligth (pa.) *sworn;* see **plighth**

yren (n.) *iron*

yslawe, yslawghe (pa.) *slain;* see **slough(en)**

ysperd, ysperred (pa.) *locked, locked up;* see **sperre(n)**

yvel (n.) *affliction; illness*

The Trials and Joys of Marriage, edited by Eve Salisbury (2002)

Middle English Legends of Women Saints, edited by Sherry L. Reames, with the assistance of Martha G. Blalock and Wendy R. Larson (2003)

The Wallace: Selections, edited by Anne McKim (2003)

Richard Maidstone, *Concordia (The Reconciliation of Richard II with London)*, edited by David R. Carlson, with a verse translation by A. G. Rigg (2003)

Three Purgatory Poems: The Gast of Gy, Sir Owain, The Vision of Tundale, edited by Edward E. Foster (2004)

William Dunbar, *The Complete Works*, edited by John Conlee (2004)

Chaucerian Dream Visions and Complaints, edited by Dana M. Symons (2004)

Stanzaic Guy of Warwick, edited by Alison Wiggins (2004)

Saints' Lives in Middle English Collections, edited by E. Gordon Whatley, with Anne B. Thompson and Robert K. Upchurch (2004)

Siege of Jerusalem, edited by Michael Livingston (2004)

The Kingis Quair and Other Prison Poems, edited by Linne R. Mooney and Mary-Jo Arn (2005)

The Chaucerian Apocrypha: A Selection, edited by Kathleen Forni (2005)

John Gower, *The Minor Latin Works*, edited and translated by R. F. Yeager, with *In Praise of Peace*, edited by Michael Livingston (2005)

Sentimental and Humorous Romances: Floris and Blancheflour, Sir Degrevant, The Squire of Low Degree, The Tournament of Tottenham, and The Feast of Tottenham, edited by Erik Kooper (2006)

The Dicts and Sayings of the Philosophers, edited by John William Sutton (2006)

"Everyman" and Its Dutch Original, "Elckerlijc," edited by Clifford Davidson, Martin W. Walsh, and Ton J. Broos (2007)

The N-Town Plays, edited by Douglas Sugano, with assistance by Victor I. Scherb (2007)

The Book of John Mandeville, edited by Tamarah Kohanski and C. David Benson (2007)

John Lydgate, *The Temple of Glas*, edited by J. Allan Mitchell (2007)

The Northern Homily Cycle, edited by Anne B. Thompson (2008)

Codex Ashmole 61: A Compilation of Popular Middle English Verse, edited by George Shuffelton (2008)

Chaucer and the Poems of "Ch," edited by James I. Wimsatt (revised edition 2009)

William Caxton, *The Game and Playe of the Chesse*, edited by Jenny Adams (2009)

John the Blind Audelay, *Poems and Carols*, edited by Susanna Fein (2009)

Two Moral Interludes: The Pride of Life and Wisdom, edited by David Klausner (2009)

John Lydgate, *Mummings and Entertainments*, edited by Claire Sponsler (2010)

Mankind, edited by Kathleen M. Ashley and Gerard NeCastro (2010)

The Castle of Perseverance, edited by David N. Klausner (2010)

Robert Henryson, *The Complete Works*, edited by David J. Parkinson (2010)

John Gower, *The French Balades*, edited and translated by R. F. Yeager (2011)

The Middle English Metrical Paraphrase of the Old Testament, edited by Michael Livingston (2011) *The York Corpus Christi Plays*, edited by Clifford Davidson (2011)

Prik of Conscience, edited by James H. Morey (2012)

The Dialogue of Solomon and Marcolf: A Dual-Language Edition from Latin and Middle English Printed Editions, edited by Nancy Mason Bradbury and Scott Bradbury (2012)

Croxton Play of the Sacrament, edited by John T. Sebastian (2012)

Ten Bourdes, edited by Melissa M. Furrow (2013)

Lybeaus Desconus, edited by Eve Salisbury and James Weldon (2013)

The Complete Harley 2253 Manuscript, Vol. 2, edited and translated by Susanna Fein with David Raybin and Jan Ziolkowski (2014); Vol. 3 (2015); Vol. 1 (2015)

Oton de Granson, Poems, edited and translated by Peter Nicholson and Joan Grenier-Winther (2015) *The King of Tars,* edited by John H. Chandler (2015)

John Hardyng Chronicle, edited by James Simpson and Sarah Peverley (2015)

Richard Coer de Lyon, edited by Peter Larkin (2015)

Guillaume de Machaut, The Complete Poetry and Music, Volume 1: The Debate Poems, edited and translated by R. Barton Palmer (2016)

Lydgate's Fabula Duorum Mercatorum and Guy of Warwyk, edited by Pamela Farvolden (2016)

The Katherine Group (MS Bodley 34), edited by Emily Rebekah Huber and Elizabeth Robertson (2016) *Sir Torrent of Portingale,* edited by James Wade (2017)

The Towneley Plays, edited by Garrett P. J. Epp (2018)

The Digby Mary Magdalene Play, edited by Theresa Coletti (2018)

Guillaume de Machaut, The Complete Poetry and Music, Volume 9: The Motets, edited by Jacques Boogart (2018)

Six Scottish Courtly and Chivalric Poems, Including Lyndsay's Squyer Meldrum, edited by Rhiannon Purdie and Emily Wingfield (2018)

Gavin Douglas, The Palyce of Honour, edited by David John Parkinson (2018)

Guillaume de Machaut, The Complete Poetry and Music, Volume 2: The Boethian Poems, Le Remede de Fortune and Le Confort d'Ami, edited by R. Barton Palmer (2019)

John Lydgate's "Dance of Death" and Related Works, edited by Megan L. Cook and Elizaveta Strakhov (2019)

The Roland and Otuel Romances and the Anglo-French Otinel, edited by Elizabeth Melick, Susanna Fein, and David Raybin (2020)

Christine de Pizan's Advice for Prices in Middle English Translation: Stephen Scrope's "The Epistle of Othea" and the Anonymous "Lytle Bibell of Knighthod," edited by Misty Schieberle (2020)

Of Knyghthode and Bataile, edited by Trevor Russell Smith and Michael Livingston (2021)

🖋 COMMENTARY SERIES

Haimo of Auxerre, *Commentary on the Book of Jonah,* translated with an introduction and notes by Deborah Everhart (1993)

Medieval Exegesis in Translation: Commentaries on the Book of Ruth, translated with an introduction and notes by Lesley Smith (1996)

Nicholas of Lyra's Apocalypse Commentary, translated with an introduction and notes by Philip D. W. Krey (1997)

Rabbi Ezra Ben Solomon of Gerona, *Commentary on the Song of Songs and Other Kabbalistic Commentar- ies,* selected, translated, and annotated by Seth Brody (1999)

John Wyclif, *On the Truth of Holy Scripture,* translated with an introduction and notes by Ian Christo- pher Levy (2001)

Second Thessalonians: Two Early Medieval Apocalyptic Commentaries, introduced and translated by Steven R. Cartwright and Kevin L. Hughes (2001)

The "Glossa Ordinaria" on the Song of Songs, translated with an introduction and notes by Mary Dove (2004)

The Seven Seals of the Apocalypse: Medieval Texts in Translation, translated with an introduction and notes by Francis X. Gumerlock (2009)

The "Glossa Ordinaria" on Romans, translated with an introduction and notes by Michael Scott Woodward (2011)

Nicholas of Lyra, *Literal Commentary on Galatians*, translated with an introduction and notes by Edward Arthur Naumann (2015)

Early Latin Commentaries on the Apocalypse, edited by Francis X. Gumerlock (2016)

Rabbi Eliezer of Beaugency: Commentaries on Amos and Jonah (with selections from Isaiah and Ezekiel), by Robert A. Harris (2018)

Carolingian Commentaries on the Apocalypse by Theodulf and Smaragdus, edited and translated by Francis X. Gumerlock (2019)

SECULAR COMMENTARY SERIES

Accessus ad auctores: Medieval Introduction to the Authors, edited and translated by Stephen M. Wheeler (2015)

The Vulgate Commentary on Ovid's Metamorphoses, Book 1, edited and translated by Frank Coulson (2015)

Brunetto Latini, *La rettorica*, edited and translated by Stefania D'Agata D'Ottavi (2016)

DOCUMENTS OF PRACTICE SERIES

Love and Marriage in Late Medieval London, selected, translated, and introduced by Shannon McShef- frey (1995)

Sources for the History of Medicine in Late Medieval England, selected, introduced, and translated by Carole Rawcliffe (1995)

A Slice of Life: Selected Documents of Medieval English Peasant Experience, edited, translated, and with an introduction by Edwin Brezette DeWindt (1996)

Regular Life: Monastic, Canonical, and Mendicant "Rules," selected and introduced by Douglas J. McMillan and Kathryn Smith Fladenmuller (1997); second edition, selected and introduced by Daniel Marcel La Corte and Douglas J. McMillan (2004)

Women and Monasticism in Medieval Europe: Sisters and Patrons of the Cistercian Reform, selected, translated, and with an introduction by Constance H. Berman (2002)

Medieval Notaries and Their Acts: The 1327–1328 Register of Jean Holanie, introduced, edited, and translated by Kathryn L. Reyerson and Debra A. Salata (2004)

John Stone's Chronicle: Christ Church Priory, Canterbury, 1417–1472, selected, translated, and introduced by Meriel Connor (2010)

Medieval Latin Liturgy in English Translation, edited by by Matthew Cheung Salisbury (2017)

Henry VII's London in the Great Chronicle, edited by Julia Boffey (2019)

MEDIEVAL GERMAN TEXTS IN BILINGUAL EDITIONS SERIES

Sovereignty and Salvation in the Vernacular, 1050–1150, introduction, translations, and notes by James A. Schultz (2000)

Ava's New Testament Narratives: "When the Old Law Passed Away," introduction, translation, and notes by James A. Rushing, Jr. (2003)

History as Literature: German World Chronicles of the Thirteenth Century in Verse, introduction, translation, and notes by R. Graeme Dunphy (2003)

Thomasin von Zirclaria, *Der Welsche Gast (The Italian Guest)*, translated by Marion Gibbs and Winder McConnell (2009)

Ladies, Whores, and Holy Women: A Sourcebook in Courtly, Religious, and Urban Cultures of Late Medieval Germany, introductions, translations, and notes by Ann Marie Rasmussen and Sarah Westphal-Wihl (2010)

Neidhart: Selected Songs from the Riedegg Manuscript, introduction, translation, and commentary by Kathryn Starkey and Edith Wenzel (2016)

VARIA

The Study of Chivalry: Resources and Approaches, edited by Howell Chickering and Thomas H. Seiler (1988)

Studies in the Harley Manuscript: The Scribes, Contents, and Social Contexts of British Library MS Harley 2253, edited by Susanna Fein (2000)

The Liturgy of the Medieval Church, edited by Thomas J. Heffernan and E. Ann Matter (2001; second edition 2005)

Johannes de Grocheio, *Ars musice*, edited and translated by Constant J. Mews, John N. Crossley, Catherine Jeffreys, Leigh McKinnon, and Carol J. Williams (2011)

Aribo, "De musica" and "Sententiae," edited and translated by T. J. H. McCarthy (2015)

Guy of Saint-Denis, *Tractatus de tonis*, edited and translated by Constant J. Mews, Carol J. Williams, John N. Crossley, and Catherine Jeffreys (2017)